Greenhill Books

1815
THE
WATERLOO
CAMPAIGN

This book is a sequel to Peter Hofschröer's *1815: The Waterloo Campaign – Wellington, his German Allies and the Battles of Ligny and Quatre Bras*, published by Greenhill Books (1998)

"The worst behaviour has come from Wellington, who without us would have been smashed to pieces. He did not keep his promises to be prepared to come to our assistance on the 16th [June], but, not considering the defeat he caused, we chivalrously came to his assistance on the 18th. We cleared his way to Paris, for without us, he would not have got there so quickly. We saved him a second battle thanks to our rapid pursuit, for it was we who scattered the enemy, so no Britons needed to fight a battle after the 18th. The man has rewarded our many services with the most contemptuous ingratitude."

Letter written by Gneisenau to Ernst Moritz Arndt, Paris, 17 August 1815.

1815
THE
WATERLOO CAMPAIGN

The German Victory:
From Waterloo to the Fall of Napoleon

PETER HOFSCHRÖER

GREENHILL BOOKS, LONDON
STACKPOLE BOOKS, PENNSYLVANIA

1815: The Waterloo Campaign – The German Victory
first published 1999 by

Greenhill Books, Lionel Leventhal Limited,
Park House, 1 Russell Gardens, London NW11 9NN

and

Stackpole Books, 5067 Ritter Road,
Mechanicsburg, PA 17055, USA

British Library Cataloguing in Publication Data
Hofschröer, Peter
1815 : the Waterloo campaign
The German victory : from Waterloo to the fall of Napoleon
1. Waterloo, Battle of, 1815
I. Title II. Eighteen fifteen
940.2'7

ISBN 1-85367-368-4

Library of Congress Cataloging-in-Publication Data
Hofschröer, Peter
1815, the Waterloo campaign : the German victory :
from Waterloo to the fall of Napoleon / by Peter Hofschröer
p.   cm.
Includes bibliographical references and index.
ISBN 1-85367-368-4
1. Waterloo, Battle of, 1815–Participation, German Sources.
2. Prussia (Germany), Heer–Influence Sources.
3. Napoleonic Wars, 1800-1815–Campaigns–Belgium Sources.
4. Napoleon I, Emperor of the French, 1769-1821–Military leadership Sources.
I. Title.
DC241.5.H843 1999
940.2'742—dc21

99-35087
CIP

Edited and designed by Donald Sommerville
Maps drawn by John Richards
Printed and bound in Great Britain

Contents

Explanatory Key to Maps

Allied Army	Allied Infantry Regiment
French Army	French Infantry Regiment
2nd — Anglo-Allied Corps	Allied Cavalry Regiment
IV — Prussian Corps	French Cavalry Regiment
1er — French Corps	Allied Infantry Battalion
1st — Anglo-Allied Division	French Infantry Battalion
11. — Prussian Infantry Brigade (equivalent of a division)	Allied Cavalry Squadron
Anglo-Allied Infantry Brigade	French Cavalry Squadron
French Infantry Brigade	Allied Skirmishers
Allied Cavalry Brigade	French Skirmishers
French Cavalry Brigade	Artillery

Illustrations, Maps and Tables

List of Maps (continued)

Sketch Map

Tables: Orders of Battle

Acknowledgements

In addition to all those kind people and helpful institutions mentioned in the first volume of this work, the following either assisted in the production of volume two only, or deserve a special thanks for their particular efforts with it.

A considerable number of man-hours were expended in deciphering the handwriting of various participants in this campaign, particularly that of the elderly Duke of Wellington. My thanks for volunteering for this task go the Marquess of Anglesey, Dr. John A. Houlding and Derek S. Mill. Lars-Holger Thümmler was also kind enough to assist me with the transcription of certain manuscripts. I am grateful to Dr. Mark Nicholls for his help in obtaining articles from back issues of the *Journal of the Society for Army Historical Research*. Bob Elmer, editor of the *Waterloo Journal*, provided important information on the genesis of Wellington's Waterloo myths and the Duke's falsification of the record, for which I thank him. Both John Schneider and Fons Libert were kind enough to allow me to promote my work on their respective web-sites.

Herr Grimm of the Stadtarchiv Gütersloh patiently allowed me to break his microfilm printer on several occasions while attempting to make paper copies from numerous rolls of microfilm. Herr Vogt of the Stadtbibliothek Gütersloh processed my innumerable and seemingly never-ending interloan requests. Bruno Nackaerts helped me solve the perplexing issue of the correct spelling of Fichermont, or was it Frichermont? Walter Rosenwald kindly helped me to locate a painting of the battle. Ute Dietsch of the Geheimes Staatsarchiv preussischer Kulturbesitz in Berlin went to enormous trouble in obtaining copies of certain papers for me, this in the midst of a reorganisation of the Archive. Dr. Charles Esdaile, Geert van Uythoven, Yves Martin, Jeffrey A. Knudsen, Steven H. Smith and Jim Woollett took the trouble of copying various articles for me, saving me much time and effort.

Drs. Christopher Bassford and Gregory Pedlow kindly shared with me their expertise on Clausewitz, particularly with regard to the issue of Wellington's 'Waterloo Memorandum' and Clausewitz's *History of the 1815 Campaign in France*. Pierre de Wit gave me the benefit of his specialist knowledge of these events, as did Derek S. Mill. Both made an important contribution to the final shape of the work. George Nafziger assisted me with my research on orders-of-battle, Rory Muir pointed me in the right direction on certain source materials and Colin Jones, Kevin J. Connolly, Rick Peterson, Ian Jackson and Frederic Pouvesle were kind enough to assist me with aspects of my researches.

Certain archives provided me with material and information for use in this volume, the Niedersächsisches Hauptstaatsarchiv Hanover, the Stedelijk Archief en Museum of Tienen, the West Sussex Record Office, the London Metropolitan Archive and the Northamptonshire Record Office. The Historisches Museum in Hanover and the Victoria & Albert Museum assisted me in obtaining certain of the illustrations used, as did Victor Powell.

10

A special thanks goes to Dr. David Chandler for his continued encouragement and support with this project.

I am also most grateful to those who took the trouble of reading all or part of my manuscript, offering me most useful advice. Those people included Colonel John R. Elting, Colonel G.W.A. Napier, Dr. John A. Houlding, Dr. Gregory Pedlow, W. J. Cook, David Hollins and Derek S. Mills. Of course, the final decision on what to include or what not to include was mine and only I can be responsible for any errors in the text.

Last but certainly not least, I am grateful to my publishers, Greenhill Books. Lionel Leventhal kindly tolerated the seemingly unending delays in the completion of this work. Kate Ryle kept a strong organisational grip on the process of turning a manuscript into a book, while Donald Sommerville again transformed my original text into something more readable. John Richards' maps again made the book what it is.

I only hope that I have not neglected to mention any of the numerous kind people without whose assistance I could never have completed what turned out to be a mammoth project.

Quotations and Sources

Most English-language accounts of the combats during the campaign are based on British sources with the occasional reference to sources in the French language. This work refers largely to German-language material such as the after-action reports given in regimental histories. This is to allow another side of the story to be told and should not be regarded as acceptance of the total objectivity of this material. Rather, readers are encouraged to compare these quotations with those from British and French participants, and draw their own conclusions as to what might really have taken place in these incidents.

I have reproduced many quotations in this book from sources not in the English language. I have translated each of these into English myself and am therefore entirely responsible for any possible mistranslation. Where sources not originally in the English language have already been translated into English, I have still tried to refer to the original work and translate the parts used into English myself. This may explain any minor differences between the wording of quotations appearing in this work and the versions used in other works.

Visitors to the Waterloo battlefield will see signs pointing towards 'Fichermont'. This is the current spelling and it is used in the body of the text of this work. However, the spelling 'Frichermont' was common in 1815, and this is used where it occurs in quotations from contemporary documents. I trust this will not cause any confusion.

In the interests of saving space footnote references to frequently cited works have been abbreviated as follows:

BL	British Library, London
GGS	Grosser Generalstab (German General Staff), Berlin
GStA	Geheimes Staatsarchiv Preussischer Kulturbesitz, Berlin
MWBl	*Militair-Wochenblatt*, later *Militär-Wochenblatt*, Berlin
NSHStA	Niedersächisches Hauptstaatsarchiv, Hanover
PRO	Public Record Office, London
WCD	Wellington, 2nd Duke of; *Despatches, Correspondence, and Memoranda of the Field Marshal Arthur Duke of Wellington* (New Series)
WD	Gurwood, *Dispatches of Field Marshal The Duke of Wellington*
WP	Wellington Papers, Hartley Library, University of Southampton
WSD	Wellington, 2nd Duke of, *Supplementary Despatches, Correspondence, and Memoranda of Field Marshal Arthur Duke of Wellington*

Comparative Table of Ranks

British	French	Prussia/German States
Ensign, Cornet	Ensigne, cornette	Fähnrich
Second Lieutenant	Sous-lieutenant	Seconde-Lieutenant
Lieutenant	Lieutenant	(Premier-) Lieutenant
Captain	Capitaine	Kapitain (infantry & artillery) Hauptmann (inf. & arty., certain German states) Rittmeister (cavalry)
Major	Chef de batallion (infantry) Chef d'escadron (cavalry)	Major
Lieutenant-Colonel	Major	Oberstlieutenant
Colonel	Colonel	Oberst
Major-General	Général de brigade (imperial) Maréchal de champ (royalist)	Generalmajor
Lieutenant-General	Général de division (imperial) Lieutenant-général (royalist)	Generallieutenant
General	Général en chef	General (der Infanterie, der Artillerie, der Kavallerie)
Field Marshal	Maréchal	Feldmarschall

Throughout this text, the rank designation in the language of the army of the person in question has been used. The above table shows their equivalents in the ranks of the British Army of the period.

Abbreviations and Conventions

Army corps and divisions in all armies have been designated following the usual style of roman numerals for corps and arabic ordinal numbers for divisions (III Corps, 3rd Division etc). Brigades in all armies, and regiments in the Anglo-Dutch and Prussian Armies, have also been designated with arabic numerals (3rd Brigade, 42nd Foot etc). Regiments and lower level French formations have been designated using the French style of ordinal numbers (2e Line etc) with battalions and any other sub-units as 2/1er Chasseurs etc. Battalions in the Prussian Army and forces of the German states have been designated in roman numbers for the musketeer or line battalions (I., II.), and with F. for the fusilier battalion (e.g. I./3rd Westphalian Landwehr). Occasionally, in the Landwehr (militia) regiments or in certain regiments from the German contingents, the third battalion was denoted by a III. Prussian cavalry squadrons have been shown with Arabic numbers, such as 2./1st Silesian Hussar Regiment. It is hoped that these conventions will avoid all confusion.

Seniority between two officers of the same name in the Prussian Army was usually indicated by a Roman numeral after the name. Thus Generalmajor von Pirch I, commander of the II Army Corps, should not be confused with his junior Generalmajor von Pirch II, commander of the 2nd Brigade in the I Army Corps.

Preface

My previous book, *1815: The Waterloo Campaign – Wellington, his German Allies and the Battles of Ligny and Quatre Bras*, describes the events that led to the outbreak of war in 1815, up to the retreat from Quatre Bras, the point at which this volume starts. Chapters cover topics such as the Duke of Wellington's relationship with his allies, the organisation of the Prussian Army and Wellington's German contingents, the Allied plans and intelligence gathering, and the combats of 15 and 16 June 1815.

This second volume continues two themes begun in the first volume. Firstly, the full role played by the German forces in this campaign is highlighted, albeit at the expense of that played by the remainder of the Allied forces and their French opponents. Secondly, the testimony given by the Duke of Wellington on his role in this campaign – particularly his report to the Earl of Bathurst of 19 June 1815 and his Memorandum of 24 September 1842 – is examined in some detail. These two documents have formed the basis of much of the Anglo-Saxon historiography of this campaign, despite both being clearly unreliable on several crucial issues.

As well as a blow-by-blow account of the actions of Wellington's German troops in the Battle of Waterloo, this work also examines the advance to the battlefield made by the Prussian forces on 18 June. Those exhausted troops were pitted against difficult terrain that was crossed with great determination, before falling on the flank of Napoleon's army and snatching victory from his hands. Thielemann's fight with Grouchy is also examined in more detail than has been seen in many previous accounts.

The role of the Prussian Army in ensuring the retreating *Armée du Nord* did not play a viable role again in the campaign is also covered. The fall of Paris – again to Prussian arms – is recounted. This volume also contains what is probably the most detailed account yet written in the English language of the numerous sieges of the northern fortress belt in France which took place after Waterloo. Again, the bulk of this fighting fell to German troops.

The final chapter of this volume concludes the central theme running throughout the two volumes of this work – that, on the Allied side in this campaign, the bulk of the marching and fighting was done by German soldiers and argues that the German role in the defeat of the 'tyrant' and in the establishment of a general peace has been too long belittled and should be accorded due credit. Likewise, credit for the victory at Waterloo, if calculated in terms of numbers present and casualties suffered, should also go to the Germans.

Waterloo was more of a German victory than a British one.

Peter Hofschröer,
Austria, 1999.

1. Central Europe on the Eve of the Congress of Vienna
(September 1814)

DENMARK

SCHLESWIG

HOLSTEIN

Lübeck

Hamburg

THE

Schweri

MECKLENBURG

E. FRISIA

Weser R.

OLDEN-BURG

Bremen

HANOVER

Hanover

Altmark

Magdeburg

BRUNSWICK

ANHALT

THE NETHERLANDS

WESTPHALIA

HESSE

Cassel

Leipzi

SAX

HESSE DARMSTADT

HESSE CASSEL

BELGIUM

Meuse R.

Rhine R.

Wetzlar

THURINGIA

Lahn R.

NASSAU

Luxembourg

Moselle R.

Frankfurt

WURZBURG

Main R.

Mainz

H.D

Darmstadt

FRANCE

BADEN

Neckar R.

BAVARIA

Stuttgart

Danube

WURTTEMBERG

Hohenzollern Principalities

Munich

Inn R.

Berchtesgaden

SAL

Lake Constance

Neuchâtel

VORARLBERG

Innsbruck

SWITZERLAND

TYROL

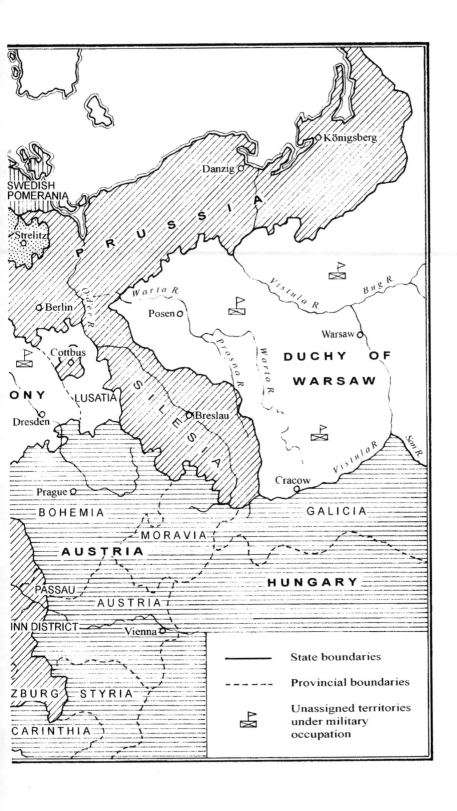

Chapter 1

The Confusion
of Battle

News of the Prussian Defeat

By nightfall on 16 June the Prussian forces had been defeated at Ligny and were retreating northwards in a state of confusion. Now, more than ever, the Duke of Wellington's intentions were crucial to the outcome of the campaign, so during that night Generallieutenant von Gneisenau, the Prussian chief-of-staff, sent Major Graf Winterfeld, one of Generalfeldmarschall von Blücher's ADCs, to take the news of the Prussian defeat to the Duke. However, while Winterfeld was riding down the cobbled road from Sombreffe to Quatre Bras, he encountered a body of French soldiers, who shot and severely wounded him.[1] The news did not get through, though somehow, the unfortunate Prussian officer managed to escape capture, and make his way to Wavre.[2]

Until then, the Prussians and Wellington had been in regular contact throughout the day. Generalmajor von Müffling, the Prussian liaison officer in the Duke's headquarters, sent reports of the developing situation at Quatre Bras to the Prussian headquarters at the windmill of Brye, with the Prussians sending reports hourly to Quatre Bras of events at Ligny. Müffling took the precaution of sending each message twice, once orally via an ADC, and once in writing by despatch rider.

The last Prussian despatch before Winterfeld's message had arrived at Quatre Bras at 8.30 p.m.[3] This communication had been sent from Brye around 7 p.m. and indicated that, despite the ferocious French assaults, the Prussians were holding their positions, and believed they would do so for the remainder of that day.[4] As the gunfire died down that night, Wellington had his troops bivouac on the ground they had defended that day with such determination, firmly in the belief that the Prussians, too, had held their own.

Between 8 p.m. and 9 p.m. the Duke and his retinue rode to Genappe, where they established their headquarters for the night. Shortly after they arrived small parties of Prussian soldiers were seen crossing the cornfields, but this was not taken as indicating a defeat.[5] Late that evening, further elements of Wellington's army arrived at Quatre Bras and probably about the same time Wellington issued orders to the 2nd Division and Reserve Artillery to move to Quatre Bras on 17 June, and the 4th Division to move to Nivelles.[6] More troops joined the army at Quatre Bras that night, so it is clear from his orders and these movements that the Duke had every intention of going over to the

---

[1] Müffling, *Leben*, p 238.
[2] Nostitz, p 33.
[3] Forbes, p 432.

[4] Müffling, *Geschichte*, p 12.
[5] *Raglan Papers*, A 24–31.
[6] *WD*, vol XII, p 475.

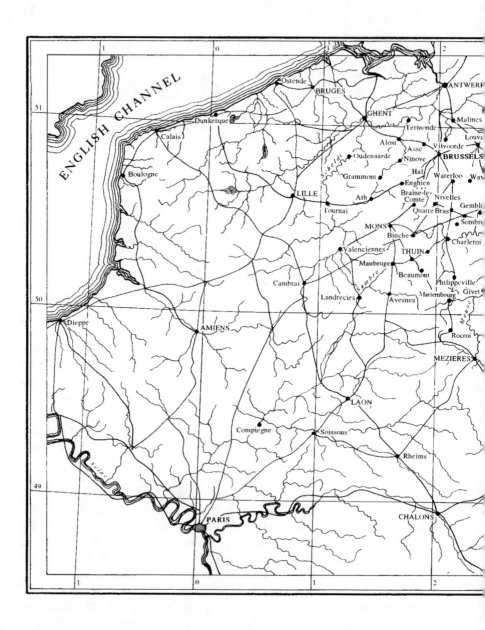

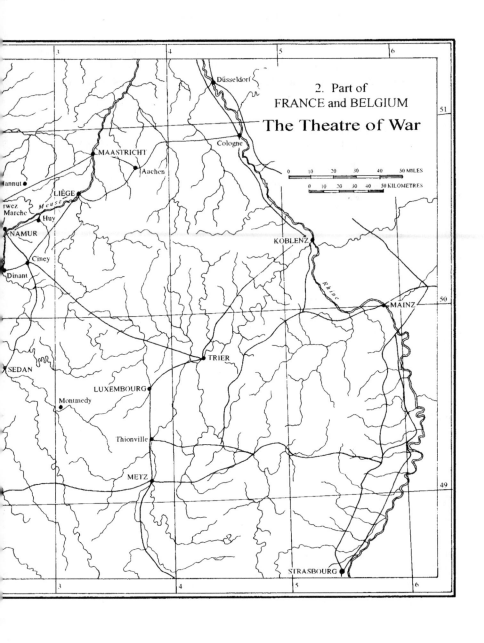

2. Part of
FRANCE and BELGIUM

The Theatre of War

offensive on 17 June. He expected Blücher, reinforced by the delayed IV Army Corps under General von Bülow, to do so as well and would be shocked when news of the true situation finally reached him in the morning.[7] All this lay ahead when the Duke went to sleep between 11 p.m. and midnight that night.[8]

Overnight, further unconfirmed reports of a Prussian defeat came in. One of these was recorded by Lieutenant-Colonel the Hon. Henry Murray, commander of the 18th Light Dragoons. He wrote,

> A Prussian officer came in there [the woods being picketed] during the night & gave account of the battle that had been fought by the Prussians, & stated the French to be very strong in Artillery & to have displayed even more than their usual spirit.[9]

Despite news of this sort, Wellington still favoured an offensive the coming morning.[10]

Muskets before Dawn

The night was far from peaceful at Quatre Bras in any case. The Reserve Cavalry under the Earl of Uxbridge started to arrive late on the 16th, parts of it only coming in after midnight. Fighting flared up again around 3 a.m., when the French outposts along the heights north of Frasnes and the Delhutte wood clashed with the Brunswickers in front of Pireaumont. An allied cavalry patrol rushed through the outposts of the Hanoverian Field Battalion York, giving the alarm. Kapitain von Elern of the 3rd Company of the Field Battalion Bremen drove off the French. Supported by the Hanoverian outposts, the Brunswickers pushed the French back into the wood, though the French then used the cover of the trees to start a lively skirmish fire.

Fighting also occurred around the Bossu wood. The report of the Field Battalion Bremen, written by Kapitain von Scriba, described this as follows,

> At daybreak, the enemy, breaking out of the wood mentioned previously [Bossu], attacked the Light Battalion Grubenhagen, which was posted there, in strength. However, after half an hour of heavy skirmish fire, the enemy was driven off. I suspected that this one isolated attack would precede a general attack on our entire position, and hardly a quarter of an hour later, we, too, were attacked by a significantly larger force. The company on picket duty was pulled back to the battalion. It was now nearly 4 a.m. Our position offered us several advantages, and we were able to defend ourselves with determination and success. After ¼ of an hour of heavy fire by files, the enemy retired, but only after being threatened on his right flank by a detachment of the Duke of York's Battalion, I think under Lieutenant von Wrede. This attack was followed by several more, interspersed with pauses, often by larger forces than our own, several times by weaker. I concluded that the enemy was trying to draw us from our positions by provoking us into a pursuit, which could have

[7] Müffling, *Leben*, p 239.
[8] *Raglan Papers*, A. 24–31.
[9] *Murray Papers*, fol 15.

[10] *WSD*, vol X, p 526; *Nineteenth Century*, 1893, p 432.

been very disadvantageous to us. However, our commander only allowed small detachments to follow the enemy, going only 400 to 500 paces from him. We lost many men in these pointless attacks. Several times, our ammunition, which was brought to us packed in little barrels, had to be replenished.[11]

Because of the darkness, the combat was at very close quarters. Korporal Bollmann of the 3rd Company of the Brunswick 3rd Light Battalion took prisoner a French skirmisher who had wounded several of his comrades from the cover of a tree. Bollmann drew the Frenchman's fire, and pounced on him before he could reload. That night, Bollmann's battalion lost two dead, two mortally wounded, and two officers, three sergeants and 21 Jäger wounded. Battalion Bremen lost two officers and 56 men. Battalion Verden, which had replaced the Lüneburg and Grubenhagen Battalions late that night, had one of its outposts mauled. Battalion York also suffered losses.[12]

The whole front line was alarmed, and the Brunswick Avantgarde Battalion moved up to the Bossu wood. General Picton, in command of the position that night, rushed to Pireaumont to find, to his relief, that the French were not launching a further offensive, but that only a clash of outposts was taking place. He ordered his men to cease fire, with the French soon following suit. By dawn, the firing had petered out.

Contact with the Prussians Re-established

Early on the morning of 17 June, Wellington left his quarters at Genappe and returned to the army at Quatre Bras. As no news of the Prussian movements had been received there either, he sent patrols out to the east to find them. One of these patrols consisted of a squadron of the 10th Hussars accompanied by Lieutenant-Colonel Alexander Gordon.[13] The regimental history of the 10th Hussars contains the following account of their activities,

> … Captain Grey's troop from the 10th Hussars was sent along the Namur road, accompanied by Lieutenant Bacon and Lieutenant-Colonel the Hon. Sir Alexander Gordon, A.D.C. to the Duke, in order to gain information. Advancing cautiously, the patrol discovered a French vedette posted on rising ground about a mile and a half beyond Petit-Marbais. Captain Grey now detached Lieutenant Bacon with a few men to explore, while with the remainder of the troop, placed in concealment, he awaited the result. On perceiving Bacon's party, the enemy's piquet mounted and galloped back to their supports. As the French showed no further disposition to advance, Captain Grey began to retire, and soon afterwards struck into a cross-road that led towards the Prussian line of retreat. Here he fell in with General Ziethen [sic], commanding the rearguard of the Prussians, retiring on Wavre. Gordon obtained satisfactory information from the general, which he immediately reported to the Duke of Wellington. The patrol, however, did not return to Quatre Bras until half-past seven in the morning.

The left troop of Howard's squadron, under Captain Wood, was also sent to

---

[11] Pflugk-Harttung, *Belle Alliance*, pp 35–6.
[12] Kortzfleisch, vol II, pp 83–4.
[13] *WD*, vol XII, p 480.

patrol in the direction of Wavre, and subsequently this officer laid claim to having been the first to convey to the Duke the intelligence of the Prussian retreat to Wavre. Hence arose a difference of opinion as to which troop was the first to give this important information... [14]

The above account is incorrect on the point that Zieten was commanding the rearguard, as the Prussian I Army Corps was already well on its way to Wavre by then. As Sohr's reserve cavalry brigade of the II Army Corps was at Tilly at this time, it is likely that Grey spoke with Sohr, and not with Zieten.[15]

Another patrol set off to ride down the road from Quatre Bras towards Sombreffe and came back after an hour with the news that the French now controlled the road.[16]

Time was passing, and Wellington was still not certain of the Prussians' whereabouts and intentions. Thus, one of Müffling's ADC's, Lieutenant Wucherer, was sent off to locate Blücher's headquarters urgently to inform him that the Duke was prepared to stay at Quatre Bras and continue the previous day's battle, if the Prussians were able to advance again. If they were not, Wellington's message added that he would fall back to the Waterloo position, and make a stand there, if he could count on Prussian support.[17] The Duke had previously reconnoitred and selected this position as being well suited for a defensive battle to cover Brussels.

At 7.30 a.m. Gordon returned with the news that he had encountered the Prussian rearguard at Tilly, where he had been told that Blücher had been beaten, and was retreating to Wavre and that, once at Wavre, Blücher intended to link up with the fresh IV Army Corps and take up a new position.[18] Not knowing that Blücher's earlier messenger had been shot, Wellington felt that his ally had left him in the lurch, an indication of how fragile Anglo-Prussian relations were.[19] It was now clear to the Duke that he would have to give up the ground defended at such cost the previous day, and instead fall back to a new position.

Wellington's men, a substantial number of whom had only arrived late the previous night or early that morning, were tired and hungry, as were the cavalry and transport horses. As there were few signs of any French activity, the Duke decided to allow his men to rest and eat before marching off.[20] He told his quartermaster, Colonel De Lancey, 'We must retire, but there is no cause to be in a hurry.'[21]

About 8 a.m. Lieutenant von Massow, a Prussian cavalry officer, rode up bringing news from Gneisenau. The Prussians were intending to go over to the offensive again once they had fed and replenished their ammunition supplies. As such a move was not likely to take place that day, Wellington did not change his decision to retire on Waterloo. He told Massow to report his intentions to the Prussian headquarters, pointing out once again that he would only offer battle on 18 June if the Prussians were to support him with two corps. If

[14] Liddell, pp 140–1.
[15] Lettow-Vorbeck, p 360.
[16] Damitz, vol I, p 222.
[17] Hofmann, pp 139–40.
[18] Müffling, *Geschichte*, p 19.
[19] Malmesbury, vol II, p 447.
[20] Müffling, *Leben*, p 240.
[21] PRO WO/12, fol 4.

they were unable to do so, he would abandon Brussels and fall back to Antwerp and the River Scheldt.[22]

Meanwhile Wucherer, according to his own account, rode cross-country, map in hand, eventually locating Blücher's headquarters in Wavre. (In view of the distances involved and the fact that Blücher was resting when Wucherer arrived it is likely that, when he wrote some years later, Wucherer's memory was at fault, and that Mellery was actually the place he found the Field-Marshal). Wherever it was, Wucherer met Graf Nostitz, Blücher's personal aide, and sought a conference with the Field Marshal. At first, Nostitz refused, pointing out that his master was exhausted and sleeping. As the next most senior officers, Gneisenau and Grolman, were away from headquarters with the corps, organising their march to Wavre, Nostitz relented, however. Waking Blücher, Wucherer was instructed to '... tell the Duke, I cannot advance again today, but tomorrow, I will come with the fresh corps, and with the others.'[23] Wucherer rushed back to Wellington with this message.

Wellington Orders the Retreat

That morning Wellington issued various orders. Lieutenant-General Lord Hill, commander of the II Corps, which had not been engaged at Quatre Bras the previous day, was instructed as follows,

> The 2nd division of British infantry to march from Nivelles on Waterloo at 10 o'clock.
>
> Those brigades of the 4th division, now at Nivelles, to march from that place on Waterloo at 10 o'clock. Those brigades of the 4th division at Braine le Comte, and on the road from Braine le Comte to Nivelles, to collect and halt at Braine le Comte this day.
>
> All the baggage on the road from Braine le Comte to Nivelles to return immediately to Braine le Comte, and to proceed immediately from thence to Hal and Bruxelles.
>
> The spare musket ammunition to be immediately parked behind Genappe.
>
> The corps under the command of Prince Frederick of Orange will move from Enghien this evening, and take up a position in front of Hal, occupying Braine le Château with two battalions.
>
> Colonel Estorff will fall back with his brigade on Hal, and place himself under the orders of Prince Frederick.[24]

It is clear from this order and the movements of the remainder of his troops that most of Wellington's forces were now being concentrated in the Waterloo position, but it is interesting to note that Wellington was already taking measures to secure his right flank by posting a substantial body of men at Hal.

---

[22] Pflugk-Harttung, *Wellington und Blücher*, pp 374–5; Lettow-Vorbeck, p 361.
[23] Hofmann, p 140.
[24] *WD*, vol XII, p 475.

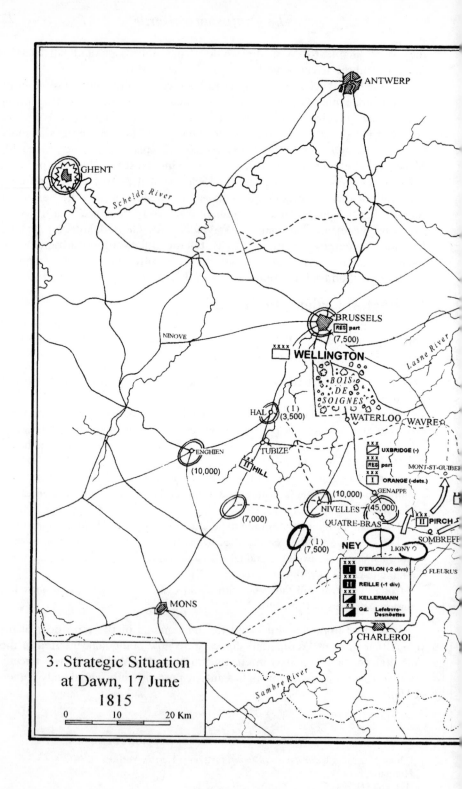

ANTWERP

GHENT

Schelde River

NINOVE

BRUSSELS
RES part
(7,500)

XXXX
WELLINGTON

BOIS
DE
SOIGNES

Lasne River

HAL (I)
(3,500)

WATERLOO WAVRE

ENGHIEN

XXX
UXBRIDGE (-)
XXX
RES part
XXX
I ORANGE (-dets.)

MONT-ST-GUIBEI

TUBIZE

II HILL
(10,000)

(10,000)

GENAPPE

NIVELLES (45,000)

(7,000)

QUATRE-BRAS

XXX
II PIRCH

SOMBREFF

(I)
(7,500)

NEY

LIGNY

FLEURUS

XXX
I D'ERLON (-2 divs)
XXX
II REILLE (-1 div)
XXX
KELLERMANN
XX
Gd. Lefebvre-
Desnöettes

MONS

CHARLEROI

3. Strategic Situation
at Dawn, 17 June
1815

Sambre River

0   10   20 Km

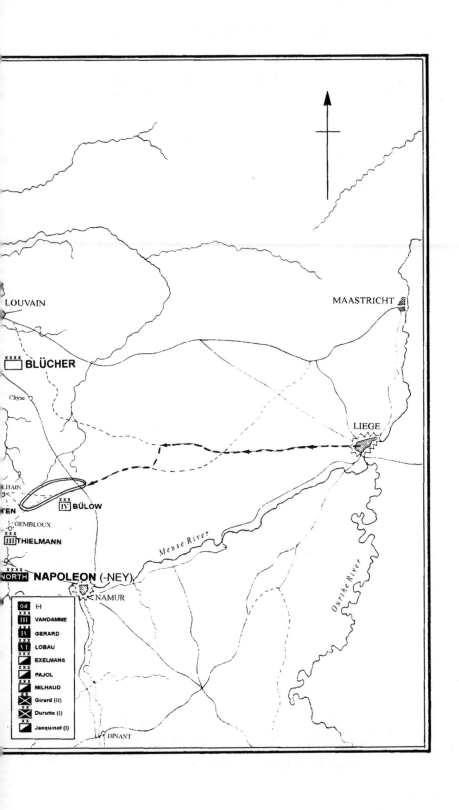

LOUVAIN

MAASTRICHT

BLÜCHER

Chyse

LIEGE

HAIN

BÜLOW

EN

GEMBLOUX

THIELMANN

Meuse River

Ourthe River

NORTH NAPOLEON (-NEY)

NAMUR

Gd (-)

VANDAMME

GERARD

LOBAU

EXELMANS

PAJOL

MILHAUD

Girard (II)

Durutte (I)

Jacquinot (I)

DINANT

Breakfast at Quatre Bras

Much of the morning at Quatre Bras was spent gathering supplies and restocking ammunition, neither of which was particularly easy. Part of the Brunswick baggage train had gone missing during the previous day's fighting, for example. The sergeant-major of the Jäger eventually found his battalion's baggage waggon in Brussels, empty in the Willebroek canal, its drivers having disappeared with its horses. The ammunition waggon was fortunately located at the far end of the city, but only by the evening of 18 June could it be brought to Waterloo. Fortunately, others of the Brunswick supply waggons that had been left at Genappe soon arrived, and their contents were quickly distributed. Oberst Olfermann, now in command of the Brunswick contingent since their Duke's death the day before, forbade any casual foraging by his troops but organised parties soon brought in cattle that were slaughtered and cooked.

Meanwhile, the Brunswickers used the time available to reorganise and replace the lost unit commanders with field promotions. Kapitain von Bülow I of the 1st Light Battalion and Kapitain von Schwarzkoppen of the 1st Line were both promoted to major and command of their battalions. Major von Wolffradt received the command of the Line Brigade in place of Oberstlieutenant von Specht, who had lost his nerve, and Major von Strombeck, former commander of the 2nd Line Battalion, was buried.[25]

Retreat to Waterloo

The withdrawal to the Waterloo position commenced at 10 a.m., undisturbed by any French activity. The light battalions of the Brunswickers remained in position to mask the movement of the remainder of the army. The 1st and 5th British Divisions marched along the main road, followed by General Perponcher's 2nd Netherlands Division, and Major-General van Merlen's 2nd Netherlands Light Cavalry Brigade. The 3rd British Division under the Hanoverian Lieutenant-General Sir Charles (or Freiherr Carl von) Alten formed the main strength of the rearguard, having thrown out outposts. Ompteda's 2nd King's German Legion (KGL) Brigade, which had only arrived the previous night, deployed in Sart-Dames-Avelines. To their north, the main bodies of Halkett's 5th British Brigade and Kielmansegge's 1st Hanoverian Brigade waited in position for their outposts to rejoin them. In addition the Brunswick Avantgarde Battalion took up positions in the Bossu wood and the light companies of the 2nd Battalions of the Coldstream and 3rd Guards moved up in support. On their flank, Ebeling's 3rd and Brandenstein's 2nd Brunswick Light Infantry Battalions drew up in Pireaumont with their guns.

Just before noon units of the British reserve cavalry relieved these infantry pickets, and the foot soldiers began their withdrawal. The rearguard fell back in four waves, not moving along the cobbled road, but rather via Baisy. Crossing the River Dyle at Ways, the 3rd Division reached the cobbled road to Brussels north of Genappe. The various bodies of the rearguard formed up at this point between 2.30 p.m and 4 p.m., including Bülow's Brunswick 1st Light Infantry and the Guards light companies.

[25] Kortzfleisch, vol II, pp 84–5.

In torrential rain, the withdrawal then continued on or near the cobbled road to Brussels, past the village of le Maison du Roi and the farm of la Belle Alliance. The 2nd and 3rd Brunswick Light Battalions covered the flank, moving along poor paths from where they could witness the British cavalry in action, supported by effective artillery fire. Brandenstein's 2nd Light Battalion even suffered a casualty. By 8 p.m. the main body of the Brunswickers had reached its position, bivouacking between Merbraine and the cobbled road to Nivelles while the rearguard also reached its allocated position south of Mont St Jean about 8 p.m.

Kapitain von Scriba of the Field Battalion Bremen, part of Kielmansegge's brigade, described his unit's part in these events,

About 11.30 a.m. the two companies named above [1st and 2nd] joined the brigade and marched off with it along a country lane. As far as Genappe, this ran almost parallel with the cobbled road from Quatre Bras to Brussels.

We noticed the enemy moving. The number of his columns at Frasnes and this side of that village was growing. The brigade continued its march on Genappe, and, about 2.30 p.m., joined the division on a large ridge about 1000 paces before Genappe. The two companies that had remained behind rejoined the brigade. We camped for an hour and a half in the blazing sunshine.

At 4 o'clock, the brigade moved off again. On moving off, a heavy rain shower began, which covered the enemy following us in darkness. The paths we continued to follow were soon flooded, in places going above the knee. At 5 o'clock, the division reached the cobbled road just before the farm of Caillou. Here, we saw our entire army falling back. The troops were marching next to each other in two columns along the wide cobbled road. The retreat took place quickly, but without any noticeable disorder. The enemy, following up in force, was, from time to time, thrown back by the English cavalry, with the artillery detached for that purpose on the cobbled road at 1000 pace intervals. It was impossible not to notice the good posture of the English cavalry, which, despite the poor conditions, filled us with admiration and confidence.

About 6.30, after going about 250 paces past the farm of la Haye, we turned left from the cobbled road and marched towards a large hill, on the crest of which the division took its place in the line of the army. During our withdrawal, several men fell behind, exhausted by the deep paths and were taken prisoner. They returned from imprisonment after [the fall of] Paris.

The enemy broke off his pursuit about 1800 paces from us, along the ridge opposite us, with their centre at the Maison du Roi. After firing about 50 to 60 artillery rounds, none of which hit our battalion, both armies camped. The battalion had not eaten the entire day.[26]

Uxbridge's troopers covered these moves, drawing up initially in three columns. The right column consisted of the brigades of Dörnberg and Grant (both a mixture of KGL and British units), the centre column of Ponsonby's and Somerset's heavy cavalry, and the left of the brigades of Vandeleur (three

[26] Pflugk-Harttung, *Belle Alliance*, pp 36–7.

regiments of British light dragoons) and Vivian (KGL and British hussars). Two of the light cavalry regiments (7th Hussars and 23rd Light Dragoons) were deployed as the rearguard for the centre column, covering the main road.

As the cavalry withdrew in turn after the infantry had moved off the two flank columns had to cross the Dyle either above or below Genappe. The centre and left columns were able to complete their withdrawal unmolested by the French. Napoleon himself attempted to delay the withdrawal of the right column with artillery fire, but to little avail. About 2 p.m., the sky darkened and a heavy rainstorm started, which hindered movement. Fortunately, the last of the Allied cavalry were able to cross the narrow bridge at Genappe before the pursuing French caught up with them. There was a brief combat, in which Uxbridge, leading his 1st Life Guards, was able to hold off the French 1er Line Lancers who were closely pursuing the 7th Hussars. The withdrawal to Mont St Jean continued thereafter without further incident.

That evening, the entire Anglo-Dutch-German Army stood to arms when most of Napoleon's army – Milhaud's cavalry corps, Subervie's and Domon's cavalry divisions, the I and VI Corps and the Imperial Guard – reached the heights at Belle Alliance. However, only an exchange of artillery fire took place, so all were able to rest as well as they could in the pouring rain that night.

That evening, Wellington wrote to Lieutenant-General Sir Charles Colville, commander of Hill's 4th Division, giving him instructions for those brigades ordered earlier to 'collect and halt at Braine le Comte',

> The army retired this day from its position at Quatre Bras to its present position in front of Waterloo.
>
> The brigades of the 4th division at Braine le Comte are to retire at daylight to-morrow morning upon Hal.
>
> Major General Colville [Colville was actually promoted lieutenant-general at the end of March 1815] must be guided by the intelligence he receives of the enemy's movements in his march to Hal, whether he moves by direct route or by Enghien.
>
> Prince Frederick of Orange is to occupy with his corps the position between Hal and Enghien, and is to defend it as long as possible.
>
> The army will probably continue in its position in front of Waterloo tomorrow.
>
> Lieutenant Colonel Torrens [one of Wellington's AQMGs] will inform Lieutenant General Sir C. Colville [the same Colville] of the position and the situation of the armies.[27]

These instructions underlined the Duke's intention to place a significant body of men at Hal, to cover his right flank.

About 9.30 p.m. Müffling wrote to Blücher from Wellington's headquarters. This letter no longer exists, but is likely to have enquired as to the Prussians' intentions the next day, and if the Duke could count on their support. About midnight, Blücher replied to Müffling, the message arriving in Wellington's headquarters around 2 a.m. on 18 June. It read,

---

[27] *WD*, vol XII, p 476.

I wish to report to Your Worship that, as a consequence of the news received from the Duke of Wellington that he intends to accept battle tomorrow in the position from Braine l'Alleud to la Haye, that I will set my troops in motion as follows:

At daybreak tomorrow, Bülow's [IV] Corps will leave Dion-le-Mont, and march through Wavre towards St Lambert to attack the enemy's right flank. The II Corps will follow it immediately, and the I and III Corps will hold themselves ready to follow this movement. As the troops are exhausted, and some have yet to arrive, it is impossible to leave earlier. I would request Your Worship to report to me in good time when and how the Duke is attacked, so that I can adjust my measures accordingly.[28]

With this assurance, Wellington decided to stand and accept battle the next day. At 3 a.m. he wrote to Sir Charles Stuart, the British representative in Brussels, telling him, 'The Prussians will be ready again in the morning for any thing.'[29] The Duke then wrote to the Duc de Berri, minister of war in Louis XVIII's court-in-exile in Ghent, warning him that,

It is possible that the enemy will turn us at Hal, even though the weather is terrible and the roads detestable. Despite that, I have positioned Prince Frederick's corps between Hal and Enghien. If the former [the French] arrive, then I beg Your Highness to march to Antwerp...[30]

Wellington's decision to deploy such a strong force at Hal is worthy of comment. Clearly, he feared his right flank being turned, and Louis' court, of which the Duke was the protector, being surprised by a rapid French movement. There were also other considerations. His use of the remaining substantial force of Netherlanders for this mission was an interesting choice. With the Prince of Orange present and about to fight at Waterloo, the rulers of the new Netherlands kingdom could claim a role in the victory, should one eventuate. In the event of a defeat and the subsequent destruction of the Prince's corps at Waterloo, then the continued existence of part of the Netherlands Army might ensure that the kingdom would not fall apart so easily. The deployment of such a substantial force at Hal would thus seem in part to have been a political decision, but Frederick's 10,000 men were going to be sorely missed in battle during the coming day.

The Prussians Recover

Blücher's promise to help Wellington at Waterloo was made little more than a day after his army began its disorganised retreat from Ligny. Partly aided by a casual and ineffective French pursuit (described in the next chapter) the Prussian forces soon began to rally and their commanders to recover control.

Major Carl Friccius, commander of the 3rd Westphalian (East Friesian-Lingen) Landwehr, described how order began to be restored to the Prussian forces in the course of the night of the 16th/17th, after the first shock of the defeat at Ligny began to wear off,

[28] Lettow-Vorbeck, p 365.   [30] *WD*, vol XII, p 477.
[29] *WD*, vol XII, p 476.

As, on the morning of the battle, I knew Wellington was at Nivelles [he means Quatre Bras], I believed the line of retreat would be in that direction, and attempted to make my way there. In one village we went through, almost entirely empty as its inhabitants had either fled, or hidden themselves, a young farmer came out of a cellar and assured us we were on the main road to Nivelles. However, he also said it was the road from Brussels to Wavre, so we took him along as a guide. Then we met Oberst von Reiche, chief-of-staff of our [I] Army Corps, who informed us that the retreat was going in the direction of Wavre, and we were on the right road. Thus, the retreat continued in wild disorder to the village of Tilly... where we were ordered to halt. The night was dark, and because of the great confusion and loud noise, the order could hardly be passed on, let alone carried out. The great column moved on. Once outside the village, the terrain opened out, becoming flat and level, I saw a field of corn to the left of the main road along which the masses of troops were moving. I stopped here with my ADC, each of us on the other side of the road from the other, and, as the confusion was growing, we both started calling in a loud voice, 'East Friesians, out to the left!'

This measure was soon successful, and a significant number of men started to gather. Everyone was pleased to find us, and everybody did their best to carry on the good work, so in less than three hours, the three battalions of the regiment, even if now only 400 men strong each, were rallied. [They started the campaign at a strength of around 750 men each.[31]] ... At daybreak [about 4 a.m.], the retreat to Wavre continued in better order.[32]

Other examples could be drawn to show that, though the Prussian Army had been beaten, it was not broken. The chaos dissipated, and spirits rose, particularly when news of Blücher's well-being spread. Bruised and battered, the elderly Field Marshal and his men set about sorting themselves out for the next battle.

Part of the Prussian Army at least, elements of the I and II Army Corps, had spent the night after the Battle of Ligny in a more orderly fashion bivouacking between Tilly and Mellery, the latter place being the location of the army headquarters. Before daybreak, these troops marched off to join the rest of the army, which was approaching Wavre. Having enjoyed a few hours rest at Mellery, Blücher rode off in the early hours of the morning, passing his troops on their way to Wavre. Nostitz described the scene,

The Prince had slept peacefully for several hours, and although the events of the previous day influenced his mood, he got up with the firm belief that with new deeds he would take away the laurels the enemy had won. As neither the Prince's servants nor his horses had arrived, he had to use the Uhlan horse, acquired so fortunately in the confusion of battle the day before, to continue the march to Wavre. Wherever the men saw him, they greeted him with loud cheers. Nowhere was the slightest impression of a beaten army after a lost battle to be found. When we approached the first columns of the IV Army

[31] GGS, *Preussisches Heer*, p 468.
[32] Beitzke, *Hinterlassene Schriften*, p 290.

Corps, standing to let the beaten I Army Corps march past, the former were heard calling out, 'Comrades! Don't worry, we'll soon avenge you.' 'You won't need to,' was the answer, 'we'll avenge ourselves.'

When I heard this, I turned to the Prince, saying, 'Your Highness can see that we have only lost ground, but not the whole battle, and with this spirit, these troops can be used any time against the enemy again.' 'That is my intention,' replied the Prince.[33]

Prince August of Thurn und Taxis, the Bavarian representative in the Prussian headquarters, noted Blücher's time of the arrival in Wavre to be 6 a.m.[34] The old Field Marshal, now totally exhausted, took to his bed for the rest of the day.

Meanwhile, the III Army Corps under Generallieutenant von Thielemann had left its positions around Sombreffe in the early hours of 17 June, and started its march on the road to Gembloux. Although French vedettes were close to the Prussian rearguard, no effort was made to pursue. It would also seem that the French only observed this initial movement of the III Army Corps to the east, and not that of the I and II Army Corps to the north. These corps were thus able to withdraw unmolested, with the French appearing to have been misled as to Prussian intentions.[35]

This seems to have occurred partly because of a strange inactivity on the French part. This was noted by Major Graf Groeben of the Prussian General Staff who observed the French activity that day, and sent regular reports to army headquarters. The first of these, timed at 6 a.m., read,

> The enemy is still in the positions taken yesterday evening, along the heights of Sombreffe between Ligny and Brye. One battalion of infantry is moving back, along the Roman road. There does not seem to be so many French as yesterday.[36]

Groeben's 7 a.m. report was equally undramatic,

> The enemy is securing [illegible], appears to be reducing his strength. He is spreading out along the heights of Brye, taking up suitable positions. Three bodies of infantry with artillery. A regiment of cavalry has disappeared behind Brye.[37]

The I Corps' chief-of-staff, Lieutenant-Colonel von Reiche, described the withdrawal of the I Army Corps,

> We arrived there [at Wavre] on the morning of the same day [17 June], going along the left bank of the Dyle, and bivouacking at the village of Bierges, the headquarters of General Zieten. Exhausted and lacking all essentials and despite the worst weather, the men were nevertheless in good spirits. Order was quickly restored, and the army corps was soon in fighting condition again.
> Shortly afterwards, the II Army Corps arrived in Wavre, followed a little later

[33] Nostitz, pp 32–3.
[34] Thurn und Taxis, p 328.
[35] Weltzien, p 204.
[36] Lettow-Vorbeck, p 529.
[37] Lettow-Vorbeck, p 529.

by the III Corps, and, towards evening, the IV Corps. The entire Prussian Army was now there.[38]

This delay in the arrival of the III and IV Army Corps can be explained by an apparent failure to communicate the intended line of retreat to their commanders. This is indicated by the following letter from Thielemann (commander of III Corps), written to Bülow (commander of IV Corps) shortly after the two had re-established contact with each other,

The army suffered greatly yesterday, and has been thrown apart and scattered. I, too, have suffered, but still have a good 18,000 men. General von Jagow of [3. Brigade of] the I Army Corps has joined me with five battalions and two cavalry regiments… I have no orders from Prince Blücher, but suspect that he is going towards St Trond. Since early this morning, there has been fighting on my right, probably with Wellington. The enemy is not pursuing us. At 1 p.m. I will, in any case, move off to join Your Excellency. However, I would ask Your Excellency to inform me of your intentions before I move off.[39]

At first, Thielemann was evidently expecting to retire eastwards, towards the Rhine. However, it seems that Bülow informed him otherwise, probably in his reply to this note, as a subsequent letter from Thielemann to Bülow explained,

I agree with Your Excellency's belief that the Field-Marshal intends to fall back on Wavre, and have decided to move in that direction. I request Your Excellency to take up a common position with me on the plateau between Corbais and Corroy[-le-Grand], and to march via Tourinnes[-St Lambert]. So that we do not get into each others' way, I will march via Walhain, but will direct my brigades behind me on the Roman road, to march directly to Tourinnes, so that they do not get in Your Excellency's way either. Should your route become full, then, so as not to get in your way, they can wait there. I consider it inadvisable to get involved in anything serious before we have joined up. I would suggest that Your Excellency only deploys a rearguard, as I am doing.

A detachment to observe the road from Namur to Louvain should be left at Office d'Incourt. I will leave a detachment around Tilly and observe the Roman road.[40]

Blücher's headquarters had in fact lost contact with the III and IV Army Corps for several hours after the battle, and only began to re-establish control over these formations later on the morning on 17 June. Around 10 a.m. Major von Weyrach of Blücher's staff arrived at Bülow's headquarters. This led Bülow to write to Thielemann again half an hour later. This letter read,

I have just received an order to move to Dion-le-Mont, near Wavre. I suspect that by the time this letter reaches Your Excellency, you will have already received the same order. The direction of march sent to you earlier has not

---

[38] Weltzien, p 205.
[39] Lettow-Vorbeck, p 368.
[40] Lettow-Vorbeck, p 369.

been changed by this. I will place my rearguard at Mont St Guibert, and its support at Vieux-Sart.

I will move off immediately and leave it to your discretion to determine the time of your departure. However, I would remark that it would be inadvisable to get involved in any significant rearguard action, as it would be better to save our strength until we are together.

The cavalry and artillery, which according to Your Excellency's report, is on your left flank, could, according to the Field-Marshal's ADC, be [those commanded by] Oberst von Borcke, coming from Namur.[41]

Weyrach's assessment was incorrect; those troops on Bülow's left were actually French cavalry, namely Berton's brigade of dragoons from Exelmans' cavalry corps. They had reached just south of Gembloux by 9 a.m., but it took the Prussians several hours to recognise them as French. Believing himself safe, Bülow did not rush to depart. Fortunately, the French did not attack him. Indeed, Exelmans did not report the Prussian positions and apparently did not notice them moving off.

At 11.30 a.m. Groeben sent off another report to headquarters. It read,

With a few squadrons, the enemy has just thrown back our most advanced picket, which was to the left front of Marbisou (Mellery). Oberstlt. von Sohr has his main body at the windmill of Gentinnes. Until now, little or no change in the enemy's positions has been noticed. The firing coming from the direction of the Duke of Wellington has either ceased entirely, or consists only of isolated musket shots.

Nothing of the enemy is to be seen on the left towards Sombreffe.[42]

Thus, the pursuit of Wellington seemed to have broken off, while the French were beginning to make their first probes of the Prussian outposts.

Once the initial confusion of the retreat began to dissipate, the position of the Prussian Army improved with every passing hour. Inspired by its charismatic leader, it was determined to make itself ready for another fight. However, gaping holes had been torn in its ranks, causing significant disruption. I and II Army Corps alone had lost over 10,000 men killed and wounded, and around 8,000 more men, many of them soldiers from German territories that had been under French rule for years, had decided for themselves and taken the route east and home. Furthermore, Jagow's brigade had become separated from the remainder of the I Army Corps, and army headquarters was unaware of its whereabouts, even though it had joined up with the III Army Corps. Lastly, in the darkness and confusion, there had been nothing to stop many individual soldiers from going absent to take refuge in the villages or quench their thirsts and still their hunger, or to sleep off their exhaustion.

This was the situation when Lieutenant von Massow arrived from Wellington's headquarters with the Duke's 8 a.m. request to send two corps to support his troops at Waterloo the next day. Now that the semblance of some sort of order was being created, and Blücher was in safety and recovering from

[41] Lettow-Vorbeck, p 369.
[42] Lettow-Vorbeck, p 529.

his injuries, Gneisenau had a chance to ponder on the events of the previous day. Despite the repeated assurances of support he had received from Wellington, not one of the promised 20,000 men had reached the battlefield of Ligny. As the French forces there had overwhelmed the Prussian Army, Gneisenau believed that the Duke could not have had more than 10,000 Frenchmen against him, which he should have been able to drive off with ease. Gneisenau's suspicions about Wellington's true intentions were renewed. What assurance did he have that, this time, the Duke was giving an honest outline of his plans, and not merely using the Prussian Army to cover his retreat to Antwerp, where he could embark his troops and make for home?

Despite those doubts, around midday on 17 June, Gneisenau wrote the following report, probably to General von dem Knesebeck in the Imperial Headquarters, now in Heidelberg,

> The IV Army Corps has been ordered here and will perhaps get here only tomorrow. The remainder of the army is behind the Dyle, one army corps on the right bank of this river. Tomorrow, the IV Army Corps will throw out its vanguard to Mont St Guibert, where Oberst Sohr is, with two cavalry regiments and half a horse battery.
>
> From the sounds heard, it seems as if the Duke of Wellington's left flank was attacked this morning, but he has not confirmed this. He wants to accept a battle at Waterloo, at the entrance to the Soignes forest, if we can give him two corps. We would do so, if we had the ammunition. However, we have no news of the ammunition of two army corps. If we can locate this, then we will take up the Duke's request, send Bülow's corps to him, along with the intact battalions of the other corps, and make up others from the rest.
>
> As the enemy only pursued us for half an hour, we assume that he is likewise exhausted. He has yet to follow us any farther, and even the battlefield [of Ligny] is only occupied by vedettes.[43]

Gneisenau's report was a little confused. At the time it was written, the III Army Corps was still in Gembloux, while the IV Army Corps had been ordered on Dion-le-Mont, not Wavre, and was probably expected there that day, not the next. It would seem that even by midday, the Prussian head–quarters was still not certain of the whereabouts and movements of over half its forces. Moreover, his reasoning seems equally confused. If the French were not attacking the Prussians, then why was he only prepared to send part of the army, and not the whole? Perhaps that indicates that Gneisenau was unaware of French intentions and that Groeben's report of 11.30 a.m. had yet to arrive. To take just the intact battalions of the remaining corps would destroy the cohesion of their formations, as would making up new battalions from the remnants of others. The only clear reason for not supporting Wellington was the missing ammunition; the troops had used up nearly all of their ammunition in the fighting of 16 June, and needed re-supply before being able to fight again.

Groeben wrote a further report from the windmill at Gentinnes at

---

[43] Lettow-Vorbeck, pp 527–8.

12.30 p.m., indicating that the French might now preparing to launch a pursuit of the Prussians. This read,

A strong column of enemy cavalry coming from Marbais is moving close by Tilly. One patrol reports that the English posts on our right have gone back a little. Otherwise, there is no firing. Nothing is happening in the direction of Sombreffe. The outpost reports that [enemy] infantry is following the cavalry.[44]

Half an hour later, however, Groeben added the slightly conflicting information that,

The cavalry has deployed behind Tilly. Judging by the clouds of dust, the number of infantry has increased substantially. They are all coming from Brye. Perhaps they are moving on the left bank of the Dyle towards Wellington. A rifleman, who, by accident, went near to Sombreffe, claims to have seen a crowd of French between there and Vieille Maison.[45]

At 2 p.m. he wrote more definitely,

My suspicions are confirmed, everything is moving past Tilly towards Genappe.[46]

Groeben was quite correct in his judgement for, by 2 p.m., the French pursuit of the Anglo-Dutch-German army had finally started to get underway, while that of the Prussians was put off. His report confirming this arrived in army headquarters about an hour later.

At 5 p.m., Groeben wrote his final report of the day. This read,

Oberstlt. von Sohr and his rearguard have just reached the position at Mont St Guibert. The enemy has continued his march along the left bank of the Dyle tributary. He has deployed a large body of cavalry to the fore in the following way:

$$\underset{\underline{\;\text{-I-}\;}}{\overset{\underline{\;\div\;}}{\text{-I-I-I-I-I-I-I-}}}\;\begin{matrix}\text{-I-I-I-}\\[4pt]\\[4pt]\text{-I-I-I-}\end{matrix}$$

The infantry is keeping its distance, apparently in three columns. When we were still on the heights of the windmill of Gentinnes, the enemy sent off detachments towards our rear via Strichon and Villers la Ville. Thus, the Oberstlt. decided to withdraw slowly to Mont St Guibert. On the heights of Haute Heuval, he left behind 60 men and an officer to report everything happening, until pushed back.

The cannonade with the Duke of Wellington began at 4 p.m. I fear that this [French] corps will attack his left flank, for it can easily slip between us and the Duke. Would Your Highness order the position at Mont St Guibert to

[44] Lettow-Vorbeck, p 529.
[45] Lettow-Vorbeck, p 529.
[46] Lettow-Vorbeck, p 529.

be held? The enemy has yet to attack the vedettes of the rearguard. The cannonade with the Duke of Wellington is continuing (it seems to be at Genappe).

Major von Ledebur has just arrived from Blanmont with a patrol from the IV Army Corps of one cavalry regiment and two infantry battalions.[47]

Gneisenau had already noted the danger of a wedge being driven between the two wings of the Allied forces, because around 3 p.m., he had already sent the following order to Zieten,

> … Your Excellency is requested to amend your orders in such a way that the area along the entire left bank of the Dyle is observed, and communications maintained with Lord Wellington.[48]

Zieten, too, had heard the cannonade coming, he thought, from the direction of Braine l'Alleud, and believed, '… that from the direction of the smoke, the English army was withdrawing.' To be certain of that, he had ordered Generalmajor von Steinmetz, commander of the 1st Brigade, to send a detachment of cavalry towards Braine l'Alleud '… so as, from there, to be able to report any events immediately.' At 6.30 p.m. Zieten reported the measure taken to army headquarters,[49] but unfortunately this report gave headquarters the impression that Wellington and his men might be falling back as far as Brussels.

About 5 p.m., however, the missing ammunition columns had at last arrived and the troops could be resupplied. One condition for agreeing to support Wellington at Waterloo the next day had now been met. The continuing uncertainty of the whereabouts of the III and IV Army Corps prevented this assurance from being made immediately, as the possibility that the French were holding them up could not yet be discounted. Moreover, no commitment could be given until the Duke's intentions were clear, and Zieten's report had cast doubts on this.

The first elements of the III Army Corps started to cross the Dyle at 8 p.m. and the main body moved on to bivouac at Bawette, to the north of Wavre itself. The rearguard, made up of the 9th Brigade and Lottum's cavalry brigade, finally reached Wavre at 6 a.m. on 18 June, remaining on the right bank. Marwitz's brigade, having retreated via Tilly, managed to rejoin the corps, as did the detachment of one battalion and two squadrons that had been left at Dinant. All that was missing now, as far as the corps' headquarters were concerned, were the three squadrons of the 9th Hussars.

The retreat of the III Army Corps was a far from straightforward process. Major von Bornstedt, commander of the Fusilier Battalion of the 1st Kurmark Landwehr Infantry, described the march of his unit, part of the 9th Brigade, in the following terms,

> Before daybreak on the 17th, the brigade commander arrived and ordered the battalion to move back to the windmill in the direction of Namur. When it

---

[47] Lettow-Vorbeck, p 529. The diagram on page 37 is a facsimile of the original.
[48] Lettow-Vorbeck, p 374.
[49] Lettow-Vorbeck, p 374.

reached the windmill, it joined up with the rest of the brigade and was placed in the rearguard. From then through the whole of the 17th into the night of 17th/18th and on until seven o'clock the next morning we had no opportunity for rest. Often, we had to make our withdrawal on paths we made ourselves through the fields of corn and wheat. Not once did we find the time to cook.

During this withdrawal, the battalion came under the command of Generalmajor von Hobe [commander of the III Corps Reserve Cavalry] and often had to deploy to guard defiles, particularly on the approach to Gembloux. In this position, the battalion had no food whatsoever – though the rest of the brigade was able to make camp beyond the town and cook – and there was too little time to forage for any, even if we had been able to as part of the rearguard. To cover the withdrawal through Gembloux, I did not just have the approach to the defile facing the enemy covered, but gave my brave Kapitain von Göhren the order to take his company to the other end, in Gembloux itself, to the point where the battalion no longer needed to fear being cut off.

After the battalion had spent about three hours in this position, keeping away the enemy scouts, it again followed the 9th Brigade. From here onwards, the march became much more difficult. The battalion often had to stand for hours while the enemy seemed to approach from several sides. The cavalry became more active and in the distance I could see that direct contact with the IV Army Corps had been established.

On top of this came a storm of torrential rain at nightfall. Both men and weapons suffered badly and were soaked through. Then, about midnight, the battalion again had to pass a large defile partly jammed with other units. Troops who had passed by earlier had lit fires here that confused us and the cavalry, who had been held up, rushed past at a trot. The paths had been washed away, so it took us considerable effort to find the right road. I tried extremely hard, despite my exhaustion, to find the right direction, so at daybreak, we got past the difficulty and saw part of the IV Army Corps camping some way away. From here on, we marched much more quickly, and at seven o'clock in the morning, the battalion reached the brigade's bivouac on the right bank of the Dyle, close to Wavre, where we were given a little bread and brandy.

It was now urgently necessary to get our weapons and ammunition into a useable condition, not only because this is the soldier's first duty, but also because the enemy might attack us at any moment. My men, however, were very tired, not only because it was their third night in a row spent in a bivouac, but also because the long march had exhausted them. Nevertheless, they were willing to obey my orders and had learned how necessary my caution was.[50]

News of Bülow's arrival first reached army headquarters at 10.30 p.m. with a message he had sent at 10 p.m. from his headquarters in Dion-le-Mont confirming that the whole of III Army Corps apart from 13th Brigade had reached there. His despatch read,

---

[50] Bornstedt, pp 12–13.

I report most humbly to Your Highness that the greater part of my corps is in the position ordered. Only the 13th Brigade, that had to rest after its forced march, is still on its way. To observe my left flank, I have left an officer with 80 troopers at Hottomont [on the road from Namur to Louvain where the Roman road crossed it]. This force has sent an outpost towards Hannut, and is patrolling towards Namur and Liège. In the latter place, I have left behind an officer and 25 troopers to observe. My outposts have seen nothing of the enemy other than patrols of cuirassiers that followed my rearguard when it withdrew from Basse-Baudecet.

... My brigades are positioned one behind the other on the road from Wavre to Bonlez where it is cut by the road from Grez to Corroy. I am thus able to move in any direction. I beseech Your Highness graciously to inform me where the other army corps are positioned, and how I am to make contact with them.[51]

The bulk of Bülow's forces in fact seem to have arrived at Dion-le-Mont during the course of that afternoon, but it appears that until he was certain that his entire corps could be concentrated there that day, he did not inform head-quarters. The time of IV Corps' arrival at Dion can be deduced in the following way. It had started to march off from Baudecet at 11 a.m. and, with an average marching speed of 3 km per hour, the head of the column would have arrived at Dion-le-Mont by 3 p.m. and the end of the column about two and a half hours later. Bülow's marching orders confirm these times.[52] Ryssel's 14th Brigade initially stayed behind in Baudecet to cover the withdrawal, while the 15th Brigade, the Reserve Artillery and Cavalry marched via Walhain to Dion-le-Mont. The 16th and 13th Brigades, being further down the Roman road, marched from their positions directly on Dion-le-Mont. Ryssel's command was reinforced with two cavalry regiments and one horse battery from the Reserve Cavalry, and formed the rearguard. From Walhain, he marched to Vieux-Sart, deploying two battalions as outposts (F./11th Infantry and F./1st Pomeranian Landwehr) and throwing out the 10th Hussars and two horse guns towards St Guibert. This force was commanded by Major von Ledebur and their arrival at St Guibert at 5 p.m. is confirmed by Groeben's report.

The 13th Brigade was the last part of Bülow's corps to reach its positions for the night. The brigade's journal described the difficulties it had met with during its march,

On leaving the paved road, the paths became very poor and, due to flooding, could in places only be crossed by planks in single file. This is why the brigade only reached Dion-le-Mont at midnight, and then totally exhausted, having left many men behind... As it was already so late at night, the men could be sent neither straw, nor wood, nor water, and had to spend the whole night out in the rain on a field that turned to mud. Neither food nor brandy could be obtained, so the men were in a rather sorry situation.[53]

---

[51] Lettow-Vorbeck, p 375.
[52] Lettow-Vorbeck, p 376.

[53] Pflugk-Harttung, *Von Wavre bis Belle-Alliance*, p 500. Cited hereafter as 'Pflugk-Harttung, *Wavre*'.

Bülow's Positions that Evening

By the evening of 17 June, the IV Army Corps had reached the outskirts of Wavre. Bülow's men were tired and hungry after their exhausting marches in the last two days. They were also furthest from Wellington's position to which they would be required to march the next day.

That evening, from his headquarters in Dion-le-Mont, Bülow ordered his men to take up the following positions,

> The IV Corps is to bivouac in Dion-le-Mont in the following manner:
> Losthin's brigade [15th] to the right of the road from Corroy to Grez… The two fusilier battalions forward in the woods, with two squadrons. One officer and 20 troopers are to be posted in Corroy-le-Grand to maintain contact with Ryssel's brigade [14th] and the cavalry of the 16th Brigade.
> Hiller's brigade [16th] left of the road, one fusilier battalion and the two squadrons to the fore; an outpost of one officer and 20 troopers before Chaumont and towards Tourinnes, to which they must patrol.
> Hake's brigade [13th] behind Cabaret à Tout Vent, right of the road.
> The Reserve Artillery behind the 13th Brigade, on the left of the road.
> The Reserve Cavalry along the road from Bonlez to Dion-le-Mont, placing an outpost of one officer and 30 troopers to the front of Le Corbeau, towards Malers. From there, this detachment is to patrol to the road from Namur to Louvain, establish contact with the officer in Hottomont, and to forward his reports.[54]

A supplementary disposition then ordered the 14th Brigade to

> … form the rearguard, which will be joined by the 10th Hussars, 2nd Neumark Landwehr Cavalry and one horse battery from the Reserve Artillery… [55]

Bülow's men spent that night in these positions expecting Grouchy to attack them at any moment.

Battle is Accepted

All that the Prussian headquarters now needed to make Wellington an assurance of support the next day was a more definite confirmation of his intention to remain in the Waterloo position. The required assurance came in the form of Müffling's 9.30 p.m. letter, mentioned above, which arrived just before midnight. In response new orders went out to the Prussian corps commanders. Bülow's version, timed at midnight on 17 June, read as follows,

> According to a report just received from the Duke of Wellington, he has taken up the following position: the right flank on Braine l'Alleud, the centre at Mont St Jean, and the left flank at la Haye. The enemy is opposite him, and the Duke expects to be attacked, so he has asked us to support him. Thus, at daybreak, Your Excellency will depart with your IV Army Corps from Dion-le-Mont, march through Wavre, and take the direction of Chapelle. If the Duke of Wellington is not heavily engaged, Your Excellency will deploy there under

[54] Pflugk-Harttung, *Wavre*, pp 418–9.
[55] Pflugk-Harttung, *Wavre*, p 419.

cover; should that not be the case, then you are to engage most strongly the right flank of the enemy. The II Army Corps will follow Your Excellency immediately, to be able to support you. The I and III Army Corps will be prepared to follow you if necessary. Your Excellency is to leave a detachment at Mont St Guibert to observe. If threatened, it is to fall back slowly on Wavre. All baggage, trains and everything that is not directly necessary for battle, are to be sent to Louvain.[56]

At the same time, Generalmajor von Pirch I, commander of the II Army Corps at Aisemont, was sent the order to follow Bülow. The two remaining corps were informed of the situation, ordered to cook, and make themselves ready to move off in the morning. Because of the exhausted state of the troops, it would not be possible for them to start earlier; Bülow's men, the freshest, were thus to move off first.

As we have seen, Blücher's message telling Wellington of these plans reached the Duke at around 2 a.m. Blücher also dictated a note to the Duke later that morning stating that, ill though he might be, he would ride at the head of his men to attack the right flank of the French immediately his troops were in a position to do so.[57]

The Prussian Army, tired as it was, was now prepared and ready to march to the fateful field of Waterloo.

[56] Lettow-Vorbeck, pp 376–7.
[57] Pflugk-Harttung, *Aus den Tagen*, p 181.

Chapter 2

Napoleon Follows Up

Aftermath of Battle

Exhausted after their exertions in the battles of 16 June, the French troops rested for the night in the positions they held at the end of the day's fighting. They knew that a significant part of the Anglo-Dutch-German Army was at Quatre Bras and that the Prussians were retreating from Ligny, but this was only part of the story and left several important questions unanswered. Was all of Wellington's army at Quatre Bras, or just a rearguard? And in which direction was Prussian Army retreating?

Napoleon received the first news of the day from Quatre Bras at 7.30 a.m., by which time news had also come in from the patrols of Pajol's 1st Cavalry Corps. The report from Quatre Bras informed the Emperor that Wellington had held his positions during the fighting the previous day, while, according to Pajol in a message sent from near Mazy at 3 a.m., Thielemann's III Army Corps had begun withdrawing from Sombreffe at 2.15 a.m. At 4 a.m. Pajol reported to Grouchy from Balâtre that the Prussians were in full flight towards Liège and Namur and he had taken many prisoners. Grouchy sent this report on to the Emperor, who received it around the same time as the news from Quatre Bras.[1]

Later, between 6 a.m. and 7 a.m., Pajol also reported the capture of eight guns and a substantial quantity of waggons and baggage, and that his intention was to pursue the Prussians with Teste's 21st Division, part of Lobau's VI Corps which was bivouacking between Brye and Sombreffe, about 8 km from Mazy. The Prussians, Pajol said, were attempting to reach the main road from Namur to Louvain via St Denis and Leez, while he was hoping to reach Leez that evening.[2]

The captured Prussian battery was Horse Battery Nr. 14 of the Reserve Artillery of the II Army Corps. Its commander, Kapitain Fritze, had lost his way the previous night, and was surprised by the French cavalry early that morning, though Fritze, one of his officers, and a few of his men had managed to escape capture. As the two howitzers of his battery and their ammunition waggons had been detached the previous evening, the French in fact captured only six of the guns of that battery, not the eight that Pajol claimed.[3]

The first indication of Napoleon's intentions for 18 June can be found in his letter to Marshal Ney, written by Soult on the morning of 17 June in the Emperor's headquarters in Fleurus. This letter read,

> Général Flahaut, who has just arrived here, reports that you are still unaware of yesterday's events. However, I do believe I have sent you news of the

[1] Houssaye, vol II, p 225.
[2] Grouchy, vol IV, p 48.
[3] Lettow-Vorbeck, p 379 fn.

Emperor's victory. The Prussian army has been put to flight. Général Pajol is pursuing it along the roads to Namur and Liège. We already have several thousand prisoners and thirty guns. Our troops fought well. An attack by six battalions of the Guard, the service squadrons and the cavalry division of Général Delort broke through the enemy line, causing great confusion in their ranks, and seized the position.

The Emperor is going to the windmill of Brye, beyond which passes the main road from Namur to Quatre Bras. It is not possible for the English army to do anything against you now. Should that nevertheless happen, the Emperor would march directly against them along the road to Quatre Bras while you attack them frontally with your divisions that must all be concentrated by now. The enemy would then be annihilated very quickly. Thus, you are to report to His Majesty exactly where your divisions are positioned and what is happening…

It is His Majesty's intention that you capture the position at Quatre Bras as ordered. If that is not possible, which seems highly unlikely, then send a detailed report immediately, and the Emperor will march to you as mentioned previously. If, on the other hand, there is only a rearguard there, then attack it and take the position.

Today, this operation is to be ended, the ammunition resupplied, scattered soldiers to be gathered together and the detachments drawn in…

The famous partisan Lützow [the former Freikorps leader of 1813–14], who has been taken prisoner, has said that the Prussian army has been destroyed, and that Blücher has, for the second time, led the monarchy to ruin.[4]

From this, it is clear that Bonaparte had considerably overestimated the effect of his victory over the Prussians. From the number of prisoners taken, guns captured and Lützow's statement, he was led to believe he had achieved another Jena. Pajol's message also seemed to confirm that the Prussians were withdrawing eastward after having suffered a total defeat.

A message of around noon from Exelmans, commander of the French 2nd Cavalry Corps, added to this impression. Exelmans' report said that one of his brigades, Berton's, was following up to Gembloux. He stated,

I have observed [the Prussians] until now, and have not seen them make a move. Their army is on the left bank of the Orneau. They have just one battalion on the right-bank, in front of Basse Baudecet. I will follow them the instant they move.[5]

Perhaps revealingly, Exelmans also complained that his dragoons were exhausted and lacked the necessary experience to perform properly the duties of the light cavalry.

Thus, two cavalry corps and one infantry division had set off that morning to establish the direction of the Prussian retreat. The reports they sent back indicated that the Prussians were retiring in the direction of Namur and Liège, and we know from Groeben's reports (quoted in the previous chapter) that the

[4] Lettow-Vorbeck, pp 377–8.
[5] Grouchy, vol IV, p 49.

French had undertaken no reconnaissance towards Wavre that might have corrected their error. Napoleon's attention was also being drawn away from the Prussians to events at Quatre Bras. He heard from Ney that strong forces remained in position there, so Lobau's corps and the Guard were ordered to move in that direction. Soult told Ney that it was the Emperor's wish that,

> ... you attack the enemy at Quatre Bras to throw them out of their positions. The corps at Marbais will support your operations. His Majesty awaits your reports with impatience.[6]

This decision confirmed that Napoleon had now allowed the bulk of the Prussian Army to slip away in the direction of Wavre and was not yet aware of this. Gneisenau, who had made the decision to retreat by this route the previous night, had managed to turn the heavy tactical defeat at Ligny into a possible strategic advantage. Each hour that passed from now until the end of the next day's battle was going to see the advantage the French had gained with their victory on 16 June diminish.

Grouchy Seeks the Prussians

After having received the reports from Pajol and Exelmans, Napoleon ordered Grouchy to move on Gembloux with those two cavalry corps, Teste's division and the army corps of Gérard and Vandamme. His orders to Grouchy read,

> Locate the enemy's direction of march and report to me his movements, so I can establish his real intentions. I am moving my headquarters to Quatre Bras where the English still were this morning. Thus, our line of communication is along the cobbled road from Namur, a direct line. If the enemy has evacuated Namur, order the commander of the 2nd Military District in Charlemont, to occupy Namur...
> It is important to find out the intentions of Blücher and Wellington, if they intend to unite their armies to cover Brussels and Liège, and if they intend to give battle. No matter what, you are to keep your two infantry corps together, no more than a lieue [4 km] apart, with several lines of retreat. To maintain contact with headquarters, you are to place cavalry posts along the route.[7]

It is interesting to note that, despite the information received from his cavalry earlier, Napoleon was now considering the possibility of the Allies uniting their forces to cover Brussels. Nevertheless, he made little effort to scout the area between Tilly and Wavre, only sending off a cavalry patrol in this direction later in the day.

Early that afternoon Exelmans passed on to Grouchy the information that the Prussians were massing at Gembloux.[8] The remainder of the right wing of the French Army then moved in this direction, Vandamme's III Corps arriving around 7 p.m., Gérard's IV Corps beginning to arrive at 10 p.m. In the meantime, the Prussians had slipped away, with Thielemann's corps breaking camp at 2 p.m., an hour before Exelmans' dragoons entered the town.[9]

6   d'Elchingen, p 44.
7   Lettow-Vorbeck, pp 380–1.

8   Houssaye, vol II, p 232.
9   Houssaye, vol II, p 252.

By now the great heat of the previous day had given way to pelting rain that discouraged a vigorous pursuit. Even so, about 6 p.m. Exelmans sent Bonnemains' brigade of dragoons off towards Sart-à-Walhain, and the 15e Dragoons towards Perwez.[10] Bonnemains' scouts spread out in the direction of Nil-Saint-Vincent and Tourinnes, which was still held by a Prussian infantry rearguard. After observing this force for an hour, the French retraced their steps, bivouacking at Ernage.

In the course of these moves Grouchy and his men obtained information from the locals which indicated that the Prussians might be retreating on Wavre. There was no clear picture yet of all the Prussian movements and intentions, but what was certain was that they were not moving on Namur, as had been suspected earlier. At 10 p.m. Grouchy reported the situation to Napoleon,

Sire,

I have the honour to report to you that I am in Gembloux and my cavalry is at Sauvenière. The enemy, about 30,000 men strong, is continuing his retreat. We have captured 400 cattle, supplies and baggage.

According to all reports, it appears that the Prussians, after meeting in Sauvenière, have split into two columns; one has taken the route via Sart-à-Walhain to Wavre, the other appears to be moving via Perwez. One can perhaps infer from that, that part of the enemy force is moving to rejoin Wellington, and that the centre, Blücher's [main] army, is retiring on Liège. A further column with artillery is retreating on Namur.

Général Exelmans has orders to push six squadrons on Sart-à-Walhain this evening, and two to Perwez. If, after their reports, it appears that the mass of the Prussians is retiring on Wavre, I will follow them in that direction so that they cannot reach Brussels, and to separate them from Wellington. If, on the contrary, my reports prove that the principal Prussian force is marching on Perwez, I will move on that town to pursue the enemy.

Generals Thielemann and Borstell, belonging to the army defeated by Your Majesty yesterday, were still here at 10 o'clock this morning, and admitted having lost 20,000 men. On departing, they asked the distances to Gembloux and Perwez. Blücher has a light arm wound, which has been dressed, and has not prevented him from leading the army. He did not come through Gembloux.[11]

Grouchy then issued orders for Vandamme to march on Sart-à-Walhain the next day at 4 a.m., with Exelmans' cavalry in the lead, followed up by Gérard at 8 a.m. The route to be taken after Sart-à-Walhain would be determined by the information received. Pajol was ordered to march from Mazy to Leez to establish if Namur had been evacuated. In the morning of the 17th Pajol had ridden through Temploux and St Denis, from where he established the presence of a body of about 25,000 to 30,000 Prussians at Gembloux. He then fell back to Mazy, and reported that there were no Prussians in Namur.[12]

[10] Houssaye, vol II, p 253.   [12] Lettow-Vorbeck, p 388.
[11] Lettow-Vorbeck, pp 386–7.

Bonnemains sent a report from Ernage to Grouchy at 10.15 p.m., informing him that the Prussians had stayed in Tourinnes until that evening, leaving at 8.15 p.m. According to the locals, there was much infantry and only a little cavalry, apparently guarding a supply train.[13]

The Prussians were continuing to escape almost unhindered.

Napoleon Arrives at Waterloo

When Napoleon's main force reached its positions around the inn of Belle-Alliance on the evening of the 17th, the artillery shot off a few rounds before Napoleon ordered a cease-fire and set his troops to bivouac on the wet fields.

The French Army took up the following positions. D'Erlon's I Corps (less Durutte's 4th Division, which only arrived the following morning) was in the front line, between the farm of Monplaisir and the village of Plancenoit, its front covered by Jacquinot's 1st Cavalry Division. Milhaud's cuirassiers (4th Cavalry Corps), the light cavalry of Domon's 3rd Cavalry Division (from Vandamme's III Corps) and Subervie's 5th Cavalry Division (from Pajol's 1st Cavalry Corps) and the Guard Cavalry formed the second line, bivouacking along the Rossomme heights. Reille's II and Lobau's VI Corps and Kellermann's cuirassiers (3rd Cavalry Corps) rested in and around Genappe. The Guard infantry left Genappe towards the end of the day and used side routes to march to Imperial Headquarters, the main road being blocked by the artillery and supply trains. They finally arrived at the village of Glabais between 11 p.m. and midnight.

For the troops on both sides it was a bad night. They were mostly wet and covered in mud after that day's torrential rain, and almost all had to spend the night bivouacking in the open. It was an uncomfortable way to prepare for battle.

---

[13] Lettow-Vorbeck, p 388.

Chapter 3
The Prussians Start for Waterloo

Wellington's Stand at Mont St Jean

The Duke of Wellington's decision to offer battle in the Mont St Jean position was determined, as we have seen, by Blücher's promise to offer rapid and substantial support. Blücher had said that Bülow's IV Army Corps would march off at daybreak on 18 June, followed immediately by the II Army Corps, to attack the French right flank, and that the two remaining army corps would make themselves ready to move in support. As the distance Bülow would have to march was less than 20 km, Wellington counted on the Prussians arriving from 11 a.m., but the first Prussian troops did not actually reach the battlefield until 4.30 p.m., and even then only two brigades came into action, with other units gradually arriving later. The reasons for this delay are the principal subject of this chapter.

Difficult Terrain

During the night of 17/18 June the Prussian Army camped in the vicinity of Wavre. The next day its intervention in the Battle of Waterloo took place between the villages of Fichermont and Plancenoit. The distances between these points, the terrain, and the type and condition of the roads and tracks linking them were obviously crucial factors.

The distance from Vieux-Sart, where the furthest part of the IV Army Corps was located, to Plancenoit was 25 km, and to the Fichermont wood, where Blücher made a halt in his march, 21 km. The distance from Vieux-Sart to Wavre is eight km, from Wavre to Chapelle St Lambert, ten, from St Lambert to the wood, three. Marching at normal speed, good troops would take about six hours to cover that distance. A forced march made when hurrying to aid an ally should have taken less. However, the Prussians actually needed 11 hours, double the time one would have expected them to take.

A level path ran along the edge of the Dyle valley from Wavre to Limal. Otherwise, the terrain was gently undulating or hilly, with the occasional steeper slope. Although this was the best route for a large body of troops to move with its heavy equipment, it had two disadvantages. Firstly, the hills obstructed the view, and any artillery units trying to haul their guns up or down them could hold up troop movements. Secondly, the route led through the narrow crooked streets of the villages of Wavre, Limal and Bierges. Of these, Wavre presented a particular problem as there was only one stone bridge across the Dyle there. Wavre was not only the location of the army headquarters with all its accompanying traffic, but also the point of concentration of the sick and wounded, supply trains, heavy equipment, and so on of the entire army. Delays caused by the heavy traffic were likely and did indeed occur.[1]

From Limal, the ground rises, and the paths meander to Chapelle St Lambert, from where the route drops again into the valley of the Lasne brook. On the far side of the valley, the ground rises again, up to the Fichermont wood. The final part of the march was the most difficult, as Prince August of Thurn und Taxis, the Bavarian representative in the Prussian headquarters, related in his diary,

> The terrain now began to get surprisingly difficult. There was a steep drop into the Lasne valley, and immediately after that, an equally steep rise on the other side. The path was very narrow and in a poor state. The defile delayed us for a very long time, and we had particular difficulty to bringing the artillery up the far height. A very small enemy detachment could have disputed its passage with us the whole day.[2]

The report of Kolonnenjäger (supply train provost) Diederichs confirmed this description. He wrote,

> ... just one sunken road ran out from the middle of the wood behind Lasne, which could only be crossed with great difficulty by the advancing troops, and particularly the artillery.[3]

The officer who reconnoitred this route earlier that morning reported,

> The route to La Haye, leading through Lasne, drops gently, but the bank on this side is much steeper. The path is long, the defile closed in by 20 foot high curves... The Lasne brook, however, is insignificant, only two to three feet deep.[4]

Thurn und Taxis also described the terrain on the other side of this rise,

> On reaching these heights, one finds the entrance to the wood of Frichermont, which gives its name to the village that lies a little further on, but whose church spire could be seen quite clearly from a vantage point. The entrance to the wood was occupied by enemy infantry.[5]

The wood was on the crest of the heights between Lasne and Fichermont, reaching almost as far as Aywières to the south, blocking any view to or from the direction of Belle Alliance. The path from Lasne to Plancenoit crossed the northern part of it.

The terrain along the route taken by the I Army Corps, more to the north, was also difficult, with the march likely to be delayed by several defiles, hills, valleys and the Lasne brook. The narrow country paths had been largely washed away by the recent heavy rain, and the heavy lime soil stuck to everything, clogging wheels and axles, sucking off footwear. The men were already

---

[1] Pflugk-Harttung, *Wavre*, p 414.
[2] Thurn und Taxis, p 331.
[3] Pflugk-Harttung, *Wavre*, p 415.
[4] Pflugk-Harttung, *Wavre*, p 623.
[5] Thurn und Taxis, pp 331–2.

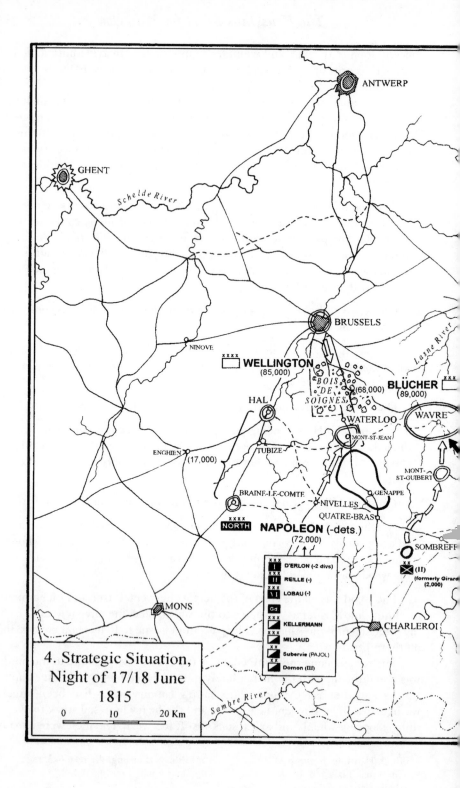

ANTWERP

GHENT

Schelde River

BRUSSELS

NINOVE

☐ WELLINGTON
(85,000)

BOIS DE SOIGNES

(68,000)

BLÜCHER
(89,000)

Lasne River

HAL

WATERLOO

WAVRE

ENGHIEN
(17,000)

TUBIZE

MONT-ST-JEAN

MONT-ST-GUIBERT

BRAINE-LE-COMTE

NIVELLES

GENAPPE

QUATRE-BRAS

NORTH NAPOLEON (-dets.)
(72,000)

SOMBREFF

I	D'ERLON (-2 divs)
II	REILLE (-)
VI	LOBAU (-)
Gd	
	KELLERMANN
	MILHAUD
	Subervie (PAJOL)
	Domon (II)

(II)
(formerly Girard)
(2,000)

MONS

CHARLEROI

4. Strategic Situation, Night of 17/18 June 1815

0   10   20 Km

Sambre River

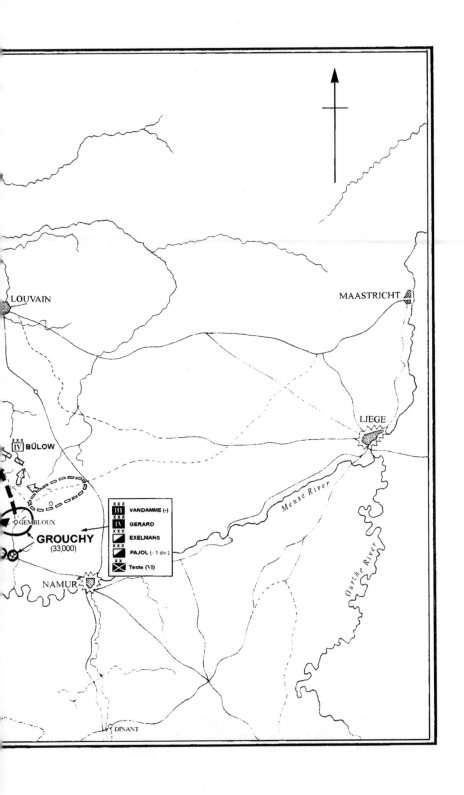

LOUVAIN

MAASTRICHT

LIEGE

×××
IV BÜLOW

GEMBLOUX

GROUCHY
(33,000)

××× III	VANDAMME (-)
××× IV	GERARD
×××	EXELMANS
×××	PAJOL (- 1 div.)
××	Teste (VI)

NAMUR

Meuse River

Ourthe River

DINANT

hungry and wet through before they started and their officers were constantly aware of the danger of a French attack, either by Grouchy or by Napoleon. In his diary, Nostitz described the situation,

> The Field Marshal's position one was of the most critical in which any commander could be. In his rear, he was threatened by an enemy corps at least 30,000 men strong, led by a veteran marshal, with whom a serious confrontation could not be avoided. Ahead was the defile of St Lambert, which would take half an hour to negotiate, and at its exit a wood that the enemy could take possession of at any moment, making any further progress difficult, if not impossible.[6]

Particular problems occurred where the road from Wavre to Plancenoit ran across a series of steep ridges. It was hard enough for the Prussian artillerymen to drag their guns and waggons up these ridges, and probably even harder to stop them sliding uncontrollably down the other side. The physical effort and care required delayed the advance by hours. Only at Plancenoit did the terrain finally begin to flatten and open out, and here Napoleon's Imperial Guard was waiting.

Bülow's Corps Moves Off

Although it was the furthest from Wellington's positions, Bülow's IV Army Corps was the freshest, and was therefore ordered to lead the Prussian march on Waterloo. Zieten's I Army Corps, the closest to their Allies, had suffered most severely, losing almost 40 per cent of its strength in the previous two days of fighting and accordingly would not have been a wise choice to lead the march. Nor would the II and III Army Corps which had also taken casualties and been disrupted by the retreat from Ligny.

Early on 18 June Bülow issued the necessary movement orders for his troops which read,

> The Corps is to move off immediately via Wavre to Chapelle St Lambert, marching in the following order:
>
> Losthin's brigade [15th] as vanguard, accompanied by the [2nd] Silesian Hussar Regiment [6th Hussars] and one 12-pounder battery. The hussars are to take the lead, and the guns are to march in front of the final battalion in the column. Hiller's [16th] brigade is to follow, then Hake's [13th], then the Reserve Artillery, then the Reserve Cavalry, which is to be joined again by the 2nd Kurmark Landwehr Cavalry. Ryssel's [14th] brigade, less Oberst-lieutenant von Ledebur's detachment will bring up the rear. This detachment will remain at Mont St Guibert unless forced back by the enemy, when it will retire on Wavre.
>
> I will be with the vanguard.
>
> All baggage trains are to march to Louvain, and Oberstlieutenant von Schlegel will organise their movement from Chapelle St Laurent. No waggons are permitted in the columns. The men must be provided with as much food

---

[6] Nostitz, *Tagebuch*, p 37.

as possible. Any outposts that cannot be pulled in quickly enough to rejoin their units are to join Ryssel's brigade.

The brigades must break camp at the same time, and be ready to move off towards Wavre one after the other.

Hauptmann Reyher will stay with Oberstlieutenant von Ledebur's detachment to keep a close eye on enemy movements, which he will have reported to me quickly.[7]

We also know when most of these units received their orders. An officer of the 3rd Silesian Landwehr Cavalry Regiment, part of the 15th Brigade, brought the orders to his brigade at 2 a.m. The 16th Brigade received theirs at 3 a.m., and the 14th at 4 a.m.

The vanguard marched off at daybreak as planned with Bülow at their head. The hussars were in front, followed by the II./18th Regiment and the F./1st Silesian Landwehr. Kapitain von Bressler commanded the Silesians, but overall charge of the two battalions was given to Major von Koschkull of the II./18th. The main body of infantry came next and the artillery brought up the rear.[8]

Major von Witowski of the 2nd Silesian Hussars was sent off to patrol the defiles of the Lasne brook in the direction of Maransart and to establish contact with Wellington's left. Major von Falkenhausen was likewise sent off with 100 men of the 3rd Silesian Landwehr Cavalry. Both patrols soon established that the French had neglected to secure their right flank on the Lasne brook.[9]

Bülow's orders thus did everything possible to ensure a rapid march to support Wellington. The cumbersome baggage was sent off elsewhere, the outposts were called in and the order of march laid down. However, delays soon ensued. The first cause was the general exhaustion of the men, exacerbated by a lack of food. Bülow's corps had marched a particularly long distance on 16 June and had another difficult march in heavy rain on the 17th, with some units, as described in Chapter 1, not reaching their bivouacs until around midnight. Matters improved little the next morning. The journal of the 13th Brigade noted,

At the same time [at daybreak], a few waggons arrived with supplies and brandy, which were given to the men immediately, raising their spirits. However, the food could not be cooked as the order to march off was received at the same time.[10]

Bülow may have ordered his men to take as much food with them as possible, but there was precious little to take in the first place, and there was no time either to look for supplies or cook them.

Though the 15th Brigade moved off first, by 5 a.m. only part of its baggage train had left for Louvain, and this meant that the 16th Brigade could only start its march at 6 a.m. The Reserve Cavalry was only able to move properly at 9 a.m., and these delays meant that the 14th Brigade, the last troops of

[7] Pflugk-Harttung, *Wavre*, pp 422–3.
[8] Wedell, pp 163–4.
[9] Lippe-Weissenfeld, p 241.
[10] Pflugk-Harttung, *Wavre*, p 502.

Bülow's corps, did not get going until 10 a.m., despite the fact that they had fallen in six hours earlier.

Hardly had the corps' rearguard started to march off when its baggage train was attacked by Exelmans' vanguard. The French cavalry had been able to approach unobserved as the Prussian pickets had been withdrawn on the main body. The 1st Silesian Landwehr Cavalry was sent back to deal with the attack, followed later by the 2nd Pomeranians. The Silesians sent out their flankers to reconnoitre the enemy's strength, with the Pomeranians supporting them, and soon established that they were facing five enemy squadrons. The French then fell back, and allowed the baggage trains and artillery to move on but the effect was that these two regiments of Prussian cavalry did not reach the battlefield of Waterloo.[11]

The IV Army Corps continued its march, passing by the bivouacs of the II and III Army Corps. Due to the proximity of French forces, it was considered too dangerous to march along the right bank of the Dyle, so the entire corps was ordered to pass through Wavre itself, waggons and all. In good weather, the village was a bottleneck, in bad weather, a muddy, slippery pass.

The corps only started to wind its way through Wavre at 7 a.m.[12] It had already taken nearly three hours to move no more than six km and further problems were ahead. The 15th Brigade crossed the bridge and marched through the town with little difficulty, although it was briefly held up by a 12-pounder cannon with a broken axle that was blocking the exit from the town. This was quickly pushed out the way.

Kolonnenjäger Diederichs' account then described a new holdup,

> Just as the vanguard reached the heights on the other side of Wavre, we suddenly noticed that the town had caught light, and were most concerned that the march could be delayed by this event.[13]

Premierlieutenant Elsner was nearer to the incident and gave a more graphic description,

> I rode a short way out of the town, along the edge of a sunken road, down which troops were marching, looking for a better route. Suddenly, I noticed that these troops started to double down the road... The cause of this unexpected movement was the outbreak of a fire in the town that threatened to make this bottleneck, down which three army corps and 300 guns [sic!] were going, quite unusable. The scene was simply dreadful. On the left of the road, clouds of smoke and flames were shooting out of a roof, and a strong wind was blowing down the street, into the town. Whole battalions were running at full pelt, the cannon and powder waggons were galloping away. Everybody was screaming and pushing.
>
> In the middle of the town was a narrow bridge over the river that cut the town into two. Now, when the infantry and artillery reached this bridge, they

---

[11] The *Journal* of Constant Rebecque contains a copy of Bülow's Report of 19 June 1815, from which much of this information is taken.

[12] Pflugk-Harttung, *Wavre*, p 506.
[13] Pflugk-Harttung, *Wavre*, p 507.

got mixed together, and there was a great danger of men being run over. A powder waggon, driven badly, blocked the bridge for a time, cutting off part of my company from the battalion, which then had to wade across the river. Finally, we got out of the town safely and the troops designated extinguished the fire.[14]

Thurn und Taxis saw things a little differently,

… just at the moment the ammunition columns started to cross the bridge over the Dyle in Wavre, a mill close to it went up in flames, creating a significant delay and danger (because of the powder). Fortunately, there were no repercussions.[15]

The fire in fact quickly spread to two houses, but was held in check by the garrison of the town, the I./14th, supported by the 7th Pioneer Company. The commander of the pioneers wrote in his report,

Called to Wavre on the morning of the 18th to stem with my pioneer company the fire that was hindering the passage of the troops, I had to devote my entire attention to this task. Having finished it, I left that place… I believe I remember that the bridge was the only crossing point in the town, and there was no ford, but that there was a place the Dyle could be crossed just below the town. I do not think that the IV Army Corps was delayed by the fire, because the troops used this passage.[16]

It is not clear from these accounts how long this fire delayed the corps, if at all, and Bülow's own report says only that,

Heavy rain had washed away the paths and the baggage trains of the various army corps directed on Wavre blocked the defile. This delayed my march and broke it up. This resulted in the 15th Brigade only managing to get to St Lambert by 10 a.m., the remainder of the corps by midday, and the 14th Brigade, due to the distance it had to march from Vieux-Sart, only by 3 p.m.[17]

II Army Corps Delayed

While the fire in Wavre probably only partially delayed the advance of the IV Army Corps, it caused the following columns to have to halt completely for several hours. Generalmajor von Brause, commander of the 7th Brigade, had his troops move off at 5 a.m. as ordered. He followed the Reserve Artillery of the II Army Corps. However,

… IV Corps' movement through Wavre delayed our march so much that, at 11 a.m., the Reserve Artillery, the 7th and 8th Brigades and the rearguard under Oberstleutnant von Sohr were still in their bivouac areas, in columns, when a report arrived that enemy cavalry was on our left flank.[18]

As the 7th and 8th Brigades now had to face front against Grouchy, they left their positions only at 2.30 p.m.

---

[14] Pflugk-Harttung, *Wavre*, p 507.
[15] Thurn und Taxis, pp 330–1.
[16] Pflugk-Harttung, *Ereignisse*, p 191.
[17] Lettow-Vorbeck, p 395.
[18] Pflugk-Harttung, *Wavre*, p 508.

In all, the march through Wavre took II Army Corps a good deal of time, the traffic jam of the supply trains which built up during the long halt for the fire mainly causing the delays. Generalmajor von Pirch I, commander of II Corps, also noted that the supply trains of the IV Army Corps blocked the roads around Bierges at 11 a.m., causing the 14th Brigade and his own corps to be delayed,[19] and Generallieutenant von Thielemann, commander of III Army Corps, reported that Pirch's men only completed their march through Wavre by 4 p.m.

On to St Lambert

After passing through Wavre the 15th Brigade halted for a time to allow the remainder of Bülow's troops to catch up and also used the opportunity to reorganise the column of march. As the 12-pounder battery with the vanguard was proving to be a hindrance, it was left behind to rejoin the Reserve Artillery. The 2nd Neumark Landwehr Cavalry moved up to replace it, so that the vanguard now had two regiments of cavalry. The Neumarkers, being on the wrong side of the fire, arrived later, after having ridden in between the marching infantry. The brigade then continued its march uninterrupted until it approached Chapelle St Lambert.

From 9 a.m., the IV Army Corps started to arrive before St Lambert, where it assembled and deployed to the left and right of the road. The journal of the 15th Brigade noted its arrival at 9 a.m.,[20] while Bülow's report gave the time as 10 a.m., so it is reasonable to assume that the brigade took an hour to assemble at this point. The history of the 18th Regiment, part of the 15th Brigade, recorded simply that, 'By 11 a.m., the regiment was deployed on the heights this side [east] of St Lambert.'[21]

Around midday the two battalions of the 15th Brigade under Major von Koschkull crossed the Lasne brook and moved into the Fichermont wood. A skirmish line deployed along the far edge of the wood and the main body of the brigade formed up behind in two lines. The first consisted of the I. and F./18th Regiment, the second of the I. and II./3rd Silesian Landwehr and the entire 4th Silesian Landwehr. The cavalry and artillery drew up behind the infantry.[22]

The remainder of the corps arrived later. Oberst von Hiller, commander of the 16th Brigade noted, 'By 2 p.m., the 16th Brigade was at the assembly area this side [east] of the village of Chapelle St Lambert.'[23] The report of the 6-pounder Foot Battery Nr. 21, attached to the 13th Brigade, recorded it having passed through Wavre by 9 a.m. It stopped briefly on the hill above the town, moving off again 15 minutes later, and arrived at the heights of St Lambert by 11.30 a.m. The 14th Brigade arrived last, completing its march from Vieux-Sart to St Lambert by about 3 p.m. The point units of the IV Army Corps therefore reached their assembly area some six hours before the rearguard.

[19] Pflugk-Harttung, *Wavre*, p 511.
[20] Pflugk-Harttung, *Wavre*, p 509.
[21] Wedell, p 163.

[22] Wedell, p164.
[23] Pflugk-Harttung, *Wavre*, p 510.

Long before then the final stages of the approach to Waterloo had begun. Diederichs' account mentioned the 15th Brigade halting for a rest at St Lambert, then hearing the sound of cannon fire starting about 11.15 a.m. Bülow's report explained what happened next,

> The Duke of Wellington had expressed the view that the IV Army Corps should remain at St Lambert until the enemy's intentions were clear. To establish direct contact with the English army, the very difficult defile of St Lambert and Lasne had to be passed. This could not be undertaken until the probable enemy movements on our left flank were established. To do so, I sent off two strong cavalry detachments to reconnoitre in this direction. One, under Major von Witowski of the 2nd Silesian Hussar Regiment went towards Maransart where it found the enemy. The other, under Major von Falkenhausen went to Seroulx [Céroux], where it was to establish contact with the detachment of Oberstlieutenant von Ledebur.[24]

Bülow also sent off several officers of the 2nd Silesian Hussars to establish contact with Wellington's forces.[25]

At last the Prussians were nearing the battlefield. Bülow's men had started off from about 4 a.m. and only completed their concentration at their jumping-off point around 3 p.m. They had taken 11 hours to cover 15 kilometres first to last, an indication of just how difficult the circumstances facing them were. These exhausted troops would have to march further and fight a battle that day, and then conduct a pursuit.

I Army Corps

Zieten's I Army Corps had taken the brunt of the fighting on the Prussian side on 15 and 16 June and in the end only the 1st Brigade of some 5,500 men and the 1,100-strong Reserve Cavalry from the corps would participate in the Battle of Waterloo. Having spent the past three days constantly fighting and marching, more than any other body of Allied troops in this campaign, Zieten's men were exhausted, hungry, wet and low on ammunition. By all normal standards, they were not fit for service. However, gritting their teeth, they, too, set out for Waterloo on 18 June, to relieve Wellington's crumbling left flank, arriving not a moment too soon.

At 2 a.m. on the 18th Zieten received the following order, timed at midnight, from Blücher,

> Your Excellency is to have the troops cook breakfast early tomorrow morning so that they can move off soon after. The II and IV Army Corps will set out at daybreak and march via Wavre in the direction of Chapelle St Lambert. Once there, they will operate against the right flank of the enemy, should, as is most likely, the Duke of Wellington be attacked in his position. The baggage, supply trains, etc. are to be directed to Louvain, with those of the I Corps going on the left bank of the Dyle to avoid the centre of Wavre.[26]

[25] *Journal* of Constant Rebecque, Bülow's Report of 19 June 1815.
[26] Lippe-Weissenfeld, p 241.
[27] Pflugk-Harttung, *Zieten*, pp 197–8.

About midday on the 18th an ADC brought Zieten an oral order actually to begin his march via Froidmont to Ohain, and thus to support Wellington's left flank. The I Army Corps was bivouacked at Bierges, that is to the south of the columns of the IV and II Army Corps, which meant that Zieten's route would cross those of Bülow and Pirch I. However, taking advantage of the delayed start of the march of the II Army Corps, Zieten's lead brigade got under way at 1 p.m., though the remainder of the Corps had to wait until Pirch's men had passed. This is why Zieten's vanguard reached the battlefield well before the remainder of the corps, and why, as will be noted later, Thielemann could still see parts of the I Army Corps in Bierges at 3 p.m.[27]

On receiving his orders, Zieten issued the following 'Disposition',

The IV, II and I Army Corps are to march in two columns in such a way that they can support the Duke of Wellington, who has his right flank at Braine l'Alleud, and his left at Mont St Jean, with a diversion into Bonaparte's right flank. The IV and II Army Corps are to form our left flank. They will march via Neuf Cabaret to St Lambert. The I Army Corps will form the right flank. It will march via Froidmont to Ohain. The order of march is as follows:

Vanguard: 1st Brigade with one horse and one foot battery. In support of the vanguard, the Reserve Cavalry, then the 2nd, 3rd and 4th Brigades, and finally the Reserve Artillery... I request that as many [units] as possible march by sections, and where the terrain allows it, by divisions [to be able to deploy into battle formation as rapidly as possible].

I will consider it one of my happiest days if, on 18th June, the same Prussian courage is shown as on the 16th, but with greater success. With officers of the quality of our brigade commanders and chiefs I am sure my wish will be fulfilled.

Major von Dendenroth will lead the head of the column of the I Army Corps. The Westphalian Landwehr Cavalry Regiment will be divided among the brigades according to the order issued. The Reserve Cavalry will maintain contact with the columns on the left flank.[28]

The I Army Corps was on its way.

---

[27] Lettow-Vorbeck, p 399.
[28] Pflugk-Harttung, *Zieten*, p 198.

Chapter 4

The Field of Waterloo

The Terrain

Like the Sombreffe position in which the Prussian Army had fought on 16 June, the Waterloo position was also one that had been selected in advance for its suitability for use in a defensive battle. Indeed, a year before the battle, Wellington had reconnoitred the area and noted this site as being well suited for holding back an advance on Brussels. On 6 June 1815 there had even been talk about digging earthworks on this site, but the Duke rejected this because he wanted to have the freedom to choose the appropriate positions.[1]

The core feature of this battlefield was a narrow ridge that ran from Braine l'Alleud in the west to Ohain in the east. The northern slope of this ridge was useful in that it hid any troops behind it from both the sight of the enemy and his artillery fire. Thus, reserves could be brought to any threatened point without the enemy being aware of this. The paved road leading to Brussels from Charleroi and the south crossed the centre of the position and a minor road ran east–west along the ridge. The first 300 metres of this minor road to the west of its crossroads with the Charleroi road were sunken, and were an obstacle particularly to the movement of cavalry. The road to the east was sunken for about 60 metres. Hedges lined the road on both sides for about 900 metres, which would again make the going difficult for mounted troops. The road from Nivelles to Mont St Jean also crossed the battlefield on its western side.

A sandpit a little south of the crossroads on the Charleroi road and the nearby farmhouse of La Haye Sainte strengthened the centre of the position. Strongly constructed buildings also secured the two flanks; the walled château and farm of Hougoumont with its surrounding wall was on the right, the farms of Smohain, La Haye and Papelotte on the left, in the valley of the Ohain brook. Both banks of this stream were steeply sloping and were lined with bushes for a little way to the southeast and another château in Fichermont.

Little had been done to prepare the formidable strongly-built farmhouse of La Haye Sainte for the defence. One of the barn gates leading into the high-walled farmyard had been burnt for fuel by the troops the night before and other measures such as loopholing, reinforcing the remaining gates and doors and removing combustible items such as hay had not been finished. Furthermore, an adequate supply of ammunition had not been secured. This farmhouse could have been turned into a fortress. Instead, its garrison was placed in an inadequately prepared building with insufficient ammunition. It is a credit to its professionalism that it held La Haye Sainte for as long as it did.

The buildings at Hougoumont were still more substantial and easily adapted for defence. A brick wall to the south and east enclosed the garden

---

[1] Lettow-Vorbeck, p 404.

and beyond that there was an extensive orchard. Unlike La Haye Sainte, the château and its farm buildings had been adequately prepared. On the evening of 17 June, firing platforms had been built, loopholing undertaken and sufficient ammunition stored.

The Fichermont château was about 1,000 metres south-east of the hamlet of Smohain. The château itself consisted of two wings and a collection of outhouses. These were all solid buildings, standing close together in a rectangle with a large courtyard in the middle. Furthermore, the château stood on a mound, so the whole structure and position was well suited to the defence. To its east and south stood Smohain, a collection of less than a dozen cottages running along both banks of the Smohain brook. The buildings to the south of the hamlet were on a slight ridge, which made them easily defensible, but those along both banks of the stream were in a hollow and thus poorly positioned. The brook itself was no significant obstacle, with its banks too low to offer any protection.[2]

Close to the hamlet of Smohain was the farm of La Haye (not to be confused with La Haye Sainte in the centre of the Allied position). The farm buildings formed a rectangle, with one garden on the north side, one on the south, surrounded by a low wall covered in bushes. A gateway led into a barn from which access to the inner courtyard could be gained. There was also a small door leading from one of the gardens to the courtyard.[3]

Less than 100 metres to the west of this stood the farm of Papelotte which also consisted of long, solid buildings. Along three sides of these buildings was a wall three metres high around an orchard. Several outbuildings stood beyond the orchard. Papelotte offered almost as much for the defence as Fichermont.[4]

The main French position was along a parallel ridge about 1,300 metres from the Allied line. From it, the valley and the rising ground to the top of the ridge opposite was both visible and within artillery range. The terrain between the two lines contained small ridges that did not greatly obstruct troop movement. Thus, the French were able to bombard the forward positions of the Allies and assault them with infantry and cavalry. The recent heavy rain had turned the soil to mud, however, hindering movement, and the tall crops, in places above the height of a man, further obstructed any attackers, though the crops would soon be trampled down.

It had been Napoleon's intention for the battle to commence at 9 a.m. that day, after his troops had rested and eaten. However, the muddy ground made him decide to wait for over two hours for it to dry out, so that his troops would be able to manoeuvre with greater ease and his cannon be brought into position and fire with greater effect. That made up in part for the delays in the Prussian advance.

Organisation and Strength of Wellington's Army

Wellington reorganised the Anglo-Dutch-German Army for that day's battle. It consisted of the following:

---

[2] Starklof, vol II, p 197.

[3] Rössler, *Geschichte*, p 86.

[4] Starklof, vol II, pp 197–8.

The *Right Wing* under Lord Hill, stationed to the west of the paved road from Nivelles. Prince Frederik's Netherlanders having been detached to Hal, the troops remaining were Clinton's 2nd Division with the brigades of Adam, du Plat, Hugh Halkett and Mitchell's brigade of Colville's division. These were joined by Chassé's 3rd Division of Netherlanders.

The *Centre* under the Prince of Orange. Drawn up between the two main roads. All that remained of the Prince's original corps were Alten's division and the brigades of Colin Halkett, Ompteda and Kielmansegge. These were joined by the brigades of Kruse and Lambert of Cole's division, and the Brunswick Corps.

The *Left Wing* under Picton. As well as the brigades of Picton's own 5th Division (Kempt, Pack and Vincke) this included Best's brigade from Cole's division, which had joined Picton's men on the march from Brussels on 16 June, and Perponcher's 2nd Division of Netherlanders with the brigades of Bijlandt and Saxe-Weimar.

The Guards remained under the direct orders of the Duke of Wellington.

The *Cavalry* were led by Lord Uxbridge, including the entire Allied cavalry force, with the exception of that of the Brunswick contingent.

The Duke of Wellington's order of battle that day reflected his habit of mixing his better troops with inexperienced units. Experienced officers were placed in command of his flanks, while the Duke himself would usually be on hand in the centre where the Prince of Orange was nominally in charge. In addition the Prince of Orange had lost control of his three Netherlands divisions and of the Guards, while some of the troops placed under his command were held in reserve.

Siborne gave Wellington's forces as having the following strengths at Waterloo:

Infantry	49,608 men
Cavalry	12,408 men
Artillery	5,645 men
Total	67,661 men and 156 guns.

These were made up as follows:

Germans	25,886 men	38% of total
British	23,991 men	36% of total
Netherlanders	17,784 men	26% of total

The 'German' units can be subdivided further as:

King's German Legion	5,824 men
Hanoverians	11,247 men
Brunswickers	5,935 men
Nassauers	2,880 men[5]

The quality of the contingents varied. While the KGL soldiers were mainly veterans of the Peninsular War, the other German units consisted largely of young, inexperienced troops. The British were well trained and

---

[5] Siborne Wm., *History*, p 230.

highly motivated, though only some were Peninsular veterans. The Netherlanders consisted in part of troops who had until recently been part of Napoleon's forces, and in part of raw militia. Many were unhappy at finding their homes being included in a new, greater Kingdom of the Netherlands consisting of a mixture of Dutch-speaking Protestants and French-speaking Catholics. Many members of this contingent had a conflict of interests. Nevertheless, two days earlier at Quatre Bras, they had shown a brave spirit, holding on to their positions against the odds.

Positions of Wellington's Army[6]

Vivian's 6th (British) Brigade of cavalry was placed on the extreme left, made up of three regiments of hussars, the 10th and 18th British and the 1st of the KGL. It was about 1,250 men strong. A picket of one squadron of the 10th Hussars was placed in the village of Smohain. The ground here was open, and the left flank did not have an anchoring point. However, as the Prussians were expected to come from this direction, that was of little consequence. Next to Vivian was Vandeleur's 4th (British) Brigade of cavalry. It consisted of three regiments of light dragoons, the 11th, 12th and 16th and was about 1,000 men strong.

The Nassauers of the brigade of Saxe-Weimar, part of the 2nd Netherlands Division, provided the main strength of the defence of the left flank, holding strong points in advance of the main position. Duke Bernhard had the II. and III./2nd Nassau Regiment, the Orange Regiment and the volunteer company of the I./Orange-Nassau at his disposal – the I./2nd Nassau having been sent to Hougoumont.[7] Of his four battalions, he posted two south of the Ohain road, with the II./2nd garrisoning the farmhouses of Papelotte, La Haye and Smohain, while the volunteer company held Fichermont. The flank company of the III./2nd Nassau occupied Papelotte. Two companies of the III./2nd Nassau garrisoned Smohain, while La Haye was probably held by detachments from the same regiment. Three guns from Stevenart's Battery (the remaining five had been damaged at Quatre Bras) stood on the ridge behind Papelotte and La Haye. A skirmish line drew up along the east–west path leading from Ohain into the Allied centre.[8] This brigade had started the campaign 4,300 men strong, but had suffered heavily on 16 June, so now certainly numbered fewer than that.

The 5th Hanoverian Brigade under Oberst von Vincke stood on the main ridge of the position, behind the Wavre road. Part of Picton's division, it numbered around 2,000 men. Immediately to the right of Vincke stood the 4th Hanoverian Brigade under Oberst Best. Part of the 6th Division, it was about 2,800 men strong. Deployed close to the Wavre road, its right rested on a knoll that marked the highest point of Wellington's left.

Bijlandt's brigade, the other of the 2nd Netherlands Division, was positioned to the south of the Wavre road, further forward than Best's men, and

---

[6] This section is based largely on Shaw-Kennedy, with additions from Lettow-Vorbeck and Wm. Siborne's *History*.

[7] Rössler, *Geschichte*, pp 84–5.   [8] Starklof, vol 2, p 198.

directly in front of Pack's. It consisted of the 7th Line Regiment (one battalion), the 27th Jäger Battalion and three militia battalions. Just over 3,000 men strong, it was in a relatively exposed position, being particularly vulnerable to French artillery fire.

Pack's 9th Brigade (British) was drawn up behind Best's. About 1,700 men strong, it consisted of one battalion each from the 1st Royal Regiment, the 42nd Highlanders, the 44th Foot and the 92nd Highlanders. Kempt's brigade (8th British), nearly 2,000 men strong, part of Picton's division, came next in the line. It consisted of one battalion each from the 28th, 32nd and 79th Regiments as well as the 1st/95th Rifles. Its right was on the Charleroi road. Three companies of the 95th Rifles occupied the knoll and sandpit 100 metres in front of the main position and almost opposite the garden of La Haye Sainte.

Next in Wellington's line of battle was the 3rd Division under Graf von Alten. The left brigade, under Ompteda, consisted of two light and two line battalions of the KGL. About 1,500 men strong, it was deployed immediately west of the Charleroi road. One light battalion of about 400 men, under Major Baring, had been detached to garrison La Haye Sainte and during the morning the I./Regiment Nassau-Usingen, one company of Lüneburg Landwehr and the Avantgarde Battalion of the Brunswick Corps moved up to support Baring's men.

Kielmansegge's brigade (1st Hanoverian) was next in the main position, and consisted of five battalions of line and two companies of Jäger, numbering around 3,000 men. On its right was Sir Colin Halkett's 5th British Brigade. About 2,000 men strong, it contained one battalion each of the 30th, 33rd, 69th and 73rd Foot.

On Halkett's right stood Major-General Cooke's 1st British Division. Immediately next to Halkett was Maitland's brigade. About 1,600 men strong, this consisted of two battalions of the 1st Regiment of Foot Guards. Next came Byng's brigade (2nd British), with two further battalions of Guards, about 1,600 men strong.

The Hougoumont farmhouse, in front of the right centre of Wellington's position, was garrisoned by the four light companies of the British Guards battalions along with the I./2nd Nassau, a company of Hanoverian Jäger and a detachment of 100 men from the Field Battalion Lüneburg.

Finally, Mitchell's 4th British Brigade was deployed on the extreme right of the Allied line. This unit was part of the 4th Division, about 1,700 men strong, and consisted of a battalion each of the 14th Foot, 23rd Fusiliers and 51st Light. It was deployed to cover the road leading from Wellington's right to Braine l'Alleud. It was supported by a squadron of the 15th Hussars. The remainder of the 4th Division was at Hal, covering the road to the Channel ports. Chassé's 3rd Netherlands Division was deployed to cover the area around Braine l'Alleud.

Three brigades of Clinton's 2nd Division were drawn up on the plateau to the south-west of Merbe Braine. Du Plat's brigade, consisting of four line battalions of the KGL, 1,700 men, stood with its left flank on the Nivelles road. Adam's brigade was a little to the rear and was around 2,500 men strong, made up of a battalion each of the 52nd and 71st Light, the 2nd/95th Rifles and two companies of the 3rd/95th. Hugh Halkett's 3rd Hanoverian Brigade, with four battalions of Landwehr, about 2,400 men in total, stood on Adam's left.

Most of the Allied cavalry were deployed initially behind the centre of the position. The main exceptions to this were the brigades of Vivian and Vandeleur already mentioned. On the right was Grant's 5th Brigade, 1,100 sabres, the 7th and 15th Hussars and the 13th Light Dragoons. The 13th were normally part of Arentsschildt's 7th Brigade but had replaced the 2nd Hussars of the KGL who had been left to guard the frontier. Grant stood behind the infantry brigades of Byng and Maitland. Behind Grant stood the Cumberland Hussars, a Hanoverian unit nearly 500 men strong.

Dörnberg's 3rd Brigade, 1,200 men strong, stood on Grant's left. It consisted of the 23rd Light Dragoons and the 1st and 2nd Light Dragoons of the KGL. It was drawn up behind Halkett's infantry. To the left of Dörnberg stood 600 men of the 3rd Hussars of the KGL under Arentsschildt.

There were two British heavy cavalry brigades. Somerset's Household Brigade, 1,200 men strong, was drawn up to the rear of the infantry brigades of Ompteda and Kielmansegge. It consisted of the 1st and 2nd Life Guards, the Royal Horse Guards (Blue) and the 1st Dragoon Guards. Ponsonby's 2nd Brigade, 1,100 men strong, consisted of the 1st Dragoons (Royals), the 2nd Dragoons (Royal North British) and the 6th Dragoons (Inniskillings). It stood to the rear of Kempt and Pack.

In army reserve were Collaert's cavalry division, the Brunswick Corps and the 10th British Brigade under Lambert. The Brunswick Corps was about 5,000 men strong, both infantry and cavalry, and was placed at first between the Nivelles road and Merbe Braine. Collaert's division consisted of the light brigades of Merlen, 1,000 sabres, and Ghigny, 1,000 sabres, and Trip's heavy cavalry, 1,300 sabres. These Netherlanders were deployed further to the rear, towards Mont St Jean. Lambert's brigade, over 2,000 men, included the 1st Battalions of each of the 4th King's Own, 27th Inniskilling and 40th Somerset Regiments. These troops only reached Waterloo after the start of the battle and were first deployed behind Mont St Jean, but were later moved to the right of Kempt's brigade.

The artillery of the Anglo-Dutch-German Army was deployed as follows: Gardiner's Troop with Vivian's brigade; Byleveld's and Stevenart's batteries with Perponcher's division; Rettberg's battery with Best's brigade; Rogers' with Kempt; Lloyd's (British) and Cleeves' (KGL) with Alten; Kuhlmann's (Hanoverian) and Sandham's (British) with Cooke; Sympher's (KGL) and Bolton's with Clinton. The two Brunswick artillery batteries remained with their own Corps. In reserve were Beane's, Sinclair's and Ross' (British), and Braun's (Hanoverian). The remaining batteries of horse artillery were with the cavalry.

Excluding Chassé's 3rd Netherlands Division, some 6,500 men, the front covered by Wellington's troops was around 5,000 metres. Their strength was around 62,000 men, that is 12.4 men per metre of frontage, which was adequate for the purpose at hand.

Although the troops had suffered considerable discomfort the previous night, mostly bivouacking in heavy rain without proper cover, the British soldiers had at least been properly fed and supplied with ammunition. Some of the Allied troops, lacking their supply trains, did not do as well. In any case, Wellington's men were better supplied, better equipped and more rested than the Prussian troops who were endeavouring to make their way to the battlefield of Waterloo that morning.

The Hal Position

Wellington deployed 20,000 men to his right rear around the town of Hal. The reasons for this decision remain a little uncertain. In a conversation on 10 December 1820, Wellington apparently explained his thinking to Charles Greville. The Duke's comments make some, but perhaps not all of the arguments for this decision clear. Greville's recollection of what he was told was that,

> In this corps were the best of the Dutch troops; it had been placed there because the Duke expected the attack to be made on that side.[9]

Wellington elaborated that,

> ... he thought that he [Napoleon] had committed a fault in attacking him in the position of Waterloo; that his objective ought to have been to remove him [Wellington] as far as possible from the Prussian army, and that he ought consequently to have moved upon Hal, and to have attempted to penetrate by the same road by which the Duke had himself advanced. He had always calculated upon Bonaparte's doing this, and for this purpose he had posted 20,000 men under Prince Frederick at Hal.[10]

These statements make a certain amount of sense, but it seems evident that far from driving Wellington and the Prussians apart, a French advance on Hal would have driven them together. Moreover, as Wellington's line of retreat was north via Brussels to Antwerp, then any troops at Hal were not there to cover such an eventuality. However, Hal was on the road to Ghent, the location of Louis XVIII's court-in-exile, and to the Channel ports. If the battle went badly the troops at Hal would have served to delay a French advance sufficiently to allow the king's escape.

In addition, it would have made great political sense not to risk the destruction of the entire Netherlands Army at Waterloo. Having part of King Willem's troops still in the field even after a defeat would help to maintain the stability of his newly establish regime. It is likely that this was one of Wellington's considerations.

---

[9] Reeve, *Greville Memoirs*, vol I, p 39.
[10] Reeve, *Greville Memoirs*, vol I, p 40.

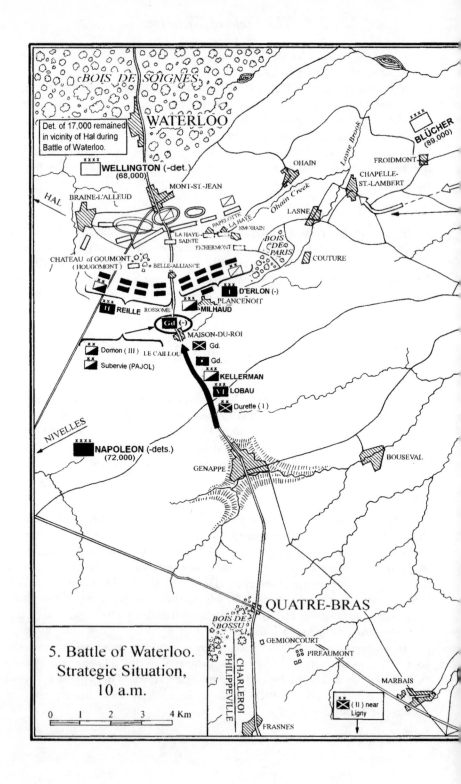

BOIS DE SOIGNES

WATERLOO

Det. of 17,000 remained in vicinity of Hal during Battle of Waterloo.

BLÜCHER (89,000)

OHAIN

FROIDMONT

CHAPELLE-ST.-LAMBERT

WELLINGTON (-det.) (68,000)

HAL

BRAINE-L'ALLEUD

MONT-ST-JEAN

LASNE

Lasne Brook

Ohain Creek

PAPELOTTE
LA HAYE
LA HAYE-SAINTE
SMOHAIN
FICHERMONT

BOIS DE PARIS

COUTURE

CHATEAU of GOUMONT (HOUGOMONT)

BELLE-ALLIANCE

D'ERLON (-)

REILLE   ROSSOME

PLANCENOIT

MILHAUD

Gd (-)

MAISON-DU-ROI

Gd.

Domon (III)   LE CAILLOU

Gd.

Subervie (PAJOL)

KELLERMAN

LOBAU

Durette (I)

NIVELLES

NAPOLEON (-dets.) (72,000)

GENAPPE

BOUSEVAL

QUATRE-BRAS

BOIS DE BOSSU

GEMIONCOURT

PIREAUMONT

CHARLEROI

PHILIPPEVILLE

MARBAIS

(II) near Ligny

FRASNES

5. Battle of Waterloo.
Strategic Situation,
10 a.m.

0   1   2   3   4 Km

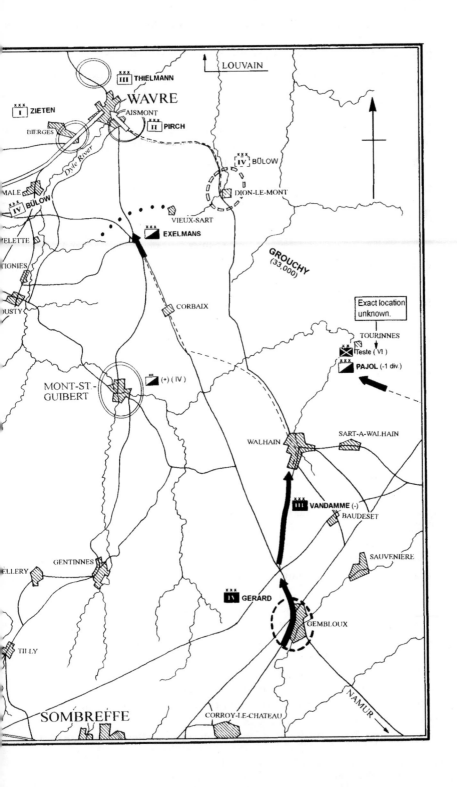

Organisation and Strength of Napoleon's Army[11]

The forces available to Bonaparte for the Battle of Waterloo consisted of the following,

Imperial Guard	Infantry	12,500 men
	Cavalry	3,500 men
	Artillery	3,300 men and 94 guns
I Corps – D'Erlon	Infantry	16,200 men
	Cavalry	1,400 men
	Artillery	1,400 men and 46 guns
II Corps – Reille	Infantry	16,000 men
	Cavalry	1,700 men
	Artillery	1,600 men and 46 guns
VI Corps – Lobau	Infantry	6,000 men
	Artillery	800 men and 30 guns
3rd Cavalry Division – Domon	Cavalry	900 men
	Artillery	170 men and 6 guns
5th Cavalry Division – Subervie	Cavalry	1,090 men
	Artillery	160 men and 6 guns
3rd Cavalry Corps – Kellermann	Cavalry	3,200 men
	Artillery	310 men and 12 guns
4th Cavalry Corps – Milhaud	Cavalry	2,600 men
	Artillery	310 men and 12 guns

Total: 50,700 infantry, 14,390 cavalry, 8,050 artillery and engineers, 252 guns.

Positions of Napoleon's Army[12]

The front line of the French positions ran along the ridge at Belle Alliance and Bonaparte's forces took some three hours to deploy there for the forthcoming battle. They formed some eleven columns, four in a first echelon, four in a second and three in a third. In front were the divisions of d'Erlon's corps on the right flank, and those of Reille on the left, deployed in battle order. The westernmost of the four columns of the first line consisted of Piré's 2nd Cavalry Division. They were deployed on the left of the second column made up of the II Corps infantry, the divisions of Jérôme, Foy and Bachelu. The third column was of four infantry divisions (Durutte, Marcognet, Donzelot and Quiot – the latter replacing the absent Général Allix) of the I Corps; and the fourth was composed of Jacquinot's light cavalry, the 1st Division. D'Erlon's four infantry divisions were drawn up with their right facing the farmhouse of Papelotte, their left against the Brussels road. Reille's three infantry divisions stood to the left of the Brussels road, next to D'Erlon's men. Jacquinot's and Piré's troopers covered the flanks.

The second line consisted of four columns. Kellermann's corps of

[11] This section is based largely on Wm. Siborne's *History*.
[12] This section is based largely on Houssaye, vol II, pp 329–34 and De Bas & T'Serclaes de Wommersom, vol II, pp 91–6.

cuirassiers stood behind Reille's divisions. Next to Kellermann was Lobau's VI Corps, with the infantry divisions of Simmer and Jeannin behind the French centre. Along the right of the Brussels road, the cavalry divisions of Domon (3rd) and Subervie (5th) formed the third group. The former had recently been attached to Lobau's VI Corps; the latter had been detached from Pajol's 1st Cavalry Corps, the remainder of which was with Grouchy. To their right, behind d'Erlon's divisions, stood Milhaud's cuirassiers, drawn up in battle order.

The third line was composed as follows. On the left was the Guard Heavy Cavalry Division, commanded by Général Guyot, the Grenadiers à Cheval under Dubois, the Dragoons under Ornans. They drew up behind Kellermann. The Imperial Guard infantry stood in reserve near Rossomme, under the command of Lieutenants-Généraux Friant, Morand and Duhesme. The third section consisted of Lefèbvre-Desnoëttes' Guard Light Cavalry, the chasseurs à cheval and lancers, who were placed behind Milhaud's cuirassiers.

D'Erlon's artillery was placed in the intervals between his brigades, that of Reille to his front and Lobau's on his left flank. The artillery of the Guard was held in the rear.

Napoleon had about 73,140 men and 252 guns at his disposal. Although he did not have a great superiority in the numbers of soldiers available, Bonaparte had a substantially larger number of artillery pieces to hand, and a solid body of high quality cavalry, advantages he could have put to better use. Even so Wellington's men would have to stand under heavy fire and face determined assaults throughout the day, while waiting for the Prussians to arrive. And this wait was going to be a longer one than they originally anticipated.

Chapter 5

The Battle Begins

A Morning of Delays

On the evening of 17 June, Napoleon had ordered his men to be in position to commence battle at 9 a.m. the next morning.[1] However, this was not to be. The troops who had spent the night at Genappe, Glabais and in the local farms needed more time to assemble, to clean their arms and cook their soup. The supply trains only caught up with their formations late the previous night or early in the morning, adding to the delays in resupplying the soldiers with food and ammunition. Furthermore, Wellington's men had passed through the villages and farms twice, leaving precious little there for the French troops to eat. Thus, they had to search for something edible further away, causing the units to become further dispersed. By 9 a.m. Reille's corps had reached only as far as the Caillou heights. A long way behind Reille, the Imperial Guard, Kellermann's cuirassiers, Lobau's corps and Durutte's division of d'Erlon's corps wound their way to the battlefield. The Guard left its bivouacs at 10 a.m. and Durutte reached his positions only about midday. These delays were making up, in part, for the time the Prussians were losing on the muddy slopes between Wavre and Lasne.

Around 44,000 men and 168 cannon were pressed together in a column about 4 km long, running from Caillou towards Genappe. Around 4½ hours would be required for all these troops to move the 6 km to 8 km required and to deploy. Add an hour or two to that to allow for the muddy surface, and a couple of hours to clean weapons, cook and eat. Thus, it would be difficult for Napoleon's orders, written by Soult and issued between 4 a.m. and 5 a.m., and themselves needing to be delivered, to be implemented before midday. The army did not complete deploying in its battle positions until 1 p.m. and the surface conditions usually described as the reason for this in fact only played a part in this delay. By the time the battle actually started, the artillery of Bülow's corps was well on its way to St Lambert, having climbed the steep slopes of the Dyle valley.

Meanwhile, having finished his breakfast, Napoleon had his troops paraded before him. Then, at 10 a.m., from the Caillou farm, he had Soult write the following letter to Grouchy,

> The Emperor has received your last report from Gembloux. You write to His Majesty of only two Prussian columns that have passed Sauvenière and Sart-à-Walhain. However, other reports mention a third column, just as strong, having passed [Saint] Géry and Gentinnes, and moving towards Wavre.
>
> The Emperor has charged me to inform you that at this moment, His

[1] Houssaye, vol II, p 316.

Majesty is going to attack the English army which has taken position at
Waterloo, in front of the forest of Soignes. Thus, His Majesty wishes that you
direct your movements on Wavre so as to move closer to us, to link your operations [with ours] and establish communication [with us], pushing before you
the Prussian army corps which has taken this direction and might have
stopped in Wavre, where you are to arrive as soon as possible.

You are to follow the enemy columns on your right with some light troops to
observe their movements and to gather up their stragglers.

Inform me immediately of your dispositions and your march route as well as
of any news you have of the enemy and do not neglect to establish communications with us; the Emperor wishes to have frequent reports from you.[2]

Napoleon's orders to Grouchy were quite clear. It is also interesting to
note that Bonaparte was aware of the possibility of a Prussian intervention in
that day's battle in the Mont St Jean position, but that he did not order
Grouchy to intervene to cut off any Prussian move towards his positions.
Rather, he ordered the Marshal to follow them, and push them out of Wavre,
from where they might otherwise march to join Wellington.

Shortly after sending this message to Grouchy, Napoleon ordered Colonel
Marbot to take up positions behind Fichermont with his 7e Hussars, and to
establish posts at Lasne, Couture and at the bridges at Mousty and Ottignies.
This regiment was clearly placed to establish and maintain communications
with Grouchy.

Napoleon's Orders

At 11 a.m. Napoleon dictated the following orders to Soult,

As soon as the entire army is deployed in order of battle, by about 1 p.m., the
attack to seize the village of Mont-Saint-Jean at the road junction will commence, when the Emperor gives the order to Marshal Ney. To this end, the
12-pounder batteries of the II and VI Corps will join that of the I Corps. These
24 cannon will fire on the troops at Mont-Saint-Jean, and Count d'Erlon will
commence the attack with his left flank division, and, according to circumstances, support it with other divisions of the I Corps.

The II Corps will advance far enough to guard Count d'Erlon's flank.

The sapper companies of the I Corps will be prepared to barricade themselves at Mont-Saint-Jean immediately.[3]

The battle was about to commence.

Fighting Begins at Hougoumont

Although it was in a rather isolated position ahead of the Allied right, the
Hougoumont country house was potentially very formidable. The light companies of the four Guards battalions of Cooke's division formed the core of the
defence. Men of Generalmajor Graf von Kielmansegge's 1st Hanoverian
Brigade supported them, including '... the 1st Feldjäger coy, a hundred men

---

2 Houssaye, vol II, pp 324–5 fn.
3 Houssaye, vol II, p 332.

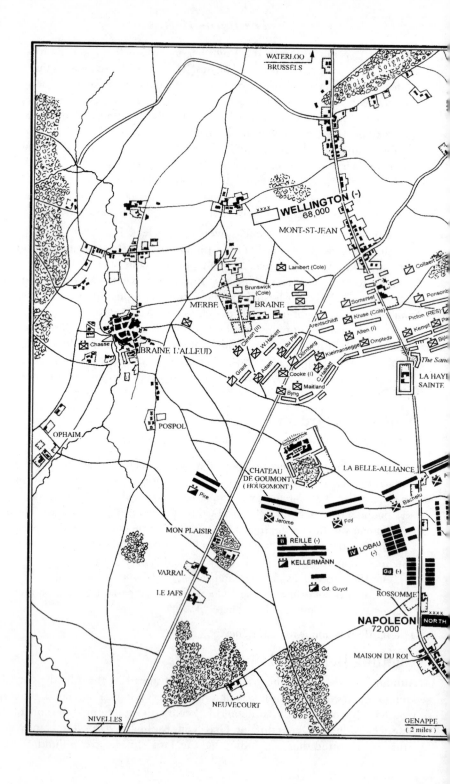

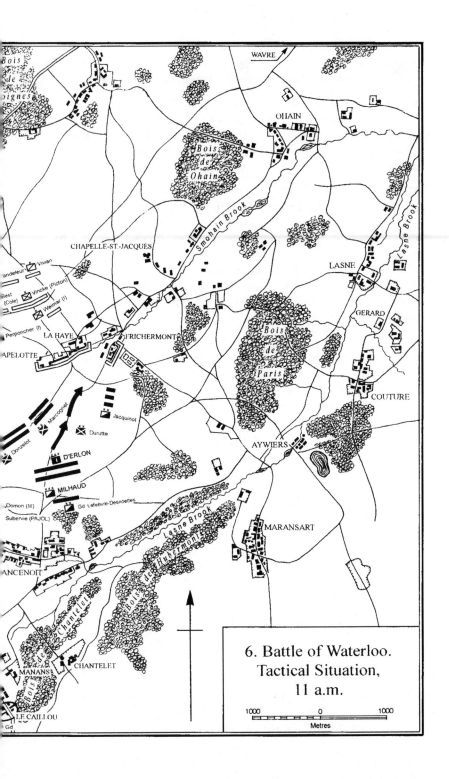

6. Battle of Waterloo.
Tactical Situation,
11 a.m.

1000   0   1000
Metres

of the Lüneburg Battalion and the same number from the Grubenhagen Battalion... '[4] The I./2nd Nassau Regiment also joined them, as General von Kruse, commander of the Nassau contingent, explained in his report,

> About 9.30 on the morning of 18th June, the 1st Battalion of the regiment (800 men under Major Büsgen), received the order to occupy the farm of Hougoumont that lay ahead of the centre of the right flank. A company of Brunswick Jäger stood along the fence of the wood near the farm and, behind the gardens, a battalion of the 2nd English Guard Regiment.[5]

Meanwhile, d'Erlon's heavy artillery was joined by more batteries, forming a line of 80 guns aimed at Wellington's centre. They opened fire. Shortly after that, Reille was ordered to advance against Hougoumont, and at 11.30 a.m. this attack opened the battle. Jérôme's division was the first to move, supported by Foy's and Bachelu's. A line of skirmishers preceded the attack columns. The French advanced boldly, gaining possession of most of the wood and orchard south of the main buildings. Bull's battery fired in support of the garrison, while Cleeves' bombarded Bachelu's troops.[6]

Major Büsgen of the Nassauers reported events in more detail,

> On the morning of 18th June, the 2nd Nassau Regiment was positioned on the left flank of the allied army. However, its 1st Battalion (800 men), under my command, was ordered to march off immediately to the farm of Hougoumont, to our right centre, and occupy it. Shortly thereafter, about half past nine o'clock, one of the Duke of Wellington's ADCs led us past the front of the army to this position. The farm was in the shape of a long, closed rectangle. The building made up three of the sides and the fourth, on the left, was made up partly by the garden wall and partly by other buildings. This rectangle was divided in two internally by the living accommodation and a wall. The upper part contained not just the large house, but also various farm buildings. The lower part contained the stalls and barns. Each section had one large gate, the upper facing towards the enemy positions, the lower towards their opponents. Joining the farm to the left was a vegetable garden with a wall five to six feet high along its front and left, and a hedge to its rear. The front wall ran into a wood and was masked by an incomplete hedge planted a few paces ahead. Left of the vegetable garden was an orchard. The vegetable garden and orchard were not joined, but the latter had a hedge along its front, running along the same line as the wall of the garden. The buildings and the vegetable garden were covered against the enemy by the wood to the south.
>
> On my arrival with the battalion, the farm and the garden were unoccupied. A company of Brunswick Jäger stood on the furthest edge of the wood. A battalion [sic] of English Guards of the Coldstream Regiment under the command of Colonel Macdonald [Macdonell] was deployed partly behind the farm, and partly in a sunken road behind the gardens mentioned, with the lower part of the Guards formed up parallel in line.

[4] Pflugk-Harttung, *Belle Alliance*, pp 76–7.   [6] Shaw-Kennedy, p 103.
[5] Pflugk-Harttung, *Belle Alliance*, pp 204–5.

From the measures of defence already undertaken (barricading of the upper gate, cutting of loop holes in it and the making of holes in parts of the garden wall), it was clear that this position was already occupied. One room of the house, as was later apparent, contained adequate supplies of infantry ammunition.

I immediately undertook the necessary deployment for the defence. I had the Grenadier Company occupy the buildings, and sent two companies to the vegetable garden next to them. I placed one company behind the hedge of the orchard, moved the voltigeurs into line with the Brunswick Jäger, and placed one company in reserve a little to the rear.

Hardly was this deployment finished when the enemy (Jérôme Bonaparte's division) began their attack on the wood with a heavy bombardment of shell and canister. Next, numerous tirailleurs moved forwards, supported by formed troops, and after meeting heavy resistance from the three companies there, pushed these back towards the farm and gardens. Under close pursuit from the enemy, the retiring troops fell back partly around the right of the buildings, partly to the left between the garden wall and the orchard hedge. The murderous fire coming from the buildings, the garden wall and orchard hedge halted the enemy. The English Guard Battalion threw them back into the wood in a state of flight, with great losses, and then advanced into the orchard. However, it proved impossible to push the enemy completely out of the wood for the remainder of the battle, as fresh troops constantly reinforced them. The English battalion therefore took up its earlier positions again. The Brunswick Jäger company, after bravely helping defeat this attack and suffering heavily, then rejoined its Corps in the main position.[7]

The French grand battery now opened a more severe and concentrated fire on the Anglo-Dutch-German centre. Jérôme renewed his assault on Hougoumont, supported by Foy. They captured the wood, and advanced as far as the south wall of the garden. Here, close range Allied musket fire forced them back once more. Artillery fire from two of Bolton's guns under Major Napier, and from Webber-Smith's Troop of RHA and Sympher's Troop of the KGL artillery supported the defence.[8]

Büsgen's report then continued,

Towards one o'clock, the enemy renewed his attack, moving against the buildings and gardens in a great rush, attempting to climb the garden wall and to seize the orchard hedge. However, the skirmisher fire from the garden wall chased him off and he was repelled at all points. In this attack, the enemy set light to several stacks of hay and straw close to the farm, intending to set the buildings alight, but this was not successful.[9]

Driven back for a second time, the French again returned quickly, regaining the woods and forcing the light companies of the Coldstream and 3rd Guards into the walled enclosure. A desperate hand-to-hand combat occurred around the gateway, with a small group of attackers getting inside before they

[7] Pflugk-Harttung, *Belle Alliance*, pp 207–8.   [9] Pflugk-Harttung, *Belle Alliance*, p 208.
[8] Shaw-Kennedy, pp 103–4.

were overwhelmed.[10] The struggle for Hougoumont would carry on for several hours to come, but events elsewhere on the battlefield had begun to overshadow it.

The Bombardment Begins

Meanwhile, Napoleon's grand battery lined up along the ridge opposite the Allied centre and started a bombardment around noon that was to continue throughout much of the day. The battery was drawn from the artillery of d'Erlon's corps reinforced by 48 12-pounders from the Guard. Its objective was to inflict such high casualties on the Allied centre that the French infantry would be able to march straight through it. A report of the activities of the 1st Hanoverian Brigade described some of the effects of this fire,

> From the beginning of the battle, the enemy undertook a massive artillery bombardment against that part of the line that the brigade was covering. The fire ricocheted into the second line, inflicting greater damage on the Nassau Infantry Regiment than on the brigade. The two batteries attached to the 3rd Division along with a third which had deployed on the crest of the hill in front of the brigade suffered heavily. Other batteries relieved them several times, but they either quickly ran out of ammunition, or were damaged and left standing. In front of the brigade, several powder waggons blew up.[11]

The report of the Hanoverian 5th Infantry Brigade written by its commander Generalmajor Vincke also described the scene,

> About noon, two enemy batteries moved up to less than 2,000 paces from the 5th Brigade. They had very heavy guns and the balls fell so far to the rear of us that the dressing station had to be moved further back. The situation soon changed and the enemy artillery severely wounded the commander of a Nassau battalion that was close to the 5th Brigade. I had my brigade surgeon dress his wound.[12]

The Battle for Papelotte Begins

Round about 12 o'clock, as the main French bombardment began, Durutte's 4th Division started to move against the Allied left. While engaging the Nassauers at the farm of Papelotte, his men also pressed on towards the brigades of Best and Vincke. Oberst Best, commander of the 4th Hanoverian Brigade, described the position and events,

> The area the brigade covered consisted of a gentle ridge running from behind the farm La Haye Sainte to behind the farm of Papelotte. In front of Papelotte the ground became steep, forming ravines, but in front of us the terrain was flat up to the enemy position, and behind us to the Soignes Forest it was also level. [The battle area] consisted of fields of planted corn, with hedges and bushes here and there. However, the columns of marching troops

---

[10] Shaw-Kennedy, p 104.
[11] Pflugk-Harttung, *Belle Alliance*, p 60.

[12] Pflugk-Harttung, *Belle Alliance*, p 95.

and their camps had trampled the lush cornfields flat. The heavy soil had been much softened by the heavy rainfall, and hindered the movements of the troops.

The enemy had taken up positions opposite us. The approach there, like ours, was favoured with a gentle rise. The distance from our line was about 900 to 1,000 paces. The right flank of the enemy opposite us consisted of the I Corps under Général Count d'Erlon, the division on his far right being that of Général Durutte. These troops, as far as I could tell, seemed to be drawn up in line, the intervals between the infantry brigades filled with cavalry and artillery. This deployment changed according to the movements undertaken, in that the infantry formed squares when attacked by our cavalry…

A detachment of enemy infantry, mainly light troops (probably the division of Général Durutte) attacked our extreme left. It attempted to take possession of the hamlet of Smohain and the farms of Papelotte and La Haye, as well as the château of Fichermont. The brave Nassauers resisted with greatest determination. Several bodies of infantry deployed in line to carry out this attack, supported by a few guns, and with skirmishers in front. I do not wish to judge if it was the enemy's intention to take our left flank. However, although he attacked with much impetuousness, and was greatly superior in numbers to the Nassauers, this particular detachment did not seem strong enough for that purpose.[13]

Rittmeister von Rettberg, although a cavalry officer, spent the Waterloo Campaign in command of a light company in the III./2nd Nassau Regiment. His report of these events read,

> Between 11 o'clock and 12 o'clock, the enemy columns and artillery drew up before us. One of the first cannon balls wounded Major Hegmann [commander of the battalion], and Hauptmann Frensdorf took command. Between 12 o'clock and 1 o'clock, a line of enemy skirmishers moved towards Papelotte. The Prince of Saxe-Weimar sent me with my company, the 3rd Flankers, against them. Shortly thereafter, a detachment of the Orange-Nassau Regiment occupied the village of Smohain and La Haye, and I linked up with them. (Papelotte, a square stone building surrounded by sunken roads and hedges, was most suitable for a determined defence.) I was then able to drive back the enemy skirmishers to the furthest hedge on the edge of the valley meadow between our position and the enemy's, and even took a few small houses there.[14]

However, contrary to Rettberg's account, in the confused fighting Durutte's men did manage to take possession if not of all, then certainly of some of the buildings of the Papelotte farm. There are only a few accounts of the desperate struggle that took place there. One of them was from Drummer May, then a 14-year-old serving with the Orange-Nassau Regiment, who fought in the skirmish line under Oberlieutenant Rath, in front of Fichermont. He wrote,

[13] Pflugk-Harttung, *Belle Alliance*, pp 84 –5.
[14] Pflugk-Harttung, *Belle Alliance*, p 211.

About three o'clock, the ammunition started to run out but, as the 2nd Battalion's men were armed with French muskets, we could not share their ammunition. So I took off my belts and ran through the firing line to the English troops standing in the rear [they were, in fact, red-coated Hanoverians] who filled my big bread-bag with cartridges. After I had distributed this load, I went back a second time. On the way back, I was hit in the right hip by a ricochet (I later found the bullet in my drawers) but that did not stop me going a third time. As I returned with my filled bread-bag, the Prince of Weimar approached me, asking how many rounds I could carry in my bag. He then told me not to go again, as the men had enough ammunition, and he would think of me. I put my belts on again and took my drum.

French guardsmen [in fact line troops] were standing opposite us. They concentrated their efforts on us so much that we were forced back somewhat. The Prince then came up to Oberlieutenant von Rath and ordered him not to fall back a step further. Hearing that, I went to the front of the line and, without any orders beat the charge. My comrades then called out, 'follow the little one, we can't leave him in the lurch!' We advanced under heavy fire, the reserves following us, and the French fell back again.

At that moment, I was shot in the throat and fell to the ground. I lay there unconscious for about half an hour, and was later told by Kapitain Götz and Lieutenant Vollrecht, themselves wounded, that I got up on my knees several times, only to fall over again. I do remember the cavalry riding over me. I sensed that I was lying on my back, so I turned over, covering my face from the frightening sight. I was not trodden on. I believe this cavalry was the Netherlands dragoon regiment that was originally to the rear of our brigade. Afterwards in hospital I heard that the Prince sent the engineers, who had nothing else to do that day, to bring back the wounded. Engineer Knetsch lifted me up and carried me off on his back to the Prussian columns which had moved up in the meantime. Here, we were made welcome and bandaged.

Some years later, Prince Bernhard came across May again, remembered the incident and awarded him the Order of William.[15]

Napoleon Observes the Prussians at St Lambert

While his brother Jérôme was attempting to storm Hougoumont, Napoleon was supervising the deployment of his grand battery from the heights of Rossomme. Around 1 p.m. he also took the opportunity to study Wellington's positions, scanning along the line from left to right with his telescope. Suddenly, an unexpected movement away to the right attracted his attention. His retinue noticed his surprise, and all trained their glasses in that direction. The distance was 9 km, and it was difficult to be certain of the details. Some could only make out the trees there, others thought they could distinguish columns of troops, either French or Prussian. As Grouchy had still been in Gembloux at 6 a.m., and no report of his moving nearer had since come in, then it could not be him. That only left one possibility. Soult was quickly told to pen the following message to Grouchy,

---

[15] Starklof, vol II, pp 202–3.

At 6 o'clock this morning, you wrote to the Emperor that you were marching on Sart-à-Walhain. Thus, it was your plan to move to Corbais and Wavre. This movement conforms with the dispositions His Majesty has communicated to you. However, the Emperor has ordered me to tell you that you must now manoeuvre in our direction and seek to come nearer to us. This is so that you may join us before a corps can push its way between us. I will not indicate to you your direction of march. It is up to you to see where we are, and to orientate yourself consequently and to join communications. You must always be in a position to attack any enemy troops that might seek to disquiet our right, and to eradicate them. At this moment, battle has been joined in the direction of Waterloo before the forest of Soignes. The enemy's centre is at Mont-St-Jean. Manoeuvre in such a way that you join our right.

The ink had not dried when a captured Prussian hussar was brought in to the Imperial Headquarters. He was carrying a letter from Bülow to Müffling indicating Bülow's intentions. Soult was accordingly told to add a postscript to the letter to Grouchy. It read,

A letter has just been intercepted saying that General Bülow is to attack our flank. We believe we have already sighted this corps on the heights of St Lambert. Thus, do not lose an instant in moving towards us to join with us to wipe out Bülow whom you will catch in flagrante delicto.[16]

Thus, before Napoleon's assault on the Allied centre had even started, he was being forced to consider the possibility of a Prussian intervention. He first moved the light cavalry divisions of Domon and Subervie to cover the various approaches to his right flank, and to establish contact with Grouchy. However, as these 2,300 troopers would obviously not suffice to hold back the Prussians, he immediately also ordered Lobau to move his VI Corps up behind the cavalry. Therefore, before the main part of the battle had begun, the Prussian manoeuvre had already tied down over 9,000 French troops. Later, more of Napoleon's reserves were to be committed to attempting to stem the blue tide that was sweeping up over his right flank. Time was running out for Bonaparte.

[16] Houssaye, vol II, pp 343–4.

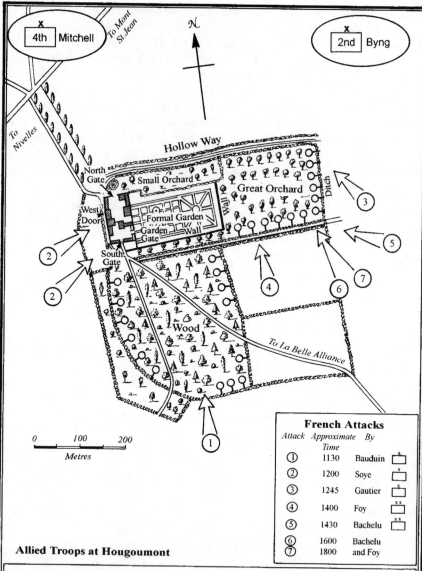

4th | Mitchell (X)

To Mont St.Jean

To Nivelles

N

2nd | Byng (X)

Hollow Way

North Gate

Small Orchard

Great Orchard

Wall

Ditch

West Door

Formal Garden

Garden Wall

Garden Gate

South Gate

③

⑤

②

②

④

⑥

⑦

Wood

To La Belle Alliance

①

0 100 200

Metres

French Attacks

Attack	Approximate Time	By	
①	1130	Bauduin	(X)
②	1200	Soye	(X)
③	1245	Gautier	(X)
④	1400	Foy	(XX)
⑤	1430	Bachelu	(XX)
⑥	1600	Bachelu	
⑦	1800	Bachelu and Foy	

Allied Troops at Hougoumont

British

Commanded by Lt.Col.Lord Saltoun
Light coy, 2nd Guards Battalion
Light coy, 3rd Guards Battalion
Deployed along the front edge of the Great Orchard

Commanded by Lt.Col.Henry Wyndham
Light coy, 2nd Battalion, Coldstream Guards
Deployed in farm and chateau

Commanded by Lt.Col.Charles Dashwood
Light coy, 2nd Battalion, 3rd Guards
Deployed in and around the Formal Garden

Lt.Col.James Macdonell was placed in overall command of the troops in the farm, chateau and Formal Garden, but not those in the Great Orchard

German

Hanoverians
1st Feldjäger Coy
100 men from the Lüneburg Battalion
100 men from the Grubenhagen Battalion
Deployed in the wood

Nassauers
1/2nd Nassau Regiment
The Grenadier Coy was deployed in the farm buildings, two companies in the Formal Garden, one company behind the hedge of the Great Orchard, the Voltigeur Coy with the Brunswickers at the southern edge of the wood, one company in reserve towards the rear of the wood

Brunswickers
Coy of Jäger
Deployed at the southern edge of the wood

7. Plan of Hougoumont

Chapter 6

Attack and Counter-attack

The Battle for Hougoumont

At Hougoumont, the struggle continued unabated. The British Guards light companies, the Brunswickers and one of du Plat's KGL line battalions fought with two of Foy's regiments. Attack was met with counter-attack. Foy took the woods, but the Guards held the farm buildings. A battery of French howitzers lobbed shells into the buildings, setting them alight. The château, the farmhouse, the sables and storehouses all went up in flames. The British fell back into the chapel and the gardener's house from where they continued to fire on the French, who were unable to make any headway because of the flames.

Major Büsgen's account, quoted in the previous chapter, continued,

Between two and three o'clock, a [French] battery drew up on the right side of the buildings and began to bombard them heavily with cannons and howitzers. It did not take long to set them all alight.

The enemy now made a third unsuccessful attack mainly against the buildings. Using the smoke and flames to his advantage, his grenadiers forced their way through a small side door into the upper courtyard. Fire from the windows of the house and the advance of a detachment of English Guards through the lower gate and courtyard drove them out. Some were taken prisoner, though the enemy also captured seven of our grenadiers. The attack, which ended about half past three, was the enemy's last serious attempt on the position of Hougoumont. The skirmish fire, however, continued almost without interruption to the end of the battle.

Neither when I was detached, nor during this period, was any commander under whose orders I was placed, named to me. No allied troops were drawn up either to our left, or to our right. If, in this account, I only mention the battalion of the Coldstream regiment of the English Guard, then this is because I saw no other troops sent to support the battalion under my command. I do not know if and what other troops were later sent to support this position. Due to the continuous fighting and the view restricted by trees, hedges and walls, I could not observe what was happening at a distance.[1]

Büsgen was correct in that four companies of the Coldstream Guards under Colonel Woodford, in addition to the original garrison, assisted in driving back the French, and some of these troops were indeed used to reinforce the garrison of Hougoumont directly.[2]

---

[1] Pflugk-Harttung, *Belle-Alliance*, p 209.
[2] Shaw-Kennedy, pp 105–6.

D'Erlon Assaults Wellington's Centre

For all its ferocity the fighting for Hougoumont was a subsidiary part of the day's events and about 1.30 p.m. the main action commenced in earnest. Napoleon ordered Ney to carry out the planned attack on the centre of Wellington's position. For about half an hour, the grand battery of 80 guns bombarded the Allied troops whose artillery returned the fire. As much of Wellington's infantry was taking advantage of the cover offered by the ridge, their losses must have been relatively low. The Allied artillery and Bijlandt's brigade, unwisely positioned to the front of the Allied centre, were the only visible targets.

D'Erlon's infantry then advanced, the grand battery ceasing fire to let it pass. The four divisions marched in echelons to the left. Allix's division, commanded by Général Quiot, formed the first echelon. Donzelot's division followed in the second, then came Marcognet's, and finally Durutte's. Ney and d'Erlon rode at the head of their men. The importance of the farm buildings of La Haye Sainte seems not to have been noticed at this stage. A more determined and more carefully directed bombardment might well have reduced it to rubble and flames. Much to the relief of the commander of its small garrison, the German Legion officer Major Baring, this did not happen.

D'Erlon's men had spent 16 June counter-marching uselessly in between Ligny and Quatre Bras and had yet to see action in the campaign. Fresh and keen, they marched towards the Allied lines crying 'Vive l'Empereur!' Several batteries of artillery moved up in support.

The first major setback suffered by the Allies that day was the defeat of Bijlandt's Netherlands brigade. While most accounts agree on the sequence of events leading to this incident, those of its results conflict considerably. Bijlandt's men, one battalion of the 7th Line, the 27th Jager Battalion, three battalions of militia and one battery of artillery had initially been placed in a relatively exposed position in front of Wellington's left but had then been moved back to join the main defence line. This brigade, consisting in part of young, inexperienced troops, had already suffered heavily at Quatre Bras two days earlier and the bombardment they had just endured from d'Erlon's grand battery did not help their already nervous disposition. The fire of Donzelot's skirmishers that immediately followed did not allow them to recover their composure. When Donzelot's columns approached, the Netherlanders beat a hasty retreat, leaving a gap in the Allied line. Whether or not Bijlandt's men recovered sufficiently from this experience to play a significant role in the remainder of the battle is beyond the scope of this work.[3] However, Bijlandt's men were certainly not to be the last to take flight in this battle. French cavalry moved up to exploit the success.

Meanwhile, on the left, the lead unit of Allix's division, Brigade Quiot,

---

[3] Shaw-Kennedy (pp 111–12) claimed the Netherlands brigade '... placed itself on the reverse slope of the position, against orders and remonstrances, and took no further part in the action!' However, the journal of Perponcher's division stated 'Several files fell, making an opening for the enemy through which his column pushed. All that faced this wide column had to fall back, while the troops on both flanks joined up cold-bloodedly with their neighbouring troops.' (Quoted in Lettow-Vorbeck, p 424).

quickly moved towards the farm of La Haye Sainte, where it engaged in a vigorous firefight with the defenders. Bourgeois' brigade, four battalions strong, moved on, forcing the 95th Rifles to abandon the sandpit they were holding nearby. Part of Kempt's brigade was the next French target.

However, Allied reinforcements were also on the move. Captain d'Huvelé, of the 1st Hanoverian 9-pounder Battery Braun, wrote the following in his report,

> About two o'clock, the battery received the order to deploy on the left of the Charleroi road at a point given by its commander next to the 5th Division of General-Major Sir James Kempt. However, the battery commander had the misfortune of being put out of action by a wound to the right thigh just as the battery was leaving its starting point. Command passed to the next most senior officer, Premierlieutenant von Schulzen. He led the battery to a mound immediately behind the ridge over which the lane from Wavre to Ohain ran. A skirmish line of Scotsmen from the 5th Division held the lane. The 5th Division was further to the rear, in column. Hardly had we reached the mound when an enemy shell set alight the limber of the howitzer and blew it up. It damaged the gun and killed one NCO, one gunner, one driver and four horses and wounded one NCO, two gunners, one driver and two horses.
>
> Hardly had the battery unlimbered in position 'B' (see sketch) [overleaf], when an assault column of about five enemy battalions came up at us from the hollow to the left at point 'C', attacking us at point 'B'. It was part of Count d'Erlon's Corps that had stood about 1,100 to 1,200 paces opposite us. Supported by the enemy artillery on the ridge opposite, of which we could see 60 to 70 guns, the head of the column reached the far side of the lane, ignoring the effects of the artillery and infantry fire. Here, the Scotsmen in the lane charged them with the bayonet from the front, while those to our left attacked their right flank. The Frenchmen were driven off.
>
> Premierlieutenant von Schulzen was mortally wounded immediately after this attack. He had to leave the battlefield and died shortly afterwards. Command of the battery passed on to his second in command. Behind the ridge that served as a breastwork, so much water had collected and the ground was so soft that the guns were now stuck fast. Furthermore, the undergrowth along the ditch blocked our view. The new commander thus decided to move the battery across the lane, placing the guns in position 'D'. We took up this position about half past two. The caissons that were not immediately needed, were placed in position 'E', a hollow, under the supervision of an NCO, while the limbers were drawn up at 'B'.[4]

Supported in this way, Kempt's men held their ground, firing steady volleys against the French infantry columns. The French had lost all their impetus and now attempted to deploy for a firefight, but instead fell into a state of confusion. After their success against Bijlandt's brigade Donzelot's men also paused to reform. Taking advantage of this situation, Pack's brigade of Picton's division moved forwards to fill the gap left in the Allied line. The

4 Pflugk-Harttung, *Belle-Alliance*, pp 182–3.

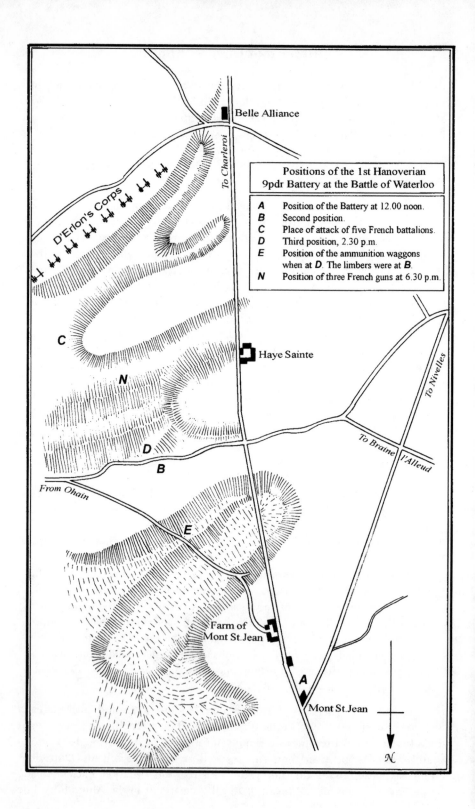

See Captain d'Huvelé's report quoted on p 83.

British veterans fired into Donzelot's flank from 40 paces with devastating effect. The French began to waver so Picton ordered his men to charge home and almost immediately was himself shot in the head and mortally wounded. Marcognet's third echelon moved up, past the confused mass of Donzelot's infantry. Pack's men blocked their way, too, his 92nd Highlanders opening fire at 20 paces, and following up their devastating volley with a bayonet charge.

All along the line the French advance now ground to a halt.

The Charge of the Heavy Cavalry

Seizing the opportunity, Wellington committed his cavalry to complete the defeat of the French attack. On the Allied left, the light cavalry brigades of Vandeleur and Ghigny threatened Durutte's right flank. In the centre, Somerset's heavies (1st and 2nd Life Guards, the Royal Horse Guards and 1st Dragoon Guards) charged at a gallop to deliver the *coup de grace* to the confused mass of Frenchmen. Soon Somerset's men came within pistol range of Travers' cuirassiers to the left of the main road to Brussels. Travers' troopers counter-charged but the British heavies pushed most of them down into the valley, the weight of numbers and the advantage of the slope prevailing.

German cavalry units supported this move. The report of the 3rd Hussar Regiment of the KGL described its role as follows,

> Between two and three o'clock in the afternoon, the regiment moved to the front of the column as the cavalry in front of it had been moved elsewhere and was otherwise occupied. Next, three companies led by Rittmeister von Kerssenbruch made a very fine attack on two squadrons of cuirassiers, threw them back and pursued them a fair distance. Before these three companies came back, Generalmajor von Arentsschildt ordered the two remaining squadrons of the regiment to attack two enemy cavalry regiments, one cuirassiers, the other dragoons, that were moving towards the English line. This attack was made, forcing those part of the enemy the two squadrons could reach to fall back. Meanwhile, as the enemy line was so much stronger, our men were overlapped on both flanks, losing significant numbers of officers, men and horses. Rittmeister Janssen, Lieutenant and Adjutant Brüggemann and Cornet Deichmann fell. Lieutenants Oehlkers and True, and Cornet von Dassel were so badly wounded they had to leave the battlefield. The regiment rallied and reformed, but not in squadrons as there were insufficient men left, only 60 files remaining of the seven companies.[5]

Meanwhile, Ponsonby's Union Brigade (Royals, Inniskillings and Scots Greys) was also thrown against d'Erlon's columns. The Royals rode down the Brussels road, pushing Bourgeois' infantry back, and allowing the 95th Rifles to reoccupy the sandpit. The Inniskillings struck Donzelot's column. The Scots Greys moved through the intervals in Pack's infantry and the 92nd Highlanders joined the mad rush forward against Marcognet's division.

---

5 Pflugk-Harttung, *Belle-Alliance*, pp 164–5. The regiment started the campaign at a strength of around 500 sabres. By now, only 120 were left, the remainder being *hors de combat*.

Receiving infantry fire to the front and being charged in both flanks by cavalry, the French columns offered little resistance. They broke and fled. Bourgeois, trying to rally by the sandpit, now also fell back in disorder. Quiot's brigade abandoned its attack on La Haye Sainte. At Papelotte, Vandeleur's light dragoons (11th, 12th and 16th Regiments) charged Durutte's division in the flank. Ghigny's Dutch dragoons and Belgian hussars followed up, and within minutes not a single Frenchman was left on the ridge of Mont St Jean.

However, the British commanders completely lost control of their cavalry. Uxbridge attempted to recall and rally his men, but on they went across the valley towards the French positions. Here, the fire of Bachelu's division mauled the Life Guards and Dragoons. The Scots Greys rode into two French divisional batteries, cutting down the gunners and riders, before moving on towards the grand battery. Colonel Martigue's lancers charged their flank and Ponsonby fell, stabbed by a lance. At the same time, Colonel Brô's lancers moved to assist Durutte, forcing Vandeleur to break off his pursuit.

Farine's brigade of cuirassiers now joined the fray. The British heavies, blown by their exertions, outnumbered and outflanked by fresh troops, were thrown back with heavy casualties all the way to the ridge. Here, the light cavalry brigades of Vivian and Merlen finally forced the French to break off their pursuit.

Wellington's German Infantry

There are various accounts of the role played by the German infantry units in defeating d'Erlon's attack. Du Plat's KGL brigade suffered particularly from the preparatory bombardment when his battalions moved up in readiness to face the expected assault. Oberstlieutenant Muller, commander of the 2nd Line Battalion of the KGL, wrote,

> ... Between twelve and one o'clock, we were ordered to form square and advance. The 1st and 2nd Line Battalions [KGL] each formed one square, while the 3rd and 4th formed a square together. After we had moved forwards in square about 1,000 paces, enemy infantry, in line, appeared diagonally to our left (I estimated their strength to be about 1,000 to 1,200), on a wave-shaped mound about 400 to 600 paces from us. The brigade manoeuvred its squares in such a way that the 2nd Battalion came on the right flank and then halted. We fired for a short time. Oberst du Plat, however, soon gave the order to advance and attack the enemy with the bayonet. They were not expecting this attack, and fell back the instant we advanced into an old oak wood that was full of ditches and abatis. (I believe that Oberst du Plat fell here, as I did not see him again). Arriving on the mound, we saw to our right front a well spread out line of infantry. In front of it was a line of French cuirassiers, 600 to 800 men, being attacked, I believe by the 2nd Dragoon Regiment of the King's German Legion. Fire from the French infantry in the wood drove our cavalry off and, followed by enemy cuirassiers, they retired back behind our squares.[6]

6 Pflugk-Harttung, *Belle-Alliance*, p 115.

In fact, it was the 1st and not the 2nd Light Dragoons that carried out the successful charge on the French cuirassiers. According to the regiment's official report, it carried out four successful charges against the French cuirassiers in the course of one and a half hours.[7]

Kapitain von Scriba of the Feldbataillon Bremen had a more difficult time,

About 1 o'clock [probably later], we formed a square along with the Verden Battalion. The enemy cavalry, cuirassiers, came on at a steady trot and suffered fire by files at about 40 to 50 paces from the side of the square facing them. They turned back without any attempt to attack us. We saw them off with a loud 'Hurrah!'...

Our square was suffering from the 'overs' from the fire directed at the artillery in front of us. Major von Schkopp (Verden Battalion) thus got Oberstlieutenant von Langrehr [commander of Feldbataillon Bremen] to move us slightly to the right, which we did immediately. This manoeuvre saved us many men because shortly after that, two powder waggons that had been just 30 to 40 paces in front of us, exploded...

A little later, we deployed again, but, as enemy cavalry moved up once more, we did not stay long in this formation. We formed square quickly and in an orderly fashion. The attackers were many, and I counted six very wide troops following each other at about quarter distance. They were cuirassiers again, and I estimated their strength at 700 sabres. All the officers in the square were very busy preventing the men from firing off too early. Our commander threatened to shoot any man doing so with his pistol. It was now a quarter past two. The cavalry came on at a trot and halted at about 70 to 80 paces away. The temptation to shoot was great, but the entire square stood motionless with weapons cocked. I saw a square to our left doing the same.

The French cavalrymen were brave, but too slow. Instead of charging the remaining distance to us, they finally trotted to the left corner of the square, wheeled left around it and passed the next side of the square and around to its right. All these sides of the square gave them heavy fire at very close range. Led by a brigade general, the cavalry passed the right side, of which I was in command, at a distance of six paces. I remark on this trivial incident only because several of my comrades and I noticed that when ordered to aim, the right side all pointed their muskets at his horse. We also noticed that he moved away from the danger.

The cavalry suffered some losses from this attack, but not as many as I would have expected from the close range. This led to me believe that our men were aiming too high, and so the officers then continuously reminded them not to do so. Nevertheless, many riderless horses were running around, and dead and wounded were all around the square. We soon began to regard the cavalry attacks as a relief as, afterwards, the devastating artillery fire began once more, and it grew continuously in force.

Our cavalry, positioned about 300 paces to our rear, now pursued the enemy cavalry, leading to a brief but sharp combat. The crews of the guns in front of

7 Pflugk-Harttung, *Belle-Alliance*, p 151.

us sheltered themselves during this cavalry attack by crawling under the cannon. To our great consternation, when the [French] artillery fire began again, we saw our neighbours on our right, the Nassauers, begin to fall into disorder. However, the brave Nassau officers, who set their men a glowing example, restored order and they returned to their previous positions. This misfortune repeated itself several times in similar circumstances. Their heavy losses were clear to see for, as mentioned above, they stood in a very close column. About half past two, our brave commander lost his horse to a cannon ball. He immediately mounted Major Müller's horse. A few minutes later, he had a riderless horse caught and gave the major his back. Less than a quarter of an hour later, the highly popular Oberstlieutenant von Langrehr had his right leg shattered by a cannon ball. He stayed on his horse, spoke a few calm words of farewell and handed over command of the square to Major von Schkopp.[8]

Generalmajor Vincke of the Hanoverian 5th Infantry Brigade had a slightly different view of events,

Behind the enemy artillery stood the army corps of the Comte d'Erlon, mainly infantry, deployed in close columns. About 12.30 p.m., a significant mass of enemy cavalry drew up in front of them. It was particularly easy to distinguish the lancers. To me, it seemed certain that this cavalry would attack us. As the left flank was not secured, and I was convinced that it would be the target of the enemy attack, I considered it my duty to take up the strongest possible position. For that purpose, the 5th Brigade pulled back a little, next to the 4th Hanoverian Brigade of Oberst Best. Thus, the place where we had camped the previous night... together with the sunken path were now in front of our position. Here, the brigade was significantly protected from the enemy artillery fire. My sharpshooters had been sent to the battery of Oberstlieutenant Heise [in fact he was a major], partly to support him, and partly to fire into the left flank of the enemy should he advance. To avoid manoeuvring at this moment, I had all eight battalions of both brigades stand next to each other in closed column. I then had the rear ranks face outwards, the flanks turn left and right so they formed in my eyes an impenetrable mass. They met the cries of the advancing enemy with a loud 'Hurrah!'

The English cavalry until then to our left and rear formed up to attack the enemy cavalry. This happened immediately and was most successful. However, the English cavalry fell back, pursued by enemy flankers, so I had to send up part of my sharpshooters, who were most effective. Lieutenant Deppe of the Hildesheim Battalion particularly distinguished himself here and an enemy cavalry officer was taken prisoner.[9]

After the cavalry charges and counter-charges the German infantry units also helped cover the retreat of the Allied horsemen. Major von Rettberg's report on the activities of the 1st Line Battalion of the KGL described his unit's part in this,

---

[8] Pflugk-Harttung, *Belle-Alliance*, pp 134–5.
[9] Pflugk-Harttung, *Belle-Alliance*, p 95.

About three o'clock, the brigade [du Plat's, from the 2nd Division] was ordered to march left forwards and after a few hundred paces, we formed battalion squares. This movement brought us closer to the masses of enemy cavalry that had thrown our cavalry back. The enemy was about to cut them down but seeing us move up at a steady pace, turned around without being fired upon.[10]

There was now a pause in the action on this part of the front while both sides tried to restore order in their ranks. Casualties were heavy on both sides.

Attacks on La Haye Sainte

Since the farm complex of La Haye Sainte stood in front of the Allied centre, it would have made sense for the French at least to mask it, but preferably to capture it, before storming Wellington's main position. However, although the French did assault the farm during d'Erlon's attack and again later, it would be several hours yet before they succeeded in taking it.

The report of the participation of the Hanoverian and KGL troops in the battle gave a good summary of the various French assaults on this vital point throughout the early afternoon,

Until about two o'clock, the brigade [2nd KGL] suffered from heavy cannon fire. When the enemy infantry and cavalry advanced, the 2nd Light Battalion [KGL] was soon surrounded in the farm and had to withdraw the 100 men in the orchard. It defended itself with great determination in the buildings; the men firing out of the windows and loopholes in the walls made with their musket butts. At three o'clock, two companies of the 1st Light Battalion, each about 100 men strong, reinforced the garrison. A little later, the Light Company of 5th Line Battalion joined them, and later still, 200 Schützen from the Nassau Regiment. The enemy attacked three or four times this day, each time in the same fashion, with two battalions or regiments. One would go straight for the buildings, the other around to their left, sending out screens of skirmishers.[11]

A more detailed account came from Major von Baring, commander of the garrison, who began by describing the buildings as follows,

The farm lies in the long valley directly on the paved road between Mont St Jean and Belle-Alliance, that is almost in the middle of the two armies. However, due to a nearby ridge, almost nothing could be seen of the enemy position. This allowed the enemy to approach unseen to musket range. The farm buildings, joined together by a series of walls, formed a rectangle. There were five entrances, that is three large gates and two doors, though one of the former, which shut a barn, had been used as firewood the previous night by the troops posted there. An orchard stood in front of the farm, in the direction of the enemy. Behind this was a small kitchen garden. A substantial hedge surrounded both.[12]

[10] Pflugk-Harttung, *Belle-Alliance*, p 112.
[11] Pflugk-Harttung, *Belle-Alliance*, p 63.
[12] Pflugk-Harttung, *Belle-Alliance*, p 106.

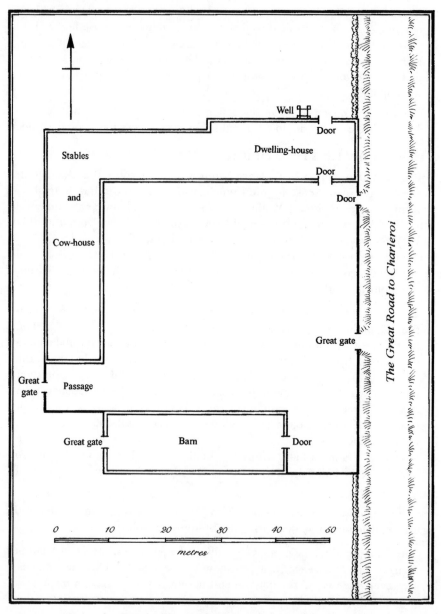

Well

Door

Dwelling-house

Stables

Door

and

Door

Cow-house

Great gate

The Great Road to Charleroi

Great gate

Passage

Great gate

Bam

Door

0   10   20   30   40   50

metres

8. Ground-Plan of the Farm of la Haye Sainte

His account then outlined the opening moves and what he saw of the repulse of d'Erlon's attack,

After the battle on 18th June began at the farm of Hougoumont, La Haye Sainte was itself attacked about 12.30 p.m [it may have been later]. The mound [to the south of the farm] hid the approach of the enemy from us, and they only appeared at musket range whereupon we fired at them. The attackers were formed in two close infantry columns, each of more than one, possibly two battalions. They advanced 'en masse' at the 'pas de charge' on the left flank of the farm and towards the orchard. The men in skirmish order behind the hedge could not withstand this charge and fell back to the buildings, but not without significant loss. They drew up beside us and fought back.

The Hanoverian Light Battalion Lüneburg moved down from the main battle line to assist us. A mass of 600 men, they had not kept the best order when moving up. Both [the skirmishers and the Light Battalion Lüneburg] now attacked the enemy, driving him back out of the orchard. Now, however, a strong line of enemy cuirassiers drew up to the right, forward of the garden. The sight of them caused the young, inexperienced soldiers to depart from the orchard in great disorder and return to the main position. Attempts to prevent men of the 2nd Light Battalion in the farm from joining this mass were fruitless. Even less successful were the attempts to bring it to a halt for its own salvation. Cavalry rode it down with severe loss. Moreover, it also had to suffer fire from the enemy column that had gone around the buildings in an unsuccessful attempt to attack the rear garden and move to our main line.

A brigade of English Dragoon Guards now moved up, threw the cuirassiers back and fell upon the two columns of enemy infantry. These had already suffered very heavily from the fire from the buildings and were now wiped out.[13]

Baring's account then continued with the next French attacks, which took place around 3 p.m.,

After the first attack that lasted perhaps one and a half hours, two companies of the 1st Light Battalion reinforced me. The tactics used by the enemy caused me to leave the orchard unoccupied and to limit the defence to that of the buildings and far garden. For about half an hour, the enemy left us to make small improvements to our defences. Then they came at us again in two columns, the first attacking the farm the same way. At the same time four lines of cavalry drew up to their right. The first consisted of cuirassiers, the second of dragoons, the third of hussars and the fourth of lancers, each about one regiment strong. While the infantry attacked us vigorously, the cavalry moved through our fire from the farm towards the position where the 5th and 8th Line Battalions of the Legion, a brigade of Hanoverians and one of English were formed up in squares. When one line was driven back, the next moved up to attack with equally little success. After their useless efforts, both the infantry and the cavalry withdrew, exhausted. We had used much ammunition and I was beginning to fear we would run out entirely. I called for more, but

[13] Pflugk-Harttung, *Belle-Alliance*, pp 107–8.

none arrived. However, the Schützen Company of the 5th Line Battalion of the Legion was sent to reinforce us.[14]

The German troops to the rear of La Haye Sainte were also having a tough struggle. It was about this time that the French cavalry managed to seize the colour of the 8th Line Battalion of the KGL. Its report described the scene,

> The battalion had formed square, but shortly afterwards was ordered to deploy against infantry, which caused the greatest disorder. But then the enemy infantry retired and their cuirassiers charged so forcefully into the battalion that it had the misfortune to lose the King's Colour in the struggle. Fähnrich Moreau, who was carrying it at first, and Sergeant Stuart, who took charge of it next, were severely wounded and left on the battlefield. Oberstlieutenant Schroeder was mortally wounded in this charge, so Major Petersdorff took command of the battalion. The battalion had been badly cut about by the cuirassiers and chased away from its designated place. However, it was soon rallied and then formed square again in its designated position, but because of the many dead and wounded, the square was now much smaller than before.[15]

Battle had now been joined along Wellington's entire front. The Allied positions were more or less holding, but the French assaults were determined and ferocious. A war of attrition had begun, and unless the Prussians were to intervene soon, the chances were that Napoleon would win it. Fortunately the Prussians were now beginning to break out of the Fichermont wood.

[14] Pflugk-Harttung, *Belle-Alliance*, p 108.
[15] Pflugk-Harttung, *Belle-Alliance*, p 126.

Chapter 7

The Prussians Approach

Scouting Reports

By late morning the Prussian IV Army Corps had assembled at St Lambert for the last stage of that day's march but, before moving on, the senior command needed to establish the lie of the land and enemy dispositions to the west, south-west and south. Two battalions of the 3rd Silesian Landwehr under Major von Krahn advanced to the edge of a wood to the left and were deployed in cover. Mounted detachments were sent to Maransart, Céroux and Mont St Guibert, and pickets were thrown out to cover the area between the Lasne and Dyle.

Furthest to the east was Oberstlieutenant von Ledebur. His detachment was supported by elements from the 14th Brigade, the F./2nd Silesians, the III./1st Pomeranian Landwehr, the 10th Hussars and two horse guns. They had gone to the important road junction at Mont St Guibert on 17 June, where they met the Brandenburg and Pomeranian Hussars of the II Army Corps under Oberstlieutenant von Sohr. All was quiet that night. From 9 a.m. on the 18th, however, small groups of French cavalry appeared.

On the morning of the 18th Major von Falkenhausen led another patrol to Céroux, south of St Lambert, but found no Frenchmen there. So he rode on, now in a south-westerly direction, via La Hutte to Les Flamandes, close to the cobbled road to Brussels, where, at 12.30 p.m., he captured some French foragers. They informed him that Napoleon was fighting Wellington, and had his Guard with him. Falkenhausen sent back this important news to his headquarters; it would seem there was no French threat to the Prussian left now. He then moved on beyond Maransart, from where he observed the French positions, which he reported to be spread out as far as Fichermont. This news was also sent to headquarters.

Next, a patrol of one officer and 20 troopers, part of Ledebur's force which had become cut off, appeared. They reported that 300 French cavalry had driven them off. Falkenhausen feared that this cavalry was the advance guard of a French flanking force and rode off to establish their whereabouts. Surprising the French, he chased them away, taking an officer and 27 troopers prisoner. Questioning them, he established that Grouchy had sent them to establish contact with Napoleon. Sending the captured officer back to headquarters along with this news, Falkenhausen rode back to the Brussels road at Passe-Avant, south of Le Caillou.

Further to the north, Generalmajor von Valentini, chief-of-staff of the IV Army Corps, had been ordered to reconnoitre the terrain west of St Lambert.

Accompanied by Major von Hedemann and Kolonnenjäger Diederichs, Valentini observed dips, rises and copses of bushes in front of a long line of heights at a fair distance, running up to the right of the Fichermont wood. Left of the wood was a village from which the main road from Brussels could probably been seen. This village could not been found on his map and there were no locals to ask. Suddenly, movement was seen in some nearby bushes. A local farmer appeared from them, and told Valentini that the village was Céroux, and the Brussels road could easily be seen from it. Diederichs was sent to Falkenhausen with an order for the latter to go there and observe enemy movements. On his way, he came across three redcoats hiding in the crops. Diederichs then rode with Falkenhausen to Céroux, and observed the events there before returning to St Lambert. By then, it was after 2 p.m., and the IV Army Corps was on the move again.

Meanwhile, Major von Witowski had ridden westwards with a squadron of the 2nd Silesian Hussars. Reaching the village of Lasne, he found it empty, so two companies of the II./18th moved up to occupy it. Riding further south-westwards, he located the French in Maransart.[1]

Between 9 a.m. and 10 a.m. a detachment of the Silesians also reached the wood of Fichermont. There were no Frenchmen around, and it seemed as if the French had taken no measures to secure their right flank. A troop of Prussian hussars drew up in front of the Fichermont wood, just at the point where one of Wellington's outposts had been earlier that day. From there the Prussians observed the movements of the French and the Allies. A patrol rode on to the village of Smohain where, about 10 a.m., they met a patrol of the British 10th Hussars under Captain Taylor. Taylor sent Lieutenant Lindsay to Wellington's headquarters with the news that Bülow was at St Lambert, and was advancing.[2]

Thus, without any significant resistance from the French, the Prussians were able to throw out a picket line covering their advance and their entire left flank. Not only would this protect them from any surprises, they had also established that Grouchy had no significant forces to their south-east, and Napoleon had none to their south-west. Even the defile of the Lasne brook, where a few men could easily have delayed the entire Prussian advance, was unoccupied by the French. The Prussians could advance unobserved and unopposed as far as the wood of Fichermont. Even at this late stage, if the French had occupied this wood, the Prussians would have had difficulty in removing them. Conversely, once the Prussians had occupied it, the French would not be able to hold up their advance easily.

A Lively Exchange of Messages

A line of communication between Wellington's and Blücher's headquarters was now established. Thus, from shortly after 10 a.m., the Duke was aware of Prussian movements and intentions. While the 15th Brigade was waiting at St Lambert, Müffling arrived there from Wellington's headquarters, along with

[1] Damitz, vol I, p 255.
[2] Liddell, *10th Royal Hussars*, p 149.

several of the Duke's officers among whom was the Hanoverian General Freiherr von Linsingen, colonel-in-chief of the 1st KGL Hussars. Müffling and these officers had a conference with Bülow and Prinz Wilhelm (commander of Bülow's Reserve Cavalry) a little before midday.[3] The plans for the day's battle were discussed. Müffling proposed that various manoeuvres be implemented according to circumstances,

> *Case 1.* If the enemy attacked the Duke of Wellington's right flank the Prussian army should reinforce him via Ohain.
>
> *Case 2.* If the enemy attacked the Duke's centre and left flank an offensive by the Prussian Army from the line of heights would be most effective, and the valley at La Haye, which would be difficult to pass, would be avoided.
>
> *Case 3.* If the enemy turned against St Lambert then the Duke should advance with his centre against Jenappe [sic] and attack the enemy in the left flank and rear.[4]

When the direction of Napoleon's attack later became known, Wellington had Bülow informed that Case 2 had occurred, and that he was to react accordingly. Bülow's acknowledgement read,

> In the event of the centre or left flank of Marshal Wellington being attacked, General von Bülow intends his corps to pass the Lasne [brook] at [the village of] Lasne, to form up on the plateau between La Haye and Aywières, and to attack the enemy's right flank and rear.
>
> My advice [to Blücher] is that another Prussian corps should go via Ohain to support the English forces at the most threatened point. A third Prussian corps could go via Maransart and Sauvagemont to cover the left flank and rear of the IV Army Corps. The remaining fourth corps will be held in reserve at Couture.[5]

Wellington agreed with Bülow's proposition, and Müffling passed it on to the Prussian headquarters with some marginal notes, including one which said, 'By 11.30 a.m., two brigades of Bülow's Corps had reached St Lambert. However, the Army Corps cannot be there until 4 p.m.'[6] Thus, at the beginning of the battle, Wellington was fully aware of the situation of the Prussian Army, and of the time at which he could expect to start to receive effective support.

Onwards From St Lambert

The Prussians had already examined the route ahead, and knew what difficulties they would have to face in moving forward. A report from one of their scouts (quoted on page 49) had arrived that morning. Despite having this information, Valentini did not want to take any chances, so he rode off to make his own reconnaissance, as described above, accompanied by Diederichs and a local farmer, who was mounted on an artillery horse. The farmer pointed out a better route, one that led through the Fichermont wood. Diederichs noted,

[3] *MWBl.*, 1907, p 2935.
[4] Pflugk-Harttung, *Wavre*, p 620.
[5] Pflugk-Harttung, *Wavre*, pp 620–1.
[6] Pflugk-Harttung, *Wavre*, p 621.

The suspicion that the enemy occupied the wood and would deny us access to it, was well founded. By doing so, he would have covered the right flank of the forces drawn up against the English... Fortunately, this very important point had escaped the enemy's attention. However, before we could be sure of this, we thought we saw the enemy nearby, as one of our despatch riders suddenly cried out, 'Halt! On our left flank, enemy lancers!' We turned about quickly to avoid capture along with our few despatch riders. However, we soon established that these lancers were part of the detachment sent out by Major von Falkenhausen. We rode through the wood, searching it thoroughly, and found it quite empty. Dismounting [on the far side], we could see individual enemy flankers ahead, but they were observing the events to their front, not in our direction. I was then ordered to inform the commander of the infantry of our vanguard that he should occupy the wood as quickly as possible. This he did, his men advancing at the double.[7]

The advance guard having now reached Fichermont wood, the Prussians started to consider the breakout. Thurn und Taxis' account continued,

From a point to the right of the road where there were a few clearings in the wood, we could see in the direction of Frichermont (from which we were only a quarter of an hour distant) to that part of the battlefield where the French right flank was attacking the English left. This attack was being made with great violence at La Haye Sainte in an attempt to force the English out of this position by bursting through their centre. This would probably make a union of, and communication between, our two armies impossible, even if the Duke knew we were so close to each other. Hard to believe as it may be, we could see into the rear of the enemy (a distance of about 1½ hours' march), and could even make out with our telescopes how the wounded were being carried back. The enemy was not gaining any ground, and officers coming as directly as possible from the Duke of Wellington, brought us the news that the English were beating off all the attacks most brilliantly. However, these attacks were getting more forceful, and a speedy diversion from us was needed.[8]

Oberst von Pfuel and Graf Nostitz of Blücher's staff were also observing these events. While Pfuel drew a sketch-map for future use, Nostitz rode back to headquarters with a preliminary report. In response Blücher ordered the III Army Corps to move towards Couture, then rode to the front with Gneisenau and Grolman (the Quartermaster-General), with Nostitz guiding the party. From their new vantage point, they observed the battle, noting the positions of Napoleon's reserves. A discussion ensued in which Gneisenau expressed the view that an intervention by the Prussians would result in Napoleon redoubling his efforts to break the Allied centre, while Nostitz feared that the French would throw their forces against the Prussians.[9] French patrols were seen on the heights left of Fichermont.[10] Blücher observed that the French reserves were more than adequate to break through Wellington's front but finally decided to continue the advance.

7 Pflugk-Harttung, *Wavre*, pp 623–4.   9 Nostitz, *Tagebuch*, p 40.
8 Thurn und Taxis, pp 332–3.   10 Pflugk-Harttung, *Wavre*, p 632.

Bülow's report described the decision to move forward from St Lambert,

The reports of Major von Falkenhausen indicated that the enemy had fortunately not moved up into positions along the Lasne brook. Thus, the Field Marshal [Blücher] decided that the IV Army Corps should pass through the defile there and secure the Fichermont wood.[11]

While their commanders were debating the next move, Bülow's leading units were able to rest for about 3½ hours. After their strenuous march, the men needed this respite before going into battle. There was no opportunity for most to cook a meal, however, not that there was much food available. All that could be done was to collect water out of the puddles. Muddy water, with some ground coffee, sugar and rum made up the main meal of the day.[12] Meanwhile, the officers tried to discern events to the west through their telescopes, but their poor position and the heavy atmosphere blocked the view.

Just after 2 p.m. the 15th Brigade led off, supported by as many light troops as possible and by the 2nd Neumark Landwehr Cavalry. As the remaining squadrons of the 3rd Silesian Landwehr Cavalry had been weakened by Falkenhausen's detachment, two squadrons from the 16th Brigade were also moved up.

The Prussians marched down the narrow Lasne valley. Mother nature again partly made up for Napoleon's failure to secure his right flank. The Lasne valley was muddy, the ground boggy. The guns sank so deep in the mud, that it was almost impossible to move them. The men found movement difficult, but Blücher personally urged them on. Eventually they struggled up the side of the far bank and stopped again at the wood between Lasne and Fichermont. It was now 3 p.m.[13] More precious time had been lost.

Finally, the brigade marched into the Fichermont wood, formed up in two lines. The first line consisted of the I. and III./18th, and the I. and II./3rd Silesian Landwehr, the second of the 4th Silesian Landwehr. Once the main body of the brigade closed up, its two fusilier battalions were sent through the wood, drew up on its far side, and occupied two houses there. The Prussians had now secured this important position.

To prevent clear information of the Prussian movements from reaching the French, pickets were deployed along every path in and out of the wood, and nobody was allowed to pass. The II./4th Silesian Landwehr were deployed along the southern edge of the wood to stop any surprise movements against the left flank. The advance continued cautiously, with van and flank guards being thrown out. Horse Battery Nr. 11 moved up in support. The 2nd Silesian Hussars were still in the wood.

Bülow commented on the situation at this point,

The enemy had begun his attack against the English army about midday. He was thrown back everywhere. Thus, from 3 o'clock that afternoon onwards, he renewed his attacks with double the determination. It was clear that he wanted to force back the English left flank and separate us from it. At the

---

[11] *Journal* of Constant Rebecque, Bülow's Report of 19 June 1815.
[12] *MWBl.*, 1907, p 2935.   [13] Clausewitz, p 109.

same time, it was favourable for us to act against the enemy right flank that he had inexplicably neglected and because he did not appear to be paying any attention to our existence.[14]

The 16th Brigade followed closely behind the 15th, reaching Lasne at 3.30 p.m. Next, the Reserve Cavalry moved up, passing through the 13th Brigade before joining the 16th. Clearing the Lasne defile, the cavalry halted behind the 16th Brigade and deployed. Since the 1st Silesian and 2nd Pomeranian Landwehr Cavalry Regiments were part of the rearguard at Dion-le-Mont, and later Wavre, the 2nd Silesian Hussars and 2nd Neumark Landwehr Cavalry had been allocated to Prinz Wilhelm's Reserve Cavalry. They formed up behind the 16th Brigade, in front of the other cavalry, and were the closest mounted troops to the French.

The 13th Brigade rested for over three hours at Chapelle St Lambert before passing through the defile to the wood of Fichermont behind the Reserve Cavalry. The 13th Brigade moved off from the heights east of St Lambert at 2.45 p.m., after the other brigades, and reached Lasne an hour later, with another short rest being taken there. Half an hour later, the march continued and it was thus well after 4 p.m. that the 13th Brigade got to the Fichermont wood.

Bülow's men thus arrived at the wood of Fichermont roughly as follows: the 15th Brigade after 3 p.m., the 16th Brigade at 3.30 p.m., the Reserve Cavalry at 4 p.m. and the 13th Brigade at 4.30 p.m. The Reserve Artillery came up later, with the 12-pounder batteries in the lead. This column straggled due to the difficult terrain. The 14th Brigade brought up the rear, being delayed by the Reserve Artillery, and arriving at St Lambert between 3 p.m. and 4 p.m., and at Fichermont by about 5 p.m. The 5th Brigade of the II Army Corps was not far behind. Once the 14th Brigade arrived, the 13th moved forward into action with it. They reached the field of battle about 5.30 p.m.

Therefore, by about 4 p.m. IV Army Corps could begin its advance into combat, though Bülow had Nostitz pass on a message to headquarters that he would only be able to commence his attack with two brigades (15th and 16th) and the Reserve Cavalry. A plea for urgent assistance arrived from Wellington at the same time as a British battery was seen limbering up and withdrawing. This was regarded as possibly an indication of the worst, so the Prussian high command considered an immediate reaction necessary. Rather than wait for the IV Army Corps to complete its concentration, Blücher decided to throw the available troops into the battle, despite Bülow's objections. He ordered Bülow to attack immediately, even if he only had one brigade in position.[15]

Bülow's deployment for battle began with the two fusilier battalions on the edge of the Fichermont wood moving forwards, supported by the 2nd Silesian Hussars. The 15th and 16th Brigades followed them, advancing along the edges of the road to Plancenoit. The Reserve Cavalry stayed in the woods in reserve, while such of the artillery as had arrived moved along the road in support.

---

[14] *Journal* of Constant Rebecque, Bülow's Report of 19 June 1815.
[15] Nostitz, *Tagebuch*, pp 40–1.

The skirmishers encountered a French cavalry patrol of about 20 men who fell back to Fichermont.[16] Hidden from sight at first, the 2nd Silesian Hussars trotted out of the wood by threes and deployed. The charge was sounded and the French patrol seen off. The skirmish line formed by the F./18th and 3rd Silesian Landwehr moved on. More French cavalry came up, forcing the Silesian Hussars to withdraw. The Prussian artillery now came into action and their fire persuaded the French to fall back in turn.[17] In this way, at roughly 4.30 p.m., the Prussian intervention began, hours later than it should have done, and with an inadequate force of tired and hungry men. It would nevertheless be successful.

Just then, news arrived in Blücher's headquarters of a column of French cavalry moving from Tilly towards Wavre. Battle was soon to be joined also in the Prussian rear.

I Army Corps Closes In

The first units of I Corps to near the Waterloo battlefield were from 1st Brigade. The 1st Brigade's order of march was follows: a vanguard consisting of the 1st Silesian Hussars and Brandenburg Dragoons, supported by Horse Battery Nr. 7 and 6-pounder Foot Battery Nr. 7, two companies of Silesian Schützen and the F./12th and F./24th;[18] next came the main body made up of the Musketeer battalions of the 12th and 24th, and the complete 1st Westphalian Landwehr; and, as rearguard, the Reserve Cavalry. When, in the course of operations the vanguard was detached, the I./24th was deployed for this purpose.[19] This happened because the path used was so poor that the men had to march in files, which led to the brigade being spread out and losing all semblance of order. Eventually, the vanguard became separated from the remainder of the brigade, and the vanguard itself drifted apart, the cavalry and guns in front leaving the infantry behind. The hussars were the first to reach Ohain where they made contact with Wellington's forces around 6 p.m.[20]

It seemed that Wellington's left wing would soon get some much needed assistance and the Duke would be able to move forces from there to reinforce his battered centre.

[16] Thurn und Taxis, p 332.
[17] Lippe-Weissenfeld, pp 241–2.
[18] Pflugk-Harttung, *Zieten*, p 200.
[19] Zychlinski, p 282.
[20] Pflugk-Harttung, *I. Korps*, p 149;
    Lettow-Vorbeck, p 433.

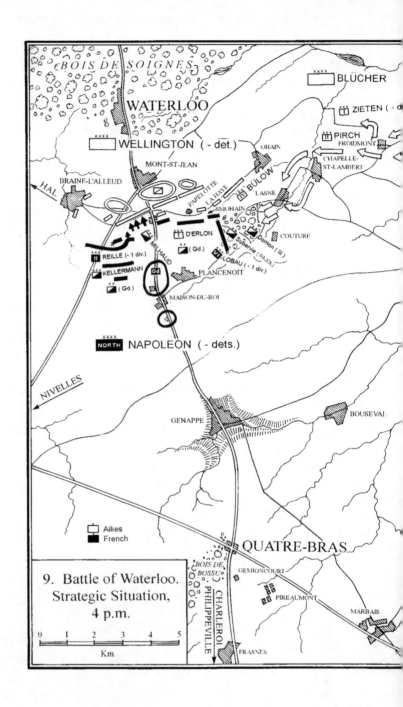

9. Battle of Waterloo. Strategic Situation, 4 p.m.

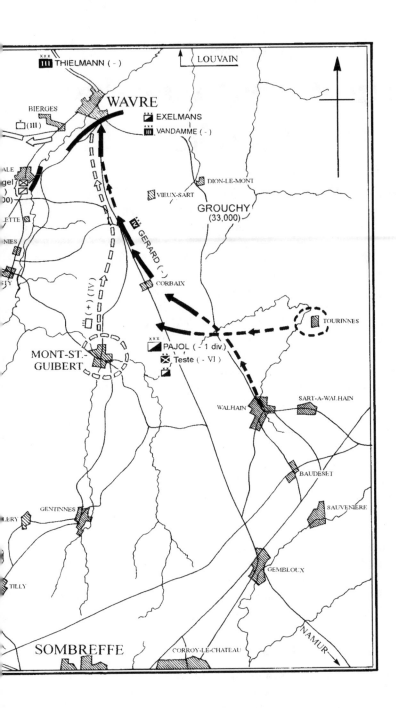

Chapter 8

The Great Cavalry Attacks

Napoleon's Options

By 3 p.m. matters were not proceeding as well as Napoleon had hoped. He was continuing to observe the Prussian movements with some trepidation and Major La Fresnaye now returned with a letter written by Grouchy from Walhain at 11.30 a.m. The news was not good. At the time of writing Grouchy was still three leagues (about 20 km) from Wavre, and had yet to establish what was going on to his left, that is between Napoleon and himself. Finally, Grouchy asked for orders to move in the direction of Chyse the following day, 19 June.[1] This clearly meant that Napoleon would have to defeat Wellington without any direct assistance from Grouchy, and would have to do so quickly because the menace from the Prussians was growing by the hour.

The situation on the Waterloo battlefield was also far from favourable for the French. D'Erlon's corps was *hors de combat* for the time being, after its losses earlier in the afternoon. Reille's corps was still heavily engaged at Hougoumont, and Lobau's had been deployed to the east to receive the expected Prussian attack. The only troops remaining were the Imperial Guard, and the large reserves of cavalry. Marshal Ney suspected that Wellington's line would not hold much longer, particularly because of the massive artillery bombardment it was suffering, and decided to send the cavalry forward against the battered but still unbroken Allied infantry lines. The French cavalry did not have sufficient infantry or artillery support, but with such a large body of high quality mounted troops and little fresh cavalry available to support the Allied infantry, the attackers still had a good chance of wearing down Wellington's centre enough for a final attack by the Imperial Guard to be decisive. Wellington's infantry now just had to sit tight and hold on until the French cavalry was a spent force. If enough of them stood, the Guard was going to have a difficult time. The next two hours were to be dramatic, but not quite decisive.

Wellington's Centre Reforms

Taking advantage of a brief respite after the earlier attacks and counter-attacks, Wellington brought up fresh formations to shore up his battered centre. Among these troops was the Hanoverian Foot Battery of Kapitain Braun. The official report of the Hanoverian and KGL troops in the campaign explained the situation,

---

[1] Houssaye, vol II, p 362.

Until three o'clock, the battery stood in reserve with the English brigade of Major-General Lambert at the farm of Mont St Jean, to the right of the paved road from Charleroi. Around this time, it moved into the first line with the infantry. The infantry deployed with their right flank on the Charleroi road, and the battery was posted in the centre of the infantry. It remained there for the entire battle, its front protected from all attacks by the sunken road, its flanks by the raised sides of the paved road. Along with the other three batteries deployed on the left flank the battery fired on the enemy's right flank and against the attack columns advancing on La Haye Sainte. The enemy artillery fire at this point was particularly heavy. One by one, most of our cannon were knocked out, but we continued to fire until the enemy withdrew. The battery also suffered heavy losses from enemy skirmish fire.[2]

Captain d'Huvelé of Battery Braun gave more detail in his report,

About half past three, an English 9-pounder battery moved up to the left of the battery. Two of its guns were knocked out very quickly and a caisson to the rear blew up. A further two caissons were so badly damaged that they could no longer be moved. The battery soon left this position, leaving us with significant fresh supplies of ammunition.[3]

Even at this stage of the battle the French fire had brought about some confusion and panic in the rear of Wellington's positions where the surgeons of the various units were attempting to treat the wounded. Among them were Dr. Lauprecht, brigade surgeon of Vincke's brigade, and his three assistants Behrens, Oppermann and Schröder of the Peine, Hameln and Hildesheim Battalions respectively. Lauprecht was at the front until about 3 p.m. when he rode to the rear to inspect his dressing station. It had gone. Oppermann had been setting up the station when he had been ordered further to the rear immediately. Oppermann's account described several panics and further moves. He wrote,

I then left the house I mentioned earlier to find out if the orders I had just heard really did indicate a retreat. I met Brigade Surgeon Schulze, who told me, 'We shall have to fall back,' which I did. After moving to the rear for about ten minutes, I met some other surgeons with whom I worked together for half an hour. However, the tumult continually increased and I had to make a quick decision, for every minute mounted men were coming up, crying out in the greatest panic, 'Back! Back! Move! Move!' This indicated the approach of great danger. I decided, without any orders or authority, to proceed with these surgeons to Brussels... [4]

In the rush their valuable medical equipment went missing. General von Vincke later put them on report and refused to accept their excuses. Small incidents and panics like these were a sign that Wellington's centre was perhaps beginning to crumble.

---

2 Pflugk-Harttung, *Belle Alliance*, pp 70–1.
3 Pflugk-Harttung, *Belle Alliance*, p 183.
4 Pflugk-Harttung, *Belle Alliance*, p 248.

The Battle for Papelotte Continues

Between 3 p.m and 4 p.m. Durutte's men renewed their assaults on the Nassau troops on Wellington's far left. A skirmish line preceded the attack columns in the usual way, and Hauptmann von Rettberg's skirmishers (3rd Flanker Company) were forced back to the main farm building of Papelotte. Supported by three other companies (10th, 11th and 12th) of the III./2nd Nassau, Rettberg then counter-attacked, forcing the French out of the sunken road at bayonet point, though French artillery fire soon forced the Nassauers to cease their pursuit.[5] Rettberg's report read,

> On my request for reinforcements, Kapitain Frensdorf placed the 10th, 11th and 12th Companies under my command and they joined the Flanker Company of the 2nd Battalion of our regiment. The enemy column was first held up by the fire from Papelotte and the small houses where the garrison was offering brave resistance. Then it was thrown back by a bayonet attack and pursued to the furthest hedge. Here, an enemy battery, not 500 paces away, fired canister at us. Although our losses were heavy, (the 3rd Flanker Company lost two officers in this position and by the end of the battle had lost half its men) the enemy did not attempt to undertake a new, serious attack. He merely conducted skirmisher fire from a hedge on the other side of the valley, at the foot of his position. It was a part of Durutte's division that attempted this attack. How strong this part was I cannot say exactly, but it was in any case significantly stronger than mine.[6]

Whether or not the entire farm fell to the French is a matter of dispute. Certainly, the Nassauers lost control of some of the buildings for some time. The nature of such fighting is that opposing forces can occupy different parts of the same building, leading to claims of its capture by the attacker, while the defender, still holding some of the building, claims a successful defence. In the confusion of battle, it is difficult to be sure of the facts. Suffice to say that the advancing Prussians of Zieten's I Corps who arrived later did think that the French had captured Papelotte, but only because they mistook the uniforms of the Nassauers for French ones.

The Battle for La Haye Sainte

After d'Erlon had finally rallied some of his battalions after their earlier defeat, Napoleon had Ney send them against La Haye Sainte again.[7] The destruction of Wellington's centre would decide the battle, and the key to the centre was this strong farmhouse. Reille also believed that Hougoumont was about to fall to his assaults, so there would soon be little to stop the French cavalry riding over Wellington's decimated battalions, followed by the Imperial Guard, opening up the road to Brussels.

Quiot's brigade advanced against La Haye Sainte where two companies of Ompteda's light infantry had reinforced its garrison. Troops from one of

---

[5] Rössler, *Geschichte*, pp 95–6.
[6] Pflugk-Harttung, *Belle Alliance*, p 206.
[7] Houssaye, vol II, pp 363 ff.

Donzelot's brigades also deployed into skirmish order and climbed the slope to the east of the Brussels road, opening fire at 20 paces on Wellington's infantry. The British returned the fire and Donzelot's men retreated. Meanwhile, Quiot's men suffered a similar fate at the hands of Baring's Germans, who fired at them from the farm buildings. The Frenchmen fell back to the orchard. In his personal account Baring described the scene,

> The enemy gave us a break of only half an hour that we used as best we could to prepare ourselves for the next attack. This happened in the same way as before, from two sides with two closed columns that advanced with great speed and almost surrounded us. The French, ignoring all danger, attacked with great force, more than I had ever before experienced. As they attacked in such a mass, every one of our shots hit home, many of them claiming more than one victim. This, however, did not prevent them from throwing themselves onto the wall and from grabbing our rifles through the loopholes, tearing them away from us. For their equally determined attempt to break through the gates and doors, many of the attackers paid with their lives. The battle was most intense around the missing barn door where they appeared to be most determined to break in. At this point 17 of the enemy lay dead, on top of each other, and protected their newly advancing friends with their bodies...
>
> The battle for the farm continued with uninterrupted violence. Nothing could break our men's courage. They followed the example of their officers, laughing at the danger. Nothing could discourage us, nothing gave us more hope than to see such behaviour.[8]

In his official report Baring, however, explained how the high morale of his men might not be enough,

> About an hour after this attack [made around 3 p.m.], the enemy attacked again with infantry in the same fashion. We were now suffering from a lack of ammunition, and my repeated demands for more remained unanswered. Nevertheless, 200 Nassau Scharfschützen were sent up. As the enemy was unable to make an impression on the farm with force of arms, he now tried to do so with fire by setting light to the barn. The small quantity of straw there quickly went up in flames, but with the help of a Nassau field kettle, we were soon able to put the fire out, although not without great sacrifice. Exhausted, the enemy now retired to gather his strength for a fourth fresh and vigorous assault that was carried out in the same way as before, but this time with more artillery support.[9]

For the time being, the German Legionnaires held on.

The First Cavalry Charge

The French grand battery resumed its violent fire against Wellington's left centre, with some of the 12-pounders of the Guard now supporting Reille's batteries. Few of the Allied troops had experienced a bombardment of such

---

[8] Baring, *Theilnahme*, p 76.
[9] Pflugk-Harttung, *Belle Alliance*, pp 108–9.

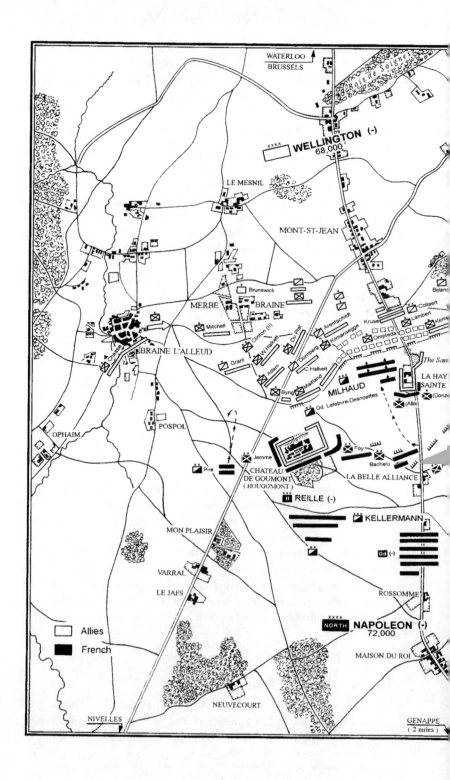

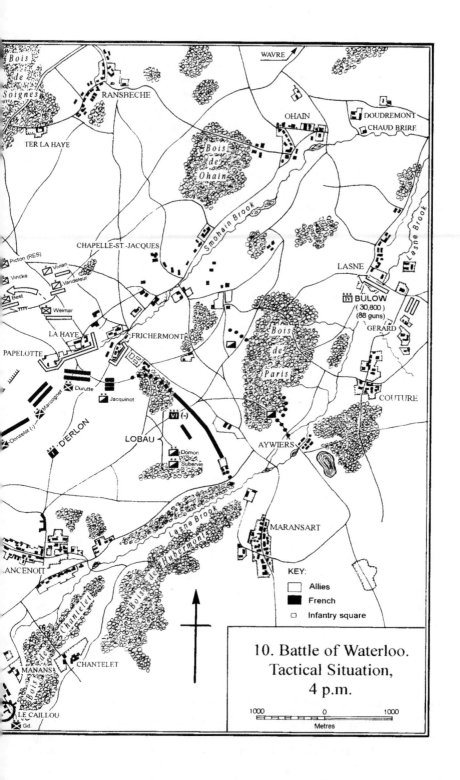

WAVRE

Bois de Soignes

RANSBECHE

OHAIN

DOUDREMONT

CHAUD BRIRE

TER LA HAYE

Bois de Ohain

Smohain Brook

Lasne Brook

CHAPELLE-ST-JACQUES

Picton (RES)

Vivian

Vincke

Vandeleur

LASNE

Best

Weimar

IV BÜLOW
(30,800)
(88 guns)

GERARD

LA HAYE

FRICHERMONT

Bois de Paris

PAPELOTTE

COUTURE

Durutte

Maicognet

Jacquinot

VI (-)

D'ERLON

LOBAU

Donzelot (-)

Domon

AYWIERS

Subervie

MARANSART

ANCENOIT

KEY:

Allies

French

□ Infantry square

Lasne Brook

Bois de Hubermont

Bois de Chantelet

MANANS

CHANTELET

10. Battle of Waterloo. Tactical Situation, 4 p.m.

LE CAILLOU

Gd.

1000   0   1000

Metres

intensity before. In the face of this hail of shot and shell, some battalions retired to more sheltered positions and groups of wounded and fugitives sought the relative safety of the Forest of Soignes. It seemed as if the entire Allied line was wavering, and a longer bombardment might well have broken some of the battalions. However, the leading elements of Bülow's corps were forming up in the Bois de Paris, on the eastern edge of the battlefield and the French were running out of time. Rather than wait for the artillery to do its preparatory work, Ney instead brought up a brigade of cuirassiers from Milhaud's corps to assault the Allied centre. Then, by about 4 p.m., more regiments, including the light cavalry of the Guard under Lefèbvre-Desnoëttes, came up in support. Baring again described the scene,

> Meanwhile, four lines of cavalry formed up to the right front of the farm. The first consisted of cuirassiers, the second of lancers, the third of dragoons and the fourth of hussars. One could not doubt for an instant that their orders were to attack the squares of our division and, by annihilating them, break through our entire line. It was equally clear what our fate would be if they were to succeed. As they rode past the farm to our main position, I had all the men I could bring up fire at the cavalry, killing many of them or their horses, but without discouraging the others. Not taking the slightest notice of our fire, they moved up fearlessly and attacked the infantry. I was able to observe all this and freely admit that my heart fell repeatedly.[10]

However, the Allied centre was far from being broken and Wellington was bringing up reinforcements. He moved four battalions of the Brunswickers to support Maitland's Guards. Mitchell's and Adam's brigades were moved in from the left, across the Nivelles road, nearer to Hougoumont and in front of the Ohain road. The four battalions of Brunswickers were placed in the second line, as were two of Adam's battalions. On sighting the French cavalry, the Allied infantry formed squares. In all, 20 steady battalions of infantry drawn up in a chequer-board formation stood to receive the charge. The artillery remained deployed on the edge of the plateau at the crest of the ridge. From there, the gunners were ordered to fire at the advancing French before abandoning their pieces at the last moment and retiring to the protection of the infantry squares. The limbers had already been brought to safety, so the French could not tow away the captured guns and it transpired that none of the French commanders thought to have artillerymen accompany their attacks equipped with spikes with which they could have put the Allied guns out of action.

The French cavalry advanced in echelons of squadron columns. On the right rode the cuirassiers, on the left, the chasseurs and chevaulégers. The right echelons manoeuvred in such a way as to gain the level part of the Ohain road, the left towards the slopes above Hougoumont. Once the cuirassiers left the protection of the hollow in which they had formed up, the supporting French batteries ceased fire, while those of the Allies opened up, pouring shot and canister rounds into the flank of the cavalry. The French troopers moved

[10] Baring, *Theilnahme*, pp 76-77.

slowly, the soft ground and remains of the tall crops delaying them. After receiving several rounds of fire at close range, Napoleon's troopers eventually reached the line of guns, driving off their crews. Then, for a few seconds, the French seemed to hesitate until the trumpeters sounded the charge and the advance continued. Raked by small arms fire, the French attempted to press home the attack but the battalions of British, KGL, Hanoverian, Brunswick and Nassau infantry stood their ground.

Kapitain von Scriba, acting commander of the Feldbataillon Bremen in Kielmansegge's brigade, was a participant in this part of the action. He wrote,

> At 3 o'clock, we deployed for the third time, but stayed in line for less than half an hour. Just before we formed square for the third time (3.30 p.m.), Major Müller was thrown from his horse by a cannon ball and wounded, whereupon command of the battalion fell to the undersigned [Scriba] from then until 19th July in the camp at Paris. Before the two battles [Quatre Bras and Waterloo], I had been the fifth officer in seniority in the battalion. The subsequent third attack by the [French] cavalry (cuirassiers again) was as violent and determined as the second. Like the first two, it was beaten off with total calmness and great success. Nothing could stop us from believing that it would be impossible for the enemy to break our ranks. Our morale was thus high, and seemed to rise and rise. During this episode, as earlier on, we had the great pleasure of seeing our most honoured divisional commander, General-lieutenant von Alten, nearby. His presence also played a role in keeping up our morale. However, the enemy cavalry stayed close to us, and we had to remain in square.[11]

The force of the cavalry charge soon dissipated. Only small groups of French cavalrymen actually tried to penetrate the squares. Others rode around poking with lances, slashing with swords, and firing off their pistols at point-blank range, gradually inflicting heavy casualties on the Allied infantry, but the gaps were quickly closed and not a single square was broken. It was now time for a counter-move.

Uxbridge's Counter-Charge

Although Uxbridge's British heavy cavalry were effectively out of action because of the casualties suffered during their earlier charge, two-thirds of the Allied cavalry were still fresh and unused. Dörnberg's light dragoons, Arentsschildt's hussars, the Brunswick lancers, Trip's carabineers, Merlen's and Ghigny's Netherlands light cavalry, some 5,000 sabres in all, were all ready, at around 4.15 p.m., to move against the confused and disorganised French horsemen.

Generalmajor von Dörnberg, commander of the 3rd Cavalry Brigade, described the situation as follows,

> At about 4 o'clock, more enemy cavalry appeared on our right, Lord Uxbridge gave me the order to detach one regiment to deal with this and I sent Oberst

von Jonquières, the most senior officer, with the 2nd Light Dragoon Regiment [KGL], though I cannot say any more about his service that day as I did not witness it.

Shortly afterwards, an enemy cuirassier regiment trotted up, moving between the squares and the battery on the ridge. As my two regiments were light cavalry, I told them to remain in column with orders that, at the instant I had the charge blown, the 23rd Regiment [British light dragoons] was to attack the enemy's left flank and the 1st [KGL light dragoons] their right. The three rear squadrons were to halt and deploy once the enemy was thrown back, with only the leading squadron of each column pursuing.

This charge was absolutely successful, with the cuirassier regiment being totally routed. However, the rear squadrons did not make a halt and everybody charged after the enemy until we came up to his reserve. It threw us back again. We had hardly begun to restore order again when another cuirassier regiment trotted up the ridge. We moved against it in line and at a gallop. The enemy regiment halted and pointed its swords at us. Our men slashed with their curved sabres, but with little success, and I heard them crying, 'Oh, if only we still had our old swords!' [Dörnberg's KGL troopers had formerly been heavy cavalry armed with straight swords.] I took a few men into the enemy's right flank and rear, but there was little we could do against these armoured horsemen. However, they did start to move to the left and then to fall back in relatively good order.

At this point, I was stabbed in the left of my chest into my lung, and blood started to come out of my mouth, making it difficult to speak. I had to ride to the rear and thus can say no more about the further actions of my troops in the pursuit of the enemy.[12]

Major Quintus von Goeben author of the report of the 3rd Hussars described a charge his unit made,

... two squadrons of the regiment... moved up to the ridge and were immediately personally ordered by the Earl of Uxbridge, the general commanding the entire combined cavalry, to charge the enemy cavalry – one regiment of cuirassiers on the right flank, one of dragoons and some lancers – about 200 to 250 paces in front of our regiment. Whether because of the enemy's great superiority in numbers – they were about three or four times our strength – or the lack of a proper commander – Rittmeister von Kerssenbruch was not present because of the earlier action [an earlier attack made in support of Netherlands cavalry], and the two squadrons had not been informed of this – in any case, the charge ordered did not start immediately. Seeing our hesitation, Lord Uxbridge shouted at the two squadrons, so there was nothing else to do but to trot forward and then without further thought charge the enemy cavalry at the gallop. The enemy were themselves advancing either at a slow trot or walk. The right-hand squadron of the regiment struck the right-hand squadron of the enemy dragoons, and the 2nd Squadron attacked the cuirassiers. The enemy line was broken at both these points, but their flanks overlapped both squadrons and took them in the rear, inflicting heavy losses.

12 Pflugk-Harttung, *Belle Alliance*, pp 102–3.

The few survivors of the two squadrons fell back under enemy pursuit to the infantry squares, where they rejoined the rest of the regiment.[13]

Despite such setbacks the Allied cavalry generally had the advantage of numbers and cohesion and drove the French from the plateau. The gunners now rushed back to their pieces to give the retiring Frenchmen a parting shot. Only the Cumberland Hussars (a Hanoverian regiment) failed to charge home, instead fleeing from the battlefield.

The First Crisis

Driven back to their starting point in the hollow of the valley below the ridge, the French cavalry quickly recovered from their shock and turned around. Moving back up the slippery slope of Mont St Jean, they again suffered terribly from the allied artillery fire. Once more, they took possession of the guns tormenting them before falling on Wellington's battered squares. Some believed the Allied infantry could not withstand a second ferocious assault.[14] The young Brunswickers were particularly nervous and likely to break at any moment.

Seeing the opportunity of achieving a breakthrough here, Napoleon reinforced Ney, but only with cavalry – four brigades of cuirassiers and carabineers from Kellermann's corps.[15] He was still unwilling to commit the Guard to the attack and the reason for that was quite simple – Bülow's leading brigades under Losthin and Hiller had just begun their move against Plancenoit. Napoleon knew he needed to take measures to protect his right rear before he could deliver the *coup de grace* against Wellington's centre. Even though the Prussians had scarcely fired a shot so far, their intervention was significantly reducing the effect of the blows against the Anglo-Dutch-German forces along the ridge of Mont St Jean. Napoleon was being compelled to divide his forces against enemies who were becoming numerically stronger by the hour.

The second cavalry attack ran much as the first. After having penetrated the line of guns, the French troopers made their way towards the infantry squares. Here, they were met with musket fire at close range and once again could not charge home. The squares held, though for a time some doubted they would. The Nassau troops were among the hardest hit and the journal of the 1st Nassauers described their difficult situation,

Very strong masses of French heavy cavalry moved up after the enemy artillery had caused havoc in numerous battalions and in our artillery. The 1st Battalion of the Duke of Nassau's 1st Regiment suffered particularly and the guns were either destroyed or out of ammunition. It must have been about 5 o'clock now. Covered by their artillery, the enemy continually attacked our infantry for over an hour. Lacking artillery support and with only minimal help from our cavalry, we only had our courage to offer. The cuirassiers broke through our first and second lines, and were only 100 paces from the first English line, defying the fire with great bravery.

13 Pflugk-Harttung, *Belle Alliance*, pp 170–1.
14 Mercer, p 168.
15 Houssaye, vol II, p 376.

A French battery moved forward through the wreckage and opened up with canister fire at short range into the 1st Battalion of the 1st Regiment. The cuirassiers, taking advantage of the smoke, rode into this battalion, wiping out 1½ companies, taking prisoner two officers (one of them badly wounded) and about 20 men.[16]

Generalmajor von Kruse's account elaborated,

The enemy commenced his movement against our right flank. Forty artillery pieces and several battalions advanced. This combat lasted at least one hour after the arrival of the artillery whose bombardment was most heavy, coming from well-manned large guns. This strong artillery fire was aimed largely against the key of our position on the plateau described earlier. On this plateau stood four or five battalions of Hanoverians, two English battalions and the Duke's [of Nassau] 1st Regiment. The I. [Nassau] Battalion stood in the front line, the other two in the second line. The entire cavalry of the army was formed up in several lines on the plain to the rear of this line of infantry. The artillery had devastated the various battalions, particularly the I. Battalion of the Duke's 1st Regiment, and our artillery was largely destroyed or out of ammunition. Then enormous masses of enemy cavalry moved up, covered by their own artillery, and attacked our infantry continuously for over an hour. Without a single cannon, and with little cavalry support, our men had only their bravery left. The cavalry halted 100 paces in front of our first line and defied its fire with great courage.

At this moment, the heavy losses caused by canister fire finally caused the I. Battalion to start wavering. The waiting cuirassiers cut it down and took several prisoners, including the brave Captains Schüler and Waitz.[17]

Some of the Hanoverian battalions fared rather better. Kapitain von Scriba of the Bremen Battalion again described his experiences,

At half past four, Major von Schkopp [of the Verden Battalion] led the square up the ridge towards the enemy. The Crown Prince of the Netherlands [Prince of Orange] followed this move in person. I believe our advance co-incided with a general movement forward of the entire army, but as smoke obscured my view, at times hardly seeming to move, I cannot be sure. Our advance and fire drove off the nearby enemy cavalry, but we then came under heavy canister fire. That and the retiring Nassau troops caused a large gap in our line, forcing our commander to fall back to our starting position. This we did in complete order.[18]

Major Müller of the Feldbataillon Bremen also mentioned a retrograde movement,

… our square was attacked by a French chasseur regiment. It received fire into its left flank from close range and was attacked in the rear by English cavalry regiments, forcing it to ride around the rear of the square. Now fired on at

[16] Pflugk-Harttung, *Belle Alliance*, p 198.
[17] Pflugk-Harttung, *Belle Alliance*, pp 201–2.
[18] Pflugk-Harttung, *Belle Alliance*, pp 136–7.

close range by our right flank, and pursued by the English cavalry, it suffered very heavy losses and was almost wiped out. The enemy cavalry, who appeared to me to be being drawn into the fire of the squares by fake attacks from our cavalry, now made a third charge, although this was much slower than the previous ones. Again, they were beaten off. On the orders of the Prince of Orange and accompanied by him, Major von Schkopp led the square against the French cavalry. After receiving well-aimed fire, a French cavalry regiment withdrew. The square continued to advance, but came under murderous canister and musket fire. That and the retreat of a square of Nassauers on our right flank, forced our square to withdraw, but only after Major von Schkopp had been wounded. A large part of the flank facing the enemy had been knocked over and wounded, killed or momentarily paralysed with shock.[19]

Wellington's centre was battered and wavering but once more a counter-charge from Uxbridge's Reserve Cavalry drove off the French horsemen. This sequence of events was repeated again and again, still the French kept surging forward and still the squares held firm.

The 3rd KGL Hussars were among the units involved in the series of Allied counter-charges. Major Quintus von Goeben of the 3rd KGL Hussars recalled how his unit tried to help the infantry,

Between 4 o'clock and 5 o'clock, on the left flank of the regiment along a hedge about 300 to 400 paces away, a battalion of the combined army, probably the 5th Line Battalion of the King's German Legion, made a bayonet attack on enemy infantry. It threw them back, but was threatened by several squadrons of enemy cuirassiers who were galloping up. Seeing this, and without any further orders, the regiment's then commander, Rittmeister von Kerssenbruch, attacked the enemy cuirassiers at a gallop in their left flank with the remainder of the regiment. Thus, he prevented any further pursuit of the infantry. However, the greater numbers and the superiority of the enemy cavalry soon made it necessary for the regiment to start thinking of withdrawing, but before this could be done our men had suffered significant losses, including Rittmeister von Kerssenbruch. The enemy came on right up to the infantry squares, mixed with the scattered regiment, but the effective fire of a Hanoverian Field Battalion quickly drove them off. Nevertheless, several enemy cuirassiers got to behind the line of squares and one of the enemy was discovered in the middle of the regiment when it was reforming. As he did not want to surrender, he was cut down, but not before it became apparent how well protected his head and body were. It took several attempts by the hussars to strike an effective blow against the cuirassier's armour.

The remainder of the regiment, now down to 40 files strong, stayed in a position just to the rear of Generallieutenant Graf von Alten's division and was now the only cavalry he had left.

At this time, several squadrons of enemy cavalry drew up in line about 300 to 400 paces away. The officers sported tall, broad bearskin hats and several of them rode up, challenging our officers to single combat. As they were much

---

[19] Pflugk-Harttung, *Belle Alliance*, pp 130–1.

stronger, the regiment could not accept this honour, and the enemy cavalry did nothing else other than offer these big bearskin hats as targets to some sharp-shooters of the Hanoverian Field Battalion.[20]

The official report of the 3rd KGL Hussars also described this action,

The infantry in this part of our line had suffered severely and could no longer hold back the enemy skirmishers who came up to close range and killed many men. A detachment of the 3rd Hussars under Rittmeister Georg Meyer moved against them, driving them right back to a safe distance...

We again took our original position next to the infantry squares. Shortly afterwards, we were presented with another opportunity to make an attack on the left flank of a cuirassier regiment that was about to cut into a battalion of infantry. The latter had just broken an enemy infantry battalion with a bayonet charge. Our charge was successful. Part of the cuirassier regiment was driven off and its attack on the infantry halted. Just a few squadrons of lancers attacked our rear and forced us to abandon our gains. We quickly withdrew behind the infantry squares while a Hanoverian Field Battalion caused heavy casualties to the enemy with its cold-blooded fire.

The regiment lost heavily in this incident and Rittmeister von Kerssenbruch fell during the charge. Even when behind the infantry squares, the regiment continued to suffer from canister and small arms fire. A canister ball smashed the left arm of Cornet Hans von Hardenberg. Many of the men were wounded.[21]

Finally Marshal Ney tried to break the stalemate by sending forward some of Reille's infantry with a renewed cavalry advance. The Allied infantry were equal to the challenge once again.

The official report of the 1st Brigade of the KGL outlined its role in events,

The brigade under the command of Oberst du Plat stood on the right flank, which was refused. It stayed there until after 3 p.m. To protect itself against the artillery fire as much as possible it wheeled into open column. When the enemy cavalry recommenced its attack on the plateau, forcing the artillery to withdraw and almost reaching the infantry squares on the left flank of the brigade, we had to change front. The English brigade in the division did like-wise. Thus, the column changed direction towards Hougoumont. However, as there was enemy cavalry on the plateau on this side of Hougoumont, the battalions had to form squares. The rear squares moved to the left from the column, still advancing steadily against the plateau. The brigade commander [du Plat] was shot dead here.

The 2nd Battalion square was in front and marching straight towards Hougoumont, firing at the line of enemy cavalry as it went. The enemy then retired because of this threat and the fire of the batteries that had moved up simultaneously. The square then moved close to Hougoumont and the enemy

---

[20] Pflugk-Harttung, *Belle Alliance*, p 171.
[21] Pflugk-Harttung, *Belle Alliance*, p 165.

skirmishers in the orchard fired at it. Our men had little choice but rapidly to assault the enemy in the ditches and seize the orchard. The battalion succeeded in capturing this broken ground bit by bit. Meanwhile, the enemy resistance grew and some battalions of Brunswickers were sent in support. The battalion fought in this area for the rest of the day with varying success. Only when the Salzgitter Battalion [Hanoverian Landwehr] came to help in the evening was the enemy totally driven away...

At first, the squares of the 3rd and 4th Battalions stayed on the plateau the cavalry had abandoned. The 1st Battalion moved into a position that some of our batteries had occupied before the enemy cavalry attacks where they found several unmanned artillery pieces. One enemy infantry column, supported by cavalry, attempted to regain this position. However, the battalion repulsed it, forcing it sideways into the wood at Hougoumont. The cavalry charged the square twice, but were beaten back.

As the 1st Battalion square had suffered heavily by then, it joined up with that of the 3rd Battalion. Shortly afterwards, the squares were again charged with force by the cavalry of the enemy Guard. The men, having double-loaded their muskets, calmly held their fire to point blank range, causing great loss to the cavalry. The two divisional batteries increased this loss, forcing the enemy horsemen back.[22]

Major von Rettberg, commander of the 1st Line Battalion of the KGL (du Plat's brigade), described his unit's role in more detail,

We then attacked the ridge in front of us (the original position of the centre of the right flank), where enemy infantry had taken control of our artillery, and drove them off in flight. A strong column of enemy infantry with cavalry support attacked us and our artillery with determination. The enemy infantry closed up to our cannon and to about 30 to 40 paces from our square. At this moment, Colonel Robertson, our commander, fell badly wounded from his horse. The enemy fire was devastating. Fortunately, we were then ordered to attack. We charged in square, threw back the enemy pell-mell, and were charged by lancers while advancing. We drove off the cavalry with some losses, while the enemy infantry withdrew into the garden of Hougoumont and took cover in a ditch. From there, they inflicted heavy losses with their musketry. Lancers and dragoons threatened us all this time and only retreated after we threw them back again with further casualties.[23]

The outcome of the battle was still in the balance. For the moment the Anglo-Dutch-German forces were holding on, but only just.

---

[22] Pflugk-Harttung, *Belle Alliance*, pp 58–9.
[23] Pflugk-Harttung, *Belle Alliance*, p 112.

Chapter 9

The Prussians Tip the Balance

The Initial Prussian Attack

The objective of the IV Army Corps was to seize Plancenoit in the right rear of the French position and from there to break into the rear of the French position behind La Belle Alliance. Advancing from the Bois de Paris down the valley of the Lasne brook, Bülow aimed to secure his right flank at Fichermont before moving on to his main objective.

Thurn und Taxis gave a clear summary of the overall situation,

> … It was about half past four, the Field Marshal [Blücher] and General Bülow… noticing that the enemy appeared to have gained some ground [against Wellington], decided to attack, even though only two brigades were available. (I think they were right to do so.) The attack began with a battery opening fire so the Duke [of Wellington] would be aware of our move, and immediately after that we marched off. On the far side of the wood [that is west of the Bois de Paris], the land dropped in step-like intervals down into the valley in which the village of Plancenoit lay. Just at that moment an enemy cavalry detachment of about 150 sabres rode out of the village and up the heights, evidently to reconnoitre them, although this was obviously a little late now. They clearly did not expect so many of our men to have already deployed. They halted, then turned about. We followed them, riding downhill into terrain that was opening up, thus giving us the advantage. Plancenoit was right in front of us… [1]

Bülow's report also described how his advance got going in this way,

> It was half past four in the afternoon, when the head of our column advanced out of the Frichermont wood. The 15th Brigade under General von Losthin deployed quickly into battalion columns, throwing out skirmishers. The brigade's artillery, along with the Reserve Artillery, followed up rapidly, seeking to gain the gentle ridge. The brigade cavalry, led by the 2nd Silesian Hussar Regiment, covered this movement. [2]

Once Losthin had moved off, Hiller's 16th Brigade 'moved out to the left, forming a line on the plateau between the sunken road of the Abbey of Aywières and the sunken road at Frichermont.'[3] Small arms fire opened up all along the line of advancing troops. The Prussians were in action.

---

[1] Thurn und Taxis, pp 333–4.
[2] *Journal* of Constant Rebecque, Bülow's Report of 19 June 1815.
[3] *Journal* of Constant Rebecque, Bülow's Report of 19 June 1815.

Bülow's account continued,

As enemy cavalry came up, the 2nd Silesian Hussar Regiment, which was in the lead, had to move quickly to the left flank of the infantry while the 16th Brigade deployed. The 2nd Neumark Landwehr Cavalry Regiment under Oberstlieutenant von Hiller moved to the right rear of the threatened infantry. Later, the West Prussian Uhlan Regiment moved up behind the right flank for the same purpose. Meanwhile, the remainder of the Reserve Cavalry formed up behind Hiller's [16th] brigade. However, it soon became apparent that the enemy cavalry was acting as a screen and that they had no serious intentions. Rather, they only wanted to cover the advance of their skirmish line that now engaged with ours in a lively fire-fight.[4]

Lobau's Defence

Two battalions of Losthin's 15th Brigade (F./18th and F./3rd Silesian Landwehr) under the command of Major von Koschkull moved down the ravine north of the Fichermont wood, securing the right flank of the Prussian advance. The Prussians had now linked up with the Nassauers. The skirmish platoons deployed in front, under Kapitain von Osten and Premierlieutenant von Wedelstädt. The brigade cavalry, the horse artillery and the brigade artillery moved on their left flank in support. This symbolic union of German soldier with German soldier marked the beginning of the end of the battle for Napoleon. If the two wings of the Allied forces were to succeed in uniting on the field of Waterloo, then the weight of numbers would almost inevitably tell. Time was running out for Bonaparte.

The history of the 18th Regiment gave a detailed description of some of the fighting which immediately followed,

Meanwhile, the brigade had moved up to the two battalions, to the left of the deployed battery. The I. Battalion of the 18th Regiment was directly behind the battalions of the vanguard. When it reached Frichermont and found the farm buildings to the left of the village occupied, it threw out its skirmishers under Kapitain von Pogwisch and attacked the enemy positions. Their front line was taken with the first, very determined, bayonet charge. Kapitain von Pogwisch's charge was a great contribution. Supported by the brigade battery and the 2nd Silesian Hussar Regiment under Oberst von Eicke, he forced the enemy to abandon this position. The hussars drove back the enemy skirmish line posted to the left front of Fichermont and forced a chasseur regiment to retire. However, a second enemy cavalry regiment attacked them in the flank, throwing them back. The [3rd Silesian Landwehr] cavalry under Rittmeister von Altenstein and the horse battery restored the situation.[5]

The Prussian advance continued. The 15th Brigade formed in two lines and pressed on to the bush-lined heights beyond Fichermont. All three battalions of the 18th Regiment became involved in a bloody battle. The Prussians quickly moved up their artillery onto the ridges just captured. The

---

[4] *Journal* of Constant Rebecque, Bülow's Report of 19 June 1815.
[5] Wedell, p 166.

12-pounder battery attached to the 15th Brigade advanced between the columns of infantry, in effect dividing the brigade into two parts. The left wing now consisted of two battalions of the 3rd Silesian Landwehr and the III./4th Silesian Landwehr, while the right consisted of the I. and F./18th Regiment and the remaining battalions of the 4th Silesian Landwehr. Major von Krahn took command of the left wing, Oberst von Massow, commander of the 4th Silesian Landwehr, the right.

The fighting on both flanks of the IV Corps now became intense. Oberst von Loebell, commander of the 18th Regiment, and Oberst von Massow led the first assaults. The I. and F./18th Regiment and the I. and II./4th Silesian Landwehr advanced on the right. The French tried to hold back the Prussians with a strong skirmish line but one by one the Prussian battalions moved up and deployed, continually trying to force their way forward. A regiment of French lancers tried to delay the advance, charging the skirmishers covering the dividing line between the brigades, but Major von Colomb moved up with the 8th Hussars and saw them off. Colomb's hussars followed up a distance before an infantry square halted them. Driven off by musketry and threatened in the flank by French hussars, they fell back, reforming to the rear.[6]

Bülow's report described this phase of the advance,

> The enemy disputed every foot of ground, but not with any great determination... Only in the village of Plancenoit and on the heights running up to our right flank did the enemy appear to want to show any serious resistance.[7]

Bülow's report then continued,

> Six battalions of the 16th Brigade now came up to assault Plancenoit. They formed three attack columns next to each other, with two battalions of the 14th Brigade that had also reached the battlefield following up in support. Just as this brigade formed up behind the 16th, the 13th Brigade under General-lieutenant von Hake arrived and moved up behind the 15th.[8]

Lobau attempted to halt the wave of Prussian blue rushing towards him. One of his four brigades was hurriedly sent to occupy Plancenoit. The other three, along with most of his 38 guns, and the two cavalry divisions, each with two batteries, were deployed in the open ground to the north of the village. Here, Lobau was able to unbalance Losthin, despite the fact that the 13th Brigade had now come up in support. For a moment, the Prussians hesitated, and could have been driven off. However, Bülow noticed the danger, and quickly moved two regiments of cavalry, the 1st Neumark Landwehr and the 1st Pomeranian Landwehr from his left, covered by the 2nd Silesian Hussars, to 'support this threatened point. With this measure, the faltering success of the battle was overcome in an instant.'[9] However, the reality was rather different from this version in Bülow's report. In truth the Prussians were now

6 Anon, *Husaren-Regiment Nr. 8*, p 5.
7 *Journal* of Constant Rebecque, Bülow's Report of 19 June 1815.
8 *Journal* of Constant Rebecque, Bülow's Report of 19 June 1815.
9 *Journal* of Constant Rebecque, Bülow's Report of 19 June 1815.

bogged down and making no headway in this part of the front. As Losthin explained more accurately in his report, 'for several hours, the enemy defended his position with determination.'[10]

The report of the 18th Infantry Regiment described this fierce struggle,

> The skirmish platoons under Premier-Lieutenant von Pastau and Seconde-Lieutenant Mittelbach had used up all their ammunition against the French Guards. Kapitän von Koschytzi called for volunteers to relieve the two platoons. The first to come forward was Lieutenant Schönfeld, who placed himself under the command of Lieutenant von Wedelstädt. The latter took command of the large number of volunteers. Both officers led from the front, their fearlessness and encouragement inspiring the men. Several shots hit Schönfeld, but he refused to go to have his wounds dressed. Only after a further ball hit him in the knee did he reluctantly leave the field of battle...
>
> Lieutenant Culemann of the fusilier battalion heard a French staff officer continually calling 'Vive l'Empereur! En avant mes braves!' to his battalion of the Young Guard. He had Sergeant Walter, the best shot, take aim at him. Just as Walter was about to carry out his order, he was shot in the left hand. Lieutenant Culemann rode up and offered Walter his stirrup as a rest. Walter used it and shot the French officer from his horse. Taking advantage of the moment, the commander of the fusilier battalion launched a bayonet charge... The charge was so violent that the Young Guard battalion, deprived of its leader, turned and fled. The 1st Uhlan Regiment immediately charged the retiring battalion.[11]

The 13th Brigade moved up to act as a reserve for the 15th Brigade troops who were holding Papelotte and the area nearby. The 1st Silesian Regiment and the 2nd Neumark Landwehr deployed for action. The brigade journal noted,

> Once the 13th Brigade, at first allocated to the reserve, had passed the [Lasne] defile and the Frichermont wood, finally gaining the field of battle, it immediately moved towards the village of Frichermont. At 5 o'clock in the afternoon, on the orders of Generallieutenant von Hake, it was deployed against the enemy as follows: the I. Battalion of the 2nd Neumark Landwehr Regiment on the right flank in the front line against the village of Frichermont, the II. Battalion to its left, with the Fusilier Battalion in front of them both.[12]

The Battle for Plancenoit

Hiller had only six of his battalions available for his first attack on Plancenoit. He had already detached one to the centre because a battalion of the 15th Brigade there had run out of ammunition and Major von Keller had taken the fusilier battalions of the 15th Regiment and the 1st Silesian Landwehr to the Bois de Virère to protect the left flank. Hiller then attacked Plancenoit from

---

[10] Lettow-Vorbeck, p 431.
[11] Wedell, pp 169–70.
[12] Rehmann, p 176.

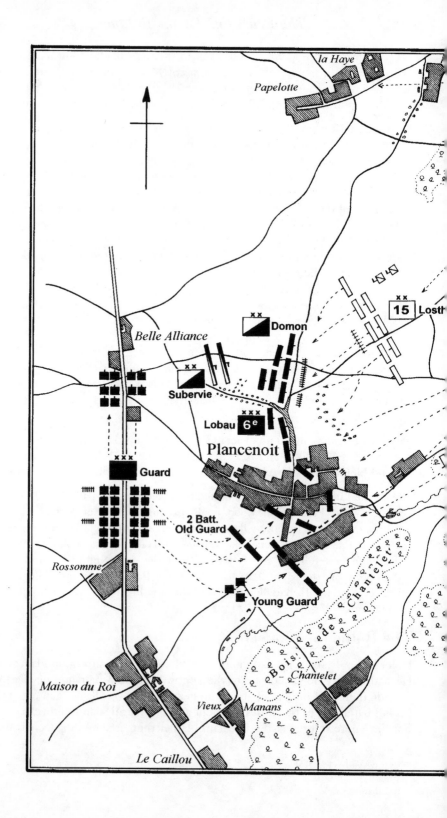

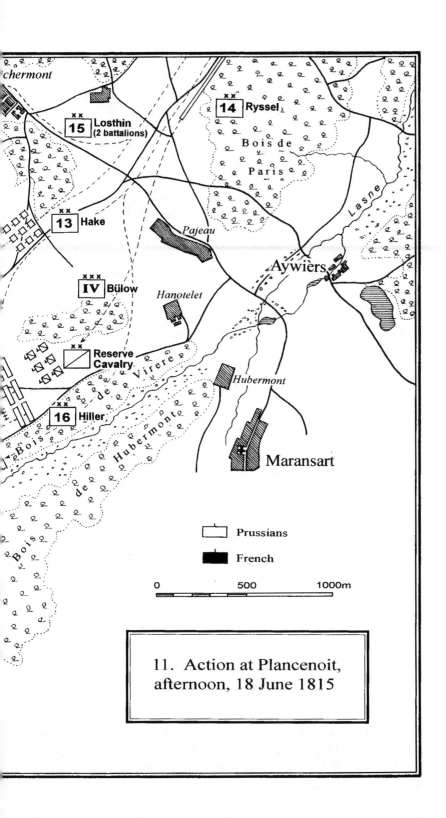

11. Action at Plancenoit,
afternoon, 18 June 1815

both sides: two battalions of the 15th Regiment from the right, two of the 1st Silesian Landwehr from the left. Several battalions of the 14th Brigade were following up, but were still some distance from the village. The two battalion columns of the 15th Regiment pushed on to the high walls of the church in the centre of the village, despite furious resistance from the French and heavy losses. They captured three cannon and took two staff officers and several hundred men prisoner.

'The open space around the churchyard,' wrote Hiller,

> was circled by houses and hedges from which the enemy, despite our every courageous effort, could not be dislodged... Only the arrival of several fresh masses of Old Guard made the men waver and, despite all my efforts, and those of the brave officers supporting me, fall back.

Accounts of the fighting for Plancenoit vary considerably in detail and the sequence of events and number of Prussian attacks is not always clear. Hiller's first attack may actually have succeeded in capturing the village, although he does not claim this, and he was certainly wrong in saying that his men were counter-attacked by the Old Guard at this stage. In fact Napoleon had sent the eight battalions of Duhesme's division of the Young Guard to help Lobau's hard-pressed corps, and it was these troops who quickly threw the Prussians out of Plancenoit. The exhausted Prussian troops rallied in the gully east of Plancenoit under the protection of Ryssel's 14th Brigade that had now moved up. Plancenoit was not proving easy to take.

Blücher, believing that the capture of Plancenoit would determine the outcome of the entire battle, directed the fighting there personally. However, just as he ordered Hiller's 16th Brigade into the fray once again, news from Thielemann and III Army Corps arrived. He reported that Wavre was now under attack by superior forces, and requested assistance. This was the crisis point of the day for the Prussian Army. Blücher's main attack was faltering, his reinforcements were coming up too slowly, his ally's defences were showing signs of crumbling under the French assault, and now his line of retreat was in danger of being cut. Blücher and Gneisenau were not deterred, however. They were now in no doubt that Plancenoit was the key to winning the battle. Gneisenau coolly dictated the answer for Thielemann to Lieutenant von Wussow,

> he is to dispute with all his strength every step the enemy makes forwards, for even the greatest losses to his corps would be more than outweighed by a victory over Napoleon here.[13]

Plancenoit Captured

Meanwhile, the battle for Plancenoit had continued. The 14th Brigade was now ready to support the 16th whose troops accordingly began a new assault. Supported by five battalions of Ryssel's (14th) Brigade, namely the I. and II./2nd Silesians (11th) and the 1st Pomeranian Landwehr, the 15th Regiment forced its way into Plancenoit a second time. The 1st Silesian Landwehr

[13] Ollech, p 196.

remained in reserve. Once again the Prussians could not hold on to their gains but in a third attack much of the village was taken and the French suffered heavy casualties, with many of the Young Guard surrendering.

The history of the 2nd Silesians described the arrival of the Young Guard at Plancenoit and the succeeding events,

Nine battalions of the Guard, including eight of the Young Guard advanced on Plancenoit with three of the Old Guard in reserve. Once Duhesme's division of the Young Guard had got into Plancenoit, it immediately took up positions in the houses and particularly behind the churchyard wall.

Taking no notice of the heavy canister and musket fire, the 16th Brigade advanced up to the churchyard. Here, hit by murderous fire and attacked by the French reserves with such force, it was forced to withdraw. It rallied outside the village and went over to the attack immediately. In this second assault, the two musketeer battalions of the 2nd Silesian Regiment took part. However, the French also beat off this attack.

The I. Battalion had been ordered to move to the right in support of the three battalions of the 13th Brigade that were in front of the lower part of the village where the II. Battalion stood. The enemy had driven off these three battalions after their assault on the village and they now stood between the 15th and 16th Brigades. The II. Battalion was in danger of being cut off. After having lost many of its officers and suffered heavy losses, it was forced to withdraw from Plancenoit.

… Thanks to their success, the French skirmishers were becoming bolder. They tried to break out of Plancenoit, but a squadron [4.] of the 2nd Silesian Hussar Regiment charged them, cutting down some of them and chasing them back. The battalions that had rallied in the meantime now followed up for the third assault. This involved not only the entire 14th Brigade, but also the 5th Brigade of the II Corps that had just reached the battlefield. This attack was decisive.[14]

The history of the 15th Regiment also described this cavalry counter-attack and then explained how the attack was renewed,

Enemy skirmishers, getting bolder now, moved up to the regiment, which was in a hollow in front of the village, and fired on it with considerable effect. The regimental commander, Major von Wittich, brought up and led a squadron of the 2nd Silesian Hussars against them, driving them back into the village.

Meanwhile, the battalions of the 14th Brigade had moved up behind the 16th Brigade in support. Our regiment, along with four battalions of this brigade (from the 2nd Silesian Infantry Regiment and the 1st Pomeranian Landwehr Regiment) undertook the second assault on the village. The 1st Silesian Landwehr Regiment remained in reserve. The enemy resisted with great determination, but the village was recaptured and a large number of enemy guardsmen were either killed or captured in the close combat.[15]

14 Ebertz, pp 200, 203.
15 Dörk, pp 130–1.

What happened was that Pirch I sent his 5th Brigade (Tippelskirch) up to support Bülow's 14th and 16th Brigades as they made another attempt to seize Plancenoit. The 15th Regiment advanced on the right of the attack, storming the village from the north. Premierlieutenant von Birkholz of the I./15th Regiment captured three cannon and a number of caissons. The F./15th, supported by a battalion of Landwehr, advanced on the left flank, its skirmishers covering a battery of artillery placed on the heights before Plancenoit. Standing under French artillery fire for a while, it then sent off three platoons, the 1st, 5th and 6th, to support the skirmishers. Their first attempt to penetrate into Plancenoit made some headway and after resting a short while the skirmishers and three platoons then supported the 14th Brigade's assault.[16]

The advance of the 14th Brigade started. The history of the 2nd Silesian Infantry continued,

> The brigade commander-in-chief General von Ryssel and the brigade commander Oberst von Funck led the I. and II. Battalions of the 1st Pomeranian Landwehr Regiment, followed by the I. Battalion of the 2nd Pomeranian Landwehr to storm Plancenoit. At the same time, Major von Aulock made a further bayonet attack on the churchyard with the I. Battalion of the 2nd Silesian Regiment. This brave officer fell at the head of his battalion, fatally wounded by a bayonet and a musket ball. Enraged by the death of their popular leader, the brave musketeers pressed on, fearing nothing. Supported by Oberst von Funck's Pomeranians, they stormed the churchyard. Here, a vicious, bloody and bitter battle took place.[17]

At last Napoleon's Young Guard were ejected from Plancenoit, and to the north Lobau's men gradually fell back towards the ridge along which the road from Charleroi to Brussels ran. The Prussians now held the key to Bonaparte's rear. Elements of the II Army Corps were coming into action and the I Army Corps was now in sight and shortly to be engaged. Time was running out for Napoleon.

Zieten's Men Join the Fray

Like the other Prussian formations, Zieten's I Army Corps did not have an uneventful march into battle, Zieten had ordered his corps to march 'via Froidmont to Ohain' but the troops did not follow this route, marching to the right to Genval, which lost precious time and took the I Army Corps much further from Bülow's men than planned.

By around 5 p.m. the 1st Brigade had reached the defile of the Lasne brook where it halted to close up its ranks and await the arrival of the 2nd Brigade. Using that time, Oberstlieutenant von Reiche, Zieten's chief-of-staff, rode on to the battlefield. On the left of Wellington's positions, he met Müffling, who informed him that Wellington was desperate for his help and could not hold on much longer without aid from the Prussians.

On rejoining the corps, Reiche found that Zieten was no longer with the

[16] Dörk, pp 132–3.
[17] Ebertz, p 203.

lead units but had ridden to the rear to speed up the march. The confusion that resulted cost valuable time, time that was running out. Reiche ordered the vanguard to ride on at a trot, while he rode forwards again.[18] Meanwhile, Zieten returned to the 1st Brigade, and had it wait until the main body of the corps was in sight before allowing the advance to continue.[19] At 1,000 paces from the French, Zieten's men stopped again. An officer was sent on to examine the situation at close quarters. He saw the many wounded and stragglers retreating from Wellington's lines, while the French seemed to be pressing home their advantage. He brought this information back to Zieten, telling him Wellington appeared to have lost the battle.[20] The Nassauers and Prussians of the 15th Brigade in Smohain and Fichermont could also be seen to be falling back, so Zieten began to be concerned that his men could be caught up in a defeat if he continued on his present route.

Just as Zieten was hesitating, Major von Scharnhorst of Blücher's staff arrived at corps' headquarters, bringing an order to turn to the left and support the IV Army Corps.[21] Bülow's men were still making little headway against Lobau and the Young Guard in Plancenoit and Blücher had decided to concentrate his efforts there. Zieten's men were all the additional troops that were available. Meanwhile, Reiche had returned from a second visit to Wellington's left. Here, the situation had deteriorated further, and on the way back Reiche had assured the Nassauers that immediate assistance was about to arrive. Scharnhorst and Reiche argued about which course of action to follow. At this point Zieten himself came back to his headquarters. Having a direct order from the senior commander of the army, Zieten felt he had no choice but to obey it. His men turned around and started marching to Bülow's aid.

Seeing the Prussians march away Müffling rode after Zieten as fast as he could. Catching up with him, Müffling persuaded him to come back, and join Wellington's crumbling left flank,[22] which Zieten now did with great haste. It was one of the crucial moments of the battle. The time was now approaching 7 p.m. and La Haye Sainte had finally fallen to the French. The Imperial Guard was preparing to march against Wellington's buckled centre, supported by parts of the I and II Corps. Durutte's division had also staged a successful counter-attack in the Papelotte area, further weakening the already hard-pressed Nassauers. Victory seemed to be in Napoleon's grasp, but the arrival of Zieten's corps meant that the Duke's left was now secure, helping him switch forces from there and his right wing to shore up his battered centre.

Another advantage this toing and froing had brought was to allow more of the I Army Corps to come up. The whole of the 1st Brigade, Reserve Cavalry and three batteries were now available. They deployed into battle order at La Lavette,[23] forming four lines: Horse Battery Nr. 7, 6-pounder Foot Battery Nr. 7 and the cavalry of the vanguard were in front, with the hussars on the

[18] Weltzien, vol II, p 212.
[19] Pflugk-Harttung, *Zieten*, p 199.
[20] Hofmann, p 119; Müffling, *Leben*, p 248. ·
[21] Hofmann, pp 118–19; Weltzien, vol II, p 212.
[22] Müffling, *Leben*, p 248; Hofmann, pp 119–20.
[23] Pflugk-Harttung, *I Korps*, p 153.

right to link with Wellington's position, then the two companies of Schützen and the F./12th under Major von Neumann. Behind them came the 24th Regiment under Oberst von Hofmann, its fusilier battalion on the far left. The reserve consisted of the 1st Westphalian Landwehr Infantry and Reserve Cavalry who also closed up towards their allies.

Major von Gillhausen, temporary commander of the 1st Westphalian Landwehr, described his experience on the final stages of the approach,

> In the afternoon, the regiment marched to the right with the 1st Brigade. When the brigade got close to the battlefield, all three of our battalions were placed in reserve. I continued to follow the road towards the enemy. The I. Battalion was to the right of it, the other two to the left. They were at a suitable distance to deploy as we were in column by the centre and marching in alignment with the second line but 200 paces behind it. By moving to the left and right [of the road], we hoped to keep the battalions out of the heavy artillery fire whose direction was constantly changing, but without deviating significantly from our objective. However, I could not prevent one cannon ball striking the left of the III. Battalion, killing two men and wounding three, and another from killing one Jäger and wounding four from the 2. Jäger Detachment.
>
> The II. Battalion, the one under Kapitain von Rappard that was performing the role of the fusilier battalion, was first deployed level with the other two battalions to advance along a deep hollow. It followed this to the left, becoming separated from the other two battalions and rejoining them only the next morning. The other battalions moved more to the right to keep in contact with the second line. Later, on the orders of the brigade general, the skirmishers of the I. Battalion linked up with the 1. Jäger Detachment in some broken ground in front, while those of the III. Battalion occupied a small copse of tall trees to the right along with the Jäger of the 2. Detachment. Meanwhile, the two battalions marched with beating drums and at the correct distances to deploy through a marshy valley and up to a ridge that opened out to the left and right. Here, we linked up with a Hanoverian and a Scottish battalion.[24]

The history of the 1st Westphalian Landwehr then recorded an incident of 'friendly fire',

> At first, the 1st Westphalian Landwehr Regiment stood in the second line. The English left flank had, as we have seen, been forced back. Thus, Kapitain Bennert was sent forward with the skirmishers of the I. Battalion and the 1. Jäger Detachment to re-establish contact. The wavering English mistook the Prussian detachment for the enemy and fired. As the Prussians did not reply, they soon noticed their error.[25]

Following this there was another more serious 'friendly fire' incident. The Nassauers abandoned Smohain because of the renewed French attacks and started falling back in the direction of the Prussians, who mistook this move

24 Pflugk-Harttung, *I Korps*, p 163.
25 Harkort, p 60.

for an attack on their positions by the French and reacted accordingly. Caught between two fires, the Nassauers departed from Smohain at great speed, leaving all its buildings to be occupied by the French. Bernhard of Saxe-Weimar, their commander and hero of Quatre Bras, was eventually able to rally his men, but first he had to rush through the Prussian fire to tell his allies of their mistake. Reiche described the scene,

> The Nassauers who were leaving the village fell back in open order on our advancing troops. As the Nassauers were dressed in the French style of that time, our men took them to be the enemy and fired at them. Their commander Prinz Bernhard of [Saxe-] Weimar rushed up to General Zieten to clarify the misunderstanding, which he did in no uncertain terms. The General, not knowing the Prince, made no excuses and calmly replied, 'My friend, it is not my fault that your men look like French!'[26]

Artillery came up in support. The journal of the I Army Corps described this,

> Despite the small arms fire coming from Smohain, Horse and Foot Batteries Nr. 7 immediately unlimbered close to it. From there, they could cover the ground running down to the left, thus taking any advancing troops in their left flank. Other artillery units drew up on the ridge opposite Smohain that the exhausted Nassau gunners had just abandoned. From there, they were able to counter the enemy artillery fire as well as deal with any formed troops coming down from La Belle Alliance. The bold deployment of our artillery gave the retiring Nassauers new courage and they joined up with our battery. This manoeuvre did not quite stop the French attack on the left flank of the English army, but it at least made it waver and thus gave the tired left flank new courage and strength.[27]

The fire of Foot Battery Nr. 7 was particularly intense. During the whole day's fighting at Ligny on 16 June this battery had fired 247 roundshot and 57 shells. In just two hours of combat at Waterloo, it fired 312 roundshot and 42 shells.[28]

Horse Battery Nr. 2 also deployed in support. Its commander Kapitain von Borowsky wrote,

> The battery was ordered to advance along with the Reserve Cavalry Brigade, and once it had reached the part of the English army under fire, to form up on the heights, between the cavalry and infantry, while detaching two guns to the left. This was done immediately with Lieutenant von Knobloch taking a position to the left with two guns and starting to fire on the enemy. As the smoke from the firing was so dense, I could only make out a few positions, and could not see the enemy columns. At this moment, the English infantry was forced back somewhat and I was ordered to occupy a ridge to the right. I did this and the enemy was soon thrown back. I detached Lieutenant Patzig with three

[26] Starklof, vol 2, pp 206–7, 212; Weltzien, vol II, p 213.
[27] Pflugk-Harttung, *I Korps*, pp 215–6.
[28] Pflugk-Harttung, *I Korps*, p 225.

guns to the right flank of the English infantry while I placed the remaining three guns between the left flank of the English infantry and the right of our cavalry.[29]

Zieten's I Corps had arrived just in time to help Wellington's men meet Napoleon's final attack.

The Old Guard's Last Triumph

As discussed in the next chapter Ney had finally managed to capture La Haye Sainte and had gained a foothold on the ridge at the centre of Wellington's position. He sent back a message to the Emperor pleading for the reinforcements he needed to finish off the British resistance but the Emperor had another problem to deal with first. As we saw earlier the Prussians had captured Plancenoit once again, despite the efforts of the Young Guard, and this put them directly behind the main French position on the ridge at Belle Alliance. The Emperor had to see to this threat first.

Napoleon moved most of the Old Guard infantry from their positions between Rossomme and Belle Alliance off to his right to face the Prussians. Two veteran battalions went forward against the village itself. Without firing a shot, and even though they were greatly outnumbered, they threw the Prussians back in disorder. With this example the Young Guard rallied from their earlier defeat and they and Lobau's men also pushed forwards. For the moment the Prussian advance was halted once more and Napoleon could turn his attention back to Wellington.

The history of the 2nd Silesians tried to gloss over the matter somewhat, recording only that,

> Général Morand brought up the battalions of the Imperial Guard held in reserve behind Plancenoit. Two of them were sent into the village. Not fearing death, they pressed on, inspiring the Young Guard again. However, despite the great determination with which the French and particularly the Old Guard defended Plancenoit, all their efforts and heroic sacrifices could do nothing to halt the attacking Prussians.[30]

The record of the 15th Regiment was rather more frank and to the point,

> However, we could not hold onto the village this time either. Napoleon sent two regiments of Old Guard under Général Morand from his reserves to Plancenoit. Two of their battalions along with the Young Guard and the remaining troops in the village took control of it again, forcing our men to withdraw.[31]

Napoleon believed he had now gained a breathing space for his final and most desperate attack of the day. The Guard could now lead one last assault, inspiring his remaining cavalry and infantry, and bursting clean through the centre of Wellington's fatally weakened line. In fact there had been a vital

[29] GStA, IV HA 434, fol 38.
[30] Ebertz, p 203.
[31] Dörk, pp 130–1.

delay. While the Old Guard were retaking Plancenoit Wellington had gained invaluable time to reinforce the weakened parts of his line by moving in troops from his right and others freed from his left by the arrival of Zieten's men. Napoleon's last reserve had also been fatally weakened since some of the Old Guard formations had to stay in position to fend off the Prussians. Only nine battalions of the élite of the élite were to remain available for the final French assault.

For the third time this day the Prussian intervention had proved crucial to the Duke's success.

Chapter 10
The Defeat of Napoleon

A Brief Respite

The first crisis in Wellington's centre had been sustained. Napoleon's chances of victory were diminishing thanks to the growing Prussian intervention. His great cavalry assault on the Allied main line along the ridge of Mont St Jean had been beaten off, if only just. The possession of the key position of Plancenoit was attracting more of Bonaparte's attention and few remaining reserves. Zieten's battered I Army Corps was limping into action, linking up with the exhausted Allied troops on Wellington's left. Both the Anglo-Dutch-German forces and Napoleon's last reserves took one final deep breath before the final dramatic assaults on the Allied centre.

Some of the troops in Wellington's line could now tell that the Prussian forces were coming into action. Kapitain von Scriba of the Bremen Battalion noticed Zieten's arrival, writing,

> At this time, we heard a growing amount of artillery and small arms fire on the left flank of the army that signalled the arrival of Blücher's army. Our square, under artillery fire again, had lost its original shape; at first, it became an irregular triangle, then a shapeless mass closed together and facing outwards on all sides.[1]

Wellington used the brief respite gained by the Prussian assaults on Plancenoit to do what he could to plug the many gaps in his collapsing centre. Thanks to the approach of Zieten's corps, he was able to pull men from his reserves from his left as well as the comparatively fresh forces from his right to plug the gaps, restoring a semblance of order.

Andreas Cleeves, commander of the 4th Foot Battery of the KGL, noted,

> Major Sympher, commander of a 9-pounder horse battery of the Legion which had been held in reserve, filled the gap. His fire against the enemy cavalry was most effective, as Oberstlieutenant Hartmann witnessed. Oberstlieutenant Hartmann ordered my battery to form up and join Major Sympher's battery. With the exception of No. 4 gun that remained where it was left and was manned again later, I managed to drag my cannon out of the chaos as we still had the limbers with us. We deployed on a field close to Mont St Jean and had the empty limbers filled again. (Captain Sandham of the Royal Artillery provided the ammunition.) I then led the battery, now joined by several odd English guns, back to the main position. The Brigade-Major, Captain Baynes

---

[1] Pflugk-Harttung, *Belle Alliance*, p 137.

of the Royal Artillery, and Lieutenant Mielmann of our regiment made every effort to reorganise the scattered artillery. They were largely successful.

When we were almost in place, I received an order, I believe from the aide-de-camp Kapitain Heise, to move to the foot of the hill and await further instructions there. At the same time, Captain Sinclair of the Royal Artillery and Lieutenant Ludowieg were given orders to advance, which they did immediately.[2]

The official report of the 1st Hussars of the KGL also recorded their move,

> About half past six in the evening, General Bülow commenced the successful attack on the enemy right flank. Part of Zieten's corps relieved the 1st Hussars who then moved quickly to the centre of the position of the English army and joined up with their brigade.[3]

Chassé's Netherlanders also moved up from their earlier position far out to the right. The crumbling centre was just about being shored up when there was a new crisis.

La Haye Sainte Falls

Pulling together battalions from the divisions of Bachelu and Foy and rallied formations from d'Erlon's corps, Ney made a new assault on the farmhouse of La Haye Sainte, the key to the Allied centre, at around 6.30 p.m. The original garrison, the 2nd Light Battalion of the KGL, had been reinforced three times that day; firstly by two companies of the 1st KGL Light Battalion, secondly about 4 p.m. by the light company of the 5th KGL Line Battalion, and finally by two flank companies of the 1st Nassau Regiment. Baring's hardy Germans, decimated, exhausted and out of ammunition, would now be ejected from the buildings they had so valiantly defended. Of the 372 men of the original garrison, only 42 were able to retreat with Baring. The role of this handful of men had been crucial to the outcome of the battle.

The official report of the Hanoverians and KGL summed up the situation in la Haye Sainte succinctly,

> By about six o'clock, the garrison [of la Haye Sainte] had used up all of its ammunition. When the enemy noticed his fire was hardly being returned, he scaled the walls and penetrated the entrances of the farm, of which there were five including one that had been free of any obstruction for the whole day. The garrison fell back into the house and withdrew by a back door closely attacked by the advancing enemy.[4]

Baring's report supplied more of the detail,

> After the enemy noticed that his fire had not been returned for a while, he climbed the walls and broke through the gates and doors, forcing us out of the farm. We retired through the rear garden to the main line where the various detachments returned to their main bodies. The 40–50 men I had left from my

---

2 Pflugk-Harttung, *Belle Alliance*, pp 178–9.
3 Pflugk-Harttung, *Belle Alliance*, p 160.
4 Pflugk-Harttung, *Belle Alliance*, p 63.

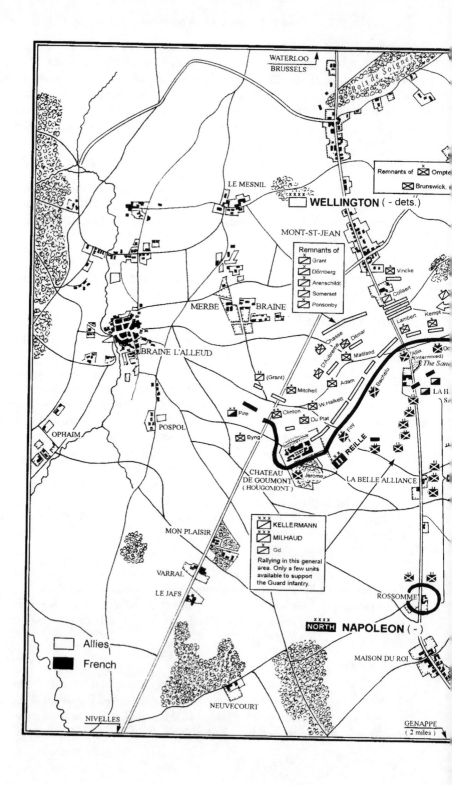

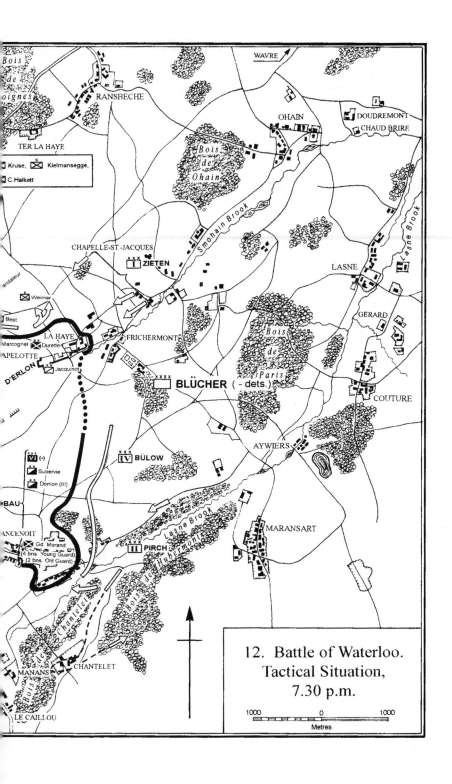

12. Battle of Waterloo.
Tactical Situation,
7.30 p.m.

battalion joined up with the 1st Light Battalion. This must have been between seven and eight o'clock in the evening.[5]

Immediately afterwards there was another setback for the allies. Oberst von Ompteda and most of the 5th Line Battalion of the KGL were ridden down by cuirassiers when advancing in a vain attempt to counter-attack. Oberstlieutenant von Linsingen, commander of the 5th Line Battalion of the KGL, was one of the few survivors and reported that, after this, his battalion could do no more,

> About half past six in the evening, both my battalion and its neighbours were ordered to take a position several hundred paces to the rear. We remained in this position until the enemy commenced his retreat.[6]

Captain James Shaw of the 43rd Foot (later General Sir James Shaw-Kennedy), then chief-of-staff of the British 3rd Division, described the situation at this point as follows,

> The possession of La Haye Sainte by the French was a very dangerous incident. It uncovered the very centre of the Anglo-Allied army, and established the enemy within 60 yards of that centre. The French lost no time in taking advantage of this, by pushing forward infantry supported by guns, which enabled them to maintain a most destructive fire upon Alten's left and Kempt's right, and to drive off Kempt's light troops that occupied the knoll in his front. By this fire they wasted most seriously the ranks of the left of Alten's and the right of Kempt's divisions; so much so that Ompteda's brigade having been previously nearly destroyed, and Kielmansegge's much weakened, they were now not sufficiently strong to occupy the front which was originally assigned to them.[7]

Success was now in Ney's grasp. Astutely, as Shaw-Kennedy says, he brought up a battery of guns which started to blast further holes from close range in Wellington's already thinned defences. Ney was using this key to open the Allied centre. The gap in the British centre was like a plug-hole down which more and more men were disappearing, pulling in those next to them. All of Wellington's remaining forces were being drawn in this direction.

Shaw-Kennedy's account continued,

> … Ompteda's brigade was nearly annihilated and Kielmansegge's so thinned that those two brigades could not hold their position. That part of the field of battle between Halkett's left and Kempt's right was thus unprotected; and being the very centre of the Duke's line of battle, was consequently that point, above all others, which the enemy wished to gain. The danger was imminent; and at no other period of the action was the result so precarious as at this moment. Most fortunately, Napoleon did not support the advantage his troops had gained at this point, by bringing forward his reserve… [8]

---

[5] Pflugk-Harttung, *Belle Alliance*, p 109.
[6] Pflugk-Harttung, *Belle Alliance*, p 125.
[7] Shaw-Kennedy, pp 123–4.
[8] Shaw-Kennedy, p 127.

Ney sent a desperate appeal to Napoleon for more infantry to complete the victory but, as described in the previous chapter, the Prussians had captured Plancenoit and the Emperor's attention was diverted. As we have seen, Napoleon moved part of the Guard to block this threat and sent two of its battalions forward to recapture the village. Wellington gained a breathing space that he used to bring up more men to steady his battered centre. He would just have enough time to shore up his defences before Napoleon's final blow.

La Garde au Feu

The Allies had now united their forces and victory was in sight if Napoleon's last effort could be defeated. Napoleon had only one card left to play, his last reserve, the veteran infantry of the Imperial Guard, but thanks to the Prussian assault on Plancenoit, it was no longer the ace of trumps. Although he had 15 battalions of this élite force in all, Bonaparte could not use all of them for the final assault on Wellington's centre. Two were left at Belle Alliance and one at Le Caillou as a final reserve and some were still committed to the fighting in and near Plancenoit. As a result, around 7 p.m., a first wave of probably only seven battalions began their march up the ridge of Mont St Jean, with others in support, for the last French attack of the day, led, for a time, by their Emperor.

It is not entirely certain which battalions and what formation the Guard used during their advance. Also, there are conflicting claims from the Allied troops involved in repelling this last assault as to who did what and when. Nevertheless, it is possible to outline the basic sequence of events. Most English-language histories concentrate on the role of the British infantry in defeating the attack but, as the accounts quoted shortly show, German units had a major part in this achievement, too.

The sight of Napoleon leading his Guard in person inspired any remaining units of his army which still had some semblance of order to follow in support. Hearing cannon-fire coming from his right, from the direction of Papelotte, Bonaparte had his aides ride up and down the line announcing that Grouchy had arrived. Spurred on by such news, false though it was, the French marched through the hail of shot and shell that greeted them from the Allied side.

The advance took place in two sections, with the one on the right (from the French side) going in to the attack slightly in advance of the second section. The leading section, of two battalions, closed on the left centre of the Allied positions. Of the second echelon of five battalions one formed a link with the leading echelon, thus appearing to some to be part of it. This may partly explain why accounts vary as to the number of battalions that participated in the final assault.

The first echelon reached the plateau and the first line of Allied troops, consisting of Kruse's Nassauers and the ever-nervous Brunswickers. These troops started to waver, but the Duke of Wellington in person steadied them. The journal of the 1st Nassau Regiment described the scene,

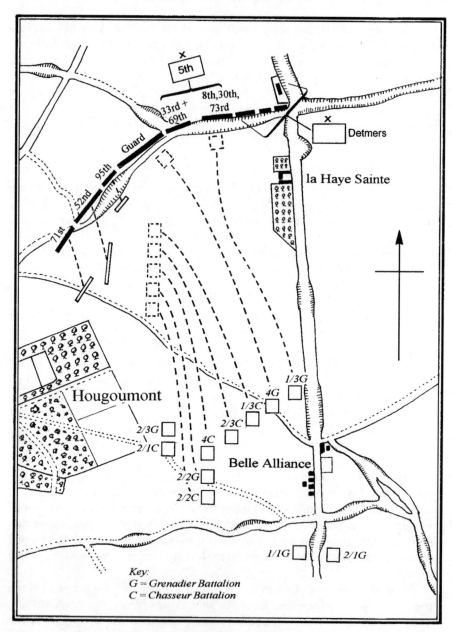

13. The Attack of the French Guard

Napoleon's Guard reached the plateau from which our infantry had withdrawn only 100 paces. A violent firefight began.

Sometime between 6 o'clock and 7 o'clock [it was later] on orders from General von Kruse, the II. Battalion of the 1st Regiment moved into the front line. The Crown Prince of the Netherlands and General von Kruse led the remnants of the I. Battalion in a bayonet charge. In this attack the Prince of Orange was badly wounded, and the attack was largely unsuccessful, but the enemy mass he struck did waver, despite its earlier well aimed and murderous fire.[9]

The issue appeared to be in the balance. General von Kruse's account was more specific,

> ... the élite of the infantry, Napoleon's Guard, reached the plateau, with our infantry withdrawing only 100 paces. A violent firefight broke out, and, showing as much courage as foresight, the Crown Prince, who had been in command on the plateau throughout the entire battle, attempted to put an end to it with a bayonet charge. For this honour, he thought of the Nassauers. Thus, he brought up the II. Battalion and led it in column. The remainder of the I. Battalion joined up with them and the attack was carried out with great bravery. I saw one side of a square of the French Guard start to waver when, perhaps because the Crown Prince was wounded, a wave of panic hit the young soldiers and at the moment of their greatest victory, the battalion fell into confusion and retreated. The remaining battalions in the first line soon followed, leaving only small bodies of brave men on the plateau. I had the Landwehr battalion and the remainder of the II. Battalion join them, but in such a way that the enemy fire could have little effect on them.[10]

Having brushed the Nassauers out of the way, the Guard moved on. Wellington had now positioned himself a little to the right where his Guards stood and where the next section of the French advance struck. At close range, his élite poured volleys into the ranks of Napoleon's men, causing them to halt. The British Guards then made a bayonet charge, pushing back this section of the attack. A volley from the 30th and 73rd Foot drove off another battalion, while the pursuing British Guards over-extended themselves and fell back in confusion, only to rally again quickly.

The second echelon of the French attack now approached Wellington's line, closing on Adam's brigade. The 52nd Foot moved against the French flank, thereby throwing part of the Imperial Guard formation into disorder. The 2nd/95th joined in and the 71st advanced in support. A bayonet charge by the 52nd settled the issue. The Osnabrück Landwehr Battalion, part of Hugh Halkett's brigade, joined this attack. Napoleon's 'invincibles' broke.

Lieutenant Richers of the Osnabrück Battalion described his unit's role,

> The battalion passed through a broad hollow, one of many in the wave-like terrain of the battlefield. It advanced in silence, tense from the large number of both enemy and friendly cannon balls flying over our heads. Nobody could

[9] Pflugk-Harttung, *Belle Alliance*, p 198–9.
[10] Pflugk-Harttung, *Belle Alliance*, p 202.

see what our destination was to be, but all knew it was towards the enemy. Once we had gone through the hollow and climbed the ridge on the other side, we saw an enemy column about 300 to 400 paces from us. It was either a regiment or battalion of the Old Guard, one could not be certain as it was a column by the centre.

Oberst Halkett cried, 'Skirmishers deploy!' I was the third officer of the second company and did not even command a division so I asked permission to go forwards with the skirmishers. Oberst Halkett and Major Graf Münster both willingly agreed.

I was now out in front and could observe everything. The events are firmly fixed in my memory. Our skirmishers deployed against the Old Guard skirmishers and a firefight began. We were advancing, but the enemy stood where he was. The centre of our skirmish chain involuntarily closed together to allow the following column to pass as it was clear we were only a few moments away from a bayonet charge. Once the advancing battalion reached the skirmish line, its pace accelerated. We moved up, the enemy skirmishers disappeared and the front ranks of the [French] column fired a volley at us. I believe we all hesitated and stood where we were.

This was the critical moment when victory or defeat, charging or retreating, were both still possible. Then Oberst Halkett spoke a short word in our ears, 'Hurrah, brave Osnabrückers!' That was enough to inspire us at this crucial time, and we followed the Oberst with trust and enthusiasm, presented our bayonets and charged forwards.

Our opponents did not engage in a bayonet fight with us. They stood for a moment longer, then wavered, turned around and retired a short distance in relatively good order. Their formation then started to break up and finally they fled in total disorder. It seemed as if we were fresher than the tired-out Old Guard because we got closer and closer to them, taking many prisoners from those who could run no further. The wild chase continued forwards towards the enemy. Both sides fired only as much as they could when running. The enemy officers did attempt to rally their men, waving their swords and shouting 'en avant!' However, that was in vain for when an officer managed to gather a few men around him, our pursuit chased them away again.[11]

The sight of the Guard retreating was a devastating blow to the morale of the French Army and, just as the Guard started to withdraw, fire from two batteries from Zieten's I Corps raked along the right flank of the French position, into Durutte's men. Clearly, Grouchy had not arrived after all, and all hope for the French was gone.

I Army Corps Breaks Through

Just as Napoleon's attempt to destroy Wellington's centre was being bloodily repulsed Zieten's advance was breaking through what was now effectively the centre of the long French line, at the angle in the French position around Papelotte between the portions of the French Army facing Wellington and those facing Blücher. Durutte's men had retaken La Haye and Papelotte

---

[11] NSHStA Hanover, Hann. 41, XXI Nr. 157.

during the final French attacks[12] but the increasing numbers of Prussian troops coming into action made a counter-attack possible. Nassau troops joined the general advance.[13]

Seeing the Prussian forces coming, the French did not wait. Instead, they fell back to the heights behind Smohain without firing a shot. Oberst von Hofmann led his 24th Regiment against their new position. It seemed at first as if he would be successful, but he was then pushed back on Smohain. The Silesian Schützen and the F./1st Westphalian Landwehr quickly moved up in support and Hofmann again went over to the offensive. The French fell back without much of a fight.

Expecting a French counter-attack, Hofmann set about preparing his position. He deployed the Silesian Schützen and the F./24th on the right flank, the two remaining battalions of the 24th under Major von Laurens on the left. At that moment, General von Grolman appeared, accompanied by Major von Lützow and Major von Scharnhorst, and ordered the advance to continue immediately. The battalion columns, supported by the West Prussian Uhlans (part of IV Army Corps) then moved on. Along the heights level with the last houses of Papelotte, the French offered a determined resistance. For half an hour, the Prussians conducted a firefight in which almost half of them had to be deployed as skirmishers. On their far right, the Prussians linked up with a battalion of Highlanders. The musketeer battalions of the 1st Westphalian Landwehr Regiment moved up in support. The advancing elements of the 13th and 15th Brigades of the IV Army Corps covered the left flank.

Major von Neumann of the F./12th (2nd Brandenburg) Regiment described his unit's role in all this,

> General von Steinmetz ordered me to take my battalion and two companies of Schützen to the village of Smohain. Here, I was to throw out the French who had just occupied it after the Nassau infantry had fallen back. Four divisions of the Schützen moved on the lower part of the village and threw out the enemy there while my fusilier battalion, led by its skirmishers, also moved through the village. Now both the Schützen and the fusilier battalion advanced against the enemy skirmishers who fought back ferociously. This struggle continued until the enemy's general withdrawal began when our cavalry followed up.[14]

The report of Major von Blücher of the F./24th Regiment was more detailed,

> ... the Fusilier Battalion marched in the vanguard along with the Fusilier Battalion of the Brandenburg Infantry Regiment and two companies of Schützen against Fichermont. My orders were to hold the village of Oué

---

[12] Müffling in his *History*, p 36 reported that French skirmishers drove the Nassauers out of Papelotte. However, Rössler, p 96 and Starklof, vol I, p 204 claim that they held it for the entire battle. It would seem that the French never entirely drove out the Nassauers, but certainly captured some of the farm buildings.

[13] Starklof, vol 2, p 207.

[14] Pflugk-Harttung, *I Korps*, p 158.

(I think that was the name of the village) [actually Smohain] against the enemy by sending my skirmishers to the far edge of the village. The main body of the battalion remained there, deploying according to the circumstances, although the Nassauers left after the enemy had thrown them back. The enemy now engaged us, and the battle became determined.

The order came to attack their line outside the village in column and we beat the enemy back in great disorder, supported by Battery Nr. 7. Our skirmishers now advanced in an open order line with the two Schützen companies, leaving behind the necessary supports. We moved towards the right flank of the IV Army Corps as their skirmishers had almost run out of ammunition. We shared out our ammunition and then attacked the enemy together with vigour. The enemy retreated from the ridge, but immediately took up positions on the next. Here, they fought fiercely before being thrown back. Shortly after that, resistance collapsed and our cavalry followed their flight.[15]

The report of the two musketeer battalions of the 24th Regiment described a slightly different sequence of events,

About 6 o'clock in the afternoon [probably later, after 7 o'clock at least], the two musketeer battalions moved into position. Both battalions, formed in close order, were ordered to take the village of Smohain that was said to be occupied by the enemy. The skirmishers surrounded it while the formed companies moved up in support. However, the enemy did not occupy it, so this attack passed through the village and into the enemy formed up outside it, who fired at the attack with great effect. The skirmishers advanced courageously and, although pushed back several times by superior numbers, counter-attacked immediately, reinforced by platoons from the main body. This way, the enemy was thrown back from one position to another, broken and beaten off in flight until the night put an end to the glorious day.[16]

The official history of the 24th Regiment provided more details and explained some of the apparent discrepancies. The artillery bombardment and Neumann's earlier attack had cleared Smohain before Major von Laurens led the two musketeer battalions, a total of 1,200 men, in their attack. As much as half of each battalion was subsequently used to reinforce the skirmish line which was commanded by Kapitain von Maltitz and Kapitain von Arnauld.[17]

The Landwehr battalions of the 13th Brigade also played an important part in the fighting in this sector, as Major von Steinmetz, commander of the I./2nd Neumarkers described,

The skirmishers entered the village of Frichermont, the battalion in support. The regimental commander, Major von Braunschweig, then gave the order for the battalion itself to move into the village and to hold the road connecting the Prussian and the English armies. As the skirmishers had meanwhile already passed through the village, Major von Steinmetz had the 1st Company sent to

[15] Pflugk-Harttung, *I Korps*, p 159.
[16] Pflugk-Harttung, *I Korps*, p 160.
[17] Zychlinski, p 283.

support them, with the 2nd Company holding the village while the two other companies of the battalion advanced to an area of ground to the left.

Major von Steinmetz received a report stating that Kapitain Sotta had moved the 1st Company at the double to join our hard-pressed skirmish line and had thrown back the enemy unit facing him.

The remainder of the battalion followed up immediately, moving about 1,000 paces from Frichermont in the direction of la Belle Alliance, led by Major von Braunschweig back to the position held earlier with the intention of holding it until further notice. The detachments did not return to the battalion until the next day.

During their advance, they found the village of Frichermont already held by a skirmisher section of the 18th Regiment [part of the 15th Brigade] along with a body of Nassau troops. As the enemy was no longer offering any serious resistance here, they moved through the village, joined by these detachments. Outside it, they again encountered enemy troops who were behind the nearby hedges and in the gardens. They attacked immediately, driving them off. From then on the skirmishers advanced continuously until late into the evening when they passed through Genappe, stopping only at the village after that, being unable to continue their pursuit in the dark.[18]

The report of the II. Battalion added,

On the orders of Generallieutenant von Hake, the battalion changed direction towards the village of Frichermont and moved towards it. First, the battalion drew up in a hollow before the village where it formed the support of the skirmishers sent up to drive off the enemy.

After a time the skirmishers practically ran out of ammunition, and the enemy began to press them hard, while odd musket shots also started hitting the battalion, wounding several of our men. Major von Grollmann then quickly sent up Lieutenants Rittwagen, Drümel and Klenke with the 5th, 6th and 7th Companies. They were soon successful because the enemy, who had already gained much ground, fell back in the face of our strengthened attack. The skirmishers then followed up with no opposition for so long that it was only possible for them to rejoin the battalion the next day. Meanwhile, Major von Grollmann was ordered to occupy the ridge left of the village. The enemy, to cover the retreat that had already begun on parts of the front, made several cavalry charges against our line, making it difficult for us to move up for a time. The Reserve Artillery of the [I Army] corps was now brought up and its lively fire here tipped the scales in our favour again.[19]

Finally, the report of the Fusilier Battalion related,

The battalion was ordered to send its skirmishers against the enemy skirmish line. Kapitain von Seydlitz took command. The attack led by this officer was carried out with such great speed and determination that the enemy skirmish line, already suffering from our artillery fire, was soon thrown back. Thus, the way was cleared to advance with success against the enemy.[20]

---

[18] Rehmann, pp 177–8.   [20] Rehmann, p 179.
[19] Rehmann, pp 178–9.

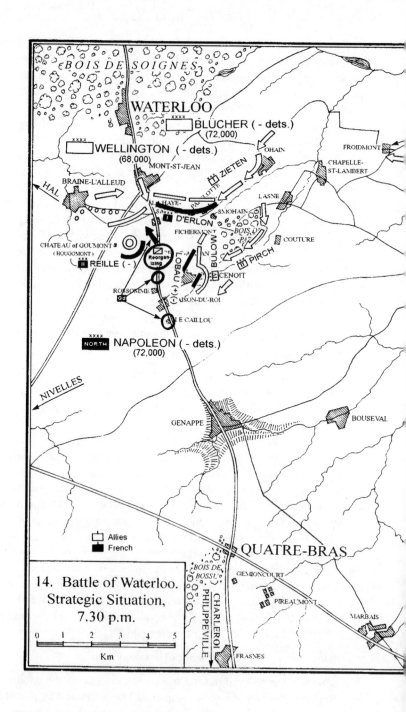

BOIS DE SOIGNES

WATERLOO

BLÜCHER (- dets.)
(72,000)

FROIDMONT

WELLINGTON (- dets.)
(68,000)

OHAIN

CHAPELLE-
ST-LAMBERT

MONT-ST-JEAN

ZIETEN

BRAINE-L'ALLEUD

LASNE

HAL

LA HAYE-
SAINTE

PAPELOTTE

SMOHAIN

D'ERLON

FICHERMONT

BOIS DE
PARIS

COUTURE

CHATEAU of GOUMONT
(HOUGOMONT)

Reorgan-
izing

LOBAU

BULOW

PIRCH

REILLE (-)

PLANCENOIT

ROSSOMME
Gd

MAISON-DU-ROI

NIVELLES

LE CAILLOU

NORTH   NAPOLEON (- dets.)
(72,000)

GENAPPE

BOUSEVAL

Allies
French

QUATRE-BRAS

14. Battle of Waterloo.
Strategic Situation,
7.30 p.m.

BOIS DE
BOSSU

GEMIONCOURT

PIREAUMONT

MARBAIS

0   1   2   3   4   5

CHARLEROI
PHILIPPEVILLE

Km

FRASNES

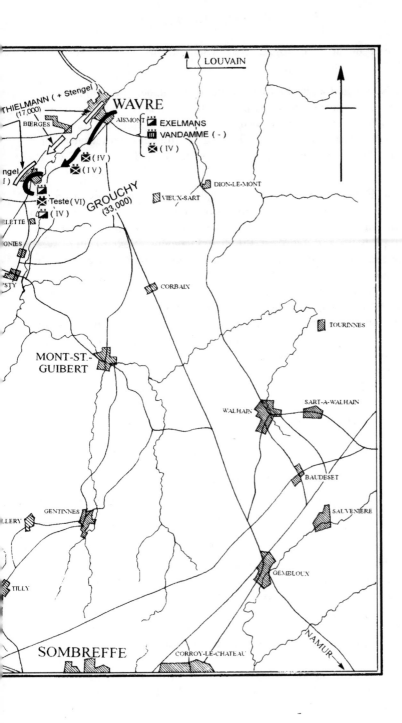

The journal of the 13th Brigade acknowledged the role of these militia-men, stating,

> The 2nd Neumark Landwehr Infantry Regiment under the command of Major von Braunschweig distinguished itself particularly on this day. Its various battalions were almost always used to cover the battery and were thus constantly under heavy artillery fire. They did not show any signs whatsoever of wavering. Their skirmishers particularly distinguished themselves with exceptional bravery.[21]

Once the French line began to disintegrate from this series of attacks Zieten's Reserve Cavalry started to move up. The main body deployed into two lines, the first consisting of Treskow's brigade – Brandenburg Dragoons, Brandenburg Uhlans and 1st West Prussian Dragoons. Next to them were elements of the 2nd Brigade – two regiments of Kurmark Landwehr Cavalry and two squadrons of the 6th Uhlans.

Some of Durutte's division still stood defiantly against Zieten's infantry and artillery. Generalmajor von Roeder, commander of the Reserve Cavalry, took the Brandenburg Dragoons and three squadrons of the Brandenburg Uhlans to the centre of Zieten's position between La Haye and Smohain. Here, they formed up for the charge. The threat alone was enough to make the French retreat once and for all. With the West Prussian Dragoons on the right flank, the 2nd Kurmark Landwehr ahead of them to the left and the remaining squadron of Brandenburg Uhlans, the Prussians broke through to the Brussels road. The artillery moved up, followed by the Silesian Hussars. Zieten and Roeder rode at the head of the Brandenburgers to the Maison du Roi. Here, with the battle won, Zieten alone took over the pursuit.

Third Time Lucky at Plancenoit

While Napoleon's attention was focused on his final effort to break Wellington's centre, at 8 p.m. Prussian troops again attacked Plancenoit, this time capturing it for good. Pirch I sent Tippelskirch's 5th Brigade up to support the 14th and 16th Brigades. The 25th Regiment from the 5th Brigade played a leading part. This unit had been formed from the Lützow Freikorps of 1813–14 and the men were still dressed in their old black uniforms. While the 25th's two musketeer battalions secured the Virère wood, the fusiliers, led by Major von Witzleben, pushed a battalion of the Old Guard (probably the 1/2e Grenadiers) out of the Chantelet wood to the south of the village. This put them in a position to threaten the flank and rear of the French in Plancenoit.

Meanwhile the remainder of the brigade was heavily engaged in the maelstrom of Plancenoit. The history of the 25th Regiment described the dreadful scene,

> Despite their great courage and stamina, the French Guards fighting in the village began to show signs of wavering. The church was already on fire with

[21] Rehmann, p 180.

columns of red flame coming out of the windows, aisles and doors. In the village itself, still the scene of bitter house-to-house fighting, everything was burning, adding to the confusion. However, once Major von Witzleben's manoeuvre was accomplished and the French Guards saw their flank and rear threatened, they began to withdraw. The Guard Chasseurs under Général Pelet formed the rearguard. The remnants of the Guard left in a great rush, leaving large masses of artillery, equipment and ammunition waggons in the wake of their retreat. These spoils of war went to the victor.

The evacuation of Plancenoit led to the loss of the position that was to be used to cover the withdrawal of the French Army to Charleroi. The Guard fell back from Plancenoit in the direction of Maison du Roi and Caillou. Unlike other parts of the battlefield, there were no cries of 'Sauve qui peut!' here. Instead the cry 'Sauvons nos aigles!' ['Let's save our eagles!'] could be heard.[22]

By 8.30 p.m. the Prussians were therefore masters of the key to the French rear. All was lost for Napoleon.

In the final stages of the struggle for the village the F./15th Regiment had moved into a copse just to the south and, once Plancenoit had fallen, the F./15th advanced again. Leaving the undergrowth, the battalion moved over a field of wheat towards the Brussels road. There, it saw a broken mass of Frenchmen fleeing. Confusion was rife, with pursued and pursuer mixed together. Cannon balls from Wellington's artillery rolled through the ranks of the F./15th, and the Prussians found it impossible to fire for fear of hitting friend rather than foe. The Imperial Guard units who had been pushed back from Plancenoit may have attempted to rally at this point to cover the retreat. However, if they did, they failed, for at that moment the Prussian assault finally broke through towards the Brussels road all along the front, into the fleeing mass of Frenchmen. Napoleon's army was now in full flight.[23]

Wellington Orders the Advance

As the Guard retreated in disorder, Wellington took advantage of the moment and ordered a general advance. Fresh regiments from his reserves of cavalry, Vivian's and Vandeleur's brigades, charged forward. The report of the 1st KGL Hussars, from Vivian's brigade, described their view of what happened next,

> The brigade moved forward at a trot. General Vivian ordered the 10th and 18th [British] Hussars to charge two squares of the French Young Guard [this is probably a case of mistaken identity]. However, he ordered the 1st [KGL] Hussar Regiment to stay in reserve, saying, 'I know you 1st Hussars, therefore I keep you in reserve.' Both squares were broken and scattered. As is known, Bonaparte said in his account of the lost battle, it was these broken Young Guards who started the cry of 'Sauve qui peut!' in his army.[24]

The infantry moved up in the wake of the charging cavalry. The journal of the 1st Nassau Regiment recorded,

[22] Stawitzky, p 106.
[23] Dörk, p 134.
[24] Pflugk-Harttung, *Belle Alliance*, p 160.

After a glorious charge by the English cavalry, the battle took a turn for the better. The Duke of Wellington had all the infantry on his right flank move to the centre. The Prussian Army now appeared on the enemy's right flank. The entire army went over to the offensive and achieved victory in less than half an hour.

The II. and III. Battalions of the Duke [of Nassau's] 1st Regiment moved into La Haye Sainte during their advance when the remaining enemy abandoned the buildings and gardens. They continued their advance at sunset along the road, which was covered in equipment and wounded men from the French Imperial Guard.[25]

Lieutenant Richers of the Osnabrückers continued his account,

One senior officer, accompanied by two other mounted officers was doing his utmost to restore order in the Old Guard. [This was Général Cambronne with the 2/1er Chasseurs.] We saw them riding up and down, encouraging the Guards, so we were told to make a special effort to shoot at these horsemen. Finally, one of the senior officers' horses fell, hit by a bullet. The rider was trapped beneath the horse and could not get free immediately. We called to Oberst Halkett, who was riding in the front of our ranks, that the officer in the distinctive uniform, on whom he was keeping an eye, had fallen. As soon as the Oberst saw this, he drew his sabre and spurred on his horse, forcing his way through the fleeing men towards the fallen rider. He was, in effect, in the middle of the enemy.

By the time the Oberst reached the fallen rider, he had freed himself from his horse and was now standing up. I believe I saw the Oberst take a cut at him. I and all skirmishers nearby rushed up since the Oberst was obviously in great danger as he could have been bayoneted or shot from any side. However, the French had no time to save their general. 'Sauve qui peut' was the rule of the day and even the general's two mounted companions had gone.

The general was now the Oberst's prisoner. The Oberst had grabbed him by the collar and dragged him towards us, over beside his horse. I was among the first of three or four skirmishers to reach them. When we got there, the Oberst stopped with his prisoner, let him go and asked who he was. The prisoner was bleeding heavily from a head wound, with the blood running down his face. He wiped it out of his mouth, saying, 'Je suis le général Cambronne.' I cannot say if Cambronne's wound was a cut from Oberst Halkett or a gunshot wound. We stopped for only a moment, for the Oberst ordered us on again. Late that evening, after the battalion had stopped, I heard that Sergeant Führing and three men had escorted General Cambronne to Brussels.[26]

Fähnrich Lyra of the Osnabrückers also witnessed these events. He wrote,

I heard repeated shouts of 'Sergeant!' and saw Oberst Halkett a short distance away, as brave as he was calm, fighting with an enemy general. I ran towards him, ignoring the calls of my captain and poked my sword bayonet into the chest of our colonel's opponent. He then cried, 'Pardon, monsieur!' and threw

---

[25] Pflugk-Harttung, *Belle Alliance*, p 199.
[26] NSHStA, Hanover, Hann. 41, XXI Nr. 157.

his sword to the ground. The prisoner had a wound above one eye and I heard the conversation between our colonel and the prisoner. The prisoner said he was a brigadier general of the Imperial Old Guard.[27]

As we shall see below, Lyra was not the only Osnabrücker who would claim to have had a sword in Cambronne's chest.

Halkett confirmed his role in this affair in several letters. In his report to Clinton, his divisional commander, he wrote, 'Majors Count Münster and Hammerstein each had a horse shot under him. I lost three myself and took General Cambron [sic] prisoner.' The next morning, he wrote to his wife that, 'I had the good luck to take a French general from among his skirmishers.' On 24 June, he confirmed to her that, 'the name of the general I took is Cambronne. Only two were taken, but I still do still do not think any notion will be taken of it.'[28] On 24 June he wrote to General von Alten, 'I was fortunate enough to take General Cambon [sic] prisoner from among his Tirailleurs in f[r]ont of the Imperial guards.'[29]

Halkett's later account of the affair read,

The moment Genl Adam's brigade advanced, I lost no time to follow with the Osnabrück Battn., then on the left of Hougoumont * * * * * The Osnabrück Battn. soon got in line, and on the right of Adam's brigade. During the advance we were much annoyed by the enemy's artillery. The 1st company of the Osnabrück Battn. broke into platoons & supported by the sharpshooters of the Battn. made a dash at the artillery on our right, and captured six guns with their horses. Some hundred yards to our right were some troops of Hussars (I believe the 10th). I rode up to them and got them to charge the head of a column of infantry which was drawing to their left in rear of the French Guards, the charge succeeded admirably & the column dispersed behind some inclosures [sic], after which I saw no more of the cavalry. During our advance we were in constant contact with the French Guards, and I often called to them to surrender; for some time I had my eye upon, as I supposed, the General Officer in command of the Guards (being in full uniform) trying to animate his men to stand. After receiving our fire with much effect, the column left their General with two officers behind when I ordered the sharpshooters to dash on and I made a gallop for the General. When about cutting him down he called out he would surrender, upon which he preceded me, but I had not gone many paces before my horse got a shot through his body & fell to the ground – in a few seconds I got him on his legs again and found my friend (Cambronne) had taken French leave in the direction from whence he came. I instantly overtook him, laid hold of him by the aiguillette and brought him in safety & gave him in charge to a Sergeant of the Osnabrückers, to deliver to the Duke. ** After this I kept in advance of Adam's brigade; we soon pushed the two French squares upon the mass of their cavalry of all descriptions, who at one moment threatened us in a most vociferous manner. However, after receiving our fire they went off in all directions. About this

[27] NSHStA, Hanover, Hann. 41, XXI Nr. 157.
[28] Plumhoff, p 28.
[29] Pflugk-Harttung, Belle Alliance, p 149.

time officers were flying in all directions seemingly with orders from a superior – some French officers, prisoners, said it was Napoleon. We had the good fortune to take 12 or 14 more guns of the Guards in full play upon us. On our advance the sharpshooters, supported by a company were sent among a mass of guns, & by their fire increased the confusion, made many prisoners & cut the horses from the leading guns. Next morning, I found marked on those guns 52nd, 71st, etc., for I had followed the enemy on the Genappes [sic] road, where I met the Prussians, and moved on with them to some houses on the left of the road near Genappes, which houses I occupied during the night, the Battalion being much knocked up, and not seeing any red coats in the rear. Soon after we halted I sent the Major of the Battn. with a company into Genappes to see what was going on; at daylight I returned to the field of battle, sent the guns & horses taken to Brussels, collected my brigade and marched with them to Nivelles. ******* [30]

Major Graf Münster, commander of the Osnabrückers, wrote on 19 June to his wife, telling her, 'I and my battalion have been given many prisoners, including a general of the Old Guard.'[31] In his report to the Duke of Cambridge, General von Alten wrote, 'Oberst Halkett was lucky enough to take General Cambron [sic] prisoner. He commanded part of the Old Guard.'[32] Halkett's version of the event was further confirmed by the account of Fähnrich Heinrich Bergmann of the 2nd KGL Line Battalion, as well as those of Lieutenant Dugald Macfarlane,[33] and Captain W. Eeles, both of the 95th Rifles. Eeles' account, written some 20 years after the battle, read,

I believe there was at the time a Column of Colonel Halkett's Hanoverians in the rear of the 71st. I cannot positively assert that I saw them, but I think I remember having done so, but I am sure that I saw Colonel Halkett himself ride forward round the right flank of the 71st and take a French officer prisoner.[34]

This contrasts with Vivian's denial of Halkett's role in this incident,

I cannot help thinking General Halkett must have imagined some of the events that he states occurred to the part of the Brigade with which he was... Where the devil Gnl Halkett found the 12 or 14 guns of the Guard in full play after he had witnessed an Attack of Hussars on a Square of Infantry I am quite at a loss to imagine. As to his Capture of Cambronne all I know is that in front of the Square of the Enemy attacked by the 10th there was a mounted officer. A man of the 10th rode by my side, & was about to cut him down. I ordered this man & an Infantryman [?] to take him to the rear. It was the affair of a moment & who this officer was I know not but I was afterwards told it was Cambronne. – Whether or not it was I cannot say – but from the very distinct

---

[30] BL Add MS 34,707 fols 44–5. The asterisks and underlinings reproduced in the body of this quotation appear in the original document but their significance is unclear.
[31] Plumhoff, p 28.
[32] Plumhoff, p 28.
[33] Plumhoff, p 28.
[34] Siborne, H.T., *Waterloo Letters*, p 307.

account given by Gnl Halkett of his first capture & subsequent chase & recapture of this said General I suppose it could have been him. Unless as it is possible may have been the case that the Attack of Infantry to which Gnl Halkett refers was the Attack of the 10th under Howard & that Cambronne after being captured by the man as I have described was again captured by Gnl H. when tottering [?] to the rear. But [word unclear] in this case where he afterwards found his 12 or 14 guns in full play I am totally at a loss to conceive because if I swore a very oath [?] I should say after the 10th charged the French square near la belle Alliance I do not recollect having perceived a shot from a French gun – but in truth every part of a field of battle must differ markedly & so must the account of every one engaged & still all may be fully persuaded of the truth of the statement they make.[35]

One wonders if personal rivalry clouded Vivian's memory. Certainly Siborne, having read Halkett's, Eeles' and Vivian's accounts, plumped for Halkett's in his *History*.

On the French side, Colonel Poret de Morvan, of the 3e Regiment of the Grenadiers à Pied of the Old Guard who was accompanying Cambronne, wrote,

Général Cambronne was wounded in the head. An English sergeant [probably Sergeant Führing of the Osnabrückers, who would have been wearing a red 'British' uniform] helped him back to his feet and was given the prisoner's purse in recompense.[36]

Lieutenant Richers of the Osnabrückers gave further details in another account in addition to the one quoted above, mentioning particularly Cambronne's words on his capture,

Sergeant Führing stuck his sword bayonet in Cambronne's chest, whereupon the latter cried 'Pardon Monsieur', and threw away his sword.[37]

Thus, it would appear that those members of the Imperial Guard involved in this episode neither died nor surrendered, but briefly attempted to resist and then ran away, with those who were unable to run fast enough being taken prisoner. Cambronne does not appear to have shouted any words of defiance, but merely surrendered. He certainly surrendered to the Osnabrückers, possibly first to Führing, who may then have handed the dazed Frenchman over to Halkett.

The advance continued. Here and there, groups of retreating Frenchmen attempted to resist, but were quickly scattered. The Duke of Wellington followed his victorious troops as far as the farmhouse of Belle Alliance that the Prussians were approaching from the east. Once there, Wellington sent the Prussians a request to cease-fire.

[35] BL Add MSS 34,707 fols 42–5. The original manuscript of this report is difficult to transcribe with certainty. Where the reading is not certain the marking [?] is used.
[36] Plumhoff, p 28.
[37] Plumhoff, p 28.

Pursuit by the Prussians

The pursuit of Napoleon's broken army now began. The only units involved were a few Prussian formations and possibly some Hanoverians. Having fought a series of battles and conducted forced marches in difficult conditions, little of the Prussian Army had sufficient energy left for such an enterprise and Wellington soon ordered his troops to break off their advance. The pursuit appears to have been improvised, with just a few squadrons and a couple of battalions participating. At some stage Gneisenau took command.

Bülow's report described how the armies joined together, putting the Prussians squarely behind the fleeing French forces and in the ideal position to chase them from the battlefield and complete the Allied victory,

> The left flank of Wellington's army... had gained a considerable amount of ground, but strong masses of the enemy with much artillery were seen around Belle-Alliance. Thus, a general wheel to the left [by the Prussian forces] was ordered and carried out in a most orderly fashion, with our right flank near Belle-Alliance linking up precisely with the left flank of Wellington's army. The Duke of Wellington had us advised that he was in the process of storming the position at Belle-Alliance and we should cease our artillery fire.[38]

The history of the 25th Regiment described the disintegration of the French forces that was then taking place,

> The indisputable bravery that the French Guard had shown in the defence of Plancenoit continued right up to this moment [of their withdrawal from the village], but did not last for much longer. Soon even the ranks of the Guard began to show signs of disorder and then to break apart completely. On the way to Caillou there was an attempt to cover the retreat with artillery, but only one gun was manned. This was overrun. Charges by some Prussian cavalry under Major von Falkenhausen forced the retreating bodies of men to form square several times, delaying their withdrawal. However, after beating off the cavalry charges the columns withdrew in a chequer-board formation.
>
> At this point Major von Witzleben exited the Chantelet wood with the Fusilier Battalion of the 25th Regiment. It advanced towards the village of Caillou, threatening the right flank of the enemy battalions. The French Guards now retired with such haste that they did not return the 25th's fire. Once they reached the main road the order maintained up until then broke down, confusion set in and they fled for their lives.[39]

The F./25th Infantry had thus broken through to the Brussels–Charleroi road, opening the way for the pursuit.

The F./18th Regiment led by Kapitain von Bieberstein pressed on as far as Genappe before Bülow ordered a halt. The remainder of the 15th Brigade followed up to the inn of La Belle Alliance supported by the 16th Brigade on its left. The 15th Brigade bivouacked close to the Maison du Roi that night.[40]

---

[38] Lettow-Vorbeck, p 438.
[39] Stawitzky, p 106.
[40] Wedell, p 170.

Wellington and Blücher met at Genappe some time after 10 pm., where they congratulated each other on their success and agreed that the Prussians should indeed take over the pursuit. It would seem that the story of their meeting at Belle Alliance was a rather romantic invention.[41] His day's work done, the Duke returned to his headquarters in Waterloo, while the Prussians spent much of the night in a wild chase of the fleeing Frenchmen.

Zieten's I Army Corps set off south along the Brussels road. General von Roeder, commander of the Reserve Cavalry, reported,

> At the moment the battle was decided, with the agreement of the commanding General von Zieten, I took the Brandenburg Dragoon and Brandenburg Uhlan Regiments forwards to pursue the enemy as far as possible. I sent orders to the other regiments to follow me as soon as they could. I went with the first two regiments to Genappe where I found General Graf Gneisenau who was pushing forwards with some infantry and driving the enemy from that place. We advanced together down the paved road, driving the enemy out of several bivouacs. In doing so, we cut many down and took a large number of prisoners. About half an hour from Frasnes, I halted to wait for the other regiments of my brigade. Graf Gneisenau, however, took the two regiments that were present on to Frasnes and sent detachments as far as Liberchies.
>
> The vigorous pursuit I believe was largely responsible for the great disorder of the enemy army. If this could have taken place with more cavalry, spread out to the left and right of the road, then more terrain would have been covered and its effect would have been that much greater.[42]

Led by Gneisenau in person, the 400 or so survivors of the F./15th pursued the French down the paved road as far as Genappe. Here, they captured 78 French cannon, along with their limbers and caissons, and took prisoner some 2,000 Frenchmen, including several generals. At Genappe, the French tried unsuccessfully to hold up the Allied advance by setting the village on fire.

Major von Keller, commander of the F./15th Regiment found Napoleon's abandoned carriage in Genappe and captured Napoleon's medals, along with a set of diamonds that the Emperor had left behind in the panic.[43] The precious stones were presented to King Friedrich Wilhelm of Prussia and later became part of the crown jewels. Keller himself was awarded the *Pour le Mérite* with oak leaves[44] and the king also expressed his own particular gratitude to the regiment.[45]

Keller's report recorded the event as follows,

> In Genappe, the enemy attempted to offer resistance again. They had blocked the entrance with overturned waggons and guns. The 15th Regiment advanced, only to be greeted by heavy musket fire. Wild cries of 'Les Prussiens! Les Prussiens!' caused Napoleon, who was close by, to leap out of his carriage, leaving behind his sword in the rush. On jumping out, his hat fell off, but he had no time to pick it up.[46]

[41] *WSD*, vol X, p 509.
[42] Pflugk-Harttung, *I Korps*, p 233.
[43] Dörk, pp 134–5.
[44] Dörk, p 147.
[45] Dörk, pp 150–1.
[46] Dörk, pp 136–7, fn.

Whether Keller was relating what he actually saw or if he was repeating what others told him later is uncertain, but it seems unlikely that he got close enough to Bonaparte's carriage to see the Emperor for himself.

Lieutenant Golz of the 2nd Squadron of the Brandenburg Uhlans was another participant, but with a rather different view,

It was already quite dark when we reached Genappe. The gate was blocked with guns and waggons, but was not manned. The 3. Squadron, in the lead, was brought to a halt by these obstacles when Prinz Wilhelm, brother of the king and Generals Zieten and Gneisenau and their entourage arrived. They asked, 'How do we get through?' Rittmeister von Stülpnagel said he would dismount and move the obstacles out of the way. 'Make it quick!' was the answer. Half the squadron dismounted, the passage was soon free and the pursuit continued. Meanwhile, the moon had come out. Along the high street of the town, which seemed to be the only one it had, stood six carriages. Each of the six was harnessed with six or eight good horses, but there was nobody in sight. To get through, the uhlans had to force themselves around the carriages and no doubt several troopers of the squadron took the opportunity to help themselves to some of the contents. However, because of the great hurry, they could not spend long there even though it would have been well worth their while. This was, after all, the Imperial baggage, and Napoleon's own carriage was among them. The following cavalry took their share, but the bulk of the prizes fell into the hands of the pursuing infantry, the Fusilier Battalion of the 15th Regiment.[47]

Golz later took Général Lobau, commander of the VI Corps, prisoner and then also captured the renowned military surgeon, Dr. Larrey, treating him roughly until he was recognised, possibly because he was initially mistaken for Napoleon himself.[48]

Elements of the 1st Pomeranians (2nd Regiment) under Kapitain von Goszicki and the Silesian Landwehr Infantry under Kapitain Ehrhardt moved up in support of the F./15th.

The F./15th reformed after the events in Genappe, with Gneisenau in the centre. On the general's instruction, the battalion sang the hymn *Herr Gott dich loben wir* ('Lord God, we praise thee'), following the song with wild cheers. The respite was only momentary and Gneisenau ordered Keller's men on again. With beating drums, playing horns and cries of 'Vorwärts! Vorwärts!' the battalion marched down the paved road to Charleroi for half an hour before again encountering the French. The French had just started to bivouac for the night when the noise of the handful of pursuing Prussians caused them to restart their flight. More prisoners were taken.

At the village of Villers Bonaparte's treasury waggon and several thousand louis d'or fell into Prussian hands, along with the entire headquarters baggage and the marshals' personal waggons. Some of the fusiliers stayed behind to guard their precious charge, while the remainder continued the pursuit.

---

[47] Guretzky-Cornitz, p 301.
[48] Elting, p 295 & fn.

The chase continued until daybreak, through Quatre Bras, Mellet and Frasnes.[49] The 2nd Kurmark Landwehr Cavalry rode the whole night down the road towards Charleroi.[50]

The Prussian pursuit after Waterloo was limited by the lack of daylight and the general exhaustion of the troops. While many stragglers were cut down or captured, and a substantial part of the artillery fell into Allied hands, not a single colour was taken, which indicates that the surviving rump of the French infantry regiments retained some sort of order and discipline. Gneisenau's leadership, however, ensured that this part of the *Armée du Nord* did not rally quickly and become a serious fighting force again. Along with his decision to retreat on Tilly and Wavre after the Battle of Ligny, this was Gneisenau's second major contribution to the Allied success.

[49] Dörk, pp 142–3.
[50] Pflugk-Harttung, *I Korps*, p 233.

Chapter 11

Grouchy and Thielemann

The Approach to Wavre

We left Grouchy with his two infantry corps (III under Vandamme and IV under Gérard) arriving in Gembloux late in the evening of 17 June, with Baron Soult's 4th Cavalry Division (from Pajol's 1st Cavalry Corps) and Teste's 21st Infantry Division (from VI Corps) spending the night at Mazy. Exelmans' dragoons camped at Sauvenière. The heavy rain of that night had turned the area over which all the troops would march into a quagmire. We have seen that Napoleon's deployment on the field of Waterloo and Blücher's march to the battle were delayed by this, so too was Grouchy's pursuit of the Prussians. In fact, as this chapter will explain, III Corps, the leading formation of Grouchy's forces, only started to reach Wavre at 2 p.m. on 18 June, with the first division from IV Corps arriving several hours later. Only that evening would all of Grouchy's men be concentrated and ready to assault the Prussian positions at Wavre.[1]

Grouchy's Advance on Wavre

Pajol set out from Mazy to Temploux and soon established that Namur had been evacuated by the Prussians. He then moved on towards Leez. During the night of the 17th/18th Grouchy had received information that the Prussians had evacuated Tourinnes, and at 3 a.m. he therefore sent Pajol orders to move on to Tourinnes after he had reached Leez. Shortly after that, news arrived of the presence of a large Prussian artillery park near Leez, so Pajol was ordered to capture this. Should his force (2,300 infantry and 1,300 cavalry) be too small to deal with any Prussian troops covering this artillery, then Pajol was promised support from troops in Sart-à-Walhain.

Following the orders issued the previous evening Exelmans' dragoons moved off from Sauvenière at 6 a.m. towards Sart-à-Walhain to where Grouchy was also moving his headquarters. Vandamme moved off at 7 a.m., followed by Gérard.[2]

At 6 a.m. Grouchy informed Napoleon that,

> All my reports and information confirm that the Prussians are falling back on Brussels, either to concentrate there, or to offer battle once united with Wellington. Général Pajol reports that Namur has been evacuated. Regarding the I and II Corps of Blücher's army, the I Corps would appear to be moving on Corbais, the II Corps on Chaumont. Both are said to have moved off from

---

[1] Clausewitz, pp 130–1.
[2] Houssaye, vol II, pp 293–5.

Tourinnes and marched all night. Fortunately, the weather was so bad, that they are unlikely to have gone far. I will move off to Sart-à-Walhain immediately, and intend moving on Corbais and Wavre. I will send you further reports from one or the other of those places... [3]

The distance between Grouchy and Napoleon being under 30 km, one would expect this information to have been with the Emperor by 10 a.m. at the latest, that is before the main battle commenced. Bonaparte thus engaged Wellington's army in the knowledge that he was likely to have to deal with the Prussians that day as well.

About 10 a.m. Grouchy arrived at Sart-à-Walhain from where he sent a second report to Napoleon, which read,

Sire!
I will not lose a moment in sending to you the news I have gathered here. I regard it as definite, and so that Your Majesty receives it soonest, I am sending Major de la Fresnaye with it...

Blücher's I, II and III Corps are marching in the direction of Brussels. Two of these corps marched either through Sart-à-Walhain or just to the right of it. They are marching in three columns more or less abreast. Their march through here lasted six hours without interruption. Those troops passing through Sart-à-Walhain are estimated as being at least 30,000 men with 50 to 60 guns. An army corps came from Liège and has joined up with the corps that fought at Fleurus. (Enclosed is a requisition form, which proves this.) Some of the Prussian troops in front of me have headed in the direction of the plains of Chyse, which is on the road to Louvain [that is north of Wavre], and two and a half lieue [about 10 km] from that town. They seem to want to mass there, either to offer battle to any troops who pursue them there, or to join up with Wellington – a plan about which their officers spoke. With their usual boasting, they maintain they only left the battlefield of the 16th to join up with the English army in Brussels.

This evening, I will be standing before Wavre en masse, and in this way, be situated between Wellington, who I assume is falling back before Your Majesty, and the Prussian army. I require further instructions, whatever Your Majesty chooses to order, as to what I should do. The terrain between Wavre and the plain of Chyse is difficult to pass; it is broken and boggy. I will be able to get to Brussels easily along the Vilvoorde road, quicker than any troops who go over the plain of Chyse, especially if the Prussians make a stop there. If Your Majesty wishes to send me orders, I can still receive them before starting my movement tomorrow.

Most of the information in this letter came from the owner of this house where I have stopped to write to Your Majesty. He is an officer who served in the French army, has been decorated and seems to support our interests. I attach some notes.

The important points in the notes that helped determine Grouchy's decisions were,

3 Lettow-Vorbeck, p 390.

The rear of the corps that marched through Sart-à-Walhain is in Corroy. The entire army is moving on Wavre. The best route to Wavre is via Nil-Pierreux, Corbais, Baraque and Lauzelle. The wounded have been sent to Liège and Maastricht. The reserves and troops that did not participate in the Battle of Fleurus are marching to Wavre, some to Tirlemont. The bulk of the Prussian army is camping on the plain of Chyse. This is confirmed, and they seem to be massing there.[4]

At just after 11.30 p.m., shortly after Fresnaye had ridden off, the sounds of cannon fire in the distance indicated that fighting was going on, probably near the Forest of Soignes, 14 km away. Grouchy rejected Gérard's suggestion to march to the sound of the guns, pointing out that his orders were to pursue the Prussians, and that the Emperor had sufficient troops to deal with Wellington.[5] Hardly were the words out of Grouchy's mouth when a report from Exelmans arrived. Exelmans and his two divisions of dragoons were now at La Baraque, about 5 km from Wavre, and his patrols had come across a strong Prussian rearguard at the Bois de la Huzelle, on the heights above Wavre.[6] This information, together with that obtained previously, indicated that the Prussians had crossed the Dyle River the previous night and that morning with the intention of joining Wellington. Exelmans reported he was considering crossing to the left (west) bank of the Dyle at Ottignies.

Retreat of the Prussian Rearguard

About 1 p.m., Vandamme's corps, now halted at Nil-St Vincent, started off again. In the meantime, Exelmans had gone to Corbais after having detached Berton's brigade to Neuf-Sart and Vincent's to Plaquerie, and left a rearguard of two squadrons at la Baraque. Returning to la Baraque, he moved off again, only to find a detachment of the Prussian 10th Hussars just outside this village. Exelmans' vanguard began skirmishing with them. The report of Oberstlieutenant von Ledebur, the commander of the hussars and that day of Bülow's rearguard, described these events,

> Early on the 18th, Oberstlieutenant von Sohr marched off with his regiments [to rejoin the main army]. General von Ryssel [commander of the 14th Brigade] sent me Rittmeister Reyher of the General Staff as an aide. Reyher also brought me an order not to leave my position [St Guibert] until forced out. Furthermore, I was not to report to Ryssel any more, but directly to General von Bülow, and not to fall back on Vieux-Sart as previously ordered, but rather on Wavre.
>
> Until about 9 o'clock, everything was quiet. Then my outposts started to report sightings of individual enemy cavalry troopers.[7]

Ledebur was unaware that he was virtually surrounded. Indeed, at 12.30 p.m. on 18 June, he sent the following message from Mont St Guibert to Bülow,

4 Lettow-Vorbeck, p 391.   7 Thielen, p 19.
5 Lettow-Vorbeck, pp 392–3.
6 Houssaye, vol II, pp 455–6.

I wish to report most humbly to Your Excellency that the enemy has not disturbed us. Here and there, we have seen enemy patrols coming from Chambry. I have despatched three patrols, one via Tourinnes, one in the direction of Gembloux and one towards Genappe. They have all yet to return. Following Your Excellency's orders, I will remain here until pushed back.[8]

Shortly after sending that report, the reality of the situation became clear to Ledebur. His report continued,

... The return of several messengers I had sent who had come across the enemy and were unable to go any further, left me in no doubt that the enemy was approaching. Thus, I had my men march off and started to move towards the road to Wavre. However, I noticed that a column of enemy cavalry was threatening my left flank in such a way that it could reach the Wavre road before me.

To keep my infantry [two battalions of fusiliers] and [2] guns out of danger on the large plain before us, I had to hurry with my regiment to gain the lead over the enemy.

Rittmeister Reyher succeeded in leading the infantry to the left, behind a ridge and to a wood just to its side [the Bois de la Huzelle]. He did this with such calmness and skill that, despite the immediate and imminent danger, they reached the defile at Wavre with no disadvantage... [9]

Needing to move quickly himself, Ledebur rode at the head of his hussar troopers and charged through the French cavalry in la Baraque, reaching the two battalions of infantry and supporting artillery that Reyher was leading via les Bruyères and Blocry towards the Bois de la Huzelle.

Ledebur's account continued,

All this time, my flankers were engaged uninterruptedly with the enemy cavalry. Although the enemy had four times my numbers, he did not pressure me unduly.

I took up position before the Wavre defile and was ordered to leave this post only in the event of an attack by superior numbers. At first, the enemy reinforced his flankers continuously, forcing me to send all my troops to support mine. However, he then pulled most of them back and my regiment suffered a lively bombardment of shot and shell that my two guns could hardly answer adequately, despite having been joined by two more. [10]

By now it was about 1.30 p.m. and the 7th and 8th Brigades of the II Army Corps were marching through Wavre. Sohr's cavalry and the 9th Brigade of the III Army Corps were still on the right bank of the Dyle but all were now alerted to the French movements. Oberst von Reckow of the 8th Brigade sent off two battalions to the edge of the wood to support Ledebur.

By 2.30 p.m. the French had brought up sufficient troops to force Lebedur's rearguard back, but in the meantime Sohr crossed the bridge at

8   Lettow-Vorbeck, p 394.
9   Thielen, pp 19–20.
10 Thielen, p 20.

Bierges, while the 9th Brigade crossed the Dyle at Bas-Wavre. Ledebur's account concluded,

> A lively advance by columns of enemy infantry forced me, after about 1½ hours, to fall back with my regiment through the defile during which I suffered from very heavy canister fire.[11]

Ledebur's detachment retired through the town, without any determined pursuit from the French.

Thielemann Defends Wavre

The town of Wavre was on the left, northern and western, bank of the Dyle River, with a suburb on the right, southern bank. Two stone bridges, one wide and one narrow, crossed the river. There were wooden bridges to the south-west at Limelette, Limal and Bierges, as well as several at Bas-Wavre to the north-east. The river was not particularly deep anywhere along this stretch, but the recent heavy rain meant that fording it was impossible. The meadows on both sides were marshy with lines of hills close by overlooking them. The hills were wooded in some places and those on the right bank were steeper, dominating the river and its crossings. The paved road from Namur to Brussels ran through Wavre, crossing the river by the larger bridge there. The recent rainfall had made the many other minor roads and tracks in the area largely unusable, and many of these in any case were sunken and unsuitable for troop manoeuvres in combat.[12]

Most of Thielemann's III Army Corps had bivouacked overnight at la Bawette and early on the 18th had been given orders for the coming day to march off after the II Army Corps and follow the rest of the army to Couture. Thielemann had instructed Generalmajor von Borcke, commander of the 9th Brigade, which was still south of the Dyle at this stage, to place a rearguard of two battalions in Wavre and then to follow the corps with the remainder of his brigade. Borcke in turn had ordered Oberst von Zepelin to cover the large stone bridge with two of his battalions, the F./30th Regiment and the F./1st Kurmark Landwehr. They were later joined by the skirmishers of the F./8th (Life) Regiment who had become separated from the rest of their battalion.

As the town itself was crowded, Borcke had his brigade cross the Dyle further down at Bas-Wavre, while leaving the skirmish platoons of the two fusilier battalions at the bridge. Having crossed the river he then sent the II./30th Infantry (former Russo-German Legionnaires) and his cavalry to reinforce the troops in the town. Mistaking the I Army Corps for the other units of his own corps, he started to follow it on its march via Froidmont with the rest of his brigade. Borcke and his men marched on in the direction of St Lambert and Ohain, with the command of the III Army Corps failing to locate them.

Thielemann had spent the night of the 17th/18th at Bawette with the main body of his corps, but as the II Army Corps began marching off early in the afternoon of the 18th, he saw strong French forces building up on the

[11] Thielen, p 20.
[12] Bornstedt, p 16.

far bank of the Dyle. He decided to draw his corps up to face them, covering the rear of Blücher's army from any attack, but this change of plan did not reach Borcke, who carried on to Ohain, as just described, in accordance with his earlier orders.[13]

Thielemann deployed his remaining troops as follows:

10th Brigade to the rear of Wavre, on the heights north-west of the town.
11th Brigade to the rear of Wavre, north of the town on the Brussels road.
12th Brigade south-west of Wavre on the heights near Bierges.
Reserve Cavalry behind the 10th Brigade, near the farm of du Ri.
The artillery to be posted in such a way as to give covering fire to the brigades and to be able to fire on any French troops in Wavre.

Believing that the Dyle was fordable in certain places, not realising the effects of the recent rain, the skirmishers of most of the corps' infantry battalions deployed along its northern bank from Bierges to Bas-Wavre. Oberst von Zepelin sent two companies of the Kurmark Landwehr to cover the bridge at Bas-Wavre. There was just about enough time to erect a temporary barricade on the stone bridge in Wavre. One company of infantry was sent to guard the bridge at Bierges. Its skirmishers deployed at both ends of the bridge. Troops taking up positions in any houses along the Dyle cut loopholes cut in their walls.[14]

In all, Thielemann had about 15,000 men at his disposal, including the 19th Infantry Regiment and the 6th Uhlans (three squadrons) from the I Army Corps, these troops being under the command of Major von Stengel. That was less than half the number Grouchy had available, though in fact only around 10,000 to 12,000 French troops would eventually attack the Prussian positions that day. The French operation was more in the form of a demonstration designed to tie down the Prussians than a determined attempt to storm and capture Wavre. Nevertheless, the day's fighting was both bitter and bloody.

The Combat at Wavre, 18 June

As he approached Wavre, Vandamme decided to try to capture the bridges there by *coup de main*. Disregarding his orders to halt on the heights, he had his men descend into the Dyle valley towards the town. Thielemann's preparations for the defence were hardly finished when, at 4 p.m., Vandamme's corps was observed moving down from the heights opposite Wavre. Two French batteries unlimbered and opened fire immediately. The battery on the right was of 12-pounders, and its fire against the town was particularly effective. A third battery moved up a little later. Vandamme sent Habert's division forward in attack columns.[15]

Grouchy then rode up, having just received Soult's 10 a.m. letter instructing him to move on Wavre. Now viewing the situation at first hand, Grouchy decided on simultaneous attacks above and below the town in addition to the

[13] Lettow-Vorbeck, pp 451–2.
[14] Houssaye, vol II, p 463.
[15] Bornstedt, p 17.

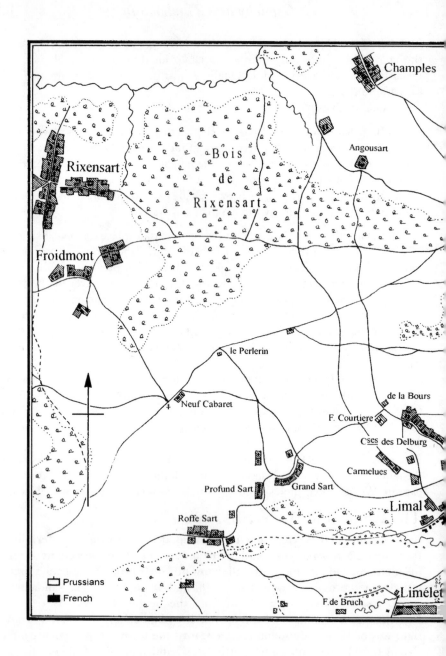

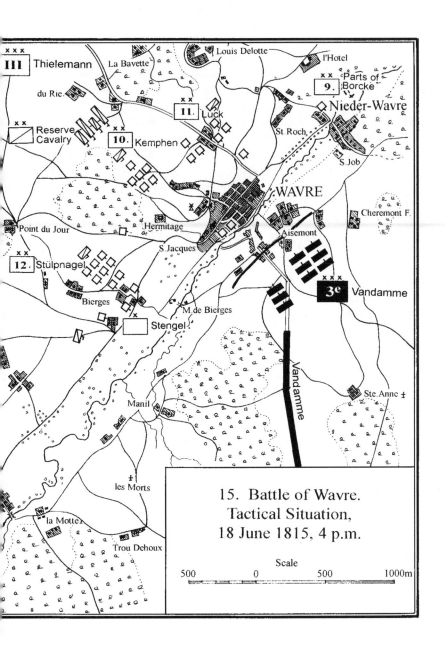

15. Battle of Wavre.
Tactical Situation,
18 June 1815, 4 p.m.

Scale
500   0   500   1000m

advance by Vandamme's men that had already begun. To that end, he sent off Exelmans with his dragoons and one battalion of infantry to Bas-Wavre, while Vandamme dispatched Lefol's division towards the bridge at Bierges. To maintain contact with Napoleon's forces, Grouchy sent orders to Pajol's cavalry and Teste's infantry division to move further west towards Limal and St Lambert.

Major von Bornstedt, commander of the F./1st Kurmark Landwehr, a battalion of Berliners, led the defence of Bas-Wavre. The French approach started before he had had a chance to destroy the bridge there, so he called for volunteers from the 9th and 12th Companies, under the command of Kapitain von Eikstedt. Militiamen Schley, a builder, and Jannot, a carpenter were the first. They were joined by Sergeant Stamm, a carpenter, and Militiamen Grohmann, Friebel and Wolff. Men from the 12th Company skilled in the use of wood also volunteered. Their work commenced under artillery fire from the French. Encouraged by Bornstedt and instructed by Eikstedt, a former artillery officer, they set about their task. Using axes and picks, they managed to remove a few timbers from the bridge, throwing them into the river while the French skirmishers approached. Under fire from the Prussians, the French attempted to replace the timbers but Lieutenants Coburg and Jaeckel led the 9th Company and engaged the French skirmishers, who fell back. Attack met with counter-attack here for some time without any change in the situation.[16]

Bornstedt rushed from one post to another. His 10th and 11th Companies, under the command of Kapitain von Göhren fought in defence of the stone bridge in Wavre. The battalion's skirmishers were posted along the Dyle to Bas-Wavre in sections commanded by Feldwebels Hold, Knack and Friedrich.

Although the Prussians had no intention of seriously defending the suburb of Wavre on the right bank, it nevertheless took the French quite some time to take it as the Prussians skirmishers fought off several attacks. Once the Prussians had been driven back, the French followed up rapidly. Moving over the stone bridge, they took the houses in the lower part of the town with a murderous street battle soon starting. The Kurmarkers held their ground, and reinforcements in the shape of a battalion of Kurmark Landwehr from Luck's 11th Brigade moved up. With this support, the F./30th and F./1st Kurmark Landwehr launched a counter-attack that drove the French back over the bridge again. Some French soldiers were caught in houses on the Prussian side. Many were bayoneted and only a few were taken prisoner. Général Habert himself was wounded.

The II./30th moved up in support as the French renewed their attacks. The French took the bridge again and advanced down the main road into Wavre. The F./30th and F./1st Kurmark Landwehr waited for them in the side streets. Hit in both flanks by fire at close range, the French hesitated. A bayonet charge saw them off, back over the bridge. The battle for Wavre continued in this way into the night, with repeated French attacks sometimes seeming to gain ground before all being ultimately thrown back.

Later French attacks on Bas-Wavre were equally unsuccessful. The Prussians eventually deployed one additional battalion, three squadrons and

16 Bornstedt, p 18.

several cannon there, along with the skirmishers of the F./1st Kurmark Landwehr on the right of the bridge and the F./30th to the left. The close-order platoons of these battalions defended the bridge while the skirmishers of the F./8th Regiment remained in reserve. A detachment of hussars covered another wooden bridge below Bas-Wavre. All attacks on the bridge in Bas-Wavre were beaten off, and the French had to be satisfied with the capture of a few houses on the right bank of the Dyle. The small arms and artillery fire continued well into the night, stopping only at around 2 a.m. on the 19th.

Lefol's attack on the windmill of Bierges was equally unsuccessful, partly because of the wet and muddy ground nearby. The windmill itself was held by one company of the 31st Regiment, supported by the II./6th Kurmark Landwehr and six guns from Horse Battery Nr. 20 drawn up on a ridge behind the mill. Later, when troops of the French IV Corps arrived, Hulot's division closed on the Prussian positions, led by Gérard in person. A shot severely wounded Gérard and the attack was driven off.

Between 6 p.m. and 7 p.m. Soult's 1 p.m. letter arrived. In this, Grouchy was told not to lose a minute in rejoining the main army and attacking Bülow. Grouchy immediately issued an order to Pajol to accelerate his march to Limal, while he himself went to la Baraque so that he could personally lead the other divisions of the IV Corps to Limal. However, when Grouchy arrived at la Baraque, there was no sign of these divisions. He waited a while, and when they still did not appear, he sent them the necessary orders before returning to Wavre. However, to his great surprise, the divisions of Vichery and Pêcheux turned up at Wavre a little later; apparently they had lost their way. Grouchy then took them along the Dyle in the growing darkness to Limal, 3 km away. Arriving there at 11 p.m., he found Pajol holding the village, having already seized the bridge there by a *coup de main*. Crossing the Dyle, the IV Corps' troops then climbed up the subsequent heights to the north where they came across Prussian troops marching to Limal, and forced them to retire.

In the report of the 12th Brigade, Oberst von Stülpnagel described the situation,

> About 8 o'clock in the evening, Major von Stengel of the 19th Regiment reported to me that he had been given three battalions and three squadrons to maintain a line of communication between his corps and the III Corps. Shortly after that, Major Simolin of the [11th] Hussar Regiment reported to me that there were no infantry in Limal and a strong enemy column had been seen moving towards it. I immediately requested Major von Simolin to occupy Limal and sent the two squadrons of the brigade there.
>
> However, I believed that the enemy had already passed the Dyle at Limal. I reported this to the commanding general, and that I was marching with the brigade on Limal and requested cavalry support. General Thielemann ordered the Reserve Cavalry to support me and ordered me to prevent the French breaking out of Limal. I then marched off, leaving all my skirmishers on the Dyle, one battalion between Wavre and Bierges, and, to protect my left flank, two battalions in Bierges.
>
> I found Limal and the heights in front of it already occupied by the enemy

and Stengel's detachment retiring to these heights. The darkness prevented a judgement of the enemy's strength. As Limal was an important position, I was of the firm belief that I should do everything to recapture it. Thus, I placed the 19th Regiment in reserve and assembled an attack from the I. and II. Battalions of the 31st Regiment, skirmishers to the fore; 50 paces behind them came the Landwehr battalions. All my troops were in column...

A sunken road obscured by the darkness forced the skirmishers to move sideways. The formed troops came up against a sunken road that separated them from the enemy who suddenly opened fire on them. Because of the sunken road we were not able to charge at the enemy, so I called up cavalry support. The enemy could not advance either, so I pulled back my troops to the heights on this side [to the north] and had the skirmishers stand in front of them... [17]

Sekonde-Lieutenant Mannkopff, commander of the skirmish platoon of the 4th Company of the 31st Regiment also described his participation in that night's fighting,

We advanced with our skirmishers out in front and a long and determined battle broke out with the enemy voltigeurs in the darkness and amid the man-high corn that covered the fields. This soon became chaotically confused, with man fighting man. In this, my men and I had to face enemy voltigeurs and cavalry sometimes to our front, sometimes to our rear. About midnight, where possible, our skirmishers pulled back to the columns and a bayonet attack was made at the charge. However, because of the darkness and high corn, it was impossible to see and keep order. Thus, this action achieved as little as the skirmish fight. Meanwhile, my skirmishers had rejoined the battalion and during this attack suddenly stumbled into a deep sunken road or ditch. At that moment, a volley of small arms fire from the opposite side struck us. However, probably because the other side of the sunken road was higher, the shots mostly went over the heads of our soldiers and unmounted officers, some of them making a loud rattling sound on hitting our bayonets. All our mounted officers were hit, though, including the regimental commander, Major von Kesteloot, and the battalion commander, Major von Tiedemann, who were wounded, as well as the battalion adjutant, Lieutenant von Aderkas, who was killed. Shortly after this bayonet charge, we broke off the battle and, without the enemy following up, withdrew to a pine forest close behind us.[18]

The cavalry came up, but as the night was now so dark, General von Thielemann, who had just arrived, considered a continuation of the combat pointless and ordered the troops to fall back further.

The 12th Brigade and Stengel's detachment took up positions in cover on the southern edge of the Bois de Rixensart. Their left flank remained in contact with the troops who had remained in Bierges, three battalions of whom had already been sent to reinforce the 10th Brigade. The Reserve Cavalry set up camp behind the wood. The French troops, Pêcheux's and Vichery's

[17] Lettow-Vorbeck, pp 455–6.
[18] Bornstedt, p 107.

infantry divisions and Pajol's cavalry later joined by Teste's infantry, bivouacked so close to the Prussians that the opposing outposts exchanged shots for most of the night.

Sekonde-Lieutenant Wehmeyer of the 31st Regiment described the night's events,

> The outposts were standing so near to the enemy that every word could be heard. Many wounded men lay just in front of the line of outposts, or even among them, and their groaning could be heard all night. Enemy patrols clashed with us constantly. The vedettes of the Landwehr cavalry in the line of outposts on the right flank fell back whenever they were shot at causing the remainder of the outposts to move back as well, so the entire chain was constantly moving. Nobody got a bite to eat and there was not a drop of water to be found to quench our burning thirst. The French were very lively. They fell back in the late evening, and butchered some pigs whose squeals accentuated our hunger they seemed likely to be so good. We remained dead quiet, only the sentries breaking this silence with their calls. Everybody else rested on the ground, musket in hand, waiting for the next battle that would begin at daybreak.[19]

Grouchy recognised the importance of this position and requested Vandamme, if he had not yet crossed the Dyle, to move to Limal immediately, leaving behind at Wavre sufficient troops only to cover the bridges. Together with Vandamme's men he hoped in the morning to fight his way through to Napoleon, who, according to rumour, had beaten Wellington.[20] That night Thielemann's headquarters received unconfirmed reports that the French had suffered a defeat. However, Thielemann apparently made no efforts to obtain further information. Thielemann claimed that he first heard certain news of the Allied victory sometime after 9 a.m. on 19 June; other sources, however, indicate that the news may have arrived at 6 a.m.[21]

Situation on the Morning of 19 June

Vandamme did not carry out his orders in full, only sending Hulot's division of the IV Corps and Exelmans' cavalry to assist Grouchy in the morning of the 19th. Although Vandamme did not undertake any offensive moves in Wavre that morning, the presence of his remaining forces there was sufficient to tie down the Prussian troops defending the town.

For the main Prussian deployment six battalions of the 12th Brigade took up positions along the southern edge of the Bois de Rixensart, three weak battalions on the road west of the Point du Jour. On the left flank towards Bierges, five battalions of the 10th Brigade linked up with two squadrons from the 12th Brigade. A further three battalions of the 10th Brigade together with their skirmishers remained in the positions along the Dyle that they had taken up the previous day. Likewise, the four battalions under Oberst von Zepelin

---

[19] Gottschalck, p 95.
[20] Grouchy, p 288.
[21] Lettow-Vorbeck, p 457 fn.

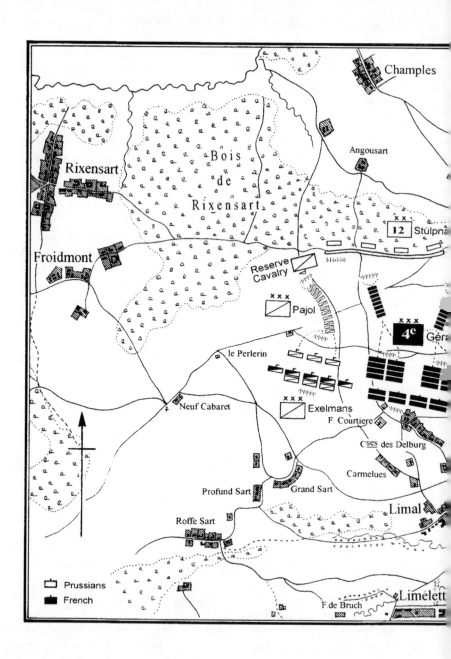

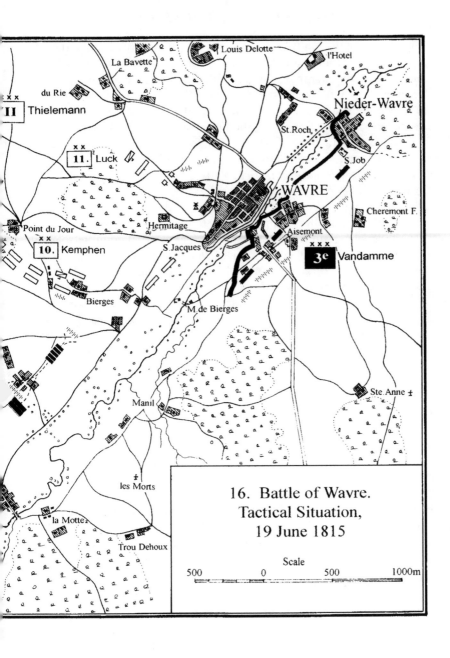

**16. Battle of Wavre.
Tactical Situation,
19 June 1815**

Scale

500   0   500   1000m

Labels on map:

Louis Delotte
l'Hotel
La Bavette
du Rie
II Thielemann
Nieder-Wavre
St.Roch
11. Luck
S.Job
WAVRE
Cheremont F.
Point du Jour
Hermitage
Aisemont
10. Kemphen
S.Jacques
3e Vandamme
Bierges
M.de Bierges
Ste.Anne
Manil
les Morts
la Motte
Trou Dehoux

(three battalions of the 9th Brigade, one of the 11th), one battalion of the 10th Brigade and two further battalions of the 11th remained in Wavre. The 3rd Kurmark Landwehr Infantry Regiment of the 11th Brigade moved up behind the Reserve Cavalry on the northern edge of the Bois de Rixensart. Thus, of the 24 available battalions, nine together with the skirmishers of some of the other battalions held the front along the Dyle and 15 plus the Reserve Cavalry faced Grouchy's main force. Grouchy had four infantry divisions and the cavalry of Pajol and Exelmans, double the Prussians' strength. The French also had more artillery available, particularly as the Prussians had deployed only two batteries in the new position.

Thielemann's force was further weakened by the loss of some of its supporting units. Presumably believing that Grouchy would have to retreat because of Napoleon's defeat, Stengel's detachment marched off to rejoin its corps early in the day. Oberstlieutenant von Ledebur's detachment had reached the defile of St Lambert on 18 June where it had covered the movement of the army's ammunition columns through the defile. Ledebur's records indicate that the French then cut him off from the III Army Corps and that by the morning of 19 June he faced three French cavalry regiments. They later moved off, in the direction of his left flank, allowing Ledebur also to march off to rejoin his corps at St Lambert and, as will be explained shortly, the main body of Borcke's 9th Brigade failed to rejoin Thielemann as well.

Thielemann's Retreat

Battle was joined early on 19 June. The 1st Brigade [12th Hussars, 7th and 8th Uhlans] and Horse Battery Nr. 18 of the Reserve Cavalry moved forwards. An artillery duel began in which five Prussian pieces were damaged, and the cavalry suffered casualties. Grouchy then sent forward his first three divisions and his cavalry, each with a battery of artillery in the lead. The Prussian cavalry and the horse battery then retired through the Bois de Rixensart and, after a short struggle, the infantry of the 10th and 12th Brigades also fell back in the face of the superior enemy numbers into the wood east of Point du Jour. However, the Prussians managed to hold Bierges against Teste's division.

Clausewitz, chief-of-staff of the III Army Corps, described the events,

> At first light, the first cannon shots fell, fired from a range of just 500 paces. A determined battle developed, in which the French moved their four divisions methodically forwards, covered by a strong line of skirmishers. The III Army Corps resisted from three positions in succession. First, the 12th Brigade and Oberst [Major] Stengel (who was still present at this time) defended a small wood. Then 14 battalions of the 12th, 10th and 11th Brigades and the Reserve Cavalry deployed between Bierges and the Bois de Rixensart. Six battalions were left behind Bierges and Wavre, and another four remained in Wavre.
>
> The resistance in the second position lasted the longest. It was here that General Thielemann heard the news of victory and that the II Army Corps had been ordered to move via Glabais and la Hutte [Bas Hutte] into the rear of the enemy.[22]

22 Clausewitz, pp 138–9.

Lieutenant Mannkopff of the 31st Regiment, part of the 12th Brigade, described the action on the ground,

... At daybreak the edge of the wood facing the enemy filled with our entire force of skirmishers, while the battalion columns formed up in support to our rear in the forest. We had hardly deployed in this fashion when some French voltigeurs, who had very skilfully crawled up to us unseen in the tall corn, opened a superior fire on us. As it was important for us to hold on to this wood, our firing line on its edge was gradually reinforced by the larger part of our battalions. Thus, we were able to hold the wood for several hours.[23]

When definite news of Waterloo arrived Thielemann immediately passed the report on to his men. Lieutenant Wehmeyer of the 31st Regiment described how he heard,

General Thielemann came up to us and said, 'Children, yesterday a great battle between Napoleon and Prince Blücher and Wellington took place. Napoleon has been totally defeated and is retreating. I have only just received this news, on my word. Now we have to stand firm and will soon receive support. Take this wood now. Long live the King! Long live the Fatherland!' Everybody was inspired by these words, and as if electrified, cried 'Hurrah! Hurrah!' between the bursts of cannon fire.[24]

Clausewitz's account continued,

As these points [Glabais and Bas Hutte] were so far from the battlefield, no direct help was to be expected, so General Thielemann could only hope that the enemy had also received news of our success in the great battle and to prevent being cut off, would quickly withdraw. Thus, General Thielemann had his men give a loud cheer and jump up and down in joy. His hope, however, was in vain.[25]

Even so the good news inspired Thielemann's men to make a counter-attack. They quickly regained the Bois de Rixensart, but held it only for a short time. Kapitain von Zurwesten of the II./31st led the battalion's skirmishers into the woods about 7 a.m. with cries of 'Hurrah!' still fresh on their lips. Major von Kesteloot, commander of the battalion, ordered Wehmeyer and the I. Battalion to advance as well, saying,

My child, take your division into this wood and, when you have reached the far end, occupy and hold its edge, for I will send you reinforcements.[26]

Led by its skirmishers, the I./31st moved back into the wood, pushing the French to its southern edge.

Instead of falling back as expected, the French renewed their efforts. French reinforcements moved up, concealed by the tall crops. Their artillery opened fire, knocking over men and smashing trees. Wehmeyer's men fell

---

23 Bornstedt, pp 107–8.
24 Gottschalck, p 102.
25 Clausewitz, p 139.
26 Gottschalck, p 103.

back. Kesteloot ordered them forward again and the struggle continued. Teste then fought his way into the village and mill of Bierges while on the other flank the French cavalry pushed the Prussians back to Champles.

The situation for Thielemann was difficult, particularly as little help could be expected from Pirch, who was still quite a distance from Wavre. Thielemann decided to withdraw, starting about 10 a.m. In his report, Thielemann explained how he now moved to his third position of the day,

> In these circumstances, I decided to quit Wavre and fall back on the road to Louvain. The Reserve Cavalry covered this manoeuvre and the corps fell back, without any more losses than the many already dead and wounded, towards St Agatha-Rode, two hours from Wavre in the direction of Louvain. Here, we took up positions on the left bank of the Dyle with our outposts in Ottenburg. The enemy did not push any further, but deployed... parallel to the Brussels road.[27]

Mannkopff's account continued,

> Suddenly, we saw the enemy make a strong attack on our left flank and rear. He had captured a village [Bierges] that formed an extension of our left flank and was occupied by a Landwehr battalion, thus taking the key to our defence and circumventing our left flank. After a determined and very confused battle in the wood that cost many lives, we had to concede it to superior numbers. A general retreat was ordered that was all the more welcome because we had almost run out of ammunition. During the battle for the wood, I had already had a quantity of cartridges fetched from a Landwehr battalion positioned behind us, as most of my men had already used all of theirs.
>
> Once they had taken the wood, the French halted and did not pursue us beyond it. Thus, the remnants of the three battalions of my regiment were able to rally out of musket range outside the wood. They were formed into a single battalion column. Like the remainder of the troops who had taken part in the combat at Wavre and were already falling back in the direction of Louvain, we, too, now joined the withdrawal in that direction. The enemy did not pursue, he merely lobbed a few shells at us.[28]

During this withdrawal, some of Vandamme's corps followed up across the Dyle, through Wavre, and cut off two battalions of the 4th Kurmark Landwehr Infantry Regiment for a short while. The Kurmarkers cleared a way through at bayonet point. However, the French captured five cannon and took prisoner some wounded Prussians who had been left behind.

Grouchy's Retreat

Now master of the battlefield, Grouchy was preparing to march on Brussels when, at 10.30 a.m., he received the news of Napoleon's defeat. Grouchy could not believe his ears. As the messenger had no precise information on the condition, position and intentions of Napoleon's army, Grouchy knew that

---

[27] Lettow-Vorbeck, p 458.
[28] Bornstedt, pp 108–9.

going further would risk being cut off. He called his senior officers together, informed them of the situation and ordered a withdrawal to Namur. Exelmans was sent off to secure the bridges across the Sambre while Grouchy directed the IV Corps via Limal and Gembloux to the Nivelles–Namur road. The troops bivouacked for the night between Mazy and Temploux. Vandamme's III Corps withdrew later, during the afternoon, crossing the Dyle at Wavre and then marching via Dion-le-Mont, Tourinnes, Grand-Leez and Gembloux. Around midnight, Vandamme and his men stopped on the heights near Temploux on the road to Namur. Pajol was left to screen the withdrawal, doing so so successfully that it was night before the Prussians noticed the French had gone. Pajol's men retreated in the evening, reaching Gembloux that night.

Thielemann's report was rather vague about all this, saying only that, '... the rearguard fell back at daybreak [on the 20th]. Thus, we did not know of the enemy's withdrawal until too late.'[29]

Clausewitz gave rather more detail,

> General Thielemann reached the area of St Agatha-Rode about noon on the 19th. He decided not to send his very exhausted men off in pursuit, as their first priority was rest. Furthermore, as the enemy rearguard was not likely to withdraw until that night anyway, a pursuit would have achieved nothing. He therefore decided to move his corps at daybreak [on the 20th] to rendezvous at Ottenburg where his rearguard stood. He thought he could follow the enemy in good time from there. However, there was an hour's delay in assembling the troops that morning and about five o'clock the cavalry started off via Gembloux to Namur. The infantry followed shortly afterwards.[30]

Oberst von der Marwitz commanded Thielemann's rearguard on the 19th, consisting of his own brigade (7th and 8th Uhlans) reinforced by six squadrons of Landwehr cavalry from the 3rd and 6th Kurmark Regiments and one battery. He was able to provide a more complete explanation still. According to his account, the French pursued the Prussians as far as Ottenburg. Here, the route ran into a defile, making it unsuitable for cavalry action. Marwitz posted one squadron to hold off what he described as 'enemy skirmishers' (he was probably referring to dismounted cavalry), while he sought more suitable ground further to the rear. This he found at St Agatha-Rode, where, to his surprise, he also found the remainder of the corps.

Marwitz immediately pointed out the importance of placing infantry in Ottenburg, but was told they were too tired. Thielemann then moved his headquarters to Neerijse, 3 km further on. Marwitz continued by noting how Grouchy deployed a 'veil of skirmishers, and this resulted in us first noticing their withdrawal the next morning, 16 hours after it had started.' Finally, Marwitz remarked that Thielemann had ordered his withdrawal from around Wavre '... because Grouchy's chances of being cut off would increase the further he followed up.'[31]

---

[29] Lettow-Vorbeck, p 459.
[30] Clausewitz, pp 138–9.
[31] Lettow-Vorbeck, p 460.

Borcke's Brigade on 19 June

After Generalmajor von Borcke's 9th Brigade passed Wavre by on the 18th and marched on it is not clear whether they kept going to Ohain or only as far as St Lambert, but they certainly spent the night in that general area. In his report on his activities on the 19th Borcke recorded that he witnessed the French crossing the Dyle at Wavre during the morning and that he therefore started to march to Limal himself to 'cause a diversion for the French, if possible'. After 'an hour', he came into contact with them, 'particularly with strong masses of cavalry that were moving from Wavre in the direction of Genappe'. He had his battery open fire, whereupon the French changed their line of march to Limal, crossed the Dyle there and covered their withdrawal with infantry. Borcke continued, 'Owing to the lack of cavalry, a pursuit was not possible, nor even an attack'. Borcke rejoined the corps the next day.[32]

Other accounts, including that of Kapitain Schlieffen, evidently one of Borcke's ADCs, supplemented this information. Schlieffen said that on the morning of the 19th several messages from Major Stengel arrived, requesting the detachment of 50 cavalry troopers. The brigade then marched on Limal, but not by the most direct route, instead rather in a curve to the north until reaching Neuf Cabaret. Here, strong detachments of French cavalry were seen at a distance. The artillery opened fire on them, but the French took little notice. Later, the French cavalry moved to Champles, but as 'one did not wish to provoke the enemy', the brigade stayed where it was. In the afternoon, an officer came from Blücher with orders to confirm the location of the III Army Corps which Blücher believed was still at Wavre. Borcke gave the officer a report to take with him, but he returned shortly after as he was unable to get through the French lines. Schlieffen then continued,

> At five o'clock, the enemy was seen moving off and, a little later, the head of a column appeared above Limal, moving up the right bank of the Dyle. A scouting party then used the cover of twilight to go to Limal and came back with the report that the village was empty. An officer was sent to General Thielemann immediately to report this to him. The next morning, he returned with orders to march via Limal to the Namur road and to rejoin the corps.[33]

All in all Grouchy had extracted himself from contact in a most skilful fashion. He had left the main body of Thielemann's III Corps well behind; he had avoided Borcke's 9th Brigade; and, as Chapter 13 (pages 185–6) will show, Pirch's II Corps also failed to intercept him on the 19th.

[32] Lettow-Vorbeck, p 461.
[33] Lettow-Vorbeck, p 461.

Chapter 12

The North German Federal Army Corps

The Lesser German States

The role played by the contingents of the lesser German states in the campaign of 1815 receives scant attention in most histories. This chapter will examine the part played by one particular corps, the North German Federal Army Corps, commanded by the Prussian General Kleist von Nollendorf.

As we saw in the first part of this work, after Napoleon's abdication Kleist was placed in command of the German forces on the Lower Rhine. His objectives were to enforce the Prussian territorial claims in that region and to observe any troop movements, particularly French, that might affect the area. When the bitter wrangling at Vienna over the shape of Europe was interrupted by Bonaparte's escape from Elba, Kleist found himself in command of the army that was most likely to have to intervene to put an end to the adventure.

Although well qualified as a soldier for the task, Kleist did not have the prestige in these new circumstances to give sufficient force to Prussia's territorial claims and desire to be recognised again as one of the Great Powers. Thus, on 19 March 1815, Friedrich Wilhelm III, the King of Prussia, sent Kleist the following order,

> As Napoleon Bonaparte's enterprise in France will probably make it necessary to take up arms against him again, I have once more given the supreme command of my army to Feldmarschall Prinz Blücher, with Generallieutenant Graf Gneisenau as Quartermaster-General... To you, however, I give the supreme command of all the Federal troops of the North German princes, namely of Hesse-Kassel, Saxony, Nassau, Mecklenburg, Anhalt and those of the lesser principalities in this area, who have at this moment been requested to provide such troops to be placed under the supreme command of a Prussian general... I have given you the command of this mixed corps in the belief that you, with your attributes, will be able to deal with the problems of such a disparate force.[1]

Kleist's response to the royal order was, 'This command is a very unpleasant task, but one has to see it through; nothing can be done about it.'[2]

Kleist's Thankless Task

This decision left a bitter taste in Kleist's mouth but, as a professional soldier, he set about carrying out his orders. These were to transform a hotchpotch

---

[1] Pflugk-Harttung, *Bundestruppen*, p 69–70.
[2] Pflugk-Harttung, *Bundestruppen*, p 69.

force of troops of mixed quality from various small German principalities into an army corps with military potential. With a nominal strength of 35,000 men, Kleist's corps was stronger on paper than a standard Prussian army corps. Reality was somewhat different, as his strength for some time was only around 8,700 men, reaching 13,000 in May and never exceeding 18,500 men. This was due to the constant bickering amongst the Allies about the allocation of the contingents, the general shortage of manpower in Germany and the wide dispersal of the constituent parts of this corps.

In effect, Kleist had been demoted, but at least he had a seemingly independent command. However, he quickly found himself needing to ask Blücher for musket cartridges and flints, both of which were in short supply, or even totally lacking, in certain contingents. This led him into a relationship of dependency on the Field Marshal. Soon Blücher was giving Kleist orders.

Faced with a myriad of such difficulties, Kleist would have been able to make good use of a capable staff to help him execute his tasks. This, too, was denied at first. Müffling, who had been his chief-of-staff, was transferred to Blücher's command and the liaison role with the British; even Kleist's personal aide, Oberstlieutenant von Watzdorff, was moved elsewhere. On 20 May Kleist sent a letter outlining his problems in this respect to the Minister of War, writing,

To date, I have done the duties of the Quartermaster, the Assistant Quartermaster, and the Quartermaster-General; I myself rode to Trier to organise various matters and have spent two entire days on horseback viewing the area.

[Major von] Legad [an officer of the Prussian General Staff and Kleist's ADC] is a very useful man, but not a staff officer or, at least, not at a higher level. He is, however, indispensable for lists and correspondence. [Oberst-lieutenant von] Perbrandt [also an officer of the Prussian General Staff] has been placed second in command, and he has been very useful on several occasions in the general staff; in Courland he served me very well. Kapitain Staedterl of the Saxons is the only other one of any use, but then exclusively for secondary matters; even then, with his bad eyes, he cannot stay outside for long (at least, at first).

I have already written about [Oberst von] Thile, but did not receive a satisfactory answer; I have asked for him, if I could not get his brother [there were two Thiles, one in the War Ministry, the other a staff officer], with which neither Müffling nor Aster [chief-of-staff of the II Army Corps] could help; he is a good man, and thanks to his conciliatory character, would be ideal to be sent to mixed company.

If there is anything you could do to help me here, I would be most indebted to you. It would do much to make me happier.

According to an order-in-cabinet, a certain Lieutenant Wulffen has been allocated to me, but I cannot use him for important reconnaissance rides, or for other serious matters.

Furthermore, the Hessian General Engelhardt, though a man of the best intentions, is over 60 years old. Should I fall ill, or be wounded, which is quite possible, then, with this man in charge, operations would have to be abandoned; I thus bring this to your attention.

See to it that an open minded, reasonable man is sent here soon. Make sure he is not one of these modern geniuses with such forceful ways of expressing himself, that he would not fit in with this colourful mixture.[3]

This sorry situation was exacerbated when Kleist fell ill with jaundice. Only then did Blücher send him Oberst von Witzleben as chief-of-staff, and Kapitain Heiden as an ADC. Kleist suspected their loyalties lay with the Field Marshal, so he saw that they did not get much involved in his affairs. When his illness got worse, Kleist sent his personal aide, Kapitain Graf von Schweidnitz of the 7th Hussars, to the king, requesting that he be relieved of his duties. Witzleben then took over the command provisionally. As the Hessian Engelhardt was actually the next senior officer, the Prussian Witzleben acted in Kleist's name. Major von Legad provided support to the bed-ridden Kleist, drafting much of his correspondence. The Saxon Captain von Staedterl carried out other duties. In the coming weeks, several more officers were sent to serve on Kleist's staff, including Lieutenant von Hymen of the 8th Uhlans, Lieutenant Adolph Fürst von Hohenlohe-Ingelfingen, Kapitain von Katte, Lieutenant von Wulffen and Volontair Lehmann. Matters were beginning to improve.

It is interesting to note that Kleist's headquarters was guarded by a detachment of Saxons consisting of one officer and 24 foot soldiers of the Saxon Guard, and 25 Saxon hussars. Despite the Saxon rebellion early that May, Kleist continued to have a high regard for these men. Moreover, in view of the heavy-handed fashion with which Blücher handled that situation, Kleist could still be sure of the personal loyalty of these men.

The Missing Contingents

A worse problem facing Kleist was the continual uncertainty as to which contingents he would get when, and at what strength. Kleist could not begin to organise his corps until these matters were clarified. Besides, he was suffering from a lack of money. As a Prussian general serving with a non-Prussian corps he considered it unwise to use Prussian funds to pay bills when it was not certain that the contingents would repay this money. In addition, those states that did provide their contingents with funds did just that and no more; they were not prepared to pay any money into corps headquarters.

It was not only on a practical level that it proved difficult to put together a North German Army Corps; there were also difficulties on the political level. The main problem was the rivalry between Britain and Prussia over the future of the states of Northern Germany, which was reflected in the fate of their military forces. This issue is covered in the first volume of this work.

As also described in the first volume of this work, a Prussian order-in-cabinet of 19 March had allocated the following contingents to Kleist: Hesse-Kassel, Saxony, Mecklenburg, Anhalt, the Saxon Duchies, Lippe-Detmold, Schaumburg-Lippe, Schwarzburg-Rudolstadt, Schwarzburg-Sonderhausen,

---

[3] Pflugk-Harttung, *Bundestruppen*, p 80.

Nassau, Waldeck and the two principalities of Reuss.[4] The issue of Saxony was to be looked at more closely once it had been decided which parts of that territory were to be annexed by Prussia, and which were to remain under the crown of Saxony, as the troops from the latter were to join the Federal Army. Had Kleist received all of these troops, then he would have commanded a full army corps. However, his corps never reached full strength. The reasons for this were firstly that only part of the expected number of troops was supplied, and then only slowly and at irregular intervals, secondly the continual shortage of artillery and cavalry, and finally because certain contingents were taken away from the corps, notably those of Reuss and Nassau (the Nassauers fought at Waterloo as we have seen), while others, such as six battalions from Mecklenburg-Schwerin, did not arrive in time.

Reuss

The rulers of Reuss objected immediately to their contingent coming under Prussian control. Their troops had previously been under Austrian command, and were expected to join the garrison of Mainz. Prince Hardenberg, the Prussian Chancellor, did his utmost to gain this contingent for Kleist. However, it marched off to the Middle Rhine, first joining the garrison of Frankfurt,[5] then later that of Mainz.

Mecklenburg-Strelitz

This state had furnished the Prussian Army with an excellent hussar regiment in the campaigns of 1813 and 1814. Kleist particularly lacked cavalry and hoped this regiment would join him. Indeed, the Congress of Vienna decided that this state would provide one-third of its contribution in the form of cavalry. Prussia came to an agreement with Mecklenburg on this issue on 25 May.[6] However, events overtook this decision and the war ended before these troops had been fully mobilised.

Oldenburg

Nominally 1,760 men strong, the Oldenburg Infantry Regiment numbered less than 1,500 when it joined Kleist. The Congress of Vienna had originally wished this contingent to be allocated to Wellington's forces, but its Duke, a relative of the Czar, instead marched to the Rhine. This small gain in manpower for the Prussians was not enough to counterbalance the losses elsewhere.

The Anhalt-Thuringian Brigade and the Hessians

The first detachments of the Hessian and Anhalt-Thuringian contingents arrived at the Rhine on 17 April. The Anhalt-Thuringian Brigade took up quarters in Neuwied and the first Hessian force camped at Langenschwalbach and St Goarshausen. The second detachment of Hessians followed shortly

---

[4] Pflugk-Harttung, *Bundestruppen*, p 111.
[5] Starklof, vol I, pp 169–171.
[6] Pflugk-Harttung, *Bundestruppen*, p 119.

afterwards and was stationed on the lower reaches of the River Lahn. The individual contingents of the Anhalt-Thuringians were amalgamated into battalions, then formed into provisional regiments and later organised into a brigade that drilled according to French regulations. The Hessians were likewise organised into a brigade that was referred to occasionally as a 'division' and even as an 'army corps'.

The headquarters of the Anhalt-Thuringian Brigade was in a similar situation with regard to staff officers as Kleist. Its commander, Oberst von Egloffstein, had to write all his own correspondence. Later, he appointed Major von Sonnenberg, from Anhalt-Bernburg, as his chief-of-staff, replacing him in due course with Kapitain von Mauderode. The Hessians had a proper staff organisation right from the beginning.

Organising the Corps

The gradual assembly of this corps with various contingents of varying sizes coming from different directions caused Kleist a number of problems. These included making sure their routes did not cross, and that they did not march through areas where heavy requisitioning had already taken place. Billets had to be found for the men, who often lacked equipment and needed further training. Kleist saw to many such matters personally, having the Weimar battalion parade before him, then visiting the Hessian troops on the Lahn and at Langenschwalbach. From here, he went on to Wiesbaden and Mainz, inspecting the Nassauers in the former place, and visiting the Austrian Archduke Charles in the latter. He then returned to Neuwied to cast an eye over the Thuringian Brigade. He had intended to inspect the remaining Hessian troops in Limburg on the Lahn on 6 and 7 May, but orders arrived from Blücher to march off, so he cancelled his plans.

During his visits, Kleist sent reports to his king. On 27 April he told Friedrich Wilhelm that he had found the Weimar Battalion in a good state and on 30 April that the Thuringian Brigade was not yet complete. On 10 May he was expecting the arrival of the Oldenburg, Waldeck, Detmold and Schaumburg contingents.

Kleist was aware of the psychological problems facing these men, some of whom had fought for the French in the Peninsula and other theatres. He tried to win over their hearts and minds, talking to each officer and sergeant he met, and speaking to many of the men. He saw to it that much of the equipment they lacked was obtained, and he implemented training programmes. Kleist had begun to turn his colourful mixture into a homogeneous body when he received Blücher's order to march towards the border on 5 May. His troops were not yet ready for action, and it would be difficult to continue their training once they were deployed on the frontier, so Kleist was not pleased with the situation.

Kleist had also not yet made full preparations for such a move. For instance, he had yet to set up a military postal system, although a military post commissioner was on his way from Berlin.[7] The route of the march would run

[7] Pflugk-Harttung, *Bundestruppen*, p 88.

through an area where supplies were sparse, and no provision for establishing magazines had been made.[8] Furthermore, the Bavarians who would cover the left flank of this march were being less than co-operative.[9] Obviously, Kleist felt that he was marching into the blue with a partially trained force.

Moving into Position

On 11 May Kleist's Hessians were the first to cross the Rhine, doing so at Ehrenbreitstein, near Koblenz. The remaining contingents crossed the next day at Neuwied. The dangers of the lack of a bridge across the Rhine became apparent during this manoeuvre. At this time the Hessians had only two infantry regiments, two of cavalry, two batteries and two supply columns, but still needed a whole day to cross the river by ferry. Were a retrograde movement ever to become necessary, the corps could find itself trapped against the Rhine. After crossing the river Kleist accompanied his troops as far as Wittlich before riding on to Trier, where he arrived on 13 May. The corps arrived at Trier on 18 and 19 May.

Next, the corps took up its cantonments. The Hessians were stationed with their right flank between the Saar and Moselle before Soest and Bibelhausen, the centre and left in front of Wiltingen, Ober-Emmel, Pellingen, Gutweiler and on the left bank of the Ruwer river. Three squadrons of hussars and two companies of Jäger deployed as outposts from Relingen and Saarburg to the heights of Kirf. They were in contact with the Bavarians. The Jäger were based at Munzingen, Sinz and Freudenberg from where they patrolled the border with France. The four hussar squadrons camped in Grevenmacher, guarding the line of communication with Luxembourg, and observing the border towards Remich.

The Anhalt-Thuringian Brigade was stationed along the left bank of the Moselle right of the Kyll and over the Sauer towards Vianden, Diekirch, Felz and Echternach, where Egloffstein established his headquarters. The Hessian dragoons attached to this brigade deployed one squadron at Diekirch to patrol the line of communication with Luxembourg and Arlon. The fortress of Luxembourg was thus at the centre of this deployment. The Hessians had by far the most dangerous positions which no doubt reflected the relative quality of the contingent.

The main objective of Kleist's corps at this point was to protect the border. An intelligence network was established along the frontier. Behind that, cannon were posted to fire alarm shots should the French attack the outposts. Assembly points to the rear were designated.

On 14 May, a letter from Blücher dated 10 May reached Kleist. This message informed Kleist that Napoleon was concentrating between Maubeuge and Condé, and that Wellington was convinced he was about to go over to the offensive. Blücher reported to Kleist that he was moving his army to counter any such invasion, and ordered him to deploy his corps around Trier and

[8] Pflugk-Harttung, *Bundestruppen*, pp 91–2, letter from Kleist to King Friedrich Wilhelm
     dated 10 May 1815.
[9] Pflugk-Harttung, *Bundestruppen*, p 89.

Order of Battle
North German Federal Army Corps[†]

Commanding General: *General der Infanterie Graf Kleist von Nollendorf*
later replaced by **Generallieutenant von Hake**

Chief-of-Staff:	*Oberst von Witzleben (Prussian)*
Commanding General, Hessian Troops:	*Generallieutenant Engelhardt*
Chief-of-Staff:	*Oberstlieutenant von Dörnberg*

1st (Hessian) Brigade   *Generalmajor Prinz zu Solms-Braunfels*
  2nd Grenadier Battalion von Lassberg
  Infantry Regiment Landgraf Karl   2 battalions[*]
  Infantry Regiment Prinz Solms   2 battalions[*]

2nd (Hessian) Brigade   *Generalmajor von Müller*
  1st Grenadier Battalion von Haller
  Infantry Regiment Kurfürst   3 battalions
  Infantry Regiment Kurprinz   2 battalions[*]
  Jäger Battalion

(Hessian) Cavalry Brigade   *Generalmajor von Warburg (Prussian)*
  Life Dragoon Regiment   4 squadrons
  Hussar Regiment   4 squadrons

Artillery   *Major von Bardeleben (Prussian)*
  Hessian 6-pounder Battery No. 1   8 guns
  Hessian 6-pounder Battery No. 2   8 guns

3rd (Anhalt-Thuringian) Brigade   *Oberst von Egloffstein (Weimar)*
1st Provisional Infantry Regiment   4 battalions
  Saxe-Weimar Line Infantry Battalion
  Saxe-Weimar Landwehr Battalion
  Anhalt-Dessau Line Infantry Battalion
  Anhalt-Bernburg-Köthen Jäger Battalion

2nd Provisional Infantry Regiment   3 battalions
  Saxe-Gotha Line Infantry Battalion
  Saxe-Gotha Landwehr Battalion
  Schwarzburg Line Infantry Battalion

3rd Provisional (Lippe-Waldeck) Infantry Regiment   2/3 battalions
  Lippe Line Infantry Battalion
  Lippe-Detmold Landwehr Battalion   *(arrived later)*
  Waldeck Line Infantry Battalion
Oldenburg Line Infantry Regiment   2 battalions

---

[*] These regiments were intended to have one fusilier and two musketeer battalions but their II. musketeer battalions were disbanded to bring the others up to strength.

[†] Vogt, pp 274–5.

Luxembourg, keeping in contact with the Bavarians. Kleist marked the letter with the dry comment, 'In current circumstances and with the number of troops, this is very difficult to achieve.'[10]

Kleist simply had too few troops to cover the area specified, and those he had were largely of too poor a quality to be able to offer any resistance to the French. If that were not enough, Trier itself was under Bavarian occupation (the land on the right bank of the Moselle had been promised to Bavaria at the Congress of Vienna), and relationships between the Prussians and the Bavarians were not friendly, so access to local resources was restricted. A second problem was that much of the Prussian garrison of the fortress of Luxembourg left to join the field army in mid-May, with Kleist having to send some of his men to replace them, which stretched his already weak force even further.

To make matters worse, Louis XVIII sent a representative, Général d'Arblay, to Trier supposedly to recruit any French deserters, but actually to observe events there. This area had been under French administration in recent years, and there were still strong sympathies for the French there. As certain of his recruits and officers might still have had leanings towards France, this could only make matters even more difficult for Kleist.

Fortunately, however, further troops joined the corps over the following weeks. On 20 May those of Waldeck, Schaumburg-Lippe and Lippe-Detmold arrived. They were formed into the 3rd Provisional Regiment of 1,200 men under Oberst Graf Waldeck. Kleist noted, 'The men of this regiment are strong and good looking, and seem to be of the best will. Their clothing and armament require some attention, which will, as far as possible, be given.'[11] They were stationed behind the Anhalt-Thuringian Brigade, forming a second line. On 29 May this was the regiment chosen to go to the fortress of Luxembourg to replace the Prussian troops who had just been called away. Two companies of Bernburg Landwehr arrived on 25 May. On 1 and 3 June the Oldenburg Regiment arrived, being allocated cantonments in Bitburg and Neuerburg. On 10 June three companies of poorly-trained Detmold Landwehr reached their designated positions, later being sent to Luxembourg. On 11 June more Hessian troops, Lassberg's Grenadier Battalion and the II. Battalion of the Regiment Kurfürst, joined their contingent. The II. Weimar Battalion was expected on 23 June.

At the front, all remained quiet. On 22 May Kleist passed on information from a conversation between Hessian hussars and the French outposts in which the French soldiers had said that they did not want to be at war. On 28 May, he reported to Blücher,

> The Prince of Hesse-Homburg has informed me that according to reports coming in, the enemy will stage a general movement towards Arlon between the 26th and 30th of the month...

Kleist was requesting help because he did,

---

[10] Pflugk-Harttung, *Bundestruppen*, pp 92–3.
[11] Pflugk-Harttung, *Bundestruppen*, p 98.

... not expect any support from the Bavarians, whose infantry are in Kaiserslautern, and whose cavalry have only posted a weak cordon. The III [Prussian] Army Corps that was on my right flank, has moved to join the army, so I have lost all contact to my right.[12]

Fortunately, nothing came of the feared French movement.

These difficulties continued to undermine Kleist's health; his jaundice grew worse. Nevertheless, he did not stop carrying out his duties. Kleist had the two companies of Bernburg Landwehr leave Luxembourg to join their line troops.[13] Wherever possible, Kleist preferred contingents from the same states to be together.

On 12 June further contingents of the Anhalt-Thuringian Brigade arrived.[14] This was small comfort to Kleist, who was having problems with some of his other allies. The Prince Elector of Hesse-Kassel was proving particularly difficult. He was obliged to provide 12,000 men, but insisted this figure was to include non-combatants. The third batch of his men arrived later than scheduled; he first sent supply trains, and then only two batteries of artillery. Gradually he give way and met his obligations.

Ready for Battle?

An army corps like Kleist's should, by definition, have been a force of mixed arms capable of independent action. This corps, with 17,000 infantry, but with only around 1,000 cavalry and eight guns, was not. It was not suitable for use as a battlefield formation.

Without greater financial resources, little could be done to compensate for these shortages. The quality of the troops was also very mixed. In a report to his king dated 30 April, Kleist described the Weimar Battalion as the best.[15] He continued by pointing out that the Bernburg Jäger were not riflemen at all, but actually musket-armed light infantry. He did not think much of the Gotha Line Battalion, although it was the largest. It trained according to the French regulations and was armed with a mixture of weapons. The infantry of the Electorate of Hesse were well trained and motivated but the cavalry was only average. The Schwarzburg Battalion was also potentially of reasonable quality but its first commander failed to maintain discipline and had to be replaced soon after the formation moved into France. Added to this great variation in capability was an equally great variation in the size of the contingents.

The troops of all the contingents were mainly young and inexperienced, even lacking practice in the use of their firearms, which was not helped by the chronic shortage of ammunition. Most units had very few veterans in their ranks, with even the officers and sergeants having little previous service. Items of uniform were in short supply, the footwear was worn out, two-thirds of the muskets were French, one-third British, supply trains were insufficient and field hospitals lacking.[16] Kleist certainly had his work cut out to turn this shambles into a fighting force.

[12] Pflugk-Harttung, *Bundestruppen*, p 98.

[13] Pflugk-Harttung, *Bundestruppen*, pp 100–1.

[14] Pflugk-Harttung, *Bundestruppen*, p 96.

[15] Pflugk-Harttung, *Bundestruppen*, p 126.

[16] Pflugk-Harttung, *Ausrüstung*, pp 380–1

The March to the Front

On 11 June a despatch dated 9 June arrived from Blücher. This ordered Kleist to be prepared to bring rations with him to supply his corps when marching to the Meuse as, 'With the infertility and exhaustion of the countryside, it is not possible to obtain supplies in this region.'[17] Blücher was making preparations for Kleist to join him in the Netherlands in the event of a French invasion, which he clearly anticipated. Kleist accordingly concentrated his forces. They received their orders to join Blücher on 16 June and marched off on the 17th. Kleist was approaching Luxembourg on 18 June when his health finally gave way. Ironically, he relinquished his command on the day that the Allies gained their major victory in this campaign. Kleist handed over command of his corps to the Hessian Generallieutenant von Engelhardt but remained with his troops until the 19th.

In the meantime the corps marched via Grevenmacher and Luxembourg to Arlon. The unpleasant weather and poor roads had their effect on these raw troops, so on 20 June they bivouacked just north of Arlon. At 3 p.m. that day Blücher's order sent from Wavre on 17 June arrived. In it, having just been defeated at Ligny, Blücher expressed his fear of a French invasion of Germany along the Lower Rhine. The North Germans were thus ordered to make forced marches to the area of Aachen and Jülich, and even to fall back on Cologne if necessary. The corps broke camp, and the troops marched off in a northerly direction, mostly reaching Martelange by late that evening, though the rear echelons only got there by midnight. At 4 a.m. the next morning, Engelhardt had them set out again and marched 20 km to the road junction at Bastogne, expecting to get as far as Eschweiler by the 24th.

Meanwhile, rumours of a French defeat started to spread. An officer sent to Blücher to obtain news confirmed the story, but only on the basis of information given by French deserters. Engelhardt therefore decided to wait for further news at Bastogne. Blücher's order, sent from Genappe on the 19th, arrived on the evening of the 21st. It read,

> Yesterday, 18th June, we won a complete victory. The enemy has been totally scattered and almost his entire artillery is in our hands. Your Excellency is thus to move on Sedan and Mézières immediately and to attempt to seize these places. The first shock can have a great effect on the French because they have no army with which to oppose us. I ask you above all to inform the Prince of Hesse-Homburg [the Prussian governor of Luxembourg] to move on Thionville with his garrison as soon as possible. Now is the time to be bold and not stick to theories and books.[18]

This clarified matters. More detail was given in a letter Blücher wrote from Merbes-le-Château on 21 June. This read,

> I must add to the news of the victory at Belle Alliance already sent to Your Excellency that the result of this magnificent day by far exceeded all our expectations. Over 200 cannon fell into our hands and the enemy escaped in

---

[17] Pflugk-Harttung, *Bundestruppen*, p 100.
[18] Voss, p 2.

the wildest flight and in total disarray with only 27. We are finding stragglers everywhere; they are offering no resistance, have destroyed their weapons and are trying to make their way home in peasants' clothing. Maubeuge has already been invested; Quesnoy and Landrecies will be today. I will be moving my headquarters close to Landrecies later today.

In such circumstances, it is most important to advance to the Meuse and to take Sedan, and I request Your Excellency to do so urgently. I will move with speed and force in the direction of Guise to exploit and increase the advantage gained. Thus, I wish Your Excellency to organise your arrangements in such a way that you link up with my left flank as soon as possible.

However, I should make you aware that during these operations by our centre, on our left flank General Thielemann has closely pursued Général Grouchy and the Armée de la Moselle via Namur. This French force is withdrawing into the Ardennes Département and I will bring General Thielemann back to me. Grouchy, fearing that his force may become surrounded, is to be expected to withdraw further into the interior of France.[19]

With these clear guidelines, Engelhardt now set off. On 22 June, he reached Neufchâteau from where he detached Egloffstein's brigade and a squadron of Hessian dragoons with two guns, sending this force to Bouillon. His Hessian brigades bivouacked at Florenville on 23 June where they were joined by the Prussian 2nd Field Pioneer Company. On 24 June his main body bivouacked at Bazeilles, while his vanguard took the Meuse crossings at Mouzon.

Kleist was not only a casualty of internal Prussian politics, but was also a victim of international political intrigues. Despite the enormous obstacles placed in his way by several parties involved in this episode, this most capable and professional commander did his utmost to carry out the task to hand. He largely succeeded in turning a mixed batch of poor recruits into an organised force. Kleist was clearly one of the most capable senior commanders of his generation, whose presence with Blücher's Army of the Lower Rhine during the difficult days of June 1815 would no doubt have significantly benefited the allied cause. However, politics prevented this talent being used to its greatest effect, though now his hard work in preparing his force for action was about to come to fruition.

[19] Voss, p 15.

Chapter 13

The Race to Paris

The Night of 18/19 June

We left the main part of the Prussian Army on the battlefield of Waterloo. On the night after the battle, parts of the army continued to move and had reached the following positions by early on 19 June. The main body of the I Army Corps was roughly in line with Wellington's army on the battlefield. The 1st Brigade was at Maison du Roi, the Brandenburg Dragoons and Uhlans under Gneisenau and Roeder were at Mellet, and the 6th Uhlans and Horse Battery Nr. 2 near Genappe. Most of the IV Army Corps remained on the battlefield, though parts of the 13th, 15th and 16th Brigades had all reached Genappe. The F./15th Infantry Regiment with small groups of infantry from the 16th Brigade and from the I Army Corps and a small part of the Reserve Cavalry were with Gneisenau at Mellet. Of the II Army Corps, the F./25th Infantry Regiment (5th Brigade), the Queen's Dragoons, Silesian Uhlans and 5th Kurmark Landwehr Cavalry under Oberst Graf von der Schulenburg had reached Genappe. The remainder of the 5th Brigade was part way to Genappe. The rest of the corps left Plancenoit at 11 p.m. and by 12 hours later had reached Mellery. The III Army Corps was still in action with Grouchy around Wavre.

The Anglo-Dutch-German Army bivouacked on the battlefield and Wellington retired to his headquarters in Waterloo. Blücher set up his headquarters at 11.30 p.m. at Genappe, from where the Field Marshal wrote a report for his king in Berlin, timed at 5.30 a.m., and sent orders to General von Kleist at 7 a.m.[1]

Orders for the Pursuit

On the morning of the 19th Gneisenau drafted orders for that day's movements. Blücher joined him at Gosselies by about 10 a.m., approved the orders and had them issued.

> I Corps is to move to Charleroi today and place its vanguard at Marchienne-au-Pont. II Army Corps is to march to Anderlues. It is to send its advance guard towards the Sambre and instruct it to cross by the bridge at Lobbes or Thuin. If the enemy should want to hold the Sambre today, then the lock gates must be opened, letting water run out so that the river can be forded at various points. If the bridges at Lobbes or Thuin have been destroyed, then they are to be rebuilt immediately. The IV Army Corps is to move to Fontaine l'Evêque today. This corps is to establish a line of communication to Mons as soon as possible.

[1] Quoted above on p 182.

Each army corps is to send a commissary to Fontaine l'Evêque. From there, when the line of communication with Mons is open, each commissary is to go to Mons, have bread baked and arrange provisions.

Headquarters is in Gosselies today. From today onwards, each army corps, once it has arrived at its designated point, is to send one officer and two NCOs to headquarters to receive orders. The 8th Hussar Regiment is to remain in Gosselies and cover the area across which the French corps moved to Wavre yesterday. The first battalion that arrives in Gosselies is to guard the headquarters and set up posts to maintain order there.[2]

Thus, three Prussian army corps were sent off in pursuit of the defeated French and the vanguards of both the I and II Army Corps were expected to cross the Sambre River on that first day, thus placing themselves between Grouchy and the most direct route to Paris. As we shall see below, only part of the II Army Corps carried out its orders. The I and IV Army Corps both moved off at daybreak, the former reaching Quatre Bras, the latter Mellet. Blücher ordered them to move on further, and at 3 p.m., they started off again, marching until evening.

II Army Corps on 19 June

It is interesting to note that Pirch I had been sent the order to cut off Grouchy's retreat before the Frenchman had heard news of Napoleon's defeat. It is also surprising that Grouchy managed to make his withdrawal to Gembloux on 19 June without interference from the Prussians, particularly as Gembloux is only a little further from Plancenoit than Grouchy's position north of Bierges that morning.

The order from Gneisenau that Kapitain Scharnhorst brought to Pirch left it up to him to react according to circumstances. According to his report, Pirch left Plancenoit at 11 p.m. on the 18th leaving behind the 5th Brigade and the three cavalry regiments that had gone part of the way to Genappe in pursuit of the French. From Plancenoit, Pirch marched via Maransart where the 7th Brigade rejoined him. By 11 a.m. on the 19th he and his men had reached Mellery, marching via Glabais and Bousval. The report of Sohr's brigade, the vanguard, says they arrived at 8 a.m., so it is likely that the entire corps, now consisting of three brigades of infantry, 4½ regiments of cavalry and the Reserve Artillery, completed its concentration by around 11 a.m. This march covered a distance of 17 km in nine hours, an indication of how tired the Prussians were after having been on their feet and almost without a break since the morning of the 18th. After their night march, a period of rest was due and was taken. Thus, one cannot attach any blame to these Prussians for having let Grouchy slip away.

The cavalry of the II Army Corps, however, came close to locating Grouchy's troops. In the afternoon of 19 June, some II Army Corps' units were only 10 km from the French in Gembloux, with Major Graf Hasslingen of the 2nd Neumark Landwehr Cavalry, part of the IV Army Corps reporting this to Gosselies. He mentioned that the II Army Corps was on his left, but did not

[2] Voss, p 2.

report the French positions to it. Thus, Grouchy made his way to Namur unhindered.

Pirch's report on the day's events read,

> I have the honour to reply most obediently to Your Excellency's order of yesterday. The patrols I sent out between Wavre and Mont St Guibert as well as the report received from Generalmajor von Borcke do not confirm the expected withdrawal by Marshal Grouchy. However, it is expected to be in the direction of Namur. Strong forces are occupying Mont St Guibert. General Borcke has six battalions between Ohain and Wavre, but has lost contact with General Thielemann. The latter has apparently withdrawn in the direction of Brussels after a battle the day before yesterday. In these circumstances, I believe I must use the freedom allowed in today's marching disposition to wait for Grouchy's movements so that I can act against him to the greatest advantage. I am also prepared to reconnoitre in the direction of St Guibert if nothing else happens. I will maintain contact with General Borcke.[3]

Grouchy did well to keep Pirch largely in the dark about his movements that day and was thus able to escape without a close pursuit from the Prussians.

Situation on the Evening of 19 June

That evening, Zieten's I Corps reached Charleroi and the surrounding area. The vanguard (Generalmajor von Jagow with the 3rd Brigade and the 1st Silesian Hussars) took up positions in Marchienne-au-Pont, while outposts spread out from Châtelet through Loverval to Montigny-le-Tilleul. The Reserve Cavalry under Generalmajor von Roeder covered the left flank at Fleurus, placing outposts along the Sambre and towards Namur.

The IV Army Corps bivouacked between Fontaine l'Evêque and Souvret. As nothing had been heard from the II Army Corps, Bülow sent his vanguard (Generalmajor von Sydow with four battalions, three cavalry regiments and one battery) towards Thuin at daybreak on the 20th. Another cavalry detachment went towards Mons. The 5th Brigade, still detached from II Corps, reached Anderlues and scouted as far as Lobbes and Thuin. Graf Schulenburg's cavalry remained at Gosselies.

The III Army Corps was at St Agatha-Rode and Limal, as described in Chapter 11.

Wellington's army followed up only slowly. It bivouacked around Nivelles. Prins Frederik's Corps moved towards the main body, and the Brunswick Corps camped at Lillois, north of Nivelles. Wellington himself had gone to Brussels where he finished writing his report to the Earl of Bathurst. He left it to the Prussians, already exhausted and battered from their previous exertions, to pursue the French.

As also outlined in Chapter 11, the French IV Corps spent that night around Le Boquet (between Mazy and Temploux), while the III Corps (Vandamme) was west of La Falize, Pajol at Gembloux and Exelmans in

[3] Lettow-Vorbeck, pp 462–3.

Namur. The remnants of Napoleon's main army were beginning to rally. D'Erlon and Reille were in Beaumont earlier in the day and Soult in Philippeville, while Bonaparte himself had left for Laon.

D'Erlon and Reille brought many of the remnants of their corps from Philippeville to Avesnes on the 19th and Morand took the parts of these corps that had gathered at Beaumont back to Avesnes. Here, he re-established order to such an extent that 12,000 men, including many from Jérôme's division who had stopped there, were in fighting condition again. Furthermore, the Imperial Guard, 5,000–6,000 men, the VI Corps and the reserve cavalry from Waterloo (Milhaud, Kellermann, Domon, Subervie and Lefèbvre-Desnoëttes) had also reached Avesnes by the evening. Soult also gathered a body of 5,000–6,000 men of all arms and from all corps at Philippeville and probably sent them off to Laon later on 19 June. The first fugitives arrived there late in the afternoon of the 20th, Soult himself on the 21st.

Though the Prussians had taken many stragglers prisoner during the 19th, they had no precise information on the whereabouts of the main French force. Despite their relatively vigorous pursuit, the Prussians had lost contact with it. In Charleroi, Zieten and his men heard rumours that Napoleon and part of his army had gone to Philippeville. Despite that, the army was ordered towards Avesnes the next day. Blücher's headquarters, still in Gosselies, issued the following disposition for 20 June,

> The I Army Corps is to leave Charleroi tomorrow, to march to Beaumont and send its vanguard to Solre-le-Château and a small observation party towards Florennes. From Beaumont, the road to Philippeville must be observed. The IV Army Corps is to march to Colleret, on the road between Beaumont and Maubeuge. The vanguard of the corps is to go towards Beaufort, cutting off Maubeuge on the right bank [of the Sambre]. Tomorrow, the 5th Brigade of the II Corps will come under the orders of Graf Bülow and is to advance along the left bank of the Sambre and around Maubeuge to cut it off. The II Army Corps is to march from Mellery to Thuin unless Général Grouchy's movements make other measures necessary.
>
> All corps are to march off at 7 a.m. Headquarters will move to Solre-sur-Sambre.[4]

Contact had been lost with the III Army Corps, but rumours of a battle between it and Grouchy at Wavre were rife.

Blücher wrote to Müffling,

> I beseech Your Excellency to do everything possible to ensure that the English army moves to Mons or Binche tomorrow, for we have to move quickly now to take full advantage of the terror of the lost battle. I also beseech you to make Lord Wellington aware that we now need the mortar and howitzer ammunition he has offered us. Please also enquire if the 6,000 rounds of artillery ammunition and the million of musket ammunition the English promised us can be sent to us at Mons, or at least designated for that place.[5]

4 Voss, p 4.
5 Voss, p. 4.

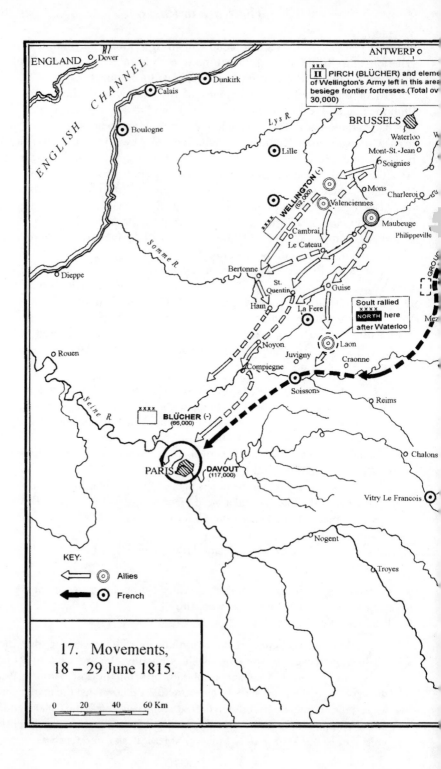

ENGLAND ⊙ Dover

ENGLISH CHANNEL

Calais ⊙
Dunkirk ⊙
Boulogne ⊙

ANTWERP ⊙

Lys R.

```
┌─────────────────────────────┐
│  xxx                        │
│  ☰ II  PIRCH (BLÜCHER) and eleme │
│  of Wellington's Army left in this area │
│  besiege frontier fortresses.(Total ov │
│  30,000)                    │
└─────────────────────────────┘
```

BRUSSELS ▨

Lille ⊙

Waterloo ○
Mont-St.-Jean ○
Soignies ○
Mons ○   Charleroi ⊙

WELLINGTON (-)
(52,000)

Valenciennes ⊙◎

Maubeuge ◎
Philippeville ○

Somme R.

Cambrai ⊙
Le Cateau ○

Dieppe ○

Bertonne ○

St.
Quentin ○

Ham ○

Guise ○

La Fere ⊙

```
┌─────────────────────┐
│  Soult rallied      │
│  xxxx               │
│  NORTH  here        │
│  after Waterloo     │
└─────────────────────┘
```

Mez

GROU

Rouen ○

Noyon ○

Compiegne ○

Seine R.

Juvigny ○

Laon ⊙
Craonne ○

Soissons ⊙

Reims ○

BLÜCHER (-)
(66,000)

Chalons ○

PARIS ▨

DAVOUT
(117,000)

Vitry Le Francois ⊙

Nogent ○

Troyes ○

KEY:

⇦ ◎ Allies

⬅ ⊙ French

17. Movements,
18 – 29 June 1815.

0   20   40   60 Km

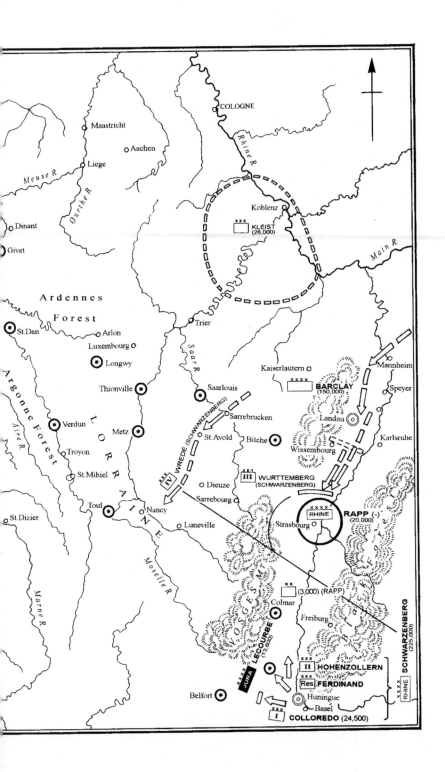

The Beginning of the Race

Hardly had the Allies defeated Bonaparte than their earlier rivalries surfaced again. Anxious to strengthen Prussia's hand at the peace table, Blücher was already thinking, early on 19 June in Genappe, what effects his advance on Paris might have and hoping to reach it before Wellington. Graf Nostitz, his ADC, recounted,

> The Prince's mood was, as one would expect, the most elated and happiest in the world. In his fantasies he painted the brightest pictures, even expressing the hope that he would rush ahead of the English army, reach Paris two days before it and enter the great city without any outside help. He even suggested that if he were able to sign the capitulation of Paris alone, he could demand reparations in which all the sums of money Prussia had earlier to pay to France would be refunded to the Fatherland. The orders for the advance were thus expressed in such a way that one could almost say that they overestimated the strength of man and beast. The great heat was becoming burdensome, as was the lack of organised supplies. Uninterrupted marching would of course increase the strain, particularly as not a single day of rest was planned.[6]

Gneisenau was of the same opinion as Blücher. He considered that a rapid advance into France and towards Paris would make the greatest military and political gains. Thus, he spoke against Grolman's suggestion that a third army corps should be sent against Grouchy, in addition to the II and III Army Corps already deployed.

In the past five days, the Prussian Army had fought two great battles and two significant rearguard actions and made several forced marches. Its supply situation beforehand was less than ideal and the marches and battles had exacerbated the existing problems greatly. The Prussian supply columns were only able to carry two days' worth of supplies and in the confusion that had arisen in the previous days, the columns had become separated from the troops, making the hungry men hungrier still. Additional supplies had been obtained from Brussels and Louvain, but these could not be moved to the troops immediately. The number of foot-sore stragglers was constantly increasing, despite harsh measures to discourage them. The circumstances spoke in favour of allowing the men a day of rest and recuperation. However, Blücher was a hard taskmaster who wanted to make the maximum gains from his recent successes.[7]

Wellington took a different approach. His 'General Order' of 20 June read,

> As the army is about to enter the French territory, the troops of the nations which are at present under the command of Field Marshal the Duke of Wellington, are desired to recollect that their respective Sovereigns are the Allies of His Majesty the King of France, and that France ought, therefore, to be treated as a friendly country. It is therefore required that nothing should be taken either by officers or soldiers, for which payment be not made. The Commissaries of the army will provide for the wants of the troops in

---

[6] Nostitz, vol II, p 46.
[7] Voss, pp 11–12.

the usual manner, and it is not permitted either to soldiers or officers to extort contributions.[8]

Wellington's 'Instructions for the Movement of the Army' of the same date read,

> The troops to march at 5 in the morning.
> The cavalry will march to the villages of Strepy [Strépy], Thieu, Boussoit sur Haine, and canton. These villages are between Rœulx and Mons. Baron Estorff's brigade of Hanoverian cavalry will canton in Givray [Givry] and Croix, and furnish outposts towards Maubeuge. The British cavalry will furnish a light brigade to do the outpost duties upon the Sambre, and the brigade will canton in Merbe St Marie, Bienne le Hapart [Bienne-lez-Happart], and Mont.[9]

When Müffling questioned Wellington on the lack of speed of his advance into France, the Duke responded,

> Do not press me on this, for I tell you, it cannot be done. If you knew the composition of the British Army and its habits better, then you would not talk to me about that. I cannot leave my tents and supplies behind. I have to keep my men together in their camp and supply them well to keep order and discipline. It is better that I get to Paris two days later than obedience break down.[10]

While Blücher was planning his advance on Paris, his men having already crossed the French border and almost commenced the investment of the fortress of Maubeuge, Wellington's troops had, on the whole, yet to regain the positions held at the start of the campaign, let alone enter France. Blücher now had his nose in front in the race for Paris. While Wellington's men were to march through what they were told to regard as friendly territory, Blücher intended to blaze a trail of destruction all the way to the enemy's capital.

As for Bonaparte, he had gone from Charleroi to Philippeville during the night of the 18th/19th with the hope of meeting Grouchy's forces. He sent out most urgent orders to Rapp, commander of the V Corps in Alsace, and to Lamarque in the Vendée, to force march their troops to Paris. Lecorbe, in the Jura Mountains, was ordered to defend Lyons, while all the fortress commanders along the Meuse River and the northern border were ordered to accelerate their preparations. Apparently, none of these orders ever arrived.

Napoleon spent some time on the 19th rallying and reorganising the fugitives arriving at Philippeville, sending out officers along all possible routes to gather everybody they could. Later, Laon was designated the rallying point. He also instructed his brother Jérôme to go to Avesnes to rally troops there as well. On 19 June, Soult issued orders designating the rallying points as follows: I, II and VI Corps at Laon; the Reserve Artillery at La Fère; the Reserve Cavalry at Marle, St Quentin, Rethel, Verviers and Rheims; the Guard at Soissons.[11]

---

8 *WD*, vol XII, p 493.
9 *WSD*, vol X, p 538.

10 Müffling, *Leben*, p 251.
11 Voss, p 7 fn.

Napoleon also wrote two letters to his brother Joseph in Paris, one for public consumption and the other more honest. The first letter admitted that a battle had been lost but the secondly spoke frankly of the disastrous state of the army. Napoleon indicated he had lost contact with Grouchy and suspected his entire force had been taken prisoner but, despite that, he intended to continue the struggle and hoped to reverse his fortunes. He then rode via Beaumont and Avesnes to Laon, arriving there on the evening of 20 June, expecting to find fresh forces to hand. Only a single battalion of National Guard awaited him, ready to defend this fortress. Napoleon was going to have to find his new army elsewhere. Grouchy's skilful withdrawal was to provide his only hope.

Orders of 20 June

Blücher had the following orders issued from Gosselies on the morning of 20 June:

> [To Generallieutenant von Pirch I]
>
> Several reports agree that the enemy will most likely have reached Namur or at least have fallen back so far that we can no longer cut him off from his retreat from the Meuse. Thus, it is now more important to carry out the intended movement on Avesnes, so Your Honour is to move the II Army Corps to Thuin, in accordance with the disposition given today. Your Honour is to have Oberstlieutenant von Sohr stay close to Marshal Grouchy with two cavalry regiments, half a horse battery and two light battalions and to have him observe the enemy's movements, while staying in contact with Generalmajor von Borcke and Generallieutenant von Thielemann. I have ordered Oberst Graf Schulenburg to lead the way to Thuin with the Reserve Cavalry of the II Army Corps.
>
> No confirmed reports have come in as to whether the bridges at Thuin and Lobbes are passable. Your Honour should send scouts to establish that the enemy has left the Sambre. In any case, the bridge at Aulne is to be passed and held by our infantry.
>
> [Choose the] weakest battalion and two squadrons of Landwehr cavalry from the II Army Corps, [and order] half to remain in Gosselies, half in Charleroi. Your Honour is to instruct [whoever is] the most senior officer with them that he is to gather any stragglers from the various corps who are disturbing the peace and restore order. He is then to send the bodies of men so gathered in detachments to join the blockading corps at Maubeuge. I have ordered Oberst Graf Schulenburg to leave two squadrons of Landwehr at Gosselies, and he is to inform Your Honour which squadrons he had chosen.
>
> Generallieutenant von Thielemann has been ordered not to follow the enemy beyond Namur. Your Honour is, however, to order Oberstlieutenant von Sohr to follow the enemy beyond Namur to establish his line of march and then to move on Walcourt via St Gérard and Florennes. Oberstlieutenant von Sohr is to send his reports directly to me via Charleroi and will be continually updated as to the whereabouts of Headquarters.[12]

[12] Voss, pp 13–14.

This portrait of Blücher, who died just four years after
Waterloo, shows more accurately how he must have
appeared around 1815 than the images painted by
romantic artists later in the century.

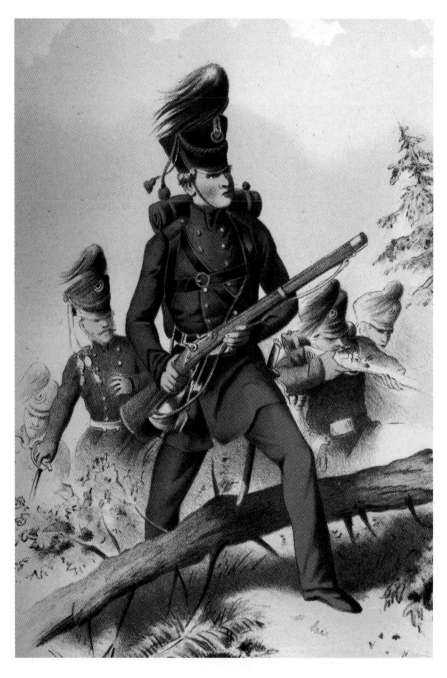

Lützow's Freikorps. This formation, raised in 1813 and dressed in black
uniforms with red facings and yellow buttons, Germany's national colours,
symbolised German nationalism in the Wars of Liberation (1813–15). It was
raised throughout the German speaking territories, but its non-Prussian members
were dismissed on demobilisation after Napoleon's abdication in 1814.
The 900 remaining veterans were employed in 1815 as the cadre for the new
25th Infantry Regiment. The veterans retained their black uniforms during the
1815 campaign but by then they must have been very threadbare.

Soldiers of the 25th Infantry Regiment in regulation uniform, 1815. It is unlikely that any members of the regiment, other than perhaps officers, wore this uniform during the 1815 campaign. As well as the black uniforms worn by the 900 Lützow veterans, the uniforms of the 3rd and 10th Ersatz (Replacement) Battalions were worn during this campaign. Their members were raw levies with no experience of war and little training. This unstable mixture of some veterans with a larger number of new conscripts was typical of Blücher's 'Army of the Lower Rhine' in 1815.

Prussian infantryman during the occupation of France, 1815–18.
This contemporary plate by Genty shows that the new regulation
uniform for the Prussian infantry did come into circulation during the
occupation and was then supplied to troops in France.

Left: The Duke of Wellington. While the Duke's performance in this campaign left much to be desired, Wellington certainly won the propaganda battle and is seen by many as the victor of Waterloo.

Left: Louis XVIII, King of France. A maligned figure, this Bourbon king was unpopular both at home and abroad. At home, he restored many of the royalists' privileges, to the annoyance of the population. Abroad, he was despised as the king of a country that had plundered Europe for a generation. He owed his throne to the Duke of Wellington whose political machinations and military success restored his dynasty to the throne of France.

Joseph Fouché, the French Minister of Police. He ran
with the foxes and hunted with the hounds. It is
possible that he was an important source of information
from Paris for Wellington prior to the outbreak of
hostilities. It is also possible that it was Fouché's
deception of Wellington that caused the Duke to delay
his movements on 15 June 1815. Fouché remained
active behind the scenes in Paris during the allied
advance on the city, still up to his double-dealing
games.

The narrow bridge at Genappe, which played a role on both
17 and 18 June. Its possession on 17 June ensured the security of
Wellington's withdrawal from Quatre Bras and slowed the French
advance. On the following evening, it delayed the French retreat
and allowed the pursuing Prussians to catch up.
Wellington Museum, Waterloo

Left: Generallieutenant Graf Carl von Alten. Alten commanded Wellington's 3rd Division, a brigade each of British, KGL and Hanoverian troops.
Historisches Museum, Hanover

Below left: The ruins of Hougoumont. This watercolour by James Rouse shows the remains of the château after the battle, viewed from the south.
Wellington Museum, Waterloo

Right: Bülow's artillery and the 1st Line Regiment of the King's German Legion. This late nineteenth-century watercolour is typical of that period.

Below: The ruined farm buildings of Papelotte, by an unidentified artist.
Wellington Museum, Waterloo

Above: The Prussian memorial at Plancenoit. Situated on the road from Plancenoit to la Belle Alliance, this monument is still standing today and has been surrounded by protective fencing.
Wellington Museum, Waterloo

Above left: Bülow breaks through at Plancenoit. The determined Prussian attacks on, and eventual capture of, this village in the right rear of the French positions, played a crucial role in deciding the outcome of the battle of Waterloo.

Left: Lithograph view of the village of Plancenoit by Jacques Sturm. The church was the focal point of the bitter Prussian assaults. The Prussian memorial can be seen at the extreme left of the picture.
Wellington Museum, Waterloo

Above: Marshal Grouchy. Napoleon's last marshal did much to keep the defeated *Armée du Nord* together and give Napoleon the option of continuing the war after Waterloo. His actions in the campaign have attracted much controversy and Grouchy wrote his own defence.

Above right: Halkett and Cambronne in the final moments of the battle. Halkett, at the head of his Osnabrückers, captures Cambronne, who is trying to take 'French leave'.

Right: The inn of la Belle Alliance, where Blücher and Wellington supposedly met at the close of the battle. The Prussian general wanted the battle named for this symbolic place. Wellington chose the name of the location of his headquarters instead. That, after all, would emphasise his own role and diminish that of his allies. Wellington also claimed, probably correctly, that, 'the meeting took place after ten at night, at the village of Genappe' (*WSD*, X, p. 509), rather than at la Belle Alliance.

Above: Francis Egerton, first Earl of Ellesmere, one of
Wellington's close advisors. Ellesmere translated
Clausewitz's history of the 1812 campaign into
English and assured Wellington of the accuracy of
Lord Liverpool's translation of Clausewitz's work
on 1815.

Right: Charles Arbuthnot. Another of Wellington's
closest advisors, Arbuthnot even had rooms in Apsley
House, the Duke's London residence. With Gurwood,
he advised Wellington on how to deal with Lord
Liverpool's translation of Clausewitz's history of
the campaign of 1815.
V & A Library Picture

John Gurwood, editor of Wellington's *Dispatches*. This painting, by James Hall, shows Gurwood in the uniform of esquire to the Duke of Wellington, as Knight of the Bath. He is holding the Duke's banner in his right hand. It was Gurwood who, more than any other, assisted Wellington in his selection of which of his papers to include in the published dispatches.

V & A Library Picture

[To Generallieutenant von Thielemann]

Your Excellency will have been informed of the glorious victory over the enemy on the 18th. The enemy is in full retreat on Beaumont. It is my intention to follow him without delay and to march to Avesnes with the army. Today, the I Army Corps has already been directed towards Beaumont, the IV Corps to Colleret on the Maubeuge road, and parts of the II Corps to Thuin. Since the report Your Excellency sent me at one o'clock in the night of the 18th to the 19th, I have heard nothing further from you. It was my intention that, if at all possible, Your Excellency should attack the enemy forces opposing you. I do not know if you have received the orders to this effect from me.

There are now two possibilities: either Your Excellency is still facing the enemy in the area of Wavre, or they have retired, probably to Namur, and you have followed them there. If it is in any way advantageous, then stay on the enemy's heels and do all the damage you can. If not, then your III Army Corps should quickly follow the movement of the main body of the army towards Beaumont. If you are close to Wavre, then march via Fontaine l'Evêque. If, on the other hand, you are nearer Namur, then march via Charleroi.

In no event is Your Excellency to follow the enemy via Namur. He will probably withdraw via Philippeville. I have ordered Oberstlieutenant von Sohr to take two cavalry regiments, half a horse battery and two battalions in the direction of Namur, marching via Florennes to Walcourt. If Your Excellency does march via Charleroi, you would be advised to make contact with Oberstlieutenant von Sohr to cover your left flank.

Today, I am going with my Headquarters to Solre-sur-Sambre.[13]

Progress on 20 June

The I Army Corps marched in two columns, expecting to encounter the French. Despite abatis on the roads and in the woods, it reached the French border without incident. (At that time, the border between France and Belgium ran further to the north than it does today). Twelve abandoned guns were taken on the way but the poor roads delayed the march. The corps only reached Beaumont that evening and bivouacked there for the night. An advance guard was sent on to Solre-le-Château and arrived there at 7.30 the next morning, having taken nine hours to cover 13 km on bad roads.

The IV Army Corps had been ordered to cross the Sambre. Information on the state of the bridges was contradictory and uncertain. Thus, in addition to the vanguard sent at daybreak to Lobbes and Thuin, a detachment was sent to the abbey of Aulne, 4½ km north-east of Thuin. After crossing the river, both parties were to link up and go via St Christophe and Colleret to Beaumont, while the main body of the corps was to march via Binche to Merbes-le-Château.

The vanguard found that the bridge at Lobbes was intact and captured it and Bülow decided to move the main body back from Binche to cross the river there. Because of this diversion, the planned march could not be completed. The vanguard only reached Ferrière-la-Petite; the lead units of the main body

[13] Voss, p 14.

(13th Brigade and the Reserve Cavalry) led by Bülow in person reached Colleret; and the rest of the corps arrived in Montignies and Lobbes late that night.

The 5th Brigade marched in front of the IV Army Corps via Binche and Villiers-Sire-Nicole. From there, in the afternoon, 100 men from the Elbe Landwehr Cavalry Regiment together with half a horse battery rode off to start observing the fortress of Maubeuge from the Sambre to the Mons road. A Hanoverian hussar regiment from Estorff's brigade coming from Binche along the road to Bavay linked up with the Prussians.

Wellington's army camped on the night of 20 June with its right flank at Mons and its left at Binche with its headquarters there. His cavalry was spread between the villages from Binche to Le Rœulx and the Brunswickers were at Soignies.

The Combat at Namur, 20 June

Pirch first had confirmation of Grouchy's withdrawal at 5 a.m. on 20 June. He had his vanguard under Oberstlieutenant von Sohr with its two hussar regiments, three fusilier battalions and one horse battery move out. The remainder of the II Army Corps followed with the 6th Brigade in front. About 10 a.m. they reached Gembloux and established that the French had now abandoned it. The Reserve Cavalry of the III Army Corps now came up from the direction of Wavre. It left the road to Namur for Sohr's men, while itself moving right down the road towards Nivelles along which the French IV Corps' baggage and wounded were withdrawing.

The Prussians caught up with Grouchy's men at the village of Boquet, throwing them out after a short fight. The situation of the French IV Corps was exposed because their supporting divisions from III Corps had fallen back in face of Thielemann's Reserve Cavalry. Grouchy had ordered Vandamme to cover the withdrawal, but he had spent the night in Namur and did not receive the order.

Grouchy therefore turned on his pursuers, the IV Corps stopped at La Falize and bought enough time to bring the wounded and the baggage trains under the protection of the old fortress walls of Namur. The French lost three guns, two of which were recaptured in a later counter-attack, in a brief combat at La Falize. Two Saxon hussar squadrons came into action here for the first time, attacking the French infantry (these units had joined Thielemann's force late on the 19th), but the French formed square and reached the safety of a wood.

From this point onwards, the terrain was unsuited for cavalry action, so Sohr now committed his three fusilier battalions, followed by the 6th Brigade. Step by step, Grouchy moved through the suburbs of Namur and behind the city walls.

At 3 p.m. Pirch received Blücher's order to march to Thuin. However, before carrying this out, Pirch came into contact with and followed one of Grouchy's columns. The French retired into Namur through the Brussels gate. Pirch attempted to storm the gate, but the French deployed strong forces there, starting an infantry battle that lasted several hours. Harkort, an officer in the 1st Westphalian Landwehr, witnessed the scene and wrote,

> With exemplary courage, the Prussian infantry columns pushed against the enemy, throwing him out of the suburbs, taking them.
>
> The French musketry was so effective that, along the long avenue where the Prussian skirmishers and columns were advancing, all the garden gates and windows were smashed, the railings broken and at man's height, all the trees stripped of bark. The blood of the fallen ran in the gutters.[14]

In his report, Pirch stated that he did not intend to stage a serious assault on Namur. Nevertheless, the 6th Brigade lost some 44 officers and 1,272 men here before Pirch broke off his attack.[15]

At 6 p.m. Grouchy started to evacuate Namur, falling back in the direction of Dinant, where most of his force had arrived by early the next day. At 8 p.m. Teste's division, the French rearguard, fell back from Namur, blowing up the Brussels gate. They reached Dinant at dawn on the 21st.

The Prussians pushed into the town following up closely at first, but broke off their pursuit when the French blocked the only bridge with piles of burning wood. The high water level prevented attempts to ford the river. Once the obstacle was removed from the bridge, a detachment of 100 Prussian cavalry moved along the right (east) bank of the Meuse on the Dinant road. This road ran into a defile and abatis blocked it at several points, so all that could be done was to take a few stragglers prisoner. On Blücher's orders, only Sohr's cavalry brigade followed after this detachment.[16]

The main body of the Prussian II Army Corps bivouacked outside the town and in the meantime the infantry of the III Army Corps had only reached Gembloux, where they spent the night. With considerable skill, Grouchy had therefore escaped from the trap the Prussians tried to set for him. He had kept his force intact and in good order. Thanks to Grouchy, Napoleon still had a formed body of men around whom he could put together a new army with which to resist the coming invasion of France.

Orders for 21st June

Contrary to Blücher's original intention the Prussian headquarters was actually moved to Merbes-le-Château on the afternoon of the 20th. From there, the 'Disposition for 21 June' was released. It read,

> The I Corps is to march as close as possible to Avesnes, with its vanguard encircling Avesnes on both banks of the Helpe. As the roads are said to be in a poor state because of the rain and enemy waggons, the corps will have to seek a road more to the right, but if possible is to advance to the Avesnes wood.
>
> The IV Corps is to march along the Maubeuge road in the direction of Landrecies as far as Maroilles. The part of the corps that has today blocked off

[14] Harkort, p 69.
[15] Lettow-Vorbeck, p 464.
[16] Clausewitz, p 142.

Maubeuge on the right bank of the Sambre is to remain there until relieved by the troops of the II Corps.

Should our troops take the fortifications at the camp of Rousies [a fortified camp near Maubeuge on the southern bank of the Sambre] today, then the infantry is to stay there until relieved by the infantry of the II Corps. The road from Maroilles to [le] Quesnoy through the Forest of Mormal is to be closely observed.

The 5th Brigade is to remain on the left bank of the Sambre river before Maubeuge, blockading it as closely as possible. The cavalry under Oberst Graf Schulenburg is to depart from Thuin and move to Maubeuge along the right bank of the Sambre to cut the town off. One regiment is to be sent to Berlaimont to observe the Forest of Mormal and to link up with the English. The remainder of the II Corps is to march as far as possible to reach the area of Maubeuge on the right bank of the Sambre, thus uniting the entire corps again.

All units are to march off at 6 o'clock.

Headquarters will move either to Noyelles or Faisnières en Thierache.[17]

To bring all available forces into play, Blücher also sent a letter to the North German Federal Army Corps on the morning of 21 June ordering it to move to join up with his left wing and then head for Sedan.[18]

The execution of these orders soon brought an unexpected success and one on the most direct and important route to Paris.

The Fall of Avesnes

Exhausted by its great efforts in the previous days, the I Corps started off at 1 p.m. on 21 June. Its vanguard (3rd Brigade with the 1st Silesian Hussars) arrived at Avesnes at 4 p.m. and Zieten immediately had all the howitzers of the Reserve Artillery brought up to commence a bombardment of the fortress. A 12-pounder battery later reinforced them. Avesnes was a formidable Vauban fort and had been equipped as the main depot for the *Armée du Nord*. The bombardment continued until nightfall and shortly afterwards the Silesian Schützen threw back a sortie by the garrison, though losing 15 men in the process. The bombardment recommenced at midnight, soon hitting the main powder magazine, which exploded. Reiche, Zieten's chief-of-staff, explained in more detail,

> General Ziethen, hoping to surprise the enemy, after having surrounded the fortress, had the brigade batteries' howitzers come up to 700–800 paces from the main wall. His demand for capitulation being rejected, he had the town bombarded until 8 o'clock in the evening, but without success. The enemy only replied with three heavy guns, which had little effect. To save unnecessary waste of ammunition, the General then had the bombardment stopped, though the enemy used this respite to make a sortie against our skirmishers, who had seen nobody on the walls. The sortie was beaten back without making the slightest change in the positions of our skirmishers.

---

[17] Voss, pp 14–15.
[18] Quoted above on pp 182–3.

We were already considering leaving a detachment at Avesnes, breaking camp the next morning and continuing the march, when the commander of the artillery of the army corps, Oberst Lehmann, an experienced gunner, expressed regret at the ending of the bombardment. At least we should not let the enemy sleep, he said, and asked permission to reopen fire at midnight. The general agreed and we went back to headquarters with no great expectations of the effectiveness of the second bombardment.

Because of lack of space, I was sharing a room with General Ziethen. We had just laid down on the straw and were about to drop off when a sudden loud explosion made us jump. It was as if a shell had landed in the house and blown it up. The night was brightly lit up. The puzzle was soon solved. A shell had landed in the powder magazine of the fortress and blown it sky high with the force of an earthquake. It was the fourteenth shot that did this.[19]

The fortress capitulated and was handed over to the Prussians the next morning. The garrison, 200 veterans and three battalions of National Guards, were disarmed, the former being taken prisoner, the latter sent home. The spoils included 47 heavy guns, 15,000 rounds of artillery ammunition and a million musket cartridges, suitable for use in the Prussian muskets, as well as large stocks of provisions. The Prussians now had a base from which to supply their operations in France. The I Army Corps then marched off in two columns, bivouacking 4 km north-east of Avesnes at the fork of the road from Maubeuge and Beaumont.

21 June

Early on the morning of the 21st, the IV Army Corps reconnoitred the fortress of Maubeuge, demanding its capitulation. Its commander refused, so the brigades left behind in Lobbes were called up. Corps Headquarters, the 13th Brigade and the Reserve Cavalry reached Maroilles, surrounding the fortress of Landrecies with cavalry and penetrating a suburb on the left bank with a battalion of infantry. The 15th and 16th Brigades reached the area between Eclaibes and Beaufort that evening, with the 14th Brigade remaining south of Maubeuge to blockade it from that side.

At 3 p.m. on the 20th the II Army Corps received the order issued in Gosselies that morning, but as it was engaged with Grouchy at Namur, was unable to carry out its instructions. However, on 21 June it moved via Charleroi to Thuin, with its leading units reaching Thuin by the end of that day. The detachment of Oberstlieutenant von Sohr (F./14th, F./23rd, 3rd Hussars, 5th Hussars, and five guns) was delayed by several barriers erected on the road running along the Meuse. It could only watch from afar as the French withdrew via Dinant. Close to Dinant, it turned right and marched to Florennes, reaching there about 2 a.m. on 22 June.

The III Army Corps marched from Gembloux via Sombreffe on the 21st, where it joined up with its Reserve Cavalry, and then to the area around Charleroi.

Both Sohr and Thielemann reported Grouchy's withdrawal to Dinant to

---

[19] Weltzien, vol II, p 235.

Blücher, whose headquarters moved to Noyelles. Sohr's report arrived first; Thielemann's only in the evening of the 21st.

Wellington's army took its first steps into French territory on 21 June, its main body moving to Bavay, its right via Mons to Valenciennes, blockading the latter and the small fort of le Quesnoy. The Duke set up his headquarters in Malplaquet, scene of the battle of 11 September 1709, and on 22 June issued a proclamation to the people of France declaring his army not to be their enemy, but their liberator.

Blücher now decided to move up the two army corps still to the rear and to use one of them to invest the fortresses in this area, while advancing further into France with the other three army corps. His headquarters had a clear idea of what it was going to do next as can be seen from the letter Gneisenau wrote to Müffling on the afternoon of the 21st,

> I report to Your Honour that tomorrow, the 22nd, the army will take the following positions:
>
> The I Corps Etrœungt, the vanguard towards la Capelle, the lead units to the Oise, Avesnes will be closely invested.
>
> The IV Corps to Fesmy [-le-Sart], vanguard at Hannapes, detachments to Guise; Landrecies closely invested.
>
> The II Army Corps is to blockade Maubeuge and to prepare to take over the blockades of Landrecies and Avesnes; one brigade is to go to Beaumont and from there to continue to Chimay and Mariembourg, clearing the immediate area and blockading Givet and Philippeville.
>
> Tomorrow's march is to be made quickly to reunite the army corps that have become separated by the difficult marches along crossing paths. No news has been heard from the III Army Corps.
>
> It is now being considered if the march should be continued to Laon and Soissons, or, leaving the Oise to the left, on Noyon and Compiègne. I consider the latter better and ask that the Duke of Wellington be told this.
>
> I enclose several captured reports on the French fortresses, particularly one on Cambrai that will be interesting to the English. Where is the siege artillery the English promised and which fortress are they going to attack themselves?[20]

22 June

The I Corps attained the positions described in the letter to Müffling. It marched off from Avesnes at midday, leaving behind two battalions to garrison that place. The main body reached Etrœungt, the vanguard la Capelle, with the 1st Silesian Hussars going to Etréaupont, sending a scouting party via Trélon to Chimay.

The IV Corps blockaded Landrecies with a detachment under Generallieutenant von Hake. This consisted of four battalions of the 13th Brigade, one regiment of the 15th Brigade, the 2nd Pomeranian Landwehr Cavalry, two squadrons of the 2nd Silesian Landwehr and one battery. Its vanguard, under Generalmajor von Sydow, consisted of the 3rd Neumark

Landwehr Regiment, one battalion of the 1st Silesian Regiment, the 8th Hussars, the 1st Pomeranian Landwehr Cavalry and half of Horse Battery Nr. 12. It marched to Hannapes, while the Reserve Cavalry advanced along the opposite bank of the Sambre-Oise canal to Étreux, bivouacking with the main body (15th and 16th Brigades and the Reserve Artillery) at Fesmy. The 14th Brigade marched off about midday, after having been relieved by the II Army Corps, but only reached as far as Maroilles.

Both corps had been instructed to send scouting parties as far as the Oise River. Those of the IV Corps reached le Cateau-Cambrésis, Wassigny and Guise. Guise was found to be unoccupied by the French, but the fort south of the Oise was found to be occupied.

In the disposition for the 22nd the II Corps received the following orders,

> The 5th and 7th Brigades of the II Army Corps are to blockade Maubeuge closely, to attempt to seize the outlying works and to make all preparations for a siege. Communications bridges are to be laid across the Sambre. The 6th Brigade is to advance sufficiently to be in a position to take over the blockades of Avesnes and Landrecies on the 23rd. For that purpose a regiment of Kurmark Landwehr Cavalry is to be attached to the brigade. One regiment of infantry, two squadrons and two guns are to blockade Landrecies. The other two regiments of infantry with one regiment of cavalry and six guns are to blockade Avesnes. The 8th Brigade with the remaining Kurmark Landwehr Cavalry Regiment is to advance to Beaumont and, on the 23rd, to Chimay and Mariembourg. They are to clear this area of the enemy and prevent the population being armed. Moreover, this brigade is required to cut off Philippeville and Givet and, if possible, to open communications with General von Kleist, who has orders to march towards Mézières and Sedan.
>
> The Queen's Dragoons, Silesian Uhlans and half a horse battery are to march to Ors, south of Landrecies, where they are to remain at the disposal of Headquarters.
>
> Generallieutenant von Pirch I will direct all these blockades, but is to concentrate on seizing Maubeuge. Oberst Graf Schulenburg is in command of the cavalry allocated to the blockades.[21]

However, the II Army Corps only received the disposition for the 21st at Thuin on the morning of the 22nd and Pirch based his subsequent orders to the troops on this. At 7 a.m. Schulenburg passed these on to his command. Those to Oberstlieutenant von Kamecke, commander of the Queen's Dragoons, read,

> As a result of orders just received from Headquarters, Your Honour is to take the Queen's Regiment to Ors, on the other side of Landrecies, today. Here, it will remain at the disposal of Headquarters, which is going to Catillon-sur-Sambre today. The Silesian Uhlan Regiment and half a horse battery have received the same instructions, but are staying with me for the time being, as I would otherwise have to leave my cannon unguarded. The II Army Corps

21 Voss, pp 19–20.

has been allocated to Maubeuge, Avesnes and Landrecies. General von Pirch will command all these sieges, and I will command all the cavalry involved and remain at Maubeuge.[22]

Because his corps was spread out over a wide area, Pirch's hope of concentrating at Maubeuge that day, as expressed in a letter to Blücher, could not be fulfilled. His vanguard reached Colleret by midday, and later relieved the 14th Brigade at Maubeuge. The 7th Brigade arrived there that evening.

Following the orders of 20 June, the III Army Corps marched to Beaumont, securing its left flank with detachments along the roads to Philippeville and Chimay.

Wellington's army, in contrast to the Prussians, continued to spread out on its march. His headquarters, II Corps and Reserve Cavalry advanced to le Cateau-Cambrésis, with Vivian's cavalry brigade going 3½ km further, to St Benin. Wellington's I Corps, now under General Byng (replacing the Prince of Orange who had been wounded at Waterloo), and the Nassau Contingent bivouacked at Gommegnies. The Reserve remained in Bavay, while parts of Prins Frederik's Netherlands Corps took over the investment of le Quesnoy and Valenciennes.

The Prussians were already one day's march nearer to Paris than Wellington.

23 June

To allow the III Corps to catch up with the main body of the Prussian Army, the I and IV Corps were allowed a day of rest on 23 June. Thielemann marched to Avesnes as ordered and resupplied his men from the captured magazines. The II Corps left one battalion and two squadrons from the 6th Brigade to secure Avesnes for the time being. Generalmajor von Dobschütz, commander of the Prussian forces in the Rhine Province, was ordered to take two of the four battalions garrisoning the fortress of Wesel on the Rhine and send them by waggon to Avesnes. They were to move via Liège and Namur and set up staging posts along the road from Namur, Charleroi and Beaumont, freeing those troops in Liège under Major von Weitershausen, particularly 6-Pounder Battery Nr. 36, which would then be able to rejoin the 1st Brigade.

The II Corps and the North German Federal Corps were now both placed under the command of Prinz August of Prussia, with Generallieutenant von Hake taking Kleist's former place at the head of the Federal Corps. Oberst von Lettow replaced Hake as commander of the 13th Brigade, while Oberst-lieutenant von Othegraven replaced Oberst von Loebell as commander of the 15th Brigade since Loebell had been appointed commandant of Avesnes. The king ordered Prinz August to take over command of the sieges. All II Corps' troops, with the exception of four cavalry regiments and half a horse battery, were allocated to the Prince's command and Pirch's corps therefore ceased to be part of the field army.

The vanguard of the IV Corps under Generalmajor von Sydow moved to Guise and invested the defences there. These consisted of the walled town

---

[22] Albedyll, p 323.

and a strong fort on a steep hill above it that served as a citadel.[23] The vanguard reported that French troops were assembling in Laon under Marshal Soult's command and that a French army was apparently marching from the Franco-German border in Lorraine. Patrols also established that the garrison of St Quentin was weak and the fortress little prepared for a siege.

Scouting parties from the I and IV Corps reported that they had located French cavalry outposts at Ribemont and Monceau-le-Neuf in the area between Guise and Laon. On sighting the Prussian patrols, these outposts had withdrawn to Crécy. According to the locals, an unspecified number of French troops had assembled there.

Blücher wrote to his king,

> ... The enemy, fleeing at great speed to Laon, can only offer resistance with the corps of Generals Vandamme and Grouchy. If the lethargy of the armies on the Rhine [Prussia's allies] allow him, he will draw on Generals Rapp and Lecorbe as he has just done with the corps in Lorraine under Gérard.[24]

There was conflicting news of Bonaparte's movements. According to reports received by Zieten on 22 and 23 June, particularly the statement of a captured colonel of the Imperial Guard, Napoleon had intended to go to Laon, but actually went to Mézières. It is noteworthy that Blücher's headquarters no longer appeared to be very interested in the whereabouts of the 'Ogre', but had its attention focused on Laon, where the main body of the French forces appeared to be. This was despite Blücher's declared intention to put Napoleon up in front of a firing squad should he ever fall into Prussian hands.[25]

Wellington's army also took a day of rest on the 23rd. The only units to move were one brigade of infantry, the 6th Hanoverian under Lyon, and one of cavalry, the 5th under Grant, and three artillery batteries. This force was under the command of General Colville, and went to Cambrai which was reported as being held by only a small garrison. Wellington's letter to Colville, written from le Cateau at 8 a.m., read

> It is reported and understood that the garrison of Cambray [sic], consisting entirely of national guards of this part of the country, have abandoned the place, leaving in it at most 300 or 400 men. I wish, therefore, that you would march thither forthwith with the troops named in the margin, and summon the Governor to surrender to the troops under my command.[26]

Wellington hoped that the mere sight of his forces would induce the commandant of Cambrai to hand the fortress over to Colville.

The Duke himself went to Blücher's headquarters in Catillon-sur-Sambre for a meeting with the Prince. It would seem that Wellington now perceived the danger of the Prussians getting to Paris first and attempted to come to an agreement with them for the continuation of operations. Müffling noted the points agreed in this conversation,

[23] Weltzien, vol II, p 241.
[24] Voss, p 23. The Gérard here, François-Joseph, should not be confused with the commander of the IV Corps, Maurice-Étienne.
[25] Müffling, *Leben*, p 252.   [26] *WD*, vol XII, pp 497–8.

1. The Prussian and the English armies are to march jointly on Paris.
2. The advance is to be made along the right bank of the Oise, as, according to reports received, the enemy army is assembling at Laon and Soissons.
3. In case of a crossing of the Oise to the left bank, bridges would have to be built. The Duke of Wellington is to bring up his pontoons as, at present, the Prussian army has only ten available.
4. The siege trains are to be brought up. The English army is to take over the investment of the fortresses west of the Sambre, the Prussian army those on the Sambre and to its east.[27]

Blücher also suggested to Wellington that he send his Netherlands cavalry as a raiding force to cut Napoleon's line of communication with Paris. The similarity of uniform between the Netherlanders and the French together with their familiarity with the French language could thus be used to great advantage. He further suggested that he should send strong bodies of Prussian cavalry to screen an Allied advance on Laon. However, nothing came of either scheme.

It is notable that, at this meeting, both Blücher and Wellington agreed that Paris was now the main objective of the campaign. It was evident to both commanders that the French Army had suffered such a blow that it would be impossible for it to stage another offensive. The remnants of the *Armée du Nord* were now assembling at Laon and Soissons, so it was considered important to get to Paris before they did. However, the joint advance on Paris did not come about. Wellington's supply and pontoon trains were slow coming up, so Blücher took advantage of this to restart his thrust to the French capital and issued the following orders,

The I Army Corps is to march to Guise, its vanguard to Origny. Cavalry detachments are to be sent to Crécy, Pont-à-Bussy and towards la Fère. According to all reports, the fort of Guise would capitulate on sight of a large body of troops. At present it is surrounded by the vanguard of the IV Army Corps. If Guise does not capitulate, then I Corps is to try to force it to do so by bombardment. If that is unsuccessful, a small force is to blockade it while the corps is to continue its march on the right bank [of the Oise]. The vanguard is then to go to Hauteville. In any event, the detachments are to go to Crécy, etc.

The III Army Corps is to march to Nouvion and send scouting parties to Hirson and Vervins. It is important to establish the movements of the corps of Vandamme and Grouchy. The III Army Corps is to leave one battalion in Avesnes until it can be replaced by one from II Corps. In any event, all troops of the I Corps in that place are to rejoin it.

The IV Army Corps is to march to Aisonville and Bernoville, its vanguard to Fontaine-Notre-Dame, cavalry detachments to St Quentin and Catillon-sur-Oise.

Headquarters will transfer to Hannapes. One battalion of the IV Corps will stay to guard it.

---

[27] Voss, p 24.

The Queen's Dragoons, Silesian Uhlans, Brandenburg and Pomeranian Hussars and one horse battery are to assemble at Étreux under the command of Oberstlieutenant von Sohr who will receive his orders directly from headquarters.

The II Army Corps is to follow the disposition given earlier and from tomorrow will receive its orders from His Royal Highness Prinz August.

Any troops of the three army corps who come up later are to assemble at Avesnes and be formed into marching groups, then sent on to the army.

The II Army Corps is to ensure that all enemy earthworks are destroyed and the roads repaired. As a priority, the road from Charleroi via Beaumont to Avesnes is to be brought to a good condition. All abatis must be cleared and the wood given to the poor inhabitants. Everything that has to do with shipping on the Sambre is to be immediately brought into good condition and anything destroyed is to be replaced.

Oberst von Loebell is appointed commandant of Avesnes. Oberst Graf Loucy will take charge of policing in all conquered provinces, Oberkriegskommissarius [a senior war office official] Precher of administration. They will direct everything from Avesnes and be in charge of supplying victuals and the other needs of the army. All sick personnel, lame horses and any items unusable by the army are to be sent to Avesnes, which is now the main depot of the army.[28]

The three army corps thus had to move towards the Oise to carry out their march. They continued their advance along several parallel routes, the I Corps on the left, east of the Sambre–Oise Canal at first, the IV Corps as the right column, the III Corps in between. It was considered unnecessary to cover the flank exposed to the French to any extent. Little effort was put into scouting.

Wellington also issued his orders for 24 June. They read,

The 2nd and 4th divisions will be in readiness to move to-morrow morning. The cavalry will be assembled in their camps and in readiness also to move.

Major-General Sir J. Byng will move the troops camped near Gommegnies, *viz.*: the 1st and 3rd British divisions, the divisions of Netherlands infantry attached to the 1st corps, the Nassau corps, and the cavalry with the Netherlands divisions (excepting the light brigade detached under the orders of H.R.H. Prince Frederick), to-morrow morning to Le Câteau [sic].[29]

In fact Wellington's forces did not make any significant movement the next day and the Prussians gained more ground in the race to Paris.

The Cavalry Detachments

Although the Prussian Army had a relatively high proportion of cavalry, it lacked a single cavalry reserve held at army level. Instead, each army corps had its own body of mounted troops. This meant that the cavalry detachments now being employed on the advance to Paris were provisional formations under various commands.

---

[28] Voss, pp 24–5.
[29] *WSD*, vol XII, p 570.

The first of these was Sohr's detachment. Following Blücher's orders, it had moved to Walcourt on the 22nd. On 23 June it moved to the fortress of Philippeville, demanding its surrender. As the fortress commander did not capitulate, Sohr remained there awaiting further orders.

On 22 June Blücher had a larger body of cavalry assembled to use as a raiding party. For this he took the Queens Dragoons and Silesian Uhlans along with half a horse battery away from the II Army Corps, which did not need this cavalry any more as it was allocated to the sieges. The Field Marshal sent this force to Ors, south of Landrecies, where Oberstlieutenant von Sohr was to take command of it with urgency. However, Sohr did not receive this order, which was relayed through the III Army Corps, until too late. He marched off with his two hussar regiments and artillery (he gave his two fusilier battalions to the 8th Brigade to use in the siege of Philippeville) to Avesnes on the 24th and thus ended up behind the army. His men had to make forced marches to regain their position in front of the army on 28 June.

On 22 June the I Army Corps detached a body of 100 cavalrymen under Rittmeister von Goschitzky towards Laon. At Etréaupont, it clashed with some French lancers (either from the Guard or from Subervie's division) and threw them back in the direction of Vervins, pursuing them as far as Fontaine. On 23 June Goschitzky continued in the direction of Vervins and Marle where he again clashed with French cavalry (Division Vathier, formerly Piré). He then followed the retiring French as far as Froidmont. Here, he came up against a body of about 800 French troopers and saw more men on the heights above Laon. Napoleon himself was said to have been present and Soult was still there with as many as 20,000 men. However, rumour had it that they would not stay there long if attacked. This information was sent back to Blücher on the morning of 24 June. The detachment continued to observe Laon until 26 June.

On 23 June Blücher allocated the 3rd Silesian Landwehr Cavalry (formerly divided between the 15th and 16th Brigades) and the two squadrons of the 2nd Silesian Landwehr Cavalry (from the 13th Brigade) to Major von Falkenhausen, an adept cavalry commander. He was to scout the area between Laon and Mézières and was particularly required to report on any troops moving from Lorraine to join the corps of Vandamme and Grouchy.

On the evening of 24 June, Falkenhausen reached the road junction 4 km north of Aubenton. From there, he reported that the *Armée de la Moselle*, that is Vandamme's and Grouchy's corps together about 25,000 men strong, was at Rocroi and Mézières that evening. Falkenhausen also reported that cavalry at Tarzy (8 km north of Aubenton) were covering their positions and 500 cavalry (Vallin's brigade) had marched from there to Montcornet, that is in the direction of Laon, at 11 a.m. The report reached headquarters the next day, but the information it contained regarding the main body of the French forces, as we shall see, was a day out of date.

Staying close to the French, Falkenhausen tried to discover the exact composition of their forces on the 25th. According to his report, they included Vandamme's corps and the *Armée de la Moselle* that he incorrectly stated as consisting of the IV and VI Corps. The French, Falkenhausen said, were marching via Rheims and Rethel to Paris. Their vanguard had indeed marched to Mézières on 22–23 June and then to Rheims on the 24th–25th. The rear-guard of Vandamme's III Corps was at Rocroi and Maubert-Fontaine from the 23rd–24th, and from the 24th–25th in Signy and Rethel. Detachments of cavalry covered their right flank, withdrawing at 10 p.m. on 24 June.

Falkenhausen's report continued,

> According to reliable information, none of the three corps [sic] is stronger than 9,000 to 10,000 men. Even in its own country, this army has resorted to plun-dering to keep up spirits as much as possible. The Battle of Belle-Alliance and the strenuous marches have exhausted it to such an extent that every night hundreds are disappearing, tired of the war and loudly calling for peace. According to reports from Laon, Bonaparte has placed 300 men in the citadel and has retired to Soissons. However, nobody believes that he will fight again outside of Paris. The local population is friendly, everybody wants the end of the war and the disturber dead.[30]

Finally, Falkenhausen's report included precise information on the corps of Rapp and Lecorbe. He was able to provide a wealth of correct and valuable details thanks to the assistance of the local population and of an officer from Vandamme's staff who had been taken prisoner at Maubert-Fontaine and was now 'playing the deserter'.

Moving down the main road from Mézières to Rethel, Falkenhausen quickly established communications with the North German Army Corps and sent regular reports of its positions and actions to headquarters. He even reported on the advance of Wrede's Bavarian Corps as well as keeping Wrede up to date on events.

Once the French rearguard had abandoned Rethel during the night of the 26th/27th, Falkenhausen reported that the French infantry were continuing their march from Rheims to Soissons, while the cavalry were moving from Neufchâtel-sur-Aisne to Cormicy. He also noted the increasing number of deserters from the French corps, particularly since the arrival of the news of Napoleon's abdication. Falkenhausen then followed up via Rheims and Damery (to the west of Épernay) into the region of Château-Thierry, thus cut-ting communications between Paris and these important towns, his men spreading terror throughout the Champagne region as they went. He intended to move on via Montmirail and Melun to rejoin the army and requested that Melun be occupied on 1 or 2 July. As that did not happen, he fell back to the area of Rheims and was ordered to Paris once the city had been occupied by the Allies.

Falkenhausen was penetrating deep into enemy-held territory, taking large number of prisoners and on 2 July even capturing four guns. However, the further he moved away from headquarters, the less relevant were his reports and the longer it took them to get there, particularly as he might not know the army's current location. He expressed particular annoyance over the

[30] Voss, p 28.

reluctance of other cavalry patrols to forward his messages. The lack of a clear system of command for these cavalry patrols was the cause of this problem.

The patrols of the cavalry of II Army Corps, although less effective, were better co-ordinated. This was because, from 25 June, Army Headquarters had direct command of this force. On the 25th these regiments moved off from Catillon-sur-Oise. The Queen's Dragoons, commanded by Oberstlieutenant von Kamecke, rode via Chauny and Coucy towards Soissons. At Coucy, they drove off about 600 French cavalry in an easterly direction and then attempted to move their outposts towards Soissons. However, French troops in the village of Guny, 4 km west of Coucy, stopped any further advance, thereby preventing the Prussians from observing the movement of a French corps from Soissons to Compiègne, as described below.

Oberstlieutenant von Schmiedeberg's orders were to take the Silesian Uhlans in the direction of Laon, spreading alarm and announcing the imminent arrival of the entire army. He was then to turn east to the heights of Montchâlons (10 km south-east of Laon) and observe the road from Laon to Soissons. Here, he was to establish above all if Vandamme's corps was moving to Rheims or somewhere else. Schmiedeberg was informed of Kamecke's and, as far as possible, of Falkenhausen's direction of march.

Schmiedeberg carried out his orders on 26 June and was able to report that Vandamme and Grouchy had apparently left Rheims with 40,000 men and were marching via Château-Thierry. A flank guard was reported marching along the Aisne River (this was Pajol's cavalry) and on the afternoon of the 26th infantry (in fact the Imperial Guard) were seen marching along the Laon–Soissons road. In addition, cavalry were seen marching from Corbeny and Craonne via Vailly on the evening of the 26th (Domon) and the morning of the 27th (Exelmans). Schmiedeberg estimated that the garrison of Laon was 6,000 men strong – both line infantry and national guards. Headquarters received the first of Schmiedeberg's reports on 27 June, with news of Domon's departure arriving on the 29th. As we shall see below, this report was correct except for the direction of march being on Château-Thierry.

Movements on 24 June

As the Prussian army corps had not been given a specific time for breaking camp, they did so at various times that morning. First to move off at 6 a.m. was Bülow's vanguard, followed by the remainder of the IV Army Corps, except for the one battalion and two squadrons left behind at Guise. A report came in that only national guardsmen were holding St Quentin and that the 500–600 regular cavalry who had been there the day before had already left for Laon. Thus, Generalmajor von Sydow departed from the letter of his orders and marched into the town. The main body bivouacked that night between Aisonville and Bernoville, and about 10 p.m. were joined by Generallieutenant von Hake's detachment from Landrecies. Oberst von Lettow's detachment came in later. It had lost around 40 men in two clashes that afternoon.

The I Army Corps moved off at 9 a.m. It relieved the troops of the IV Army Corps who had bombarded the fort in Guise the previous night and

Zieten made a new demand for surrender that was eventually accepted. Reiche described the events,

> Although we were instructed only to blockade this place with a small force should it not capitulate, we were expected to make one attempt to gain its surrender. We made our demands, threatening to raze the place to the ground and grant no concessions to the garrison, and they were rejected. We then immediately brought up our howitzer battery and deployed it in front of the walls. It would seem that the commandant, a Colonel d'Erlon, was merely waiting for this to happen so that he could feel comfortable about capitulating. No doubt, news of the terrible catastrophe at Avesnes played no small role in this. Our emissary, Major Graf Westphalen, and the commandant soon agreed on the capitulation.[31]

The Prussians took 18 officers and 350 other ranks prisoner, along with 14 cannon, 2,500 rounds of artillery ammunition, 2,850 muskets, 705,500 cartridges and 9,700 pounds of powder as well as large quantities of supplies. Meanwhile, the 3rd Brigade, the vanguard for the corps, continued the advance on Origny, reaching there at 9 p.m. The 1st Silesian Hussars were thrown forward to Ribemont.

The III Army Corps pitched camp at 4 p.m. in Nouvion, sending out detachments to Hirson and Vervins. The corps also patrolled the road from Aubenton to Montcornet and Laon.

At 9.15 a.m. Goschitzky reported from Verneuil, about 6 km north of Laon, that the road to that town was free of French troops and that apparently 30,000 to 40,000 men 'not quite properly reorganised' had left that morning for Soissons, leaving behind only a small garrison. Zieten sent the news on to Blücher whose headquarters were moved that day to Hannapes. This report did not arrive on the 24th, but another message from Goschitzky with news from Paris did. Général Morand had appeared at Marle on the 23rd, introduced himself as commander of the rearguard of the French Army, and presented Goschitzky with a letter. This letter contained the news that Napoleon had abdicated and that the Chamber had sent emissaries to the Allied monarchs. Referring to Wellington's proclamation of 22 June in which he declared himself the liberator of France, Morand called for a cease-fire. Zieten forwarded this letter to Blücher from la Capelle at midday, but neither Blücher nor Wellington took any notice of it.

Wellington's 4th Division commenced its bombardment of Cambrai, the shellfire causing a small fire. The town's fortifications were in a poor state of repair and in places had fallen down. That evening, Wellington ordered the town to be stormed. The resistance was minimal. While Colville's men scaled the walls, royalist sympathisers attacked the garrison from within. The Allies lost one officer and 30 men. They took 150 prisoners and several cannon. The commandant still held the citadel, but entered into negotiations, capitulating on 25 June on the condition that the fortress be handed over to Louis XVIII, which indeed happened.

---

[31] Weltzien, vol II, pp 241–2.

Events of 25 June

According to the disposition issued by Prussian headquarters for 25 June the III Army Corps was to cross the River Oise. It marched via Homblières. The I Army Corps moved to Cerizy, its vanguard to Fargniers and its scouts as far as la Fère. Flooded ditches prevented direct access to the fortress there, but the scouts established that by crossing the Oise below the town and gaining the heights of Charmes, the fortress could be bombarded.

The IV Army Corps moved its vanguard, as ordered, to Jussy and the Reserve Cavalry to Lizerolles and Montescourt. However, the heavy rain delayed the movement of the main body, only part of which reached Essigny-le-Grand, the point to which it had been ordered. The remainder of the Corps quartered along the line of march, some even in St Quentin.

Detachments from both corps went on to Crépy (-en-Laonnois), Chauny, Genlis, Beaumont-en-Beine and Ham. A small group of wounded French soldiers was found in the last place.

Blücher originally intended to move his headquarters to Itancourt, but once he heard that St Quentin had fallen, he went there instead. Two weak battalions guarded headquarters, and the two companies of the I Army Corps who had been left in Guise came up. These detachments were ordered to maintain communications with the blockading corps.

Wellington's army also restarted its march that day. The Duke issued the following instructions for movement:

> Lord Hill will be so good as to march the two brigades of the 4th division now at Le Câteau, on receipt of the order, towards Cambrai, where they will join the other brigade of the division. His Lordship is requested to order a brigade [two batteries] of 9 pounders (one of those attached to the 2nd division) to move with the two brigades of the 4th division.
>
> Major-General Sir J. Byng will halt the troops marching from the camp near Gommegnies, at Forest, upon the road to Le Câteau, and then camp them between the village of Croix and Bousies.
>
> The cavalry will remain at Le Câteau in readiness to move.
>
> Major-General Sir J.O. Vandeleur will continue to keep the outposts upon, and to patrol, the roads towards St Quentin and towards Le Castelet [Catelet] and Honnecourt, and the right joining with the patrols of the cavalry sent towards Cambrai under Sir C. Colville.[32]

Wellington's vanguard, Vivian's cavalry brigade, reached Gricourt, 5 km north of St Quentin. The 2nd Division, the Nassau Contingent and the Reserve Cavalry moved into the area of Joncourt, the I Corps marched to Serain and Prémont and the Reserve to Maretz, while the troops sent to Cambrai remained there. Wellington was clearly not keeping up with the pace of the Prussians, who, day by day, were gaining ground on him.

A number of reports came in to Blücher's headquarters on 25 June in addition to that from Goschitzky mentioned above. A patrol led by Rittmeister von

---

Braunschweig of the III Army Corps sent in a report from la Capelle, confirmed by a letter from Clausewitz, Thielemann's chief-of-staff, that Vandamme had left Aubenton early on 24 June and had marched to Rethel and Rheims. He was said to be at Rozoy at midday, and would probably reach Laon on the 25th. Copies of Paris newspapers sent to the IV Army Corps also indicated that the French were concentrating on the Oise. Blücher decided to accelerate the movement of his troops on the 26th, issuing these orders,

The I Army Corps is to march to Noyon, with the vanguard going to Compiègne where it is to attempt to secure the crossing [of the Oise]. Detachments are to go to Verberie to prepare everything for a crossing there as well, and towards Soissons. An attempt will be made to force la Fère to capitulate. If that is not successful, an observation party will remain on the right bank of the Oise.

The IV Corps is to march to Lassigny, the vanguard to Gournay. Detachments are to be sent to Clermont, Creil, Pont-Ste-Maxence and Verberie. There, the crossings over the Oise are to be examined and everything done to prepare them.

The III Corps is to leave two weak battalions to garrison St Quentin and is to march to Guiscard. A detachment is to be sent to Chauny on the Oise and is to place outposts via Coucy towards Soissons. The III Corps is to send its company of engineers to the IV Corps, as this corps has none.

Headquarters will move to Genvry, this side of Noyon.

St Quentin will now become the main depot of the army and everything in the way of men and horses that can no longer be employed is to be sent there, as are any superfluous pieces of equipment, muskets, drums, etc. Any empty waggons blocking the march of the various corps are to be sent back to St Quentin as well, where they will be loaded with provisions for the army and returned to it.

The general administration of the conquered French provinces and the police headquarters will move to St Quentin. Staatsrat [state councillor] von Ribbentrop will take over the administration, Oberst von Loucy the police.

Likewise in St Quentin, Guise, etc. a number of horses are to be obtained from the surrounding countryside. These are to be employed to maintain communications between the operational army and the blockading corps as well as for despatch riders to use for expresses and stage posts.[33]

With the Brunswick Corps

Throughout this period Dr. Ferdinand Drude, a surgeon attached to the Brunswick Jäger companies, kept a journal which gives some idea of what an ordinary soldier's experiences might be during this part of the campaign. Dr. Drude noted,

... the [Brunswick] Corps went through Mons [on 21 June], a rather large but old and not very nice town, whose inhabitants really seemed pleased about the

[33] Voss, p 35.

success of the Allied expedition, then on to Malplaquet. Here, we bivouacked on a large meadow. That night, it rained and being hungry and cold, we slept little.

… Wet through, on 22nd June we continued to Bavay. A little old town (as were most towns from now onwards) next to which, we bivouacked on a hill. The weather was wonderful that night.

… [We spent] the 23rd June and following day here [Bavay] until 8 o'clock in the evening. The I. Jäger Battalion [sic] camped near le Quesnoy, a small fortress, and we camped next to a hamlet. Along with Major von Hollstein, Hauptmann von Bülow, Adjutant Sommer and several other officers and I spent the night with a surgeon. We bivouacked in his garden. It rained heavily that night.

… Early on the morning of 24th June, we went to Harcourt where we were billeted in a house with Major Mahn and were well looked after. We bivouacked in an orchard where there was an abundant supply of cherries. I bought an old horse from Fähnrich Fricke for six louis d'or, including saddle.

… On 25th June, we marched very slowly with the English army, reaching our bivouacs in Marets at 12 o'clock that night. We lodged in an empty house where we found nothing alive other than a six-month old calf that I had slaughtered. On the floor, hidden in the straw, I found two large loaves of bread and some bran and oats to which we helped ourselves.[34]

26 June – Compiègne, la Fère and Péronne

La Fère was a particularly important crossing point as it stood at the junction of the Rivers Oise and Serre as well as the Sambre–Oise Canal. Its potential usefulness was no doubt evident to both Blücher and Zieten. At 4 a.m. Blücher's order to try to force this fortress to capitulate arrived and Zieten accordingly instructed his 1st Brigade to attempt to seize the town. Reiche described the events,

> While the corps marched to Noyon as ordered, the 1st Brigade remained behind along with the heavy [10-pounder] howitzers of the corps and a 12-pounder battery to make an attempt on la Fère. Oberstlieutenant Lehmann was to command the bombardment. The heights of Charmes on the left bank of the Oise offered a most advantageous position for an artillery bombardment. However, as it was considered difficult to cross the bridge at Beautor, the guns were deployed on the right bank of the Oise on a ridge between Fargniers and la Fère. Here, gardens and undergrowth masked the guns.
>
> The commandant rejected our demands to surrender, so the bombardment of this place began between 10 o'clock and 11 o'clock in the morning and continued until 1 o'clock in the afternoon. Some of the houses in the town itself were set on fire and the bombardment of the fort was lively and effective. This was despite the fact that the position of our guns was not so advantageous that success was inevitable. General Ziethen therefore ordered a cease-fire and

34 GStA, IV HA, 434, fol 10.

about 2 o'clock, the 1st Brigade and the guns marched off from la Fère, reaching Chauny that evening, where they stayed that night. One battalion of infantry [F./12th] and one squadron of [Brandenburg] Uhlans remained at la Fère.[35]

At 7 a.m. the 3rd Brigade broke camp from Fargniers, leaving behind only a small detachment to wait for the 1st to move up. It marched via Chauny to Noyon, a distance of 25 km, obtained supplies there, and continued its march later that afternoon, going a further 12 km to Cambronne, where it arrived around midnight. The point unit, the 1./1st Silesian Hussars led by Major von Hertel, got within 3 km of Compiègne, leaving the remainder of the regiment behind in Clairoix under Major von Engelhardt. At 8 p.m. Hertel reported from Clairoix,

> I wish to report most humbly to Your Honour that I have just arrived here. I immediately went to the town hall where the sub-prefect presented me with a letter from the commanding general-in-chief at Soissons. In this letter, he states he surrenders the town where he has sufficient provisions for 10,000 men ready. Despite this letter, all measures for its defence are being taken. The mood of the inhabitants here seems to be very good. All are shouting: 'Vive le Roi!' The prefect merely requested that we get to the town before the French army to avoid a battle. I have covered the roads to Soissons and Paris and have just sent a patrol to Soissons.[36]

When he received this report at midnight at Cambronne, Generalmajor von Jagow decided to take the entire vanguard to Compiègne immediately, even though he was already 24 km away from the main body of the I Army Corps. If the French really were moving up 10,000 men, then he would be in great danger. Even the nearest detachments of the IV Army Corps, if they had indeed reached their objectives, were in Gournay and Lassigny, 14 km and 22 km distant respectively. Jagow reached Compiègne at 4.30 a.m. on 27 June and immediately took measures to secure the place and scout the area.

Towards evening, while he rushed to rejoin the main body of the army, Zieten spoke with Général Tromelin whom the Queen's Dragoons had captured at Coucy. This officer had a letter from Grouchy and one from a Minister Bignon for Wellington. Zieten remained in Chauny and sent them to Blücher.

The Reserve Cavalry of the I Army Corps along with the 2nd and 4th Brigades and the Reserve Artillery marched in that order via Fargniers and Chauny, camping at Noyon late that afternoon. On receipt of the report from Clairoix, Treskow's brigade of the Reserve Cavalry was sent there in support, but only got as far at Cambronne that day.

Bülow, aware of the importance of forcing this march, instructed that it be carried out at all costs. The vanguard under Generalmajor von Sydow broke camp at 4 a.m. It reached Gournay (-sur-Aronde) about 10 p.m., throwing back a French cavalry patrol there and taking a few prisoners. That night, scouts were sent off towards the river crossings. Locals told the Prussians that the

---

[35] Weltzien, vol II, pp 246–7.
[36] Voss, pp 35–6.

bridge at Creil was in order, but that at Pont-Ste-Maxence was impassable for waggons as it had been blown up the previous year. The Reserve Cavalry, less the 10th Hussars who were now attached to the main body, stopped at Ressons. Of the main body, the 14th Brigade and the Corps Headquarters reached Cugny and Guiscard by 7.30 p.m., the rest of the troops bivouacking at Lassigny at 10 p.m.

Bülow's report of that day's activities arrived in Blücher's headquarters in Genvry that evening, while Zieten's arrived the next day.

The III Army Corps marched behind the IV Army Corps, mostly moving via Jussy, though the 11th Brigade, reinforced by parts of the Reserve Cavalry and some howitzers from the Reserve Artillery, marched via St Quentin and Ham. The commandant of the fort in Ham rejected a call to surrender, but after a short bombardment let the Prussians march through the town unhindered. Two companies remained to guard it.

Thielemann bivouacked at Guiscard and Berlancourt, 2 km to its northwest. Only the 10th Brigade went as far as Genvry. The detachment sent to Chauny and Coucy came across a French outpost at Coucy. It consisted of cavalry from Subervie's division, supported by 300 infantry.

Having let his troops rest two days before starting the next stage of his advance into France, Wellington now became more energetic, issuing the following orders for movement to his troops for 26 June,

The infantry camped near Nouroir [Nauroy] and Magny will assemble across the canal by the side of the road to Vermand, with their baggage, at daybreak. The cavalry will assemble with its baggage at the same time. The two brigades at Villerets [Villeret] and Bellenglise upon the road to Vermand, in front of the infantry. The remainder of the cavalry will assemble in such situation and be so placed as to follow the infantry as soon as they can be admitted into the column.

This column will move in the following order, and is to commence its march at 5, and camp near Beauvoir [Beauvois] and Lanchy: the brigade of British Life Guards, the 2nd division, the Nassau troops, the remainder of the cavalry. The baggage of the different corps is to follow the column in the same order in which it is directed to move.

The troops camped near Serain and Premont [sic] will be assembled at daybreak with their baggage, by the side of the chaussée leading to Vermand, in the following order, *viz*.: the Belgian cavalry, the 1st division, the 3rd division, the Netherlands infantry attached to the 1st corps. They are to march at 5, and camp near Caulaincourt and St Martin des Prés. The baggage of the different corps is to follow the column in the order of its march.

The troops camped at Marets [Maretz] will assemble at daybreak with their baggage on the side of the chaussée in the following order, *viz*.: the Brunswick cavalry, the 5th division, the 6th division, the Brunswick infantry, the reserve artillery. They are to march at 5, and camp near Nouroir, Magny, and Bellenglise. The baggage of the different corps will follow the column in the order of march.

Head quarters will be at Vermand.

The pontoon train is to move to-morrow from Le Câteau to Estrées, and join the army on the road to Vermand.[37]

The greater part of Wellington's army moved to Vermand, while Vivian's brigade rode to Matigny with his outposts going as far as the Somme. A patrol of the 10th Hussars under Lieutenant Smith established that the French had abandoned Roye the previous night. It came across Général Lauriston at Nesle who told them he was on his way to Louis XVIII on whose behalf he had unsuccessfully attempted to intervene in Paris.[38]

Major-General Byng went with Maitland's brigade and a Netherlands battery to the fortress of Péronne. Here, after a short bombardment under Wellington's personal command, the outwork on the Cambrai road was scaled and taken at 7 p.m. The royalist population of the town forced the commandant to capitulate, but he did so on condition that the disarmed garrison would be sent to its homes. Thus, another crossing of the Somme was gained.

The Prussian Army, taking little rest and making forced marches, was gaining ground in the race to Paris. Blücher was making great headway in his ambition to be there first.

---

[37] *WSD*, vol X, pp 589–90.
[38] Liddell, pp 169–70. Lauriston had fought many campaigns for Napoleon, but remained loyal to Louis XVIII in 1815.

Chapter 14

Grouchy and Vandamme

Grouchy's Withdrawal

We left Marshal Grouchy's forces on 21 June withdrawing almost without Prussian interference via Dinant to under the protection of the walls of Givet. Here, Grouchy's men ate their first freshly baked bread for three days but could not replace the ammunition they had used as the fortress had too little. Napoleon had yet to send Grouchy any orders.

Left to his own devices, Grouchy decided to attempt to re-establish contact with the main army in the direction of Laon should the Prussians pursuing from Namur not force him to fight on the Meuse. On 22 June he marched with the IV Corps, now under Général Vichery, to Rocroi. The III Corps together with Teste's division formed the rearguard, moving to Fumay.

Vandamme was unhappy with Grouchy's decision to move the entire army down one road to Rocroi, particularly as this was a continuous defile and suggested that it would be advisable to secure the western flank with cavalry. Thus, Pajol, Exelmans and Vallin sent detachments to Philippeville, Mariembourg, Chimay and Hirson to screen the march.

On 22 June Grouchy received reports of the massing of Prussian forces at Thuin (II Army Corps), Gerpinnes (vanguard of the III Army Corps) and cavalry at Walcourt (Sohr's detachment). Furthermore, according to a letter he sent to Vandamme on the 23rd, he had finally received a direct order from Napoleon the previous evening to march via Rheims to Soissons.

Instead, on 23 June Grouchy had the IV Corps start for Laon, sending the artillery via Mézières where it could be resupplied with ammunition, and had the III Corps move as vanguard via Rocroi to Maubert-Fontaine. As flank guards, Pajol's cavalry went to la Neuville-aux-Tourneurs, Vallin to Aubenton and Exelmans to Rumigny. Exelmans also left a brigade of dragoons at Rocroi at Vandamme's disposal as Vandamme's own cavalry brigade, Domon's, had been detached (and had fought at Waterloo).

Reports came in to Grouchy's headquarters on 23 June indicating strong Prussian forces of all arms in la Capelle (I Army Corps) and outposts at Hirson, Vervins and Marle (Goschitzky's detachment). This supported the supposition that the Prussians were marching on Laon. This was even more reason to follow the more easterly line of march ordered by Napoleon. This pleased Grouchy who did not want his men to mix with the broken remnants of the main army as this might have been detrimental to the discipline of his troops. He decided to change direction accordingly and sent Soult news of this, adding that his forces would only be united on 25 June at Rethel.

On 24 June Grouchy went with the IV Corps to Rethel. He had ordered the III Corps to move closer to him, but still to maintain a detachment at Maubert-Fontaine. Exelmans had been told to guard the rear on the main road at Signy and to the north. Vallin was ordered to Montcornet, and Pajol was to secure the west and communications with the main army that Grouchy expected to find still at Serre, near Marle.

However, Grouchy's plan did not come fully to fruition. Vandamme, an awkward subordinate, marched only as far as Singy-l'Abbaye, and refused to come to a personal conference. Vallin broke camp only at 11 a.m., while Pajol, following an earlier order from Grouchy, moved to Sévigny and westwards, closer to the infantry. Exelmans received his orders late, after having decided to move on his own initiative in the direction of Laon and Marle to re-establish contact with the main army. He spent the night at Rozoy and eastwards.

When he reached Rethel, Grouchy received news of the events in Paris, especially of Napoleon's abdication, along with a letter dated 22 June from Marshal Davout, the minister of war, outlining the situation. Davout concluded with the words,

> At this important moment, France is counting on you, on Général Vandamme, on Général Gérard, and on all generals and officers. I repeat, the arrival of your army will make a great impression in Paris.[1]

Grouchy immediately replied to Davout, agreeing to unite his forces at Soissons with the remnants of the main army under Soult. To secure his line of march on 25 June he moved his entire cavalry to the Aisne crossings: Pajol to Berry-au-Bac, Vallin to Neufchâtel-sur-Aisne and Exelmans to Château-Porcien. He ordered them to scout the roads via Corbeny to Laon and on the Vesle downstream to Soissons. Vandamme was supposed to march via Rethel to the Suippe but, apparently because of bad weather and the fatigue of his troops, only got as far as Rethel.

On arriving in Rheims, Grouchy received the news that the Provisional Government had appointed him supreme commander of the French forces in the north. These were to be formed into two corps, the first under Reille, consisting of the remains of the I, II and VI Corps, and the second under Vandamme, consisting of the III and IV Corps. Each corps was to consist of three or four divisions. Kellermann was to command the entire cavalry, but part of it was to be allocated to each corps. Nothing was said about who was to command the Imperial Guard. This new organisation does not seem to have been implemented, however, as the old numbers continued to be used. Moreover, at Grouchy's specific request, d'Erlon remained at the head of his corps despite the fact that the Provisional Government had not allocated him a position.

Marshal Soult, now leaning in the royalist direction, resigned as chief-of-staff. Davout suggested Grouchy for the position, but he declined. However, he did take over supreme command of the army (for the moment at least), handed his two corps and Vallin's cavalry brigade to Vandamme and rushed to

[1] Voss, p 41.

Soissons in the night of 25/26 June. He arrived at 8 a.m. on the 26th and waited for Soult, with whom he was due to have a conference.

Soult's Forces, 21–25 June

The troops that d'Erlon and Reille had managed to rally marched with some semblance of order to Vervins on 21 June and to Laon the next day. Here, the troops Soult had managed to gather at Philippeville joined them. The I Corps under d'Erlon consisted of 4,132 men, the II Corps under Reille of 7,418 men. The 3,008 men from the VI Corps were split up between them. Of the Imperial Guard, 5,211 infantry under Morand, 1,887 cavalry under Lefèbvre-Desnoëttes and 876 gunners had rallied. The surviving 879 cavalry of the 2nd Cavalry Corps who had retired via St Quentin and Guise were ordered to Crécy and Pont-à-Bussy, those of the 3rd Cavalry Corps to Corbeny and Craonne.[2]

On his arrival in Laon, Marshal Soult had about 20,000–25,000 men at his disposal, about one-third of whom lacked arms, along with only 30 cannon and their ammunition waggons. However, two batteries of the Young Guard arrived and three newly-formed batteries were brought from la Fère. Muskets and ammunition were available in Laon and Soissons and were handed out as necessary.

The Marshal did his utmost to re-establish some sort of order in the confused masses of troops who arrived in Laon. Military discipline had largely broken down and needed to be restored. As the Allies had yet to attack Laon, Soult had a short breathing space. On 21 June Soult wrote to Bonaparte,

> I have spent several hours in Rocroi where some bodies of troops have begun to gather. However, I could not keep the men there, and instead they disappeared in all directions at the first opportunity… The cavalry shows better order and is in better condition. The infantry is totally demoralised and is saying the most unbelievable things. It will be easy to gather the artillery in la Fère with a much better chance to restore its morale.[3]

On 22 June Soult again wrote to Paris, saying that Napoleon could no longer rely on his generals and senior officers. There was talk of a new government being formed and most would support it. Lacking leadership, large numbers of the men were deserting, from both the field army and the national guard. Furthermore, the farmers were refusing to hand over the supplies required, so the army had only one-fifth of the necessary provisions. Soult doubted the army would withstand an Allied assault on Laon, which, in any case, lacked sufficient supplies to be the army's base. He favoured a withdrawal on the Aisne. The cavalry was ordered back to Crécy (1st Division) and Marle (2nd Division) on the 22nd, and was to continue its march via Rheims to Soissons the next day.

Having restored order, Soult began his withdrawal on 23 June. Headquarters and the II Corps moved down the main road to Soissons

---

2 Voss, p 43.
3 Voss, p 43.

followed by the 5th Cavalry Division and the Guard Infantry under Morand. Morand and his men remained as the rearguard south of Etouvelles, while the I Corps and the Guard Cavalry under Lefèbvre-Desnoëttes took a parallel road to the west to Anizy-le-Château. Two infantry regiments of the II and VI Corps remained in Laon as its garrison. The three cavalry divisions of the I, II and III Corps secured a line around Laon from the west to the north and east. This ran from Crépy to south of Froidmont to Craonne and Corbeny. It was Soult's intention to hold this position until the allies brought their superior numbers into play, forcing him to withdraw on Soissons.

On 24 June Soult had the I Corps move to the south of Soissons, leaving only the Guard infantry and cavalry on the two roads south of Etouvelles. The cavalry screen across the road north of Laon to Marle fell back in the direction of Laon. Subervie's division extended this screen to the west to Coucy-le-Château to observe the roads north to Chauny and la Fère. The cavalry corps of Kellermann (3rd) and Milhaud (4th), both over 1,000 men strong, were ordered to move to Soissons immediately. Soult ordered Domon's 3rd Cavalry Division to move there as well, as soon as Grouchy's cavalry had relieved them at Craonne and Corbeny. Soult did not send out troops to secure the Oise crossings to the west because he feared that most of them would desert if they were not kept with the main body. Instead, he hoped that Paris might send troops for that purpose. Thus, he now ordered Domon to rest at Soissons for only three hours and then to march on to Compiègne, 35 km further. He was then to scout and defend the Oise crossings at Noyon, Roye and Montdidier to Creil. However, Domon did not move off until 26 June and only got as far as the area of Soissons. Milhaud's and Kellermann's cavalry were sent in the same direction and reached Châtelet and Ambleny respectively.

The *Armée du Nord* under Grouchy

According to Soult's 25 June report, the troops assembled in the area of Soissons amounted to 27,760 men and 7,790 horses, not including Milhaud's men. This therefore gave an overall total of around 29,000 men, including 6,000 cavalry. Little artillery was available.

Napoleon's abdication had been announced to the army in an order of the day of 23 June. This led to a further decline in morale and a rise in the already high rate of desertion. On 24 June 1,000 Guard infantry left for Paris, saying they could serve Napoleon better there. The national guardsmen were also deserting in droves, and it seemed unlikely that the commandant of Laon, Général Langeron, would be able to keep control of his garrison. Grouchy complained bitterly about this in a letter of 26 June, writing,

> The disorganisation of the army that we are trying to reform here is still very depressing. No matter what orders I give, no matter what measures I undertake, I cannot prevent the soldiers leaving the colours and committing the most damaging acts. The Imperial Guard is also leaving, inflamed by rabble-rousers who are attempting to tell the men they can still serve the Emperor's interests in Paris. They are using this excuse to leave the ranks and rush to the capital...

The troops in Soissons do not appear to me to be capable of fighting, though the cavalry is in a better mood than the infantry and one can still get something from it. However, it is not possible to consider using such demoralised infantry in a battle. Those in the government saying otherwise would not, I believe, take it upon themselves to lead these men in combat.[4]

Grouchy's own force was in much better condition. The rate of desertion remained relatively low until it joined up with Soult's men. When Grouchy united his forces with Soult's, Soult rapidly departed for Paris, taking his entire staff with him. This left Grouchy without a proper command structure for the army and led to him writing another letter of complaint,

I have to report to you that the departure the Duc de Dalmatie [Soult] has totally disrupted and disorganised the office personnel of the staff of the army. They are all trying to outdo each other in the rush to get to Paris, using the excuse that he has authorised them to do so... Please send me Général Guilleminot [as chief-of-staff], who must bring officers and clerks with him.[5]

Grouchy's already troubled situation was not helped by the constant and at times conflicting orders Davout sent him. For instance, at 4 p.m. on 25 June Davout ordered Grouchy immediately to send the corps under his direct command to Paris by the shortest route, using forced marches . He was himself to remain in Soissons to supervise the defence of the Oise line. A few hours later Davout cancelled the order, instructing Grouchy to make his own decisions about the withdrawal and then, at midnight, sent two more orders, one specifying in detail the forces, strong points and defences of the Oise line, the other telling Grouchy to avoid battle and fall back to defend Paris.

At 3 a.m. on 26 June Davout wrote to Grouchy telling him,

I heard this moment that yesterday afternoon the enemy was between Compiègne and Noyon.

The Duc de Dalmatie, with whom I spoke this evening, told me he has directed cavalry and artillery to Compiègne. I fear that these troops have been sent too late... It is crucial... to prevent the enemy pushing between you and Paris. Thus, on receipt of this letter, you are to order your troops in good time to move in forced marches without any disorder [to Paris]... Should the enemy already be in Compiègne, then you must send the most reliable generals and troops you have to Senlis and Crépy to cover your movement... [6]

Grouchy himself appears to have considered an attack in the flank of the advancing Allied forces the best way of halting their advance at least temporarily. He suggested the route between Creil and Pontoise. Although he thought his actions were too little too late, he sent those troops immediately available, d'Erlon's corps (4,600 infantry and six guns) to move to Compiègne. At the same time, Kellermann and Milhaud were to scout the far side of the Oise towards Noyon and Montdidier. He also sent an engineer company with

4   Voss, p 47.
5   Voss, p 48.
6   Voss, pp 48–9.

the cavalry to Compiègne to make the town ready for defence, prepare to blow up the bridge and to destroy all means of crossing the Oise between Soissons and Compiègne.

Frustrated by the hopelessness of his position and the lack of clear leadership from his superiors, Grouchy then tendered his resignation that day. He also reported the positions of his army at 5 p.m. as follows:

Jacquinot's cavalry division in the suburbs of Laon.
Guard infantry and cavalry between Laon and Soissons.
Reille's corps at Soissons, marching to Compiègne on 27 June.
Domon, Kellermann, Milhaud and d'Erlon on the march to Compiègne.
Exelmans between Corbeny and Craonne, scouting to the Laon–Soissons road.
Pajol behind Exelmans.
Vandamme to arrive in Soissons on 27 June.[7]

Grouchy was in error on some points. He had actually withdrawn the Guard Infantry to Chavignon. Because of the evacuation of Coucy by Subervie, Lefèbvre-Desnoëttes retired to the junction of the road to Coucy and Laon. Domon was not on his way to Compiègne and Pajol was actually at Vailly.

Battle with the Prussians was about to be joined.

[7] Voss, pp 50–1.

Chapter 15

The Fate of France

Napoleon's Abdication

Bonaparte's *coup d'état* on his return from Elba in March 1815 was successful largely because of the support he received from the army. The result of the 'four day war' in the Low Countries was that much of the army was either destroyed or totally demoralised. Without its support, Napoleon was lost. On 22 June Napoleon therefore abdicated in favour of his son. The 'Hundred Days' were over, in effect, though the war was to continue for a while yet.

Despite Napoleon's hopes for his son, a provisional government was formed in which neither Napoleon II nor any member of the Bonaparte dynasty played a role. Those wishing to maintain their positions and power now prepared for the return of Louis XVIII. However, these people were not a unified force, but represented differing interests. Their political conflicts hindered Marshal Davout's attempts to continue the military struggle with some degree of success to help in the negotiations with the Allies which were obviously to come.

Wellington, Blücher and Louis XVIII

When Napoleon returned to France from Elba the Great Powers had refused to recognise the legality of the re-established Bonapartist regime. Instead, on 15 March 1815, they declared Napoleon an outlaw and made public their aim to re-establish the Bourbon dynasty with Louis XVIII as head of state. The Allied coalition was formed to enforce this policy at bayonet point and war was declared, not on France, but on Bonaparte.

The Duke of Wellington, as Britain's representative in this issue, took on the role of protector of Louis' court-in-exile and, as we have seen, entered France declaring his army as the liberator of the French people. Anxious to maintain a favourable balance of power in Europe, Britain merely wanted to see the overthrow of Napoleon and not the weakening of France.

Prince Blücher, on the other hand, as Prussia's leading representative, had other objectives. Clearly, Louis XVIII was too ineffective to be trusted to maintain his position against Napoleon and ensure the security of Europe and there was no point in supporting his government. Instead France had to be weakened to such an extent that she no longer posed a threat to Prussia. The compensation Prussia had received after Napoleon's abdication in 1814 was considered inadequate and a larger sum was required. Furthermore, Blücher had taken a personal dislike to Louis and held his entourage in contempt.[1]

On the advice of his supporters, Louis XVIII crossed the border back into France from exile on 22 June, accompanied by his 'army' of 1,000 men.

---

[1] Nostitz, vol II, p 69.

Indeed, Wellington had set this move in train two days earlier.[2] On 24 June Louis reached le Cateau-Cambrésis where Wellington organised a public celebration of his return to France. Müffling, as Prussian representative in the Duke's headquarters, did his best to avoid becoming involved in this display of support for Louis. However, Wellington accepted no excuses from him and an unwilling Prussian was seen in public with a king his chief despised.[3]

The northern provinces of France welcomed their king. The people of Paris tended to continue to favour Bonaparte. France was divided and local conflicts between the supporters of the two parties were common. However, the government in Paris was now attempting to achieve an end to hostilities, sending negotiators to Wellington and Blücher. The Duke welcomed such a move and contact between Paris and Louis was established, but the Prussians turned away the representatives the French government sent to them.

The French Peace Mission

Acting on Soult's instructions, Général Morand delivered a letter to Goschitzky on 23 June (see page 207 above). This gave the Allies the news of Napoleon's abdication and pointed out that, as the Allies had declared war on Bonaparte and not on France, then his departure would surely restore the state of peace. This letter was passed on to Blücher who took delivery of it in Hannapes on 24 June. The Field Marshal instructed Zieten to reject these overtures, pointing out that such matters were not for him to decide, as any cease-fire would have to be agreed by the Allied monarchs. Blücher then wrote to Müffling to inform him what actions he was taking. This letter read,

> I enclose to Your Honour herewith a copy of a letter that the French Général Morand wrote to General Zieten today. I attach so little worth to the content of this letter and to all the suggestions made by those dishonourable traitors that I have ordered General Zieten simply to continue his march on Guise and to bombard the fortress most heavily. I beseech you to convince Lord Wellington to listen as little as myself to those deceitful pleas produced by treason and fear. It is my opinion that we should continue our advance on Paris without delay, to refuse all negotiations, and to show that dishonourable and vain nation that we know it and thus despise it.[4]

Wellington replied that he was also in favour of continuing the advance on Paris. Blücher sent copies of Morand's letter to his king and to Knesebeck, the Prussian representative in Imperial Headquarters, along with letters of his own. To his king, he pointed out,

> I will never accept such insidious terms, but will continue my tireless advance on Paris unless the death or handing over of Bonaparte, the surrender of the fortresses on the Sambre, Meuse, Moselle and Saar, and the evacuation of the provinces to the Marne gives us the security to negotiate with such a treacherous nation.[5]

2 *WD*, vol XII, p 492. Letter to the Duc de Feltre dated 20 June 1815.
3 Müffling, *Leben*, p 254.
4 Voss, p 63.   5 Voss, p 64.

The Provisional Government continued its efforts to obtain a cease-fire. Five representatives, none of whom continued to support the Bonaparte regime, were appointed as negotiators. They were the Marquis de Lafayette, Comte d'Argenson, Doulcet de Pontécoulant, Comte de Laforest and Général Sébastiani, with Benjamin Constant as secretary. They left Paris on 24 June and wrote to Blücher on the 25th from Laon, asking him to forward their letter to Imperial Headquarters and to send a representative to Laon to negotiate.

Blücher did not refuse, he merely repeated the terms under which he was willing to open talks. These included: the handing over of Napoleon; the surrender of Paris; and the surrender of all fortresses on the Moselle, Meuse and Sambre, including Laon, Soissons and la Fère.

Blücher sent his aide Nostitz to Laon with this message on 26 June. Nostitz delivered the terms one after the other in the prefecture. The first term was greeted with surprise, though not rejected, but, on hearing the second term, Sébastiani declared he would rather die on the barricades than hand the city over to the Prussians. The talks ended at that point. Nostitz took the opportunity of observing the French forces in Laon and their intentions. His report noted,

> They knew nothing whatsoever about the condition of our army and nobody had the slightest idea that we were already so close to the capital. On my departure, I could not help telling the gentlemen that I was very convinced our army would reach Paris before them and I would then be most pleased to welcome them back from their journey.[6]

On Nostitz's return, Blücher sent Müffling a letter outlining the events and stating simply that, 'Their request for a halt and cease-fire was rejected.'[7] Gneisenau enclosed with this letter a list of demands the Prussians had in return for an opening of negotiations. These included: the handing over of Bonaparte, dead or alive; the evacuation of fortresses on the Sambre, Meuse, Moselle and Saar, including Longwy; the occupation of the provinces up to the Marne; evacuation of the château of Vincennes; the return of all the art treasures looted by France; and the payment of reparations for the cost of the war.

The Prussians were in no mood for compromise. The French then approached Wellington, sending Général de Tromelin to see him. The Duke rejected their advances, at least for the time being, pointing out that he had no authority to negotiate. This did not stop him beginning to make arrangements for the handing over of Bonaparte to Britain.[8] He was not, as Blücher wished, going to be executed on the spot where he had had the Duc d'Enghien shot.[9]

Although the Allied forces were now converging on Paris, their war aims were as disparate as ever. The war was not yet over, the march to Paris would continue and more blood was to be spilled before peace could again be established. Battle was joined the next day.

[6] Ollech, pp 299–300.
[7] Ollech, p 300.

[8] For Wellington's correspondence on this issue, see *WD* vol XII, pp 512–16, and *WSD* vol X, pp 583–97.
[9] Ollech, p 301.

Chapter 16

The Advance to the Gates of Paris

I Army Corps, 27 June

We left the forces under Grouchy's command preparing for a withdrawal to Paris, but unaware that the Prussians were advancing there so quickly.

Blücher's orders issued for 27 June read,

> The I Army Corps is to march tomorrow [27 June] through Compiègne and across the Oise, then through the Bois de Compiègne on the road to Crépy [-en-Valois] as far as Gilocourt. If the enemy did remain at Soissons today, then General Zieten is to send his vanguard to Villers-Cotterêts and make ready to support the vanguard in its attack on the corps falling back from Soissons to Paris and cut it off.
>
> The III Army Corps is to march to Compiègne and is ordered to support the I Army Corps. It is to push a strong detachment towards Soissons to observe the enemy and to cause him apprehension if he withdraws.
>
> If the IV Army Corps can pass the Oise at Verberie, Pont-Ste-Maxence or Creil, then it is to do so and send its vanguard to Senlis and detachments to Luzarches, Louvres and Dammartin. If there are no crossings over the Oise available at these points or close to them, then the corps is to march to Compiègne and from there to Verberie, the vanguard then attempting to reach Senlis.
>
> I expect immediate reports on the possibilities of crossings and on their condition. Headquarters is going to Compiègne.[1]

When the 3rd Brigade of I Army Corps reached Compiègne at 4.30 a.m. on 27 June after a hard march, Generalmajor von Jagow had the town immediately made ready for defence. The main part of the town lay on the left, eastern, bank of the Oise, with roads leading off from it towards Senlis and Paris, to Soissons and to Crépy (-en-Valois). There was a royal palace on the eastern side of the town with its garden and park eventually joining into the Bois de Compiègne, a large area of forest which made a concealed approach close to Compiègne from Soissons possible.[2]

Premierlieutenant Gericke of the 29th Regiment described the exhaustion the constant forced marches caused,

> The short campaign of 1815 was full of forced marches, but none more so than that to Compiègne. An hour from Compiègne we halted for a short while and everybody collapsed and slept. When we were about to start off again, we

[1] Voss, p 69.
[2] Weltzien, vol II, p 249.

noticed that the commander of the 11th Company had fallen asleep on his horse and that the horse had laid down without waking its rider. Only the noise of our starting off and laughing about this woke him up.[3]

The F./29th Infantry covered the roads leaving the town to the south-west for Paris and south for Crépy. The F./2nd West Prussians covered the area between the road to Crépy and the palace. Two companies of the Silesian Schützen covered the palace gardens and half a horse battery deployed on the road to Soissons. Behind the artillery, the III./3rd Westphalian Landwehr took up positions at the la Chapelle gate. The II./2nd West Prussians drew up between the palace and the Oise, with their left flank resting on a small farm. The I. Battalion waited on the market place, in reserve. Three squadrons of the 1st Silesian Hussars went off to scout the road to Soissons, while one went in the direction of Paris. The remainder of the brigade stayed on the right bank of the Oise, partly as garrison of the suburb there, partly as reserve behind the bridge. The 6-pounder Battery Nr. 8 was deployed on the right bank in such a way that it could enfilade the road to Soissons.

Gericke's account continued,

On arriving at the bridge at Compiègne, it became clear to everyone how important and useful this strenuous march had been and how many lives the possession of this point would have cost if the enemy, whom we knew to be very close, had arrived before us… The 11th Company was ordered to cross the bridge and then to move to the right in the direction of the last houses of Compiègne and the farm beyond and occupy them. The troops sent to the farm reported they could see nothing of the enemy, but had found masses of eggs and bacon that they were now busy preparing, not just for themselves but also for their comrades in Compiègne. The company commander replied to this report with several crates of champagne and bread, accompanied by a warning not to forget to observe the enemy on the left flank where a lively skirmish fire had broken out.[4]

The French I Corps under d'Erlon spent the night of 26/27 June about half way between Soissons and Compiègne, that is around Châtelet. About 3.30 a.m. d'Erlon's men observed the Prussian cavalry moving into Compiègne. Grouchy's orders to d'Erlon were to march to Senlis as fast as possible and to stop the Prussian advance there. D'Erlon was also to occupy Verberie and Pont-Ste-Maxence and destroy the bridges so that Vandamme's march south from Soissons would be secured. This flanking march was to be undertaken even in the event of the Prussians having already got infantry into Compiègne, which was considered most unlikely. In an emergency, d'Erlon was to turn towards Gonesse, where he could join up with Reille.

The Combat at Compiègne, 27 June

Hardly had the Prussians completed their deployment in Compiègne when, at 5 a.m., reports came in of a French column approaching from Soissons. About

---

3 Wellmann, pp 135–6.
4 Wellmann, p 136.

an hour later, French skirmishers moved out of the Bois de Compiègne, and a little later a battery of four guns and a column of infantry came up the road. The French began a rather half-hearted attack on the Prussians at 6 a.m.[5]

When the half horse battery, the Silesian Schützen, and the battery on the opposite bank opened fire this forced the French to withdraw. They made three more weak attempts at attacking the Prussian positions, followed by 1½ hours of skirmishing after which the French infantry and artillery disappeared back into the wood. Lieutenant von Thadden of the 2nd West Prussians chased after the French from the royal park, leading 50 volunteers and 20 Schützen from his own regiment and 14 troopers of the 2nd (West Prussian) Dragoons. In this pursuit, Thadden took numerous prisoners, captured two good horses and the empty carriage of a general.[6]

As far as the Prussian patrols could determine, the French were moving to the south, and an assault on the town from this direction was expected to follow. This did not occur, and instead the Prussians next believed that the French were withdrawing back along the south bank of the Aisne towards Soissons. The Silesian Hussars who had gone in this direction did not come across them, however, and the 3rd Brigade was too exhausted to follow. When the remainder of the corps arrived in Compiègne about 2 p.m., the 2nd Brigade moved into the lead as vanguard.

When he established that the Prussians had occupied Compiègne in force and observed that another column was moving to Compiègne from Noyon (actually the rest of the I Army Corps), d'Erlon actually withdrew through the wood to the south. By 3 p.m. he had reached Gilocourt, where he called up the cavalry under Milhaud and Kellermann and then started for Senlis, moving first towards Néry. From Gilocourt, he reported to Grouchy that the Prussians would mostly continue their advance from Compiègne. 'Thus, I think, M. le maréchal, that Your Excellency has no time to lose in executing your move.'[7]

The Marshal waited in Soissons until 5 p.m. on the 27th, expecting to receive a report from d'Erlon and hoping that this would say he had moved into Compiègne and secured it. Grouchy was also waiting for Vandamme to arrive, but so far, only Vichery's division had appeared and that at 8 a.m. About that time, Grouchy had Reille march off to Nanteuil, followed at 2 p.m. by the Guard infantry and cavalry under Morand. Jacquinot's 1st and 2nd Cavalry Divisions were ordered to join them, riding as far as Villers-Cotterêts. The 2nd Division does not appear to have followed that order because at 5 p.m. Pajol was ordered to move to the villages between Soissons and Villers-Cotterêts to cover the movement of the divisions of Subervie and Piré, if they could be located. Between 3 p.m. and 5 p.m. Vichery's infantry and Domon's cavalry also marched off to Villers-Cotterêts.

Grouchy sent Vandamme no fewer than five orders that day. Vandamme was instructed,

Every moment, the movement to Paris is getting more urgent as the enemy is marching along the Oise to the capital. Thus, you are to direct all divisions of

5 Weltzien, vol II, p 249.   7 Voss, p 71.
6 Lewinski & Brauchitsch, vol I, p 157.

your army corps, wherever they are, to la Ferté-Milon, Lizy and Dammartin [that is on a more easterly route to Paris, avoiding the Prussians]. You do not have a minute to lose in carrying out these orders. The government has put us in a most unfortunate position by calling us to Soissons. I will wait for you here until 5 o'clock this afternoon, then I will go first to Villers-Cotterêts, then to Dammartin.[8]

On his arrival in Soissons, Vandamme apparently did not want to accept the gravity of the situation. Grouchy accordingly sent him another order in a similar vein,

The enemy's movement on the capital makes it unavoidable that we hurry there. As you are now massed in Soissons, you must break camp at 2 o'clock in the morning and march via Villers-Cotterêts and Crépy to Senlis and Paris.[9]

As well as Vallin's cavalry division, Domon's cavalry division and Exelmans' cavalry corps were now placed under Vandamme's command. Domon was to await Vandamme's arrival at Villers-Cotterêts the next morning. Exelmans was to march from Fismes via Oulchy-le-Château to la Ferté-Milon on 27 June.

The Guard infantry and headquarters spent the night of the 27th/28th in Villers-Cotterêts, with Lefèbvre-Desnoëttes bivouacking close to the town, Domon to its south, and Vichery and Pajol to the north-east on the road to Soissons. Grouchy was in Villers-Cotterêts when he finally received d'Erlon's report on the events at Compiègne. The marshal sent this information on to Vandamme that evening commenting '… there is not a moment to lose in conducting your movement to Paris.'[10] Grouchy also ordered him not to march via Crépy and Senlis as previously planned, but on the direct route via Nanteuil.

The Cavalry Action at Crépy, 27 June

Zieten's main body, with the Reserve Cavalry at its head, had moved off from Noyon at 7.30 a.m. on the 27th without waiting for the arrival of the 1st Brigade (delayed by the bombardment of la Fère). By midday, it had reached Compiègne, where Blücher had arrived earlier. The Prince ordered Zieten to continue marching through the Bois de Compiègne. The Reserve Cavalry reached Gilocourt just as the last troops of d'Erlon's corps finally withdrew across the bridge over the Automne. The 1st West Prussian Dragoons, followed by the Brandenburg Uhlans and Horse Battery Nr. 2 under Generalmajor von Treskow chased after the retiring French, catching the French rearguard before Crépy and throwing it back in disorder to Nanteuil.[11]

At 4 p.m. Zieten ordered the 2nd Brigade, reinforced by the Brandenburg Dragoon Regiment and five guns from Horse Battery Nr. 10, to follow the Reserve Cavalry to the south side of the Bois de Compiègne at Morienval. From there, it was to send its outposts to Villers-Cotterêts with the main body going to Longpré, 4 km to the north-west of Villers-Cotterêts.

The 3rd Brigade and Treskow's cavalry bivouacked that night to the north

8   Voss, p 72.   10 Voss, p 72.
9   Voss, p 72.   11 Weltzien, vol II, p 250.

of Crépy with outposts south-east of the town towards Lévignen and Gondreville. During that night, one squadron of Brandenburg Uhlans under Rittmeister von Lupinsky rode west to Senlis where it established contact with the IV Army Corps and then reported the withdrawal of d'Erlon from Senlis (discussed below). A further squadron under Rittmeister Graf Roeder went east to Vaumoise during the night because of rumours of the presence of strong French forces at Villers-Cotterêts. Roeder made contact with a body of French infantry and cavalry early in the morning and reported that the French were marching in several separate detachments in the direction of Lévignen, but not to Crépy. Zieten thus received the first news of the events in Villers-Cotterêts.

The Raid on Villers-Cotterêts, 27–28 June

Generalmajor von Pirch II intended to halt his 2nd Brigade once it had reached a point south of the wood on the approach to Villers-Cotterêts. This wood covered a large area north and west of the Soissons–Villers-Cotterêts road. However, the roads between this wood and the valley of the Automne to the south were too difficult for a night march. Thus, Pirch was obliged to move along the old road through the forest from Compiègne to Villers as far as the junction with the road from Vivières to Haramont. He reached Longpré about 1 a.m. on the 28th. A report then came in from a squadron of dragoons, telling Pirch that a French artillery park had stopped close to Villers-Cotterêts. He had the 9th Company of the 1st West Prussians and the 4./Brandenburg Dragoons under Kapitain von Oppenkowsky move up. The French cavalry and artillery, part of the forces under Lefèbvre-Desnoëttes, were totally surprised. They fell back to the town in disorder, leaving 14 guns, 24 caissons and many prisoners in Prussian hands.[12]

Taking advantage of the situation, Pirch sent up the remainder of the dragoons, supported by two howitzers. At daybreak, they opened fire on the town. The West Prussian Fusiliers then assaulted it, driving back the Guard infantry in total confusion. Some fled to Paris, some back to Soissons. According to Grouchy's account, those who headed for Paris rallied only at Bondy, on the outskirts of the French capital. Grouchy himself narrowly escaped capture thanks to a steady company of engineers who protected him.

Lefèbvre-Desnoëttes managed to keep control of the Chasseurs à Cheval of the Guard, who acted as rearguard and this gave Grouchy the chance to restore order to several battalions. He drew them up along with Domon's cavalry division on a windmill hill 3 km south-west of Villers-Cotterêts and sent an ADC with a cavalry escort around the town to Vandamme to tell him what had happened. Pirch sent two battalions to attack Grouchy's positions.

Zieten's Main Body Moves Up, 28 June

Blücher's 'Disposition' for 28 June intended a forceful blow. It read,

> The I Army Corps is to march via Crépy to Nanteuil, leaving significant obser-
> vation detachments in Villers-Cotterêts and la Ferté-Milon to observe the

---

[12] Kraatz-Koschlau, p 195.

movements of the French corps at Soissons. If news arrives that the French corps coming from Soissons to Paris is on the move, then the I Corps is to form up to attack the enemy on the march. It is also to report this immediately to the III Army Corps, which is then to march to Crépy in support.

The IV Army Corps is to move its last troops across the Oise and march to Marly-la-Ville, the vanguard to Gonesse. If the enemy is not holding St Denis, then this important place is to be captured.

The III Army Corps is to march via Verberie to Senlis. However, should the I Army Corps require support, then it is to march to Crépy. The detachment sent out towards Soissons is to accompany the enemy continuously and follow his march.

Headquarters is going to Senlis.

Each army corps is to form a detachment of all those men who cannot march further and send them to Compiègne to garrison it. The IV Army Corps is to appoint a staff officer as commandant of Compiègne who is protect the palace from looters as well as prevent the removal of any items by its officials. He is to obtain an inventory from them.[13]

Combat of Villers-Cotterêts, 28 June

The hussar squadron leading the three sent out towards Soissons now reported Vandamme's approach. He had left Soissons at 2 a.m. as he had been ordered. Pirch II had two battalions and a foot battery deploy among the château gardens at the edge of the wood north-east of the town. The unexpected sight of the Prussians caused a panic in Vandamme's ranks, with many of his men fleeing to the protection of the woods to the east and south of Villers-Cotterêts, in the direction of la Ferté-Milon. Keeping control of his cavalry and artillery, Vandamme moved his cavalry against both the Prussian flanks as well to the north of the woods, via Mont Gobert. He also brought up 20 or so guns. Between 8 a.m. and 9 a.m., Vandamme's infantry attacked, forcing back the West Prussian fusiliers, ejecting them from Villers-Cotterêts and the château gardens. His main body then skirted round the town to the east and south.

Because of the apparent superiority in strength of Vandamme's forces, Pirch withdrew the 2nd Brigade some 3 km to the north into the wood. From there, the Prussians could see further French columns marching through Villers-Cotterêts apparently in the direction of Nanteuil, though actually they were moving to la Ferté-Milon.

At 8 a.m., while all this was going on, Pirch received Zieten's orders to move via Crépy to Nanteuil. He set off to comply but the roads were so unsuitable that he had to take a slightly indirect route via Eméville to do so. After a delay of several hours, he crossed the Automne at Fresnoy-la-Rivière, 3 km east of Gilocourt. He reached Nanteuil at 9 p.m.

Pirch's men had now been on the move since early on the 27th, with only six hours' rest, and both days had been hot and sunny with little water available to the men. Because of the difficult terrain, formations had broken down into small groups. They had marched 92 km and fought an action. In all this,

13 Weltzien, vol II, p 252.

they had lost fewer than 50 men, dead, wounded and missing and had taken 14 guns. Despite these enormous efforts, the French had managed to avoid being cut off, and were on their way to Paris.[14]

The Cavalry Action at Nanteuil, 28 June

At 9 a.m. Zieten received news of the French attack on Villers-Cotterêts and of the movement of strong forces from there to Nanteuil. He set off immediately towards Lévignen from his bivouacs north of Crépy with the 3rd Brigade and Generallieutenant von Roeder's cavalry – two squadrons of the 1st West Prussian Dragoons, two of the 6th Uhlans, the 1st and 2nd Kurmark Landwehr Cavalry, the 1st Silesian Hussars and Horse Battery Nr. 2. He had his infantry occupy Lévignen and Crépy while his cavalry moved on. The French force under Grouchy – his infantry with the cavalry of Lefèbvre-Desnoëttes and Domon – had, however, gained so much of a lead that all Zieten could do was lob a few shells at them as they passed through Lévignen towards Nanteuil.

Grouchy's rearguard, consisting of about four regiments of cavalry, made a stand north-east of Nanteuil at Boissy-Fresnoy where its carbine fire drove off the first attack by the West Prussian Dragoons. However, the Prussian artillery opened fire on the French flank and this was followed up by a flanking attack from the Silesian Hussars which threw the French back through Nanteuil. The French lost 60 prisoners and two guns. Prussian losses were insignificant.

Meanwhile, the 1st Cavalry Brigade of the III Army Corps and Horse Battery Nr. 20 under Generalmajor von Hobe had moved up via Crépy on the road directly to Nanteuil. To support the advance of the I Army Corps, Hobe bivouacked between le Plessis-Belleville and Nanteuil on the night of the 28th/29th. However, by then his 12th Hussars and half a horse battery under Oberstlieutenant von Czettritz had joined up with a detachment of the 6th Uhlans under Major Graf von der Groeben and Kapitain von Scharnhorst of the General Staff and moved on Dammartin. Here, they came across Grouchy again who was hoping his cavalry could have a brief rest. However, it was forced to move once more, this time going to Claye. Groeben entered Dammartin at 6.15 p.m. He reported that the main body (Reille) had marched directly to Paris, but the rearguard (Grouchy) had fallen back on Claye and that, other than these, no French troops were to be seen.

Czettritz rode on towards Claye and at 2 a.m. on the 29th reported that the French troops who had gone there, 1,500 cavalry, 500 infantry and 15 guns, had marched on to Paris that night. They had burned the bridge over the Ourcq Canal north of Claye but Groeben established that five bridges nearby were intact. Czettritz then retired to Compans, receiving an order there at 3.30 a.m. to move to la Villette. Screened by the cavalry in this way the I Corps drew its brigades together north of Nanteuil for the night of the 28th/29th.

IV Army Corps Moves Up, 27 June

As we have seen, on the morning of 27 June Bülow was ordered to cross the Oise at Pont-Ste-Maxence or Creil or, failing those, at Compiègne. He broke

[14] Voss, p 76.

camp at 6 a.m. and marched via Ressons where the roads to Compiègne and Pont-Ste-Maxence separated. The previous evening, Pioneer Company von Rohwedel of the III Army Corps had come up in waggons and joined the vanguard of the IV Army Corps. Rohwedel reported that he would need only eight hours to repair the bridge at Pont-Ste-Maxence and that there were two large ferries there as well. On receipt of this news, the main body continued the march to Pont-Ste-Maxence via Gournay. The leading unit of the 14th Brigade, the 2nd Pomeranian Landwehr Cavalry, crossed the river and took up positions on to the commanding heights to the south. The remainder of the corps arrived late that evening and bivouacked on the north bank, where the 2nd Pomeranians then joined them.

The vanguard marched to Creil with one squadron of the 8th Hussars and 100 infantry in waggons under Rittmeister von Eisenhart taking the lead. At Creil, these troops clashed with a French cavalry detachment coming from Luzarches and quickly drove it away. The main body arrived at Creil that evening and was sent on to Senlis after leaving one battalion behind to guard the bridge. It arrived at Senlis after 10 p.m.

Combat at Senlis, 27 June

That afternoon, a patrol of the 1st Pomeranian Landwehr Cavalry was sent ahead to Senlis from where it drove off a detachment of French chasseurs. The Pomeranians remained in Senlis until 8.30 p.m., when they rejoined the vanguard on the road to Creil. They then rode towards Verberie, intending to go on to observe the I Army Corps in action at Crépy, but were soon ordered back to Senlis.

On arriving there at 10 p.m. they found the town empty of French troops. Hardly had the regiment dismounted on the market place to bivouac when an outpost sent to Crépy returned in full flight. Hot on its heels was a detachment of cuirassiers from Donop's brigade of Roussel's division, from Kellermann's corps. Since many of the Pomeranian troopers had had no time to remount, the commander of the cuirassiers demanded their surrender. Major von Blankenburg decided otherwise. Leading those men who were mounted, he charged the cuirassiers, taking advantage of the fact that they were bottled up in one of the streets and thus unable to manoeuvre. The Pomeranians cut down the front rank of the cuirassiers and drove them out of the town through the gate by which they had entered. A detachment of the 2nd Silesian Hussars supported the attack with carbine fire.

Meanwhile, the carabineer brigade of the French cavalry division moved up. Blankenburg noted their superiority in numbers and realised that they could cut his force off from Creil or Pont-Ste-Maxence, so he started to fall back towards Pont-Ste-Maxence.

At this moment, Generalmajor von Sydow and Major von Colomb arrived at the other entrance to the town from Creil with the vanguard cavalry and F./3rd Neumark Landwehr. Wachtmeister Meyer of the 2nd Silesian Hussars described the scene in his journal,

We entered the town at night. The French were still in it. They fired at us, as did the inhabitants from their windows. The order to turn and trot was sounded. Unfortunately, a cannon was in the gateway and it could not be moved either forwards or backwards. There was a terrible panic. However, the French were very frightened and did not attack us. Otherwise, not many of our men would have got away. With great effort, the cannon was moved out of the way. We rode into the town again, threw out the French and took several prisoners.[15]

In a combat lasting three-quarters of an hour, the vanguard cavalry finally drove the French cavalry from the town along with the few hundred infantry that had come up in support. At 11 p.m. the vanguard bivouacked on the road from Senlis to Pont-Ste-Maxence, at the Forêt d'Hallate. Blankenburg arrived there the next morning.

Closing in on Paris

The IV Army Corps' objective for 28 June was Marly-la-Ville about 16 km south of Senlis, its vanguard's Gonesse about 12 km further on. Once the vanguard had got to Gonesse, it was ordered to scout as far as St Denis, and if this important town was empty, to occupy it with infantry.

Expecting to have to fight the French that day, Bülow had allocated a substantial number of men to the vanguard, including the entire Reserve Cavalry and the 14th Brigade. Prinz Wilhelm was given the command and gathered these troops together at Senlis. As the Reserve Cavalry had spent the night north of Pont-Ste-Maxence, this was accomplished with some delay, at between 10 a.m. and 11 a.m. Meanwhile, Sydow, on orders from Bülow, had at daybreak taken the cavalry of the former vanguard via Luzarches and Gonesse to St Denis. They encountered French outposts at le Bourget and Stains.

During Prinz Wilhelm's advance, news of I Army Corps' action at Villers-Cotterêts came in, along with reports of French columns moving from Nanteuil to Paris so he decided to take his entire cavalry towards Roissy, a little further east than planned. However, only the 10th Hussars managed to make contact with the French. Moving via le Mesnil-Amelot, they encountered about 300 stragglers from d'Erlon's corps before meeting the French outposts late that evening at Claye and Livry. Oberstlieutenant von Ledebur described this in his report, writing

> … I was ordered by His Royal Highness Prinz Wilhelm of Prussia to take the regiment under my command to the east towards the enemy rearguard. I was told that artillery and baggage had been seen with it, and I was to attempt to capture these and inflict as much damage as possible. At the same time, I was to advance via Dammartin along the road to Nanteuil and establish communications with the III Army Corps. Thus, I went with the three remaining squadrons of my regiment [one had been detached earlier]… towards the village of le Mesnil that lay on the main road to Dammartin. During this, I became convinced that all that was to be seen of the enemy were odd detachments from their rearguard along with some baggage but no artillery. I sent

one squadron towards the village of Mitry and one to its right to observe the road running from Soissons to Claye and to capture anything of the enemy.

Arriving at le Mesnil, I found Rittmeister von Hagen with the 3rd Squadron who had taken over 200 prisoners and captured four waggons with equipment and provisions.[16]

The 3./2nd Silesian Hussars also encountered the French that day, taking 40 prisoners from Grouchy's corps on the road from Dammartin to Paris. The vanguard also chased away a small detachment from Gonesse to le Bourget.

The 14th Brigade and the Reserve Cavalry bivouacked around Gonesse that night, placing some infantry in the town. Sydow's detachment bivouacked close to Bonneuil and the main body of the corps at Louvres, because the allocated place at Marly-la-Ville was too far from the main road and lacked sufficient supplies of water. The rearguard arrived at the bivouac at 10 p.m.

A party of French peace envoys appeared and demanded to be taken to the Duke of Wellington, but Bülow had them held in Chenevières awaiting instructions from Blücher.

III Army Corps on 27 and 28 June

The III Army Corps reached its allocated position at Compiègne in good time on 27 June. Its main body bivouacked on the eastern bank of the Oise, the 12th Brigade on the western. Two squadrons of the Reserve Cavalry were posted at Breuil to relieve the 1st Silesian Hussars from I Army Corps, who had been covering the road to Soissons. Two battalions of the 10th Brigade followed up in support and to observe the lower Aisne.

On 28 June Thielemann had his Reserve Cavalry move via Verberie from where it would be able to support the I Army Corps, and when news arrived from Zieten of the combat at Villers-Cotterêts, Thielemann ordered his Reserve Cavalry to go on to Crépy. His infantry brigades and Reserve Artillery marched to Crépy also. From there, he sent on one brigade of cavalry to Villers-Cotterêts, and the other (Hobe's, as mentioned above) towards Nanteuil. The brigade sent to Villers-Cotterêts arrived too late to get involved in the fighting. The III Army Corps bivouacked that night with the 12th Brigade and Reserve Artillery in and around Crépy, Corps' Headquarters in the town itself, and the remaining brigades beyond the town to the south-east, towards Ormoy on the Nanteuil road.

Wellington's Army on 27 and 28 June

Probably noticing the relentless Prussian advance on Paris, Wellington finally started to accelerate his pace. On 27 June he crossed the Somme at Villecourt. His vanguard – 2nd Division, the Nassauers and most of his cavalry – camped at Roye, his main body level with Nesle, along with his headquarters, and the Reserve at Ham and to the rear. His orders for the the 27th had read as follows,

> The infantry camped near the villages of Beauvoir and Lanchy will assemble near the road to Nesle with their baggage at daybreak. The cavalry will assemble with their baggage at the same time. The two light brigades at Douilly and

[16] Thielen, pp 25–6.

Ugny l'Equippe [Ugny l'Equipée] upon the road to Nesle, in front of the infantry. The remainder of the cavalry and Colonel Estorff's brigade will assemble in such manner and be so placed as to follow the infantry in the column.

The column will move, crossing the Somme at Willecourt, [Villecourt] by Nesle upon Roye, in the following order, *viz.*: the two light brigades of cavalry, the 2nd division, the Nassau troops, the remainder of the cavalry, Colonel Estorff's brigade. The baggage of the different corps will follow in the order of the column.

Lieutenant-General Sir C. Colville will march the [4th] division from Gouy through Péronne towards Roye, halting at the village of Puzeaux.

The troops camped near Caulincourt and Marte Ville will be assembled with their baggage at daybreak on the road to Nesle in the following order, *viz.*: the Belgian cavalry with the corps, the brigade of the 1st division, the 3rd division, the Netherlands infantry attached to the 1st corps. These troops are to march at 5, crossing the Somme at Willecourt through Nesle, and camp near the villages of Cressy, Billencourt [Billancourt], and Breuil. The baggage of the corps will follow in the order of the column.

Major-General Sir J. Byng will be so good as to direct two battalions of the Netherlands brigade now at Péronne to occupy that place. The remainder of the brigade of Guards at Péronne are to march at 7 through Nesle to the village of Cressy, and join the 1st corps.

The troops camped near Nouroir and Magny will assemble at daybreak with their baggage near the road leading by Vermand to Ham, in the following order: the Brunswick cavalry, the 5th division, the 6th division, the Brunswick infantry, the reserve artillery. The column will march at 5: the Brunswick cavalry and the 5th division with the reserve brigade of howitzers upon Ham; the remainder of the column will camp between the villages of Douilly and Villers. The baggage of the corps will follow in the order of the column.

The pontoon train will move from Estrées, and follow by Vermand and Beauvoir the head quarters of the army.

Head quarters will be at Nesle.[17]

On 28 June, Wellington continued his march, moving down the two main roads from Roye. His 'Instructions' for that day read,

Lieutenant-General Lord Hill will be so good as to march the 2nd corps of the army by Montdidier to Petit Crevecœur, on the road to St. Just.

Order of march for the 2nd corps: Baron Estorff's cavalry, the 2nd division, the Nassau troops. The baggage of these corps in the order of the column. The 4th division will be ordered to march also from Puzeaux by Montdidier to join their corps at Petit Crevecœur. The British cavalry now in column with the 2nd corps will march from their camps near Roye, upon the road of Senlis, and camp near La Taulle [Lataule] and Ressons. The above troops will assemble at daybreak, and march at 5.

Head quarters will be at Orvillé [Orvillers].[18]

[17] *WSD*, vol X, pp 599–600.　　　　[18] *WSD*, vol X, p 614.

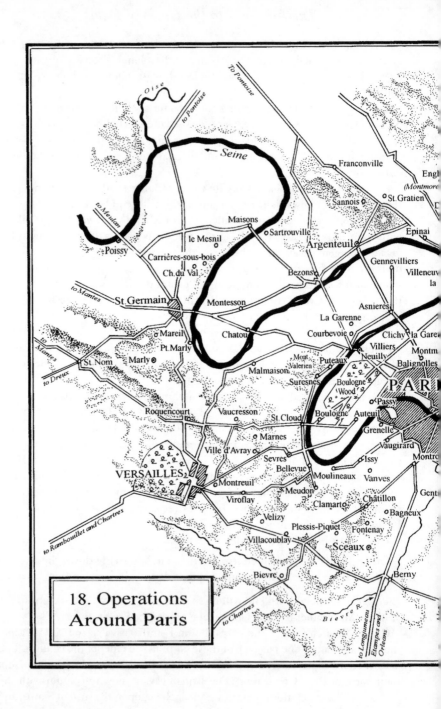

18. Operations Around Paris

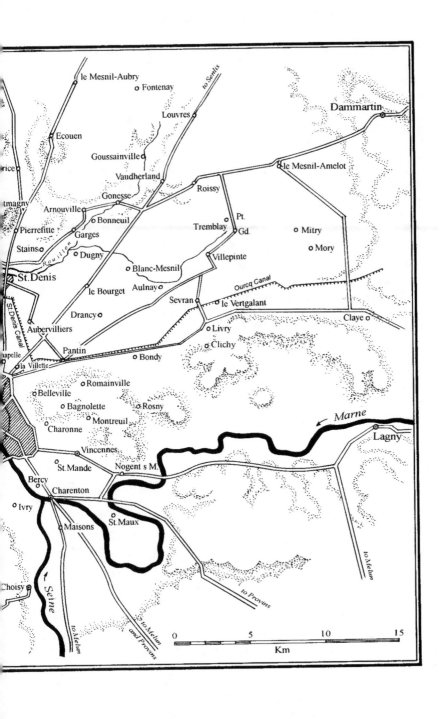

le Mesnil-Aubry
o Fontenay
to Senlis
Dammartin
Louvres
Ecouen
Goussainville
Vaudherland
Roissy
le Mesnil-Amelot
Gonesse
Arnouville
o Bonneuil
Pt.
Tremblay Gd.
o Mitry
Pierrefitte
Garges
o Mory
Stains
o Dugny
Villepinte
St.Denis
Blanc-Mesnil
le Bourget Aulnay o
Ourcq Canal
Sevran o
le Vertgalant
Drancy o
Claye o
Aubervilliers
o Livry
Pantin
o Clichy
la Villette
o Bondy
o Romainville
o Belleville
o Bagnolette
o Rosny
Marne
o Montreuil
Charonne
Lagny
Vincennes
o St.Mande
Nogent s M.
Bercy
Charenton
o Ivry
to Melun
Maisons
St.Maux
Choisy o
to Provins
Seine
to Melun and Provins
St.Denis Canal

0   5   10   15
Km

Of Wellington's other units, Vivian's hussar brigade advanced to Antheuil in the course of the 28th, and the Reserve moved to Roye. The 1st and 3rd Divisions, the Netherlanders and the British cavalry camped that night at Conchy, Lataule and Ressons. The bulk of Wellington's army was thus 40 km to the rear of the Prussians.

Dr. Drude of the Brunswick Corps noted the effects of this accelerated pace in his journal,

> On 27th June, a very hot day, we marched to Ham, an old town, next to which is a strong castle, almost entirely surrounded by marsh. The Prussians had taken it two days earlier. It was very cold that night and we slept in the open air on the bare ground on the main road, covered in a heavy dew.

The next day the march began to take its toll. Dr. Drude recorded,

> On 28th June, I brought 22 sick members of the corps to Ham for treatment. I then quickly returned to the corps. At Roye, I came across its bivouac. That night, I slept with my horse in a barn.[19]

French Movements 27–29 June

On 27 June, as ordered, d'Erlon had restarted his march on Senlis, fighting the brief combat at Compiègne en route. Kellermann's pause at Gilocourt at d'Erlon's request was the reason why he could no longer reach Senlis before the Prussians and clashed with the 1st Pomeranian Landwehr Cavalry Regiment there as described above.

In the meantime d'Erlon retired to Borest, arriving there at 1 a.m. on the 28th. Here, he allowed his men to rest for three hours after their march of some 60 km. To follow Grouchy's orders d'Erlon first intended to continue toward Louvres. However, he changed his mind because of the reports that the Prussians were at Creil and could possibly reach Louvres before him. Thus, he decided to take a more easterly direction, towards le Mesnil.

During the 28th d'Erlon reported his situation to Grouchy as follows,

> ... Yesterday evening, I was not able to occupy Senlis. Général Kellermann made contact with the enemy there and clashed with him. Because of this, I attempted to gather my entire force at Borest. The men were totally exhausted... I did not get in to my bivouac until 1 o'clock in the morning. Several cavalry regiments have arrived from different directions, but I do not have more than 600 horses from the comte de Valmy [Kellermann] with me. As I could not get through at Louvres, I have turned towards le Mesnil-Amelot... Because most of the train soldiers have deserted, my artillery is useless, as there are no drivers. I have had to have the infantry pull the guns. If I do not get through at la Patte d'Oie [the crossroads east of Gonesse], then I will try to reach the road to le Bourget via Tremblay. I only have a few men left and I cannot rely on them... [20]

---

[19] GStA, IV HA, 434, fols 10–11.
[20] Voss, p 82.

Reille's corps had fewer problems at this stage and marched via Gonesse to le Bourget without having to fight the Prussians. Reille and his men arrived in Paris during the night of 28/29 June. The Guard, marching via Claye, arrived there the same night. Following the action at Villers-Cotterêts on the 28th, Vandamme and Exelmans had, as mentioned earlier, moved away to la Ferté-Milon. That evening Vandamme reported that his troops were on the road from there to Meaux. After the alarm at Dammartin Grouchy retired via Claye late on the 28th. He had at least some of the troops he brought with him break camp that night to march on Paris, but remained there himself to deal with the stragglers. He feared the Prussians might reach St Denis before Reille and d'Erlon and thus ordered them in such a case to retire east of Paris to the Marne. However, this was not necessary in the event.

The position of the French forces can best be summarised by Grouchy's letter to Davout of 29 June. It read,

> I have the honour to report to you that I have gathered here at Claye 4,000 infantry and 1,800 horses of the Guard, Jacquinot's division the 2nd Cavalry Division and two regiments of Général Pajol. Because of a combat around Nanteuil, some of the corps has been scattered and has yet to rejoin me. Général Vandamme has fallen back via la Ferté-Milon and will not be able to reach Paris tomorrow. The comte d'Erlon is at Bondy with the remnants of his corps. Including both infantry and cavalry, it cannot be more than 1,500 men strong.
>
> The troops I have here and those of the comte d'Erlon are so demoralised that they would scatter at the first musket shot. Twelve guns were lost on the march, six more in combat. As a consequence of this situation, the government has only a very inadequate number of men available, none of whom has shown any inclination to fight, and who are totally disorganised. I consider it my duty to inform you in all haste of this tragic situation so that the government does not delude itself over the forces available for the defence of Paris that I am to lead.
>
> I will move off from here to Paris at midday. I have the enemy on my north flank at Tremblay. I very much regret that Général Vandamme could not reach me. He will only be able to join me in 24 hours if the enemy following him does not move on to the southern bank of the Marne.[21]

On 29 June most of Grouchy's troops retired behind the line of fortifications to the north of Paris. Vandamme marched via Meaux and Lagny to Vincennes, his infantry reaching there at midnight on 29/30 June. Vandamme's cavalry continued around the capital as far as the heights of Gentilly and Montrouge to the south. Grouchy rode into Paris and finally resigned his command, not wishing to serve under Davout.

The Prussians had reached the gates of Paris before Wellington, but only after a considerable effort and much hard marching. Blücher's prize now lay before him.

[21] Voss, p 83.

Chapter 17

The March South
of Paris

Paris' Defences

As far back as 1 May Napoleon had sent Davout the first of a series of orders regarding the preparation and reinforcement of the defences of Paris. The Navy was instructed to bring 300 heavy ships' cannon to Paris; 5,000 labourers were given the task of building four redoubts on Montmartre; 30 field batteries were to be made ready, these being crewed by the students of the Polytechnic, St Cyr, Alfort and the School of Medicine; gunnery and sharpshooter training for these students was to begin immediately. The planned garrison of France's capital city was to consist of 30,000 National Guardsmen, 20,000 sailors, 20,000 depot personnel brought to Paris, and 20,000 tirailleurs fédérés. These included foresters, gendarmes and any citizens who wanted to join up. They were to gather at designated positions on the sound of the alarm bells, to defend essential points and to operate in the flanks and rear of an invader.[1]

The defences were extended as far as St Denis to the north of Paris. The damming of the Rouillon brook and the River Seine running to the west helped to strengthen this position. The Ourcq Canal flanked this position and hindered any advance along the routes from the north. The city walls were prepared for defence and the gateways covered by earthworks as were all the canal crossings over both branches of the canal from St Denis to Bondy. The bank on the Paris side of the canal was made into a breastwork with firing ports cut for cannon. A line of individual earthworks ran from Bondy via Rosny to Nogent-sur-Marne. A second line was established on the dominating hills of Montmartre and Belleville. Montmartre was crowned with a double row of earthworks, as was Charonne to the east. The fortifications east of the city at Vincennes were brought to a good condition and strengthened by the fortification of the hamlet of la Pissotte to the north. A strong bridgehead protected the crossing of the Marne at Charenton and earthworks running back from Bercy linked it with the city walls.

These works, although not completed, were in a defensible condition. The works planned for the left bank of the Seine had hardly been begun, however. The volunteers of the National Guard had started their labours with great enthusiasm, but this waned very quickly.

To the west of the city the Seine bridges at Bezons and Chatou had been destroyed on Davout's instructions. Those at Maisons and St Germain were not, as the detachment of National Guard ordered to do this had refused to

[1] Lettow-Vorbeck, p 116.

obey its orders. The bridges at St Cloud and Sèvres were made impassable, while earthworks on both sides covered that to Neuilly.

Theoretically, some 90,000 men were available for the defence of Paris. In reality, there were only 78,000 men on hand, and these were partly demoralised, partly unreliable and partly untrained. They had 600 artillery pieces at their disposal and ammunition was plentiful, however. The National Guard of Paris was only partly uniformed and armed, had little interest in fighting and was thus of little use.

Napoleon had appointed Marshal Davout, his Minister of War, as Governor of Paris, commandant of the 1st Military Division, and supreme commander of the National Guard. On 24 June the Provisional Government confirmed Davout as supreme commander of the army but put Général Caffarelli in charge of the 1st Military Division, Général Durosnel in charge of the National Guard and Général Darrican in charge of the levée. Marshal Masséna was given the national supreme command of the National Guard.

On 28 June the Chamber declared a state of siege in Paris. The National Guard was to maintain order in the city, while the *Armée du Nord* was to be brought back to defend it. All old soldiers were called up. The armies on the eastern border were to continue to resist the allied invasion while a new Reserve Army was to be formed behind the River Loire. Some troops, including two regiments of the Young Guard, were returning from the Vendée.

Davout's orders of that evening read,

> All military personnel currently in Paris, whether armed or not, are to report to the following places: those from the I, II and VI Corps in front of the heights of the five windmills at la Chapelle; those from the cavalry, mounted or not, on the road to St Denis at the point where the road from Clichy crosses it; those of the III and IV Corps at the telegraph station on the heights of Belleville; those of the Guard Infantry on the heights of Vincennes, near Petite Charonne. At each of the named points, a depot of 4,000 muskets is available.[3]

At the same time, all generals and staff officers not employed on other duties were ordered to Davout's headquarters in la Villette. Through the city authorities, he announced that citizens caught sheltering soldiers would suffer severe penalties. In addition, he ordered the National Guards posted at the city gates not to let any soldier, no matter his rank, into Paris without the appropriate pass. All inhabitants of Paris were required to work to complete the fortifications and to bring all the provisions possible into the city.

On 29 June Davout moved his headquarters to la Villette, but continued to spend most of his time in Paris. Vandamme was given command of all troops on the left bank of the Seine.

The Prussian Army on 29 June

Thanks to the reports that came in up to the evening of 28 June, Blücher's headquarters in Senlis was reasonably well informed of the movements of the

3 Voss, p 88.

French forces towards Paris and their deteriorating condition. However, not a single report mentioned that significant parts of Vandamme's corps were still far away, near la Ferté-Milon and could have been cut off by a thrust to the east. Instead the Prussian commanders' attention was clearly focused on Paris and they had also been misled to some extent by a report from Kapitain von Scharnhorst sent from Gondreville at 3 p.m. on the 28th. This stated that prisoners of Vandamme's and Grouchy's corps taken at Boissy claimed that together these forces numbered about 15,000 men and were marching via Nanteuil to Dammartin and that no regular troops were marching on Meaux. The first mention of this last possibility was in the message sent at 10.30 a.m. on 29 June from IV Army Corps. It passed on the statements of country dwellers that only the head of the corps coming from Soissons appeared to have reached Paris, and that the main body had been forced towards Meaux and the Marne. This message arrived too late to influence Blücher's orders for the 29th. Bülow's message from Louvres on the evening of 28 June reporting that all reconnaissances indicated that the French had fortified St Denis had also yet to arrive at Headquarters before the orders for the 29th were issued. These read,

> The IV Corps is to march on St Denis and to occupy that place if the enemy is not holding it. It is then to patrol as far as Montmartre to view the enemy's positions. If the enemy disputes St Denis, and it is not likely that it can be taken, then all measures are to be taken to cross the Seine west of St Denis towards Argenteuil.
>
> The I Corps is to march via Dammartin towards Aulnay and le Blanc-Mesnil, detachments to Bondy and Pantin. The III Corps is to march to Dammartin, the Reserve Cavalry to Tremblay to support the I Corps, a detachment to Claye.
>
> Headquarters is going to Gonesse.[4]

Early on 29 June, new orders were sent to the IV Army Corps. These read,

> Your Excellency is requested to send immediately a good officer with one cavalry regiment, two battalions and ½ a horse battery via Argenteuil and Chatou to Malmaison to capture Bonaparte, who is said to be there with an escort of 400 men. The greatest speed is recommended and it is vital to cross the bridge at Chatou quickly. Your Excellency is further requested if possible, to accelerate the building of a bridge at Argenteuil or nearby. Unfortunately, we do not have any pontoons here, but there cannot be a lack of ships on the Seine. I am in agreement with the idea of leaving St Denis to the right and moving against Montmartre. However, that will only be possible if the enemy does not defend the line of the Ourcq Canal between la Villette and St Denis. This can best be observed from the village of Aubervilliers.[5]

These orders were executed without any difficulties. The main part of the vanguard of the IV Army Corps under Prinz Wilhelm arrived at le Bourget at

---

4　Voss, p 89.
5　Voss, pp 89–90.

midday and occupied the village with two battalions. His cavalry moved to la Villette and Pantin on the one side and to St Denis on the other. The 10th Hussars provided the outposts on the left flank. At midday, a battalion of infantry moved up to Drancy in support. The remainder of the 13th Brigade bivouacked north of le Bourget. The main body broke camp at 7 a.m. and marched from Louvres to Patte d'Oie. From there, a force under Oberst-lieutenant von Schill consisting of two squadrons of the 2nd Silesian Landwehr Cavalry, the F./2nd Silesians and two horse guns was detached. It rode via Arnouville and Stains, where it encountered some French cavalry. The Prussians chased them back to St Denis and established outposts only some 700 paces from the town. The French tried to drive them off several times, but the Landwehr cavalry held their ground, pursuing their attackers as far as the walls. However, the sight of strong French forces under the protection of the line of the Rouillon brook on the north side of the town deterred Schill from making a serious assault.

At the same time Rittmeister von Below of the general staff took one battalion, two squadrons and Rohwedel's pioneer company via Deuil to Argenteuil to prepare the laying of a bridge. Below arrived there late that evening and established that it would be possible to lay a bridge from the right bank if not disturbed by attacks from St Denis. However, he found that the French had taken away all the boats.

Colomb's March

Major von Colomb was instructed to take his men to Malmaison on the mission to capture Napoleon. This order did not arrive until that afternoon when he was with his regiment, the 8th Hussars, at le Bourget. He joined up with the infantry attached to him (I. and II./15th Regiment) at 4 p.m. To minimise the risk of being observed, they marched through the night of the 29th/30th via Deuil, St Gratien, Sannois and Sartrouville to Montesson, 40 km from the bivouac at Louvres. Exhausted, they then rested a while.

From information obtained from the local people and patrols, Colomb established that the bridge at Chatou had definitely been burned down and that in any case Napoleon had left Malmaison at midday and was now out of reach.

Nonetheless, Colomb recognised the importance of gaining a crossing over the Seine below Paris, and as Bülow had drawn his attention particularly to St Germain, he rode there. Reaching the bridge at 6 a.m. on 30 June, he found it barricaded and held by about 60 French infantrymen who were even then trying to remove its planks. Major von Wittich and Kapitain von Arnim immediately attacked them, driving them away after a fight lasting half an hour. Once over the bridge, the Prussians pushed on into the town, which was defended by about 200 men, and saw them off as well. The 8th Hussars threw out a line of outposts and sent patrols to Poissy, Versailles and towards Paris itself. Colomb then sent Major von Zglinitzky with his squadron from Montesson to Maisons. Zglinitzky found the bridge there intact and with only a weak guard which he drove off with two dismounted troops.

Forces Defending Paris
1 July 1815[1]

North of Paris

Unit		Infantry	Cavalry	Artillery/ Engineers
Imperial Guard Drouot	Grenadiers	2,159		
Headquarters at Villers	Chasseurs	2,254		
	Young Guard	1,353		
Cavalry Lefèbvre-Desnoëttes	Cavalry		3,392	
	Artillery			1,864
3rd Cavalry Corps Kellermann			1,641	
Headquarters at Neuilly				
II Corps	} Reille	7,057	1,248	513
VI Corps		2,790		?
Headquarters at la Chapelle				
1st Cavalry Corps Pajol				1,991
Headquarters at la Villette				
I Corps d'Erlon		4,309	1,064	133
Headquarters at Belleville				
Total		19,922	9,336	over 2,510

Men from the Depots and Stragglers

Commander and location	Infantry	Cavalry	Artillery/ Engineers
Allix in St. Denis	1,848	–	485
Meunier in Aubervilliers[2]	1,939	–	–
Ambert in la Villette	3,209	–	84
Beaumont in Belleville	1,683	–	–
Total	8,679	–	569

Bülow's report of late that afternoon showed that he was as yet unaware of these events. However, he had personally inspected the French positions on their northern front and had sent off Major von Royer from his staff to St Denis as a negotiator, though Royer had yet to return. The report described Bülow's own positions and the sending of a detachment to Argenteuil and outlined the situation to the north of Paris in some detail. That section of his report read,

I have the honour to report to Your Highness that the infantry of the vanguard of the IV Army Corps has occupied le Bourget. This afternoon, I made a reconnaissance with my cavalry along the Ourcq Canal.

In general, I did not see many troops occupying the terrain west of this canal. Bondy is occupied by infantry, as is Pantin. Between these two villages, there is an insignificant camp. La Villette is occupied by infantry. Where the cobbled road leading to La Villette crosses the canal, the road is blocked with abatis and covered by a trench. The haze made it impossible to determine what measures the enemy has taken on the other side of the canal. Reports

South of Paris

Unit	Infantry	Cavalry	Artillery/ Engineers
4th Cavalry Corps Milhaud	–	1,127	together
IV Corps Vichery	8,366	1,200	about
III Corps Vandamme	9,854	about 600	2,600 men
2nd Cavalry Corps Exelmans	about 2,600	2,000	
Total	18,220	about 4,927	2,600

Formed from the Depots

Commander & Location	Infantry	Cavalry	Artillery
Pully in Boulogne	2,031	334	–
Tilly in Bercy	492	–	58
In the Paris barracks	1,102	–	–
Total	3,625	334	58

National Guards

From Paris	6,000 men
2 mobile battalions, Indre Département	432 men
1 mobile battalion, Indre et Loire Département	400 men
(arrived on 3 July 1815)	
2 mobile battalions, Haute-Marne Département	631 men
(armed but not uniformed)	
Total National Guards	7,463 men

Overall 57,819 infantry 14,597 cavalry 5,848 artillery & engineers

Grand Total 78,264 men

[1] Based on Charras, vol II, pp 219–22.
[2] Charras is incorrect here. The troops in Aubervilliers left during the night of 29/30 June.

from the locals indicate that trenches have been dug at various points along the canal but I was not able to determine if there is really artillery emplaced in them. The locks have been shut to fill the canal with water, but the canal has not been made totally impassible to infantry as the water only comes up to waist level.

St Denis appears to contain strong enemy forces. The walls are loop-holed and flèches have been built in front of the Beauvais and St Rémy [?] gates. Inside the town, I am told the churchyard has been prepared for defence.

I did not notice any troops on the heights of Belleville. Trenches can be seen at the foot of and half way up Montmartre. The locals say that they are not finished. Artillery is said to be there and digging is still going on. A lot of people and a sizeable camp can be seen. The enemy is still occupying Aubervilliers with some infantry.

Reports from Paris say that Général Grouchy has arrived there with several regiments. A patrol sent this afternoon to Claye returned with a statement from one local that some of these troops actually passed through Claye yesterday evening. They did not take the main road via Livry to Bondy, but rather that towards Vincennes. Furthermore, Général Vandamme with 5,000 men is said to have crossed the Marne at Meaux to reach Paris via Lagny.

The wooden bridges over the Seine, particularly those at Bezons and Chatou are said to have been burned down. Those at St Germain still exist and there are no troops there.[6]

Zieten's I Army Corps broke camp at 8 a.m. and marched via Dammartin to its designated points at Aulnay and le Blanc-Mesnil without contact with the French. The vanguard (1st Brigade) provided outposts at Drancy. On the left flank, the Reserve Cavalry bivouacked at Savigny (between Aulnay and Villepinte) but sent detachments across the Ourcq Canal to Livry with patrols going on to Pantin, Bobigny and Bondy. The local population had fled and all supplies had been removed, leaving little for the advancing Prussians.

Thielemann bivouacked as ordered in Dammartin and the surrounding villages, his Reserve Cavalry at Tremblay. A squadron sent to Claye found the town and surrounding area unoccupied by the French. The closest French cavalry outposts were only discovered at Meaux. According to the locals there were 4,000 men there and they had orders to march via Lagny to Paris during the next day.

Prussian Orders for 30 June

As it was evident that the French would make a stand to the north of Paris, Blücher now decided not to suffer any delays here and lose his lead over Wellington. Instead, his army would move around the city to the west, crossing the Seine there and moving in from the unprotected south; he would leave Wellington to deal with the stronger north. This was an astute move with which Blücher hoped to gain control of Paris himself while tying down his ally outside for as long as possible. Thus Blücher's disposition for 30 June read,

> It is important to check the enemy's intentions.
>
> Tonight the IV Army Corps will therefore make a probing attack near Aubervilliers and on the entrenchments on the Ourcq Canal between St Denis and la Villette. If the enemy falls into disorder, the crossings of the Ourcq Canal are to be taken. The I Army Corps is to do the same between Pantin and la Villette.
>
> The attacks must be made at 1 o'clock in the morning and will be undertaken by light infantry with some cavalry from one [infantry] brigade and part of the reserve cavalry of each army corps in support. If the crossings of the Ourcq Canal are gained, then the cavalry is to move forward immediately on the plain between St Denis and Montmartre and spread panic. The infantry are to secure the bridgeheads while the army corps move forward in support.
>
> If this operation is not successful, then all corps are to prepare to march off to the right and are to start off as soon as possible. The outposts of the I and IV Corps are to remain in position until midday and are then to follow the rest of their corps. The IV Corps is to march to Argenteuil, but is to move its artillery against St Denis during the march and bombard it, leading the enemy

[6] Voss, pp 93–4.

to believe that a serious attempt to assault that place is being made. The I Corps is to march via Gonesse and Montmagny to Argenteuil.

The III Army Corps is to break camp at 5 o'clock in the morning, march down the road from Dammartin as far as the point at Gonesse where it joins the road from Senlis to Paris, and then follow the I Corps.

The object of this manoeuvre is to attack Paris from its weak, southern side while the English army moves into our positions of today.

In the event of not being able to carry out his assignment and finding the bridge at Chatou so badly damaged that it cannot be repaired, Major von Colomb is ordered to march on St Germain to take the bridge there as it is said still to be intact.

I expect rapid reports on the work at Argenteuil.

All the large number of waggons that are with the army corps are to be held in the rear during the crossing of the Seine and are to follow the last troops. The I Army Corps is also to send its pioneers to Argenteuil.[7]

At the same time, orders were sent to Oberstlieutenant von Sohr whose two hussar regiments were in Goussainville and Fontenay (north of Gonesse). These read,

Tomorrow morning at 5 o'clock, Your Honour is to break camp and take your two hussar regiments via Montmorency to St Germain where you are to cross the Seine. The day after, you are then to direct your men so that you come onto the road between Paris and Orléans to cut communications between Paris and the interior. If the raid on the enemy positions planned for tonight is not successful, then I will also attempt to cross the Seine with the army to attack Paris from the south. Thus, it is important to hold the bridge at St Germain and to collect all barges, which I also order you to do.[8]

The First Combat at Aubervilliers, 30 June

Bülow received his copy of these orders at 10.45 p.m. on 29 June. He ordered Generalmajor von Sydow to assault Aubervilliers with four battalions of the 13th Brigade and three cavalry regiments. The remaining battalions of the 13th Brigade and one of the 14th and the artillery at le Bourget were to remain there in reserve while the rest of the corps was to stand to in readiness.

As the orders went out late, the four battalions of the 13th Brigade under Oberst von Lettow only assembled at le Bourget at 1 a.m. To mask St Denis, Lettow sent his three Landwehr battalions to la Courneuve (2 km north-east of Aubervilliers). He then designated the 1st Silesian Infantry to lead the attack, followed by two battalions of the 3rd Neumark Landwehr. The Silesians formed up in columns to attack Aubervilliers. The two Landwehr battalions followed up. The right column consisted of the F./1st Silesians, the left consisted of the II./1st Silesians, but it lost its way in the dark, moving into the centre of the village.[9]

---

[7] Voss, p 95.

[8] Voss, pp 95–6.

[9] Ebertz, p 74.

At daybreak, the F./1st Silesians under Major von Sanitz pushed to the right, quickly removing some abatis and the II./1st Silesians entered Aubervilliers from the left, moving into the centre of the village. Lettow sent the II./3rd Neumark Landwehr, and later the I. Battalion towards the south. Despite the barricades erected everywhere there was little resistance to the Prussian advance. The attackers lost one officer and 22 men dead, four officers and 83 men missing and wounded, but took 200 prisoners. Musketeer Heinrich Wiederholdt of the II./1st Silesians also captured a French colour. Two battalions occupied the village and three reformed to the east.

The canal and some French artillery drawn up beyond it prevented any further pursuit and a strong force of French infantry was visible nearby. This consisted of recruits from the Young Guard who had just been issued with small arms and rushed to la Villette and were now commanded by Davout in person along with his whole staff.

At the same time, Oberst Graf Dohna took the F./1st Pomeranian Landwehr and the 10th Hussars (the left flank of the outposts) towards la Villette. The cobbled road in front of the canal was blocked with abatis and defended by infantry. Although the Prussian skirmishers drove them back after a long firefight, the strong French artillery on the far side prevented the attackers from crossing the canal. The Prussian skirmishers then retired to their outpost line. The report of Major von Krüger, commander of the Pomeranian Fusiliers, described the events,

> At daybreak on 30 June, we took the village of les Vertus on our right by storm. Following up our success, Oberst Graf Dohna went forwards over the heights of the cobbled road for 500 paces to a house on the other side. Using the cover provided by two rows of trees, our skirmishers closed up to 200 paces from the enemy, supported by the cavalry flankers.
>
> Premierlieutenant Hoeppner, commander of the skirmishers, had one section from each of the skirmish platoons to deploy. The enemy resisted our firing line with a determined defence. The supports were called up, and the charge sounded. We fell on the enemy with cries of 'Hurrah!', throwing him back far beyond the abatis blocking the road and into the battery, scattering that as well.
>
> Once Oberst Graf Dohna was certain of the enemy's strength and that our position was untenable, he ordered our skirmishers to fall back to their previous position. We did this under constant fire, and the enemy, recovering his earlier positions, did not dare follow us.
>
> The skirmish chains fired on each other all afternoon. However, they stopped when I gave the order not to fire unless fired upon, and only to fire if fired upon by the enemy and when certain that the shot would hit. Some enemy skirmishers who moved up against our left flank towards our cavalry were forced to retire by our skirmishers.
>
> Towards midday, the French fired a round from their battery on the cobbled road, but it was without effect. That afternoon however, they drew up a few guns diagonally to our left flank, using the cover provided by the village of la Villette. They fired six shots, killing or severely wounding five hussar horses.

What happened here was that one squadron had been sent forward to cover the remainder of the 10th Hussars who had dismounted to feed their horses. While this was going on, the French used the cover of some trees to move up several guns and deploy them behind the main road. These guns shot off several rounds, killing five horses, and causing great confusion as some of the other hussar horses were unbridled with their riders away foraging and cooking. The support squadron soon chased the French away, however.

Krüger's account then concluded,

> Oberst Graf Dohna then withdrew the cavalry and infantry to behind the house mentioned earlier. At dusk, everybody except a picket was ordered back to le Bourget.[10]

Although Zieten received Blücher's orders before midnight, he was concerned about making a night attack on the villages of la Villette and Pantin on the far side of the Ourcq Canal. Thus, he contacted Bülow to confer with him on, 'how the dispositions of the Field Marshal would be best carried out'.[11] He then carried out the demonstration attack ordered in the early hours of the morning. Steinmetz's brigade made the attack, covered by three battalions of the 3rd Brigade on the canal at Bondy, to the north of Bobigny and at Sevran. However, the French defences were found to be strong and alert and this operation made as little headway as Dohna's.

Blücher's New Orders

As it was clear that the line of the Ourcq Canal could not be crossed without heavy fighting, the Prussian headquarters now decided to implement its plans for a move to the west. However, as the I and IV Army Corps were in contact with the French and could not easily be withdrawn until Wellington had moved up, only the III Army Corps at Dammartin was available initially. That afternoon it received the following orders,

> Your Excellency is immediately to move your Corps towards St Germain where Major von Colomb is holding the bridge. The vanguard must rush as fast as possible to St Germain to support Major von Colomb and maintain this bridge. Your Excellency is likewise to send a detachment to Maisons, where the bridge is intact, to maintain this bridge also, so that, if the bridge at St Germain should be lost, the corps can cross the Seine at Maisons. The enemy has destroyed the bridges at Bezons and Chatou and at Argenteuil and we lack the materials to build a bridge of our own.[12]

That morning, Zieten and Bülow had been given oral instructions to remain where they were. They were now sent written orders. Those to Zieten read,

> Your Excellency is to move the Corps under your command at 10 o'clock tonight via Gonesse and follow the III Army Corps to St Germain. The

[10] Thielen, pp 28–9.
[11] Voss, p 97.
[12] Voss, pp 97–8.

outposts are to remain where they are until relieved by the English. The campfires are to be kept burning to conceal our march from the enemy. The enemy has destroyed the bridges at Bezons and Chatou and we do not have the materials to repair them. Thus, it is most important to reach the bridges at St Germain and Maisons that have not yet been destroyed. Major von Colomb is holding the first of these with two battalions, half a horse battery and a cavalry regiment. Oberstlieutenant von Sohr with two cavalry regiments has already been sent there this morning. The IV Army Corps is to remain where it is until relieved by the English and is then to follow via St Germain or to try to cross the Seine at Argenteuil. I will move my headquarters to St Germain tomorrow.[13]

Those to Bülow read,

Owing to the difficulty of repairing the bridges at Bezons and Chatou and laying a new bridge at Argenteuil, I have just sent the III Corps to St Germain. Major von Colomb is holding the bridge there, and the enemy has not destroyed the one at Maisons. The I Corps is to start off at 10 o'clock tonight and follow the III Corps. Your Excellency is to maintain your present positions until relieved by the English. Likewise, the outposts of the I Corps will remain where they are with the bivouac fires kept alight. Your Excellency could reinforce the brigade of Oberst von Hiller with another and gradually shift everything to the right, in preparation for the general move in that direction. The English vanguard is already in Vaudherland and the Duke of Wellington himself is in Louvres. Our seven pontoons have just arrived and been sent to Argenteuil. Your Excellency should use your own discretion whether to follow the two corps to St Germain or to attempt to make a crossing at Argenteuil. In the latter event, Mont Valérien is your objective. The other two corps are advancing on Sèvres.

Headquarters will be moved to St Germain tomorrow.[14]

Orders for reconnaissance in other directions were also issued. Those to Oberstlieutenant von Kamecke, commander of the Queen's Dragoons read,

As it is most important to observe enemy movements from Châlons to Paris, Your Honour is to take your regiment towards Château-Thierry and la Ferté-sous-Jouarre and from there, to send out raiding parties towards Montmirail and Sézanne. If the enemy has garrisons in those places, then they are to be ignored. The regiment has to change its base often and tell everybody it is the vanguard of a corps. Oberstlieutenant von Schmiedeberg has the order to go to Châlons and patrol the area between the Marne and the Aube. All reports are to be sent to Gonesse and are to be addressed both to Prince Blücher and General von Müffling, who is with the Duke of Wellington.[15]

In the same way, Schmiedeberg was ordered to Châlons with his Silesian Uhlans and instructed to patrol deep into the Champagne area and to cover the area between the Marne and Aube.

13 Voss, p 98.   15 Voss, pp 98–9.
14 Voss, p 98.

Wellington's Army on 29 and 30 June

Wellington issued the following 'Instructions for the Movement of the Cavalry' on 29 June,

> The British cavalry will move from their respective bivouacs upon Pont St Maxence [sic] in the following order: Major-General Sir H. Vivian's brigade will move from Antheuil and Monchy at 3 a.m., and enter the high road by the most convenient route in the direction of Estrées St Denis. The 7th brigade will move from La Taulle [Lataule] at 3½ a.m. [sic], and will, if possible, find a road to enter the chaussée to Pont St Maxence in front of Gournay, and will follow Major-General Sir H. Vivian's brigade: these two brigades will form the advance guard under the command of the senior officer.
>
> The 3rd brigade will assemble at Gournay so as to be in readiness to march at 5, and follow the 7th brigade. Major-General Sir C. Grant's brigade and the 4th brigade will march from Ressons and Ricquebourg at 3½, and enter the high road to Pont St Maxence at Gournay, and will follow the 3rd brigade.
>
> The heavy cavalry will move from Cuvilly precisely at 5, and will proceed on the high road to Pont St Maxence, following the 4th brigade. The 4 troops of horse artillery will move from Mortemer at 4½, so as to be able to close up and move with the heavy cavalry as above.
>
> The baggage will follow in rear of their respective brigades to Pont St Maxence, when further orders will be given.
>
> Head quarters of the army to be at Le Plessis Longueau.[16]

His 'Instructions for the Movement of the Army' of 29 June read,

> Lord Hill will be so good as to move the 2nd corps of the army from Petit Crevecœur to Clermont. Order of march for the 2nd corps: Baron Estorff's cavalry, the 2nd division, the 4th division, the Nassau troops, the baggage of these corps in the order of the column. The 4th division, if it has not reached Petit Crevecœur this day, will follow the 2nd corps to Clermont. The troops are to assemble at daybreak, and march at 5.
>
> The British cavalry will move from its camp near La Taulle to Pont St Maxence.
>
> The 1st corps will move from its camp near Cinchy by Estrées St Denis on the great road to St Martin Longueau. Order of march for the 1st corps: Netherlands cavalry, the 1st division, the 3rd division, the Netherlands infantry, baggage of the troops in the order of the column. The above troops will assemble at daybreak, and march at 5.
>
> The troops camped near Roye will move to Gournay on the road to Pont St Maxence. Order of march for the troops near Roye: the Brunswick cavalry, the 5th division, the 6th division, the Brunswick infantry, the reserve artillery, the baggage of the corps in the order of the column. These troops will assemble at daybreak, and march at 5.
>
> The pontoon train, the hawser bridges, to Estrées St Denis. The reserve ammunition to Orvillé [Orvillers]. The civil departments will move to Orvillé.

---

[16] *WSD*, vol X, pp 621–2.

Head quarters will be at Le Plessis Longueau.

The cavalry to draw their resources from the following villages: Les Ageux, Pont St Maxence, Saron [Sarron], Beaurepaire, St Genoux.[17]

That day, Wellington's army had reached the following positions: the vanguard cavalry (Vivian's and Arentsschildt's brigades) Senlis; the Reserve Cavalry Pont-Ste-Maxence; the I Corps St Martin-Longueau; Headquarters le Plessis-Longueau; II Corps and the Nassauers Clermont; Reserves Gournay; the pontoon trains Estrées-St Denis.

That evening and not the 30th as Nostitz stated in his account,[18] Wellington went to Gonesse to confer with Blücher on the response they were going to give to the French pleas for a cease-fire. These are fully examined in the next chapter. During this meeting plans for the continued movements of both armies to Paris were also discussed, but without a firm agreement being made. On his return to his headquarters, the Duke began contemplating a movement to the west around Paris for his own army, with the Prussians tying down the French army on the north of the city. Thus, on 30 June, Müffling, then en route to Louvres with the cavalry of Wellington's vanguard, wrote to Gneisenau,

> The Duke of Wellington informs me he has received the news that his pontoon train has reached its designated point. As he now has to issue orders for tomorrow's march, he is considering the entire situation and believes it would be better if he were to move to the right tomorrow to cross the Seine at Poissy.
> 1. He does not believe that a crossing at Argenteuil can be made without the enemy noticing and [responding] with a deployment in or around Mont Valérien, making the march between the loop in the Seine difficult.
> 2 Our entire objective would be revealed as soon as the Prussian Army was seen marching off.
> 3. The order of battle and the lines of communication would be maintained as soon as the Duke crosses the Seine.
> I replied that I would inform Your Excellency of this with haste and believe that you would accept these reasons.[19]

From the military perspective, this plan had a number of advantages, as Wellington suggested. However, as Wellington's army was far to the rear, two days would be lost in waiting for him to come up and, more importantly for Blücher, his rival would end up entering Paris first That was clearly not acceptable to the Prussians and so Gneisenau replied to Müffling,

> Today [30 June] Major von Colomb has taken the bridge at St Germain with two battalions, half a horse battery and one cavalry regiment. The bridge at Maisons is also intact. Thus, the III Corps is already on the march to St Germain where it will arrive tomorrow morning. The I Corps will follow tonight as will the IV Corps once it has been relieved by the English. Thus, it is impossible to change this march that has been undertaken as decided this morning. Thus, I request you to tell this to the Duke and all the more so as

17 *WSD*, vol X, pp 622–3.   19 Voss, pp 99–100.
18 Nostitz, p 61.

his plan to march via Pontoise and Poissy will separate the armies for four days and give the enemy that amount of time to destroy the bridge at Poissy. That, and because we move more quickly, is the only reason to undertake this operation. Of course, it would be much easier for us to remain here, to rest our troops and to allow our baggage trains to come up. As soon as we reach St Germain, we will try to advance on St Cloud, and then it will be necessary to lay a bridge at Argenteuil and repair those at Bezons and Chatou.

What is now most important is to get IV Army Corps relieved by Wellington's army as soon as possible.[20]

Gneisenau was thus presenting Wellington with a *fait accompli*. There was no way he was going to allow the Duke to be in a position to make any reasonable claim to lead the way into Paris. That honour was to be for the Prussians and the Prussians alone.

Wellington issued the following 'Instructions for the Movement of the Army' for 30 June,

Lord Hill will be so good as to move Baron Estorff's cavalry by Creil and Chantilly to Luzarches; the infantry of the 2nd corps are to move to Chantilly.

Order of march for the 2nd corps: Baron Estorff's cavalry, the 2nd division, the Nassau troops, the 4th division, the baggage of the corps in the order of the column. These troops are to assemble at daybreak, and to march at 5.

The British cavalry will move from its camps near Pont St Maxence to Louvres, and camp in the plain about that place. The cavalry should march at 5.

The 1st corps will move from its camps near St Martin-Longueau and move by Pont St Maxence: the head of this column will be carried as far as La Chapelle, the rear will rest upon Senlis.

Order of march for the 1st corps: Netherlands cavalry, 1st division, 3rd division, Netherlands infantry, baggage of the corps in the order of the column. These troops will assemble at daybreak, and march at 5.

The troops camped near Gournay will move and cross the river Oise at Pont St Maxence; the head of the column will be carried as far as Fleurines, on the road to Senlis; the rear will rest upon Pont St Maxence.

Order of march for the troops camped near Gournay: the Brunswick cavalry, the 5th division, the 6th division, the Brunswick infantry, the reserve artillery, baggage of the corps in the order of the column. These troops will assemble at daybreak, and march at 5.

The pontoon train and hawser bridges will move to Senlis. The reserve ammunition to Pont St Maxence; the civil departments, Pont St Maxence.

Head quarters will be at Louvres.

The British cavalry will draw resources from the villages of Vauderlan [Vaudherland], Goussainville, Le Thillay, Louvres, Epiais, and Chenevières.[21]

On 30 June Wellington's vanguard cavalry duly reached Vaudherland, headquarters and the Reserve Cavalry Louvres, and the Hanoverians Luzarches, having marched via Creil and Chantilly. The II Corps was behind

[20] Voss, p 100.
[21] *WSD*, vol X, pp 628–9.

them, as far as Chantilly, and the I Corps along the paved road from la Chapelle to Senlis, the Reserves from Fleurines to Pont-Ste-Maxence.

The Prussians Move to the Right

The Prussians now executed their move around the west of Paris to its relatively undefended south from where they planned to enter the city. Following his orders, Thielemann gathered his corps together to the west of Dammartin early in the morning of the 30th. It assembled in the following order in the direction of Patte d'Oie: 9th Brigade, 10th, 11th, 12th, Reserve Artillery. The Reserve Cavalry took the lead from Tremblay with the 12th Hussars at the point.

As far as Argenteuil, the terrain would conceal Thielemann's movement from the French but from there onwards, Thielemann realised, it would be open to view from the church tower of St Denis. Thus, Thielemann rested his troops on the way while an alternative route was sought. Late that afternoon, following Blücher's order to hurry to St Germain, the III Army Corps moved off again, marching down the Montmorency valley. The Reserve Cavalry only rested once it had gone through Argenteuil, doing so to the west of the road. It then marched on via Maisons, with Thielemann himself, along with the 12th Hussars, arriving in St Germain late that evening. Here, Thielemann heard that Sohr's cavalry brigade had already crossed the Seine in front of him and gone on to Marly (-le-Roi). Thielemann therefore ordered Colomb's detachment to go there as well along with a battalion and half a 12-pounder battery Bülow had sent on to him, giving them orders to occupy Marly with infantry.

After having detached two battalions to secure the bridge at Maisons, the 9th Brigade arrived at St Germain at 6 a.m. on 1 July, and took control of the bridge over the Seine. Thielemann's final brigade and the Reserve Artillery arrived about 10 a.m., having been delayed en route by abandoned waggons. There were many stragglers after this march of over 50 km. Once across the Seine, the corps bivouacked in battle order, with its left flank resting on St Germain, the right on the heights of Mareil, and the front towards le Port-Marly.

The seizure of the bridgehead at St Germain was an important coup for the Prussians. As Thurn und Taxis put it in his journal,

> The position at St Germain is most suitable for a determined defence. I believe that if the enemy had had only a few thousand men there, then we could not have taken it without very significant losses. It is probable that the French did not anticipate this very bold move in which we gave up our basis of operations.[22]

Zieten's I Corps was also on the move. The troops formed up at le Blanc-Mesnil at 10.30 p.m. on the 30th. Major von Engelhardt was given command of the 6th Uhlans and 2nd Silesian Hussars with two horse guns and the outposts of the Reserve Cavalry at Sevran, Livry, Bondy and Bobigny supported

[22] Thurn und Taxis, p 352.

by the F./2nd West Prussians at Nonneville. They were ordered to keep the campfires burning to deceive the French as to their real movements until relieved by Wellington.

The order of march was with the 1st Brigade of the Reserve Cavalry at the point, followed by the infantry brigades in numerical order, the 1st supported by a battery of 12-pounders, then the Reserve Artillery, and the 2nd Brigade of the Reserve Cavalry forming the rearguard. The route taken passed south of Gonesse then went through the Montmorency valley via Franconville, Cormeilles and Sartrouville and over the bridge at Maisons. The corps reached Château du Val and Carrières-sous-bois, about half way between Maisons and St Germain, about midday on 1 July and bivouacked there, with the Reserve Cavalry behind le Mesnil and the Reserve Artillery at Maisons. The bridge at Maisons was guarded.

The I Army Corps marched over 34 km that night and, like the III Army Corps, had left many stragglers behind. These losses were in part compensated for by the arrival of the 19th Regiment, part of the 4th Brigade, which had been left behind earlier at Avesnes.

Sortie from St Denis

As it was so close to the French positions, the planned move was potentially most difficult for the IV Army Corps. As there was no sign of the approach of Wellington's forces, the IV Army Corps remained largely where it was on 30 June, though the vanguard under Sydow moved towards Argenteuil to maintain contact with the III Army Corps. Bülow did what he could to alleviate the situation by securing the front against St Denis by reinforcing Schill with three battalions, two squadrons and a 12-pounder battery under Oberst von Hiller. The 14th Brigade relieved the 13th at Aubervilliers and the I./2nd Pomeranian Landwehr garrisoned that village. Two battalions were placed nearby on the road to la Courneuve where the main body of the 14th Brigade bivouacked. To the right, a post at Merville (on the Rouillon brook half way between Dugny and St Denis) maintained the 14th's communications with Hiller. To its left, on the road to la Villette, it kept in contact with Dohna's detachment.

If the French were to attempt to interrupt the movement of the IV Army Corps, then the line of outposts was to fall back to the line from Merville to la Tourterelle (just to the south-west) and defend there. The line of the Rouillon brook with its undergrowth and the substantial local manor houses offered a good position for about six battalions, while the remainder of the brigade was to mass on the cobbled road to le Bourget, covering the left flank.

At 3 p.m., possibly having noticed the III Army Corps marching to Gonesse, the French staged a strong sortie from St Denis onto the road to Stains, and a weaker one against Pierrefitte and Épinay. Oberst von Hiller deployed the Schützen of the F./2nd Silesians and the II./2nd Pomeranian Landwehr, supported by two squadrons and two horse guns. The remainder of his men stayed in Stains on alert. The fighting was heavy at times, and the firefight continued until about 9 p.m. when the French fell back, allowing the Prussian outposts to take up positions beneath the walls of St Denis again.

During the course of the day reports also arrived from Rittmeister von Below and Kapitain von Rohwedel. They stated it would not be possible to lay a bridge at Argenteuil without pontoons, but that it might be possible within 48 hours at Chatou where a number of river barges could be brought from St Germain. Bülow only received the report of Colomb's success that afternoon, somewhat later than Blücher's headquarters. He immediately ordered Oberst von Hiller to take one battalion and half a battery of 12-pounders to secure the bridge. (These are the troops Thielemann later sent on to Marly, as described on page 252 above.) Blücher's written orders to Bülow, quoted on page 248 above, only arrived that evening.

The Second Combat at Aubervilliers, 1 July

It remained quiet along the entire front on the night of the 30th/1st. At 6.30 a.m., however, the French began a heavy bombardment of Aubervilliers from St Denis, following this up with an advance over the canal bridges against the village by a strong body of skirmishers. In the heavy firefight that ensued, the I./2nd Pomeranian Landwehr put up strong resistance. Generalmajor von Ryssel, commander of the 14th Brigade, ordered the II./2nd Silesians to move immediately from Courneuve to the windmill near Aubervilliers and the battalion remained there in readiness for about one and a half hours. The firefight lasted until about midday when French reinforcements succeeded in driving the Pomeranians back to the village church. Ryssel ordered the 5th Company of the 2nd Silesians into the village, while the remainder of the battalion drew up behind it in reserve. He then personally led the 5th and 8th Companies of the 2nd Silesians to support the Pomeranian Landwehr. Meanwhile, the I./2nd Silesians, in reserve behind Courneuve, were ordered to move up in support. The commander of the 2nd Silesians, Major Graf Reichenbach, now came to lead his men in the battle. Premierlieutenant von Montbach led the 5th Company in a successful charge. Its skirmishers, led by Lieutenant Theremin, recaptured the church. A general advance by the Prussians cleared the village and forced the French back over the canal. Their counterattacks were beaten off and the Prussians remained in Aubervilliers until relieved by Wellington's troops at 9 p.m. The skirmish fire continued for a while and in all the Prussians lost 32 men in the day's combat.[23]

The IV Army Corps Moves to the Right

Expecting to be relieved by Wellington, Bülow had ordered his men to move to the right at midday on 1 July. The Reserve Cavalry were to move first, via Dugny and Pierrefitte, with the 15th Brigade and Reserve Artillery following. The 13th Brigade was to remain in position north of le Bourget until further orders, while the 14th Brigade was, when relieved by Wellington, to go back to le Bourget immediately and also await further orders. Oberst von Hiller, with the 16th Brigade, was to wait until the 14th and then the 13th Brigades had marched past Pierrefitte before following on as the rearguard. Oberstlieutenant von Schill's outposts were to remain until Wellington moved up.

[23] Ebertz, p 213.

Wellington's vanguard arrived at le Bourget at 2.30 p.m. Ryssel was again ordered to withdraw all his outposts, including Dohna's, to behind le Bourget and to mass west of the cobbled road before following via Dugny and Pierrefitte. His orders continued,

> I am counting on you having gathered all your men behind le Bourget before evening and then being able to march off, as it is crucial that you rejoin the corps at Argenteuil as soon as possible and be at its disposal.[24]

Bülow's main body had marched off from le Bourget at 2 p.m., reaching Argenteuil between 10 p.m. and 11 p.m. and halting there to await the arrival of the remainder of his men. After the combat at Aubervilliers, Ryssel and Schill only reached Argenteuil at 5 a.m. on the 2nd. Ryssel's men were so exhausted that they had to be allowed to rest for several hours. Before then, at 10.45 p.m. on the 1st, Bülow reported to Blücher that,

> … All measures have been taken to lay a bridge at Argenteuil tonight. Several matters, however, cause me, with Your Highness' permission, to suggest my own choice of a place to cross; I am thinking of Chatou. We are working flat out on the reconstruction of the bridge there that the enemy destroyed and I believe we will be finished tomorrow. I think it will be better to cross at Chatou because the Neuilly Bridge is so near the line of march from Argenteuil to Mont Valérien that my flank would therefore be exposed if I were to debouch via Argenteuil. At daybreak, I will move off from here to Chatou and will cross the Seine as soon as the bridge is ready.[25]

With his troops now well on their way to the right or already across the Seine, Blücher moved his headquarters to St Germain at midday on the 2nd. The Prince had had his way, and the Duke was left following in his wake.

Wellington's Orders

Wellington's 'Instructions for the Movement of the Army' of 1 July read,

> Lord Hill will be so good as to assemble the 2nd corps and to move it upon the great road towards Pierrefitte, and its left to the great road of Senlis.
>
> The 2nd corps will relieve the Prussian corps at Aubervilliers. Lord Hill will be so good as to send on before his corps to General Bülow to concert with him the relief of the Prussian troops and ascertain the position they occupy. The 2nd corps is to assemble at daybreak, and march at 5.
>
> Order of march of the 2nd corps: Baron Estorff's cavalry, 2nd division, Nassau troops, 4th division, baggage of the corps in order of the column.
>
> The cavalry will be camped and cantoned about the villages of Le Thillay, Goussainville, Vauderlan, and Roissy.
>
> Major-General Sir J. Byng will be so good as to move the 1st corps by Louvres past Gonesse on the great road. The 1st corps is to relieve the Prussian corps now occupying a position having its right upon the great road behind Le Bourget, and its left upon the Forest of Bondy. The 1st corps is to relieve the Prussian post at Le Bourget.

---

[24] Voss, p 104.   [25] Voss, p 104.

Sir J. Byng will send on before the 1st corps to the General commanding the Prussian troops on the above position, in order to concert with the Prussian General the relief of the Prussian troops, and to ascertain the position they occupy. The 1st corps will be assembled at daybreak, and will move at 5.

Order of march of the 1st corps: the Netherlands cavalry, the 1st division. the Netherlands infantry, the 3rd division, baggage of the corps in order of the column.

The corps camped between Pont St Maxence and Fleurines will move by Senlis and Louvres, and camp between Louvres and Vauderlan.

Order of march of the above corps: Brunswick cavalry, 5th division, 6th division, Brunswick infantry, reserve artillery, baggage of the corps in order of the column. These troops will assemble at daybreak, and march at 5.

The pontoon train and hawser bridges will move from Senlis at daybreak, and proceed by Louvres to Sarcelles on the road by Chantilly to Paris.

Colonel Nicolay is requested to send forward an officer to examine the best road from Louvres to Sarcelles, who should be back in time to turn off and to conduct the train on its arrival at Louvres to Sarcelles.

Reserve ammunition to move to Louvres. Civil departments to move to Senlis.

Head quarters will be at Gonesse, but the heavy baggage belonging to it will remain at Louvres.[26]

Wellington's Army Arrives

The Anglo-Dutch-German Army relieved the Prussians on the northern front of Paris on 2 July. Its right flank, consisting of the II Corps with the Nassau Contingent and Estorff's brigade of Hanoverian cavalry, took up positions around Pierrefitte and towards the road from Vaudherland to le Bourget, their right resting on the wooded hills there. The I Corps and the Netherlands cavalry took up positions from le Bourget to Bondy, with their outposts along the Ourcq Canal. The Reserve Cavalry camped in and around Vaudherland and the Reserve from there to Louvres. Wellington set up his headquarters in Gonesse.

The three light companies of Colville's 4th Division designated to relieve the Prussian outposts at Aubervilliers did so under fire from the French, moving to the far side of the village. Here, the French commander suggested a local armistice which was agreed to by Lieutenant-Colonel Neil Campbell who saw no advantage to either side in crossing the canal.

No other incidents of note occurred during this movement which was so successful because of the initiative gained by the strenuous efforts of the Prussian forces, particularly their night marches.

With the Brunswickers

Dr. Drude, marching along with the Brunswick Corps among Wellington's reserves, again provided an account of the ordinary soldiers' experiences throughout this period,

[26] *WSD*, vol X, pp 636–8.

On the 29th, we marched to Gournay, a small town. We bivouacked in a valley between a limestone quarry on one side, and a hill with buildings on it on the other. Almost everywhere was deserted and had been plundered by both the Prussians and the English...

On the 30th, we marched to Pont-Ste-Maxence, a rather pretty town on the Oise, a navigable river in a romantic area. Here, the Oise is crossed by a magnificent stone bridge that the French had destroyed the year before [during the campaign of 1814]. We bivouacked in a wood to the right. I slept with the Major, etc. in a farmer's cottage where we found wine, bread, beer and meat...

On 1st July, we marched eight hours to Senlis, then to Louvres. Both were bad towns, Senlis a bit better. Louvres has a royal palace. We bivouacked west of Louvres, but I slept with the Major, etc. in a big warehouse where we found nothing to eat. I set up a field station here...

On 2nd July, we marched through Gonesse for two hours, which is 1½ hours north-east of Paris, which we could see as we marched, along with Montmartre. Around noon, we heard firing coming from Montmartre to the west, where the Prussians were having an encounter with the French.[27]

Sohr's Raid

Oberstlieutenant von Sohr and his raiding party of two regiments of hussars, some 650 men, were resting in quarters north of Gonesse on the night of the 29th/30th when their orders arrived to raid along the left bank of the Seine. From 25–29 June they had ridden a total of 170 km and since 15 June they had been marching and fighting almost continuously, which was taking its toll both on man and beast and may partly account for what was to follow.

Sohr's detachment rode off at 5 a.m. on the 30th as ordered, heading first for St Germain, where it met Colomb's force, and then on to Marly where it camped. Shortly after midnight Major von Brandenstein of the III Corps staff arrived with the news that his corps had taken the bridge at St Germain and had crossed the Seine and that Colomb was approaching Marly. Sohr decided to move via Versailles to Longjumeau to cut communications between Paris and the Loire. Arriving in Versailles at 10 a.m. he wrote to Blücher that,

> I have the honour to report most humbly to Your Highness that I occupied Versailles today. On my approach, an insignificant number of [French] infantry with a few cavalry, using the broken terrain, took the opportunity of withdrawing along the road to Paris. The 1,200 men of the National Guard here sent a negotiator to us, opened the gates, declared themselves for the king and requested our protection. I agreed on condition that they remove the tricolour cockades from their hats and that Your Highness' permission be sought.
>
> According to reports received here, Napoleon departed on the afternoon of 29 June via Rambouillet and Chartres to Cherbourg where two frigates are waiting for him to embark.
>
> I will continue my march to Longjumeau and have already sent off patrols along all the roads to Paris and the interior of France.[28]

27 GStA, IV HA, 434, fol 11.
28 Voss, p 107.

Sohr had no information on any French forces nearby until the patrols he had sent out returned. In the meantime, as it was a hot day, he had his regiments dismount on the *place d'armes* in front of the palace of Versailles to have a meal and rest. Sohr also took the opportunity to disarm most of the National Guard in the town and replace some of his troopers' saddles and belts from the stores discovered in a cavalry depot. At 4 p.m. he continued his march towards le Plessis-Piquet and Longjumeau.

The Combat at Versailles, 1 July

Meanwhile, Exelmans received news in his bivouac south-east of Vaugirard that two Prussian hussar regiments, coming from St Germain, were on the main square of Versailles and seemed to want to have a long rest there. Exelmans immediately reported this to Vandamme and Davout, requesting permission to drive them off. Exelmans had his 2nd Cavalry Corps with eight regiments of dragoons available along with Domon's and Vallin's divisions and was joined by Vathier's division of four regiments early in the day.

Apparently about 11 a.m. Exelmans took all this cavalry and probably three battalions of the 44e Infantry Regiment – other accounts say only one battalion, and the 33e Regiment – first to the south to the main road from le Plessis-Piquet to Versailles, then in the direction of Versailles. Domon's division went around the south of the town, while Vathier, accompanied by the infantry, went towards Roquencourt to block the line of retreat, followed by Vallin's division.

The 5e and 6e Lancers of Vathier's division moved along the main road from Paris to Versailles. The 6e Chasseurs rode via Sèvres to the road south of Ville-d'Avray leading to the north of Versailles. The 1er Chasseurs, the three battalions of infantry and half a battalion of National Guard volunteers moved from Sèvres via Ville-d'Avray to Roquencourt and occupied the wooded ridge to Versailles and Trianon. A detachment of 100 chasseurs was sent to cover the rear towards St Germain, but the Prussian outposts covered every road in the direction of Versailles. A patrol of one sergeant and eight troopers of the 8th Hussars took the chasseurs prisoner at a tavern before they had got far. Another 150 chasseurs, followed by two companies of infantry, pushed forward to the northern entrances to Versailles.

A detachment sent by Sohr to Plessis-Piquet reported to him that the head of a French cavalry column was coming up there. Sohr sent off his vanguard squadron, reinforcing it with the Jäger squadron of the Brandenburg Hussars when it reached the heights of Vélizy and met the French at Villacoublay.

The French vanguard was thrown back in the first clash. Behind it, however, the 5e and the 13e Dragoons deployed out of the wood of Verrières. Sohr charged them with his two regiments, the 5th Pomeranians from the south of the main road, the 3rd Brandenburgers from the north. One squadron of the Brandenburgers followed up in reserve. The French dragoons were driven back and fled to Villacoublay with the Prussians cutting many of them down and capturing their mounts. Sohr attempted to rally his pursuing troopers before they reached Villacoublay.

Meanwhile, Exelmans had found another way into the village for his following regiments and the 20e Dragoons with an unlimbered battery appeared in the flank of the Prussian hussars before they had reformed. The hussars had to retreat, but quickly rallied and counter-charged the French, forcing them back to Villacoublay as well. Despite this success, the Prussians could see they were outnumbered and retired to Versailles. The French pursuit was so vigorous that the rearguard, the Brandenburg Hussars, had to make several charges to try to force Exelmans to break off.

Sohr reached Versailles again at 7 p.m., having already taken heavy losses. His rearguard, using the cover offered by the town gate, held the pursuing French off for a while with carbine fire. The remaining men rode on through the town towards the exit to St Germain, being fired on from some of the houses as they went. A party of National Guards who had not been disarmed awaited the fleeing Prussians and Colonel Simonneau arrived with his 1er Chasseurs to support them. The leading hussar squadrons hesitated a moment, then charged towards the gate, scattering the National Guard and chasseurs and taking Colonel Maubourg prisoner. However, the French infantry had by now blocked every exit from the town, while Vathier's regiments had moved up from Roquencourt and le Chesnay and deployed for the attack. By this time Exelmans' entire force was moving through Versailles from various directions and the Prussians were caught in a trap. Sohr, now severely wounded, was taken prisoner while small groups of his men attempted to cut a way out. Only a few escaped, among them Major von Wins, commander of the Pomeranian Hussars, who rallied the remains of his unit and led them towards St Germain.

Major von Klinkowström, commander of the Brandenburg Hussars, who still had 150 of his troopers under command, described their unfortunate experiences in searching for an escape,

> But this way, too, we came across a bridge with houses next to it that were filled with enemy infantry who fired upon us. This additional obstruction forced us to look for another way out so we tried, cost what it might, to clear a way through the village of le Chesnay. Hardly had we chased off the enemy outposts and found a way through when we ended up on a road lined with high walls. Here, enemy artillery and infantry fire greeted us. We tried to go back the way we had come, but enemy cavalry rode to meet us, cutting us off. In the hopeless bloody battle that followed many of us fell. Even our brave leader, Oberstlieutenant von Sohr, refusing to surrender, was severely wounded by a pistol shot when at my side. All that I had left in my hand after one blow was the hilt of my sabre. On my left, a brave hussar was bleeding in a hopeless struggle.
>
> We fell into the hands of the enemy! Major von Cosel of the General Staff along with several officers of both regiments, namely Rittmeister von Sydow and von Ditfurth of the Brandenburg Hussar Regiment, both severely wounded after a desperate struggle, suffered the same fate.[29]

[29] Schöning, pp 498–9.

Exelmans pursued the scattered Prussians via Marly towards St Germain but in the evening he clashed with the Prussian 9th Brigade which immediately deployed the Fusilier Battalion of the Life Regiment to block the French advance. The F. and I./30th Infantry Regiment joined the action later. Together, they held off the French cavalry attacks, and then repelled an assault by a couple of battalions of infantry supported by artillery, pushing them back to the crossroads at Roquencourt. After this Exelmans kept his corps and Vathier's division at Versailles and fell back to Montrouge early the next morning. The 9th Brigade followed up to Roquencourt, leaving its cavalry bar one squadron behind. The patrols sent forward that night reported Versailles had been abandoned at 3 a.m.

It is difficult to be certain of Sohr's losses as the badly wounded men who had been left behind in Versailles were returned to Prussian hands the next day, and the prisoners were handed back on the fall of Paris. However, on the evening of 2 July, the regiments were of the following strength:

| *Brandenburg Hussars* | 11 officers, 159 other ranks, 10 unmounted personnel. |
| *Pomeranian Hussars* | 13 officers, 125 other ranks, 12 unmounted personnel. |

Once the prisoners had been returned, the regiments recorded the following casualties:

Brandenburg Hussars	Dead	1 officer	15 other ranks	76 horses
	Wounded	7 officers	36 other ranks	35 horses
	Missing		4 other ranks	167 horses
Pomeranian Hussars	Dead	1 officer	57 other ranks	56 horses
	Wounded	4 officers	77 other ranks	25 horses
	Missing			243 horses [30]

An early report mentioned two staff officers being captured, plus 11 officers and 287 other ranks from the Brandenburgers and 8 officers and 225 other ranks from the Pomeranians. However, these figures include many wounded later discovered in Versailles. According to French sources, 437 hussars, including officers, were taken prisoner. In any case, the loss was heavy. The 9th Brigade lost 7 dead, 1 officer and 74 men wounded, and 22 missing. Sohr had clearly underestimated the French strength and determination and was expecting the supporting infantry to have moved up into Versailles sooner.

After rallying his survivors Major von Wins went to report the defeat to Blücher, who was colonel-in-chief of the 5th Hussars. Nostitz described the scene,

> Blücher was in his room on a sofa, enjoying a brief rest and I was sitting in front of the house on a bench when a small troop of hussars of the 5th Regiment led by Major von Wins unexpectedly rode up and stopped. The major dismounted, and recognising me from earlier, came up to me, saying in a very excited voice, 'What you see here is all that is left of the two hussar regiments. Everyone else is either dead or taken prisoner. Even Oberst-lieutenant Sohr has been badly wounded and taken prisoner.'

[30] Voss, p 111.

I was very surprised. I thought it was impossible for two such excellent and brave regiments to suffer such a defeat and I said I could not believe it. Major von Wins assured me it was true and demanded to be taken to the Prince. I tried to stop him, telling him his reception would be highly unpleasant. However, that did not help and I had to announce him.

The Prince heard the report in growing anger and then cried out in rage, 'Lord! If what you are saying is true, then I wish the devil had fetched you too!' With those words, Wins was sent off. The Prince was greatly outraged and shocked.[31]

Blücher had suffered his one great setback in this stage of the campaign.

Events of 2 July

Blücher's intention for 2 July was to advance on a broad front against the south-west of Paris with his two leading corps, the I and III. While doing so, he would observe the terrain on his left flank that rose up to Mont Valérien and the bridge at Neuilly which was still in French hands. The IV Army Corps was to remain behind the centre in reserve. His orders read,

> The III Army Corps is to march off at daybreak tomorrow via Marly to Roquencourt, the vanguard to Versailles. It is to remain there until the I Corps has moved up and then move on from Versailles to Plessis-Piquet with the vanguard going to Châtillon.
>
> The I Army Corps is also to set off at daybreak and march via St Germain and Marly to Roquencourt. From there, it is to move via Vaucresson and Sèvres to Meudon, the vanguard to Issy. A flank detachment is to move along the main road to Paris, via Malmaison to St Cloud.
>
> The IV Corps is also to move off at daybreak and march via St Germain to Versailles.
>
> Headquarters is going to Versailles.
>
> Care is to be taken when marching through this broken, wooded terrain. The woods to the left and right are to be patrolled and observed. The IV Corps is to send a detachment of infantry and cavalry to Poissy to occupy the bridge there, and another detachment to St Nom to observe the road from Versailles to Nantes from the other side of the Marly wood.
>
> When the bridges at Chatou and Argenteuil are ready, detachments are to remain behind to guard them until relieved by the English.[32]

The Prussian movements of 1 July must have made their intentions clear to the French. They reacted accordingly. On 2 July the Imperial Guard moved to the Champ de Mars, on the left bank of the Seine in what was then the south-western part of the city, to act as the reserve. A pontoon bridge was built nearby and a 24-gun battery was placed on the heights of Auteuil on the right bank of the Seine. From there it could enfilade the plain of Grenelle, the possible line of attack from Meudon. To protect this battery, Général Pully's troops, men from the depots, deployed to defend the crossings at St Cloud and

[31] Nostitz, pp 61–2.
[32] Voss, p 113.

Sèvres. The remainder of the French troops on the southern front maintained their positions. The IV Corps drew up on the right at Vaugirard, the III Corps and Exelmans' cavalry from Montrouge to Gentilly. The villages of Issy and Vanves were placed in a state of defence. Outposts took up positions in Sèvres, St Cloud, Clamart and Châtillon. Davout transferred his headquarters to the *barrier d'enfer* in the south of Paris and issued a new decree to all military personnel in Paris to report forthwith to the Champ de Mars.

Following its orders, the III Army Corps marched off at daybreak. The vanguard, the 9th Brigade, reached Versailles without opposition and the main body arrived at Roquencourt where it halted. The I Army Corps moved off at 7 a.m. The vanguard under Steinmetz consisted of the Brandenburg Uhlan Regiment, the 1st Brigade reinforced by one 12-pounder battery and all the 10-pounder howitzers of the corps as well as a brigade of the Reserve Cavalry. The three other brigades followed, then came the Reserve Artillery and finally the remainder of the Reserve Cavalry. To be particularly careful, Zieten sent patrols into the wooded and broken terrain as far as Meudon. The I./1st West Prussians, one squadron and two horse guns, under Kapitain von Krensky, marched via Malmaison to St Cloud.

At Roquencourt the vanguard turned towards Vaucresson, Marne and Ville d'Avray where a French picket was chased off to St Cloud. The Prussians observed that the bridge at St Cloud had been blown up, but the French were attempting to repair it and had a strong body of troops, probably Milhaud's cavalry, in the Bois de Boulogne. Zieten then had the 3rd Brigade move to the left through the park of St Cloud towards the French position to cover the left flank while his vanguard and main body continued their march on Sèvres.

Sèvres, like all the villages around Paris, consisted of solid buildings. The line of houses here ran from east to west in a valley with the surrounding heights being covered with woods, vineyards and walled manor houses. Another part of the village was about 1 km east, by the Seine bridge. The village of Bellevue was roughly the same distance to the south, at the junction of the roads from Versailles to Issy and St Cloud to Meudon. Three battalions of French infantry held Sèvres and Bellevue.

The Combats at Sèvres and les Moulineaux

At 3 p.m. on the 2nd the 1st Brigade encountered the French. The close terrain hindered the Prussian movements to such an extent that only one gun of Foot Battery Nr. 7 could be brought up, and that with great effort. It fired on Sèvres as well as on Billancourt, on the far side of the Seine. The advancing Prussian troops often had to climb the walls of the vineyards to see where they were going and in an attempt to find better paths. In doing so they risked being fired upon at close range by French skirmishers. Despite this Kapitain von Rexin led the two skirmish companies and the skirmishers of the F./24th forward against the French taking cover in various buildings. Charges by small battle columns cleared them, and the Brandenburgers pushed into Sèvres.[33]

Two companies of the Silesian Schützen advanced frontally against the

---

[33] Zychlinski, p 232.

French while the F./24th Regiment attempted to move around to the right. The Prussians slowly forced the French back through the streets and up to and over the Seine bridge. The French threw away the loose planks on the bridge and the exchange of skirmish fire continued across the river. Meanwhile, Steinmetz ordered the skirmish platoons of the II./24th along with the entire Fusilier Battalion and some of the Silesian Schützen to continue on in the direction of Issy.

Four or five battalions of French infantry stood on the far side of the Seine, in Billancourt, with some in St Cloud and a strong skirmish line deployed along the river bank. Rexin deployed his skirmishers with such skill that the bridge was covered by crossfire. Kapitain von Wentzel then took it with the supports of the 12th Company of the 24th Regiment. The Prussians held on to this bridge all night.[34]

Once Steinmetz had established that the III Army Corps had cleared the area to the south of the wood between Chaville and Meudon, he ordered the main body of his 1st Brigade to move on via Bellevue to Meudon. Zieten now directed the 2nd Brigade under Pirch II up the heights of Meudon to the right of the 1st. Its right flank reached to Clamart. He sent the I. and II./2nd Westphalian Landwehr and half of Foot Battery Nr. 3 against les Moulineaux and moved a further battalion to a hamlet north-east of Meudon, just south of the bend in the Seine on the cobbled road to Issy. The 1st Brigade took up positions at the château of Meudon and occupied the hamlet of le Val one km to the east with the 12th Regiment. Some of the 24th Regiment and 1½ companies of Silesian Schützen advanced on les Moulineaux and took it with the first attack. Parts of the 1st and 2nd Brigades accordingly became mixed together by this sequence of moves.

The right flank of the 2nd Brigade attempted to establish contact with the III Army Corps, while in the meantime the infantry of the 2nd Brigade dragged half a 12-pounder battery up the windmill hill between le Val and Clamart that they already held. This was the highest point in the area and this artillery dominated the plain leading down to Issy and engaged in counter-battery fire.

A message arrived from the III Army Corps stating that its main body was in line with Vélizy and its vanguard was standing before Châtillon. However, because of the proximity of the main French force at Montrouge, Zieten ordered the 1st Brigade not to move via les Moulineaux at first.

After Generalmajor von Jagow was sure that the French were not moving forwards from St Cloud and that Krensky's detachment would suffice to secure it, he moved his 3rd Brigade from the left flank via Sèvres to rejoin the corps. It drew up behind the 2nd Brigade at Meudon along with the Reserve Cavalry. For the time being, the 4th Brigade was held back at Sèvres, then later deployed at les Moulineaux.

A large force of French troops, about 15 battalions with strong cavalry and artillery support, in fact what was left of the IV Corps, was observed at Issy. The vineyards in front were filled with infantry. Vandamme himself was in

---

[34] Zychlinski, p 233.

command and had his fresh troops attack les Moulineaux from Issy. The defending forces from the intermingled 1st and 2nd Brigades suffered heavy losses, but drove off the French assaults despite an ever-dwindling supply of ammunition.

As soon as the sound of cannon-fire coming from Châtillon indicated the advance of the vanguard of the III Army Corps had made his right secure, Steinmetz could counter-attack. He ordered Oberst von Stutterheim to take the I./12th and the Brandenburg Uhlans from le Val to the west of Issy, the 24th Regiment against Issy itself and the 1st Westphalian Landwehr against Vanves. Those parts of the 1st and 2nd Brigade which were already engaged, followed by the combined battalion of the 4th Westphalian Landwehr, from the 4th Brigade, also joined this forward movement.

Major von Wietersheim led six platoons of the 12th Regiment towards the heights of Issy. Noticing that the French were making great efforts to defend the main road from Sèvres to Issy, he turned towards it. Two platoons deployed as skirmishers, moving to the right of the road towards the walls and hedges along the outskirts of Issy. Wietersheim took three platoons along the road, with the 6th Platoon behind in reserve. The French fell back into Issy.

A battalion of Landwehr now moved along the main road, so Wietersheim moved the 6th Platoon to the left to make a flanking attack, since it might prove too difficult to stage a frontal assault. Wietersheim and his men charged and even a barricade on the road at the entrance to the village did not stop them. The French fell back, fighting, but the Prussians were able to set up a line of outposts beyond the village. By 10.30 p.m. Issy and Vanves were in Prussian hands and prepared for defence, while the French were falling back on Vaugirard in disorder. Général Vichery was wounded in this combat.[35]

Late that evening, Général Revest, Vandamme's chief-of-staff, rode up and requested a cease-fire. Zieten turned him away, knowing Blücher's views on this issue, telling Revest that he had no authority to make such a decision.

The Prussians Take Châtillon

During the day the III Army Corps had advanced as ordered from Versailles to Châtillon. The 9th Brigade reached Châtillon that evening and occupied it. Leaving four squadrons behind to cover Montrouge, the French forces withdrew and Borcke moved up his outposts to the road junction between Châtillon and Montrouge.

The bulk of the IV Army Corps had started out for St Germain at 5 a.m., the 14th Brigade and Dohna's detachment at 10.30 a.m. At 5 p.m. the corps moved on from St Germain to Versailles, leaving its baggage train north of the Seine. One battalion stayed in St Germain, another was sent to Poissy. Two squadrons went to Garches, placing outposts across the Gennevilliers peninsula in a line from Rueil to Suresnes, and patrolling to Neuilly. Owing to the closed terrain, the corps took every means of security necessary. The 16th Brigade and the Reserve Cavalry bivouacked east of Versailles at Montreuil, the 13th at Viroflay, and the 14th at Roquencourt. Battalions were deployed on

35 Mueller, pp 187–8.

the roads from Roquencourt to St Cloud, from Versailles to Ville d'Avray and to Sèvres. To the south, Buc and les Loges were occupied and a cavalry detachment was sent down the road to Chartres. The 15th Brigade bivouacked in Versailles, guarding its gates, while the Reserve Artillery camped to the north of the town.

Thus, on the evening of 2 July, the Prussian Army and allied forces were in the following positions:

I Army Corps
The vanguards of the 1st and 2nd Brigades in Issy and Vanves respectively, at arms and near the French forces. The main body of the 2nd Brigade was between Vanves and Clamart, that of the 1st between Issy and les Moulineaux. The 3rd Brigade and the Reserve Artillery and Cavalry were between les Moulineaux and Meudon, the 4th behind les Moulineaux, holding that place with the F./19th.

III Army Corps
Two battalions in position in each of Châtillon and Fontenay-aux-Roses, one each in Clamart and Sceaux. A smaller force held Bagneux and another Châtenay on the right. Cavalry guarded the crossroads at Berny. To their rear, the remainder of the 9th and 12th Brigades drew up along the heights on the line Clamart–Sceaux, the Reserve Cavalry at Plessis-Piquet and the 10th and 11th Brigades in front of Vélizy. Headquarters was in Villacoublay.

IV Army Corps
Camped in and around Versailles where Blücher's headquarters later arrived.

Other Prussian units
Krensky's detachment held St Cloud, while Colomb's moved to St Nom, 7½ km south-west of St Germain from where it hoped to observe a suspected French move from Normandy. Wins' hussar brigade (the remains of Sohr's former command) advanced as far as Poissy and linked up with a detachment of the 12th Hussars from the III Army Corps that had remained behind on the north bank of the Seine. Both detachments reported stories from the local inhabitants telling of a French move along the Lower Seine to Versailles. According to Wins' report, it was 1,000 infantry and 400 cavalry strong. However, these reports were not true.

Anglo-Dutch Forces
Wellington's army remained largely in the positions it had taken up during the previous day.

Final Preparations

Once Prussian pioneers had completed the bridges at Argenteuil and Chatou using British pontoons, detachments were sent to Villeneuve, Asnières, la Garenne, Courbevoie and Suresnes on the night of 2/3 July. Thus, communications between the two Allied armies were established. The stage was now set for the capture of Paris.

Chapter 18

The Fall of Paris

Negotiations with the French

As the Prussians approached Paris in late June, various factions within the French ruling circles made overtures towards them, hoping to attain a cease-fire. Blücher rejected their requests. We have already seen how talks in Laon between the Prussians and the French failed really to get started (see page 222). The same emissaries also approached the Duke of Wellington from whom they received a more favourable hearing.

On the morning of 27 June the French government appointed five new commissioners to negotiate with the Allies. Three of these, the Comtes de Valence, Boissy d'Anglas and Flaugergues, favoured the duc d'Orléans for the crown, Général Andreossy was a Bonapartist at heart and the Comte de la Besnardière a supporter of Louis XVIII. They were authorised to go so far as to hand over one fortress on the conclusion of a cease-fire; Blücher had already demanded as many as nine. They were also to attempt to get Wellington's support by offering the crown to the duc d'Orléans, Blücher's acquiescence was to be achieved by offering it to the King of Saxony, thus allowing the Prussians to achieve one of their important war aims – the annexation of all of Saxony and not just the part allocated by the Congress of Vienna. They also took with them a letter from Fouché, the minister of police, to Wellington claiming that the French people desired a constitutional government as in Britain and saying that the Chamber was already working out suitable arrangements.

The Commissioners rode off towards Senlis, and at noon on 28 June, just outside Gonesse, they came across the vanguard of the IV Army Corps under Sydow. Not wanting them to be able to observe the Prussian movements, Bülow sent them to the village of Chenevières, 3 km away, where, under the watchful eye of Premierlieutenant von Auerswald of Bülow's staff, they awaited Blücher's response.

The wily and duplicitous Fouché was concerned by the delay that had taken place and had already sent another message to Blücher at 2 a.m. on 28 June. In it, he offered Blücher an immediate cease-fire in return for the evacuation of one fortress. An officer from Davout's staff by the name of Laloy was ordered to take this message to Grouchy, for Grouchy to have it handed over to the Prussians. Early on the morning of 28 June Laloy met Grouchy on the retreat from Villers-Cotterêts.

After taking receipt of the letter, Grouchy considered it best to open negotiations directly with Blücher and had a letter of his own drafted. As all his staff officers were already occupied taking orders to his corps, he had his chief-of-staff, Général Sénécal, take it to Blücher. It read,

I have the honour to report to Your Highness that I have been authorised by the French government to negotiate a cease-fire on the basis of the demands that the Allied powers have made to the French envoys. I have the honour to request Your Highness to send me a senior officer with whom I can establish the conditions for such a cease-fire. I further request Your Highness to interrupt the marching of your troops and to end all hostilities. More fighting would be pointless as the wishes of the Allied powers have already been fulfilled. I do not doubt that Your Highness will make haste to permit my request and thus avoid any further bloodshed. The glory that Your Highness has achieved can only be made greater by the cessation of hostilities.[1]

On receipt of Bülow's report of the arrival of the French Commissioners, Blücher had sent his aide Nostitz to Chenevières to commence the negotiations. On his way to Chenevières Nostitz met Sénécal just outside Louvres. Nostitz acknowledged the French general and immediately began talks in the hope that he would be able to gain Paris quickly for the Prussians without any further fighting. He had no direct instructions from Blücher, but Nostitz knew his master's mind, so made the following proposal subject to later approval from Blücher:

1. The cease-fire is between the Prussian Army and the corps of Marshal Grouchy. It applies only to those troops directly under the command of the Marshal.
2. The corps of Marshal Grouchy is to march without stopping to the far side of the Loire where the Marshal has the choice of either taking up positions or sending his troops into cantonments.
3. Marshal Grouchy agrees that the march to the Loire is to be undertaken as far as possible from Paris. Both parties are to appoint officers to agree the details.
4. Marshal Grouchy agrees on his word of honour to provide no assistance whatsoever to the defence of Paris, nor to place any obstacles in the way of the operations of the Prussian Army.
5. Marshal Grouchy is to hand over Laon, la Fère and Soissons which are held by his corps.
6. Hostilities may recommence three days after both parties have given notice of such.[2]

Although the capitulation of Paris was not agreed directly, the one reliable body of French troops would have been neutralised by an agreement in these terms, but it remained doubtful that Grouchy had sufficient control over his men to put such a deal into operation. Sénécal sent a copy of this draft to Grouchy and accompanied Nostitz to Louvres. Here, Nostitz met a group of royalists who claimed that the Provisional Government had proclaimed Louis XVIII king and that the army had welcomed this. Sénécal objected, saying that only Grouchy's army mattered, and that had not recognised the king, nor would it do so.

Nostitz continued to Chenevières where he met the Commissioners. He

---

[1] Voss, pp 131–2.
[2] Voss, p 132.

informed them of Blücher's demands, which they rejected and then demanded to be taken to Wellington. Blücher refused to continue negotiations with them and allowed them to go to the Duke's headquarters.

Meanwhile, Gneisenau authorised Nostitz's agreement with Sénécal, saving the exception that a larger number of fortresses would be required to be evacuated and their garrisons placed under Grouchy's command. At that moment, news of the second combat at Villers-Cotterêts came in, upsetting Sénécal, who said that nothing would now become of the agreement as Grouchy was sure to be dismissed from his command. Sénécal then left the Prussian headquarters, crossed the Prussian lines under escort and joined Vathier's cavalry division.

When the men of the 1er Chasseurs heard the news of his negotiations, they stormed Sénécal's carriage, accusing him of treason. Vathier and Exelmans rescued him. Major von Brünneck, who was accompanying Sénécal, had Exelmans take him away for his own safety. The draft agreement thus never reached Grouchy for acceptance, but instead was handed to Davout in la Villette. Fouché, hearing of the agreement, had Davout arrest Sénécal but he was released on 30 June, after Grouchy's intervention.

Early on 29 June Wellington received the Commissioners in Estrées St Denis. The Duke repeated that the abdication of Napoleon was insufficient reason for a cease-fire, and only a viable government that could guarantee the security of Europe would be acceptable to the Allies. Furthermore, he would not be prepared to recognise Napoleon's son as head of state, neither would any other prince be acceptable (a reference to the duc d'Orleans). After consulting with Blücher, Wellington confirmed this position to the Commissioners in writing that night.[3]

The Commissioners sent an officer to Paris with this information. He reached the IV Army Corps early on 30 June during the combat of Aubervilliers, was sent under flag of truce towards the French outposts, but was fired on, slightly wounded, and turned around. Thus it was only during the evening of 2 July that a courier from Louvres arrived in Paris, bringing the news that the proposed cease-fire had not been confirmed. However, the French leaders did not see Wellington's statement as conclusive and in any case Wellington maintained both oral and written communications with the Commissioners over the next few days.[4]

Despite its overtures of peace to the Allies, the Provisional Government declared a state of siege in Paris on 28 June. Meanwhile, a faction in the Chamber of Deputies tried to drum up support in the army for the claim of Napoleon II. Fouché, on the other hand, sought support for Louis XVIII. Lack of a determined government led to order breaking down on the streets of the capital.

During the afternoon of 29 June another delegation from Paris arrived at Bülow's headquarters. He declined to enter into negotiations, but instead sent a letter from Davout the delegates brought with them to Blücher. This letter

---

3 See *WD*, vol XII, p 522.
4 See *WD*, vol XII, pp 525–39.

pointed out that, as Napoleon had abdicated, any reason for continuing the war had gone, and thus requested a cessation of hostilities.[5] On the 30th Davout sent a similar letter to Wellington and Blücher, to which both replied. Contrasting their replies gives a good example of their different perspectives on this issue. At 10 a.m. on 1 July Wellington wrote,

> I have just received Your Excellency's letter of 30th June in which Your Excellency sent me news of the armistice [on the Italian front] that [the Austrian] Général Frimont has concluded with Field-Marshal the Duke of Albuféra [better known as Marshal Suchet].
>
> I have already informed the French Commissioners sent to the allied powers in writing and the French Commissioners sent to me verbally of the reasons that prevent me from ceasing my operations and that – as I have every reason to believe – will be fully adopted by the allied powers of my sovereign, whose armies I have the honour of commanding.
>
> I have every reason on earth to stop the loss of blood by the brave troops I command. However, this can only take place under conditions that assure the establishment and stability of the general peace.[6]

Blücher's reply read,

> It is wrong that all causes of the war between the allied powers and France ceased when Napoleon abdicated. He did so only conditionally, in favour of his son, and the resolution of the allied powers excluded not just Napoleon, but all members of his family from the throne.
>
> Just because Général Frimont considers himself empowered to conclude a cease-fire with the general opposing him, this is not a motive for us to do the same. We are pursuing victory, and God has given us both the means and the will to do so.
>
> Be careful, My Lord Marshal, of what you do. Do not condemn a city to ruin, for you must know what bitter soldiers would do if they were allowed to storm your capital. Do you want Paris to be cursed as much as Hamburg was? [A reference to Davout's governorship of Hamburg in 1813–14.]
>
> We want to enter Paris to protect decent citizens against the looting threatened by the mob. Only in Paris can there be a reliable cease-fire. You, Lord Marshal, should not forget our relationship to your nation.
>
> I should also draw to your attention, Lord Marshal, that if you really want to negotiate with us, then it is strange that you break international law by holding on to officers we send with letters and missions. [Blücher was referring here to Majors von Brünneck and von Royer whom Bülow had sent off, but who had yet to return.][7]

Blücher's bitter threats clearly contrast with Wellington's more conciliatory tone and a letter Blücher sent his king the same day described the armistice with the Austrians as 'treachery'. These letters are a good example of the

---

5 Voss, p 137 has the text of the letter.
6 *WD*, vol XII, p 524–5.
7 Voss, p 138.

differing war aims of the two powers. Not surprisingly, Davout replied only to Wellington. He wrote,

> Animated by the same desire as Your Excellency, I only wish to know what the conditions would be for peace between us and request you to let me know them.[8]

Before Davout had written this letter, Wellington had let Fouché know through one of his agents that only a declaration for Louis XVIII would suffice to permit a cease-fire.

Müffling was keeping Gneisenau informed of events in Wellington's headquarters, writing to him on the morning of 1 July,

> After the Duke of Wellington had read the despatches and passed them on to the Commissioners, they requested a meeting. They asked the Duke, since Napoleon had left Paris yesterday, to allow them a few days before proclaiming Louis XVIII [as head of state] so that they could restore order in the army. When the Duke answered that the army must quit Paris immediately and retire on the Loire, the deputies unanimously agreed that they could not force the army to do so. Moreover, if he were to demand that, then Paris would be lost to the king and country as the mob would loot and destroy everything.
>
> The Duke took me into his confidence, saying that rather than get involved in such an affair, which would cost perhaps between 6,000 and 10,000 men, he would be in favour of simply surrounding Paris, thus cutting off its supplies, and waiting for Marshal Wrede [commander of the Bavarian contingent] to arrive. The English troops in his army were the only ones he could trust to do anything worthwhile and the English parliament would hold him responsible for Napoleon's escape, if he were to employ more than about 1,000 men for this affair, as in four or five days, the matter would be over anyway. I persuaded the Duke to answer the deputies that anything Napoleon might say is not a guarantee, that Marshal Davout had not mentioned Napoleon's departure, and that other reports received yesterday evening placed him at Montmartre. Thus, our movement had to continue.
>
> Monsieur [the duc d'Artois, brother and heir to King Louis] has arrived. The very thought that his beautiful Paris might suffer caused him to tremble and he begged the Duke to spare the city. The five deputies paid homage to him.
>
> I beg Your Excellency to send reports of our operations to me in Gonesse every two hours. At the same time, please instruct me as to how to react should agreement on an armistice seem likely. When the Duke of Wellington asked me what your intentions were, I answered that I hoped he had discussed all this with Your Excellency yesterday, as that was the intention of the journey. He answered that one meeting was insufficient for such matters, as it was necessary to put something down on paper and that, since the commissioners from the provisional government were sent on to here by the Prince, he must have determined under which conditions he would accept a proposal for a cease-fire...

[8] *WSD*, vol X, p 645.

P.S. The Duke is still reading the report [from Bülow] of the reconnaissance of the enemy positions and I will send it to Your Excellency with the next communication.

The Duke found the answer to Marshal Davout [above] very good. He has received the same from him.[9]

Müffling was clearly in a difficult situation. Blücher did not intend to agree to a cease-fire until his men had entered Paris and the city was firmly in Prussian control. He had rejected the overtures of the representatives of the provisional government because he regarded them with contempt. Wellington, no doubt realising this, was astute enough to attempt to turn this situation to his advantage. His Prussian rivals may have beaten him to the gates of Paris, but he had the best contacts in that city and, if he were to agree a cease-fire now, he would be pulling the rug from underneath Blücher's feet. Blücher evidently did not respond to Wellington's first overture sent via Müffling, so the Duke wrote to the Prince personally on 2 July.[10] Gneisenau's annotations on the copy received give a clear indication as to his thinking at the time. The Duke's letter arrived in Blücher's headquarters that evening and read as follows (with Gneisenau's comments shown in *italic* type),

I requested General Müffling to write to your Highness yesterday, upon the subject of the propositions which had been made to me by the French Commissioners for a suspension of hostilities, upon which I have not yet had a positive answer from your Highness.

It appears to me that, with the force which you and I have under our command at present, the attack of Paris is a matter of great risk. I am convinced it cannot be made on this side with any hope of success.

[1. Our armies are 105,000 men strong. If their commanders did not feel able to master 60,000 enemy troops, it would show they had little faith in their brave armies. The Prussian attacks yesterday demonstrate sufficiently that that is not the case. Likewise today's combat.]

The army under my command must then cross the Seine twice, and get into the Bois de Boulogne before the attack can be made; and even then if we should succeed the loss would be very severe.

[2. Granted, to operate from the side of the bridge at Neuilly, Wellington's army must cross the Seine twice. But he does have six bridging trains and the enemy cannot operate against them in strength as he is being held here by us, so crossing the Seine twice would not be difficult. If the enemy were to occupy the Bois de Boulogne in appropriate strength, then he would need more troops than he has spare. An attack on the bridge at Neuilly on the left bank of the Seine and through the Bois de Boulogne on the right bank of the river would cut off the defenders from the bridge at Neuilly and probably throw the defences into confusion if we were to attack the troops on the south of Paris and an attack on St Denis coincided with it.]

---

[9] Voss, p 119.
[10] See *WD*, vol XII, p 525, Letter of evening of 1 July from Wellington to the French Commissioners. '... I have still not had a reply from Marshal Blücher to the letter I sent him this morning on the armistice.' See also p 528, letter of 7 a.m. of 2 July '... I still do not have a response from Marshal Blücher.'

We must incur a severe loss, if it is necessary, in any case. But in this case it is not necessary. *[3. If it is ever advisable not to avoid losses, then this is the case here. It is a matter of the honour of the army and of the fright we want to give the French nation. 4. A delay of a few days would give the enemy a chance to regain his senses, to consolidate his defences, to raise the morale of his troops, and we would loose more blood then than if we were to attack now. Why await the uncertain arrival of other Allied troops?]* By the delay of a few days we shall have here the army under Marshal Prince Wrede, and the Allied Sovereigns with it, who will decide upon the measures to be adopted, and success will be certain with a comparatively trifling loss; or, if we choose it, we can settle all our matters now by agreeing to the proposed armistice. *[5. An armistice that did not give us Paris would dishonour the army.]*

The terms on which I think this armistice can be made, and on which alone I will consent to make it, are these:

First; that we shall remain in the positions we now occupy. *[6. Why not make use of the advantage of our position?]*

Secondly; that the French army shall retire from Paris across the Loire. *[7. We agree to that.]*

Thirdly; that Paris shall be given over to the care of the national guard till the King shall order otherwise. *[8. Paris must be handed over to us.]*

Fourthly; the time to be fixed for notice to break off this armistice. *[9. Only when we are in Paris can an armistice be agreed that does not have to be broken off.]*

By adopting this measure, we provide for the quiet restoration of His Majesty to his throne; which is that result of the war which the Sovereigns of all of us have always considered the most beneficial for us all, and the most likely to lead to permanent peace in Europe. *[10. To strive for the aim whereby the sovereigns take their peoples' well-being to heart is a prerequisite of not needing to fear being overwhelmed with war by a restless neighbouring nation. Any other peace would be a betrayal of one's self and suicide. Who is going to stop Bonaparte, after having fled to America for two years, coming back and causing new unrest? It is easy for the English to be satisfied with just the restoration of the Bourbons. Their islands are safe from attack.]*

It is true we shall not have the vain triumph *[11. This is no vain triumph, but rather the duty of the commanders to achieve honour for their troops. Only such a conviction will bring victory.]* of entering Paris at the head of our victorious troops; but, as I have already explained to your Highness, I doubt our having the means at present of succeeding in an attack upon Paris; and, if we are to wait till the arrival of Marshal Prince Wrede to make the attack, I think we shall find the Sovereigns disposed, as they were last year, *[12. We suffered enough from not having made better use of our victory last year.]* to spare the capital of their ally, *[13. Louis XVIII cannot be regarded as a faithful ally of Prussia as he only recently entered into an alliance against us.]* and either not to enter the town at all, *[14. That is certainly not their intention.]* or enter under an armistice, such as it is in your power and mine to sign this day.

I earnestly urge your Highness, then, to consider the reasoning which I have submitted to you on this occasion; and to let me have your decision whether you will agree to any armistice or not; and, if you will, I beg you to name a person to treat in your name with the French Commissioners. If you will not, my conduct will be guided by your decision.[11]

There was no way the Prussians were going to sit and wait for other Allied powers more sympathetic to Wellington to arrive at Paris and dictate the future course of action. Furthermore, the Prussians clearly regarded entering Paris as a matter of honour, and the stability of Louis XVIII's regime was not one of their priorities. Gneisenau penned a temporising reply in which he gave no indication of his real intentions. It read,

> Field Marshal Prince Blücher has already retired, and as the propositions you, My Lord Duke, have made to the Field Marshal, require considerable deliberation, then I will have to wait until the morning for the Field Marshal's instructions regarding your suggestion. I trust Your Grace will permit this delay.
>
> Our troops fought gloriously today and, although they were always less in number than the enemy, they repelled the enemy at all points he attacked, and then even chased back the Imperial Guard. Many people left Paris today to watch the fighting, and the Parisians witnessed the defeat of their troops. The positions that two of our army corps reached today were on the plateau of Meudon, a very strong location.[12]

Meanwhile, the 'sleeping' Field Marshal was having the dispositions for the next day, 3 July, drawn up. Recognising his men were too exhausted to push on into Paris, he ordered them to remain where they were. The disposition read,

> Until further orders, the I Army Corps is to wait at Meudon, vanguard at Issy. Cavalry will reinforce the flank detachment that has gone off via Malmaison to St Cloud and is pushing on towards Mont Valérien and the bridge of Neuilly to observe what there is of the enemy on this side of the Seine. It will also find out if the English have finished the bridge at Argenteuil and advance to there.
>
> The III Army Corps is also to remain in its positions, vanguard towards Châtillon and Bagneux, a detachment to Bourg-la-Reine, patrols to Chevilly and Villejuif.
>
> The IV Army Corps is to remain at Versailles. It is, however, to send a cavalry regiment under an intelligent commander over the Seine at Corbeil or another point. This officer has the task of operating as a partisan between the Marne and Seine. He will also observe the movement of any French reinforcements as well as Marshal Wrede's advance. He is also to attempt to establish communications with the Queen's Dragoon Regiment that should have advanced via Château-Thierry. Small detachments are to go towards Rambouillet, Dourdan and Longjumeau.
>
> Headquarters will remain in Versailles provisionally. I expect precise reports on the enemy's positions, fortifications and artillery as soon as possible.[13]

---

[11] Wellington's letter is in *WD*, vol XII, pp 526–7; Gneisenau's comments can be found in Delbrück, vol II, p 256–60.

[12] *WSD*, vol X, p 651.   [13] Voss, p 121.

That evening, Wellington wrote a long report on the events of recent days and the current situation to Bathurst, the Minister of War in London. In it, he stated,

> … If Prince Blücher consents to suspend his operations, which I imagine he is as sensible as I am to the necessity of doing, till joined by Prince Wrede, I shall urge him to adopt the terms which I propose, without which I will not consent to any suspension.[14]

Clearly, Gneisenau's letter had succeeded in misleading the Duke as to the Prussians' real aims. Wellington considered Blücher not rash enough to push into Paris alone and believed he could dominate their discussions. He misjudged the situation as the lack of movement planned by the Prussians for the next day did not indicate their acquiescence to the Duke's wishes, but merely a pause for breath before taking the plunge.

The Combat at Issy, 3 July 1815

News of Exelmans' success at Versailles on 1 July had arrived in Paris the same evening, causing a discussion between the army's high command and the politicians as to how well Paris could resist the Allies. The next morning, on receiving a negative answer from the council of war, the Provisional Government decided to agree to a cease-fire in return for an evacuation of Paris. The army was not so keen on the idea, however. Handing over the nation's great capital to the enemy without even token resistance was considered dishonourable, so one last show of force was deemed necessary.

On the night of 2/3 July, Davout moved his headquarters and the Guard to Montrouge. On the left flank, along the road to Orléans, Lefol's division of the III Corps drew up level with Montrouge. Teste's division occupied the village, and Exelmans' cavalry corps along with the divisions of light cavalry covered the right. Berthezène's and Habert's divisions stood behind the centre of the French line, between Montrouge and Vaugirard.

At 3 a.m. 20 of Vandamme's guns began a heavy bombardment of Issy. Zieten moved the 1st Brigade there and the 2nd to Vanves, correctly anticipating that an assault would follow. He then reported to headquarters that, although he could not determine the positions and strength of the French because of the morning mist, if he were being attacked in force, he would have to move up both the 3rd and 4th Brigades and was thus requesting that the IV Army Corps should occupy Sèvres and Meudon.

Vandamme attacked Issy with one division at first. The 12th and 24th Regiments, supported by half a 12-pounder battery, held their ground, despite suffering heavy losses from the French artillery fire. At 5.30 a.m. a second French attack commenced, large columns of infantry from two divisions being supported by artillery. This attack caused Zieten to report that he feared he might have to evacuate Issy. However, the 1st and 2nd Brigades managed to drive back the French, with the 2nd Westphalian Landwehr playing a role. Coming up from Moulineaux just in time, the Combined Battalion of the 4th

Westphalian Landwehr forced a French battery to limber up and withdraw. The battery's losses were heavy. Prussian skirmishers followed up the retiring French to the city's edge. Neither the main body of the French forces deployed at Montrouge, nor the Prussian III Army Corps became involved in this combat.

At the same time that the French were storming Issy, their forces at Neuilly had launched an attack on Krensky's detachment. Supported by detachments from Wellington's army that had moved on to the peninsula by the Neuilly bridge, Krensky's men drove the French away. The firing across the Seine continued for some time. Other than that, Wellington's forces did little else that day other than bring up the Reserves to a bivouac between Bonneuil and Arnouville.

Thus, it was the I Army Corps, which had fired the first shot at the start of hostilities on 15 June that also had the honour of firing the last shot at the decisive point on the front. The corps' losses on 2 and 3 July amounted to 1 officer, 256 other ranks and 27 horses dead, 29 officers, 779 other ranks and 13 horses wounded, 206 other ranks missing, a total of 30 officers and 1,241 other ranks.

At 7 a.m. the French artillery ceased firing. Général Revest appeared a second time and, offering the surrender of Paris, requested a cease-fire. Zieten immediately reported this to Versailles. Blücher's answer read,

> Having received Your Excellency's most welcome report, I will now go to St Cloud and will also invite the Duke of Wellington there. I intend having the capitulation signed immediately. Your Excellency can send Marshal Davout's chief-of-staff and the deputies of the city of Paris to St Cloud.[15]

Later that day the Convention of Paris was duly signed.

The French Withdrawal from Paris

The French Army marched out of Paris in eight columns. Three went via Artenay, two via Pithiviers to Orléans, two to the west, one to Blois, the other to Beaugency, and the last, consisting of the troops in Belleville under d'Erlon, to the south-east via Fontainebleau to Gien. This movement lasted from 5 to 11 July. Meanwhile, Masséna maintained order in the city with the National Guard.

The 1st Pomeranian Landwehr Cavalry Regiment under Major von Blankenburg observed the French withdrawal. Blankenburg received the following orders from Gneisenau on 4 July,

> The garrison of Paris has capitulated and will go to Orléans. Move off immediately and take up positions on the main road from Paris to Orléans. As soon as the French corps has started off, follow the rearguard and ensure that no marauders or stragglers are left behind. Any deviation from the main road by the French army is to be reported immediately. When you get to Angerville [65 km south of Paris on the road to Orléans], you are to wait there until

further orders. You are to send out patrols from there towards Orléans and Blois and maintain communications with the III Army Corps. You are to take great care. Assume nothing from the behaviour of the locals. You are to report to General von Bülow.[16]

Blankenburg marched to Bourg-la-Reine on 4 July, following the French columns to Étampes, then to Angerville, where one battalion and one more squadron joined him.

As agreed in the Convention, Wellington's men occupied the northern and western suburbs of Paris on 4 and 5 July. On 6 July Zieten deployed three battalions, one squadron and one battery at each of the 11 gates to Paris on the left bank of the Seine. The same day Blücher transferred his headquarters from Versailles to St Cloud and ordered Prussian pioneers to repair the bridges at Sèvres and St Cloud. He also detached one cavalry regiment from each corps to restore order in the rear of the army. They went to Compiègne, Senlis and St Germain.

Meanwhile, it was discovered that no agreement had been made over the fate of the fort of Vincennes. It held large quantities of weapons and supplies, some of which had been sent there in contravention of the Convention. Vincennes was garrisoned by 1,400 men and its commander, Général Daumesnil, was a declared Bonapartist. Fearing, therefore, that the fort could be used as a base for an uprising, Wellington sealed it off.

Only the question of the entry into Paris now needed to be decided. Early on 5 July Wellington had Müffling write to Blücher expressing his concerns as to Blücher's wish to billet his troops on the inhabitants of the city. The Duke's objections included the unsuitability of the housing, the linguistic differences, the sensitive nature of the Parisians and the need to avoid confrontation. Wellington suggested that, because the low pay of the Prussian officers and soldiers meant they could not afford Paris prices, they should instead draw their supplies from the magazines at the expense of the French government. This would of course not be necessary for the British troops as they enjoyed considerably higher pay. Müffling had already informed the Duke that Blücher interpreted this point as a matter of honour, since the French had billeted their troops in every Prussian village during their occupation of Prussia. It came as no surprise, then, when Blücher answered Wellington as follows,

1. Our soldiers are not a separate stratum of our society, but an important part of the nation itself. I do not accept their separation from other classes and consider this a great insult.
2. The army was greatly insulted by its treatment in Paris a year ago[17]... Now, after it has achieved more than then, no general can repeat this. It is the opinion of our parliament and a matter of honour, and not a question of money, but
3. On the other hand, I am not intending to be quartered in Paris for a long time. All I want is [then follows a list of suggestions of how Blücher intended

---

16 Voss, p 141.
17 Blücher is referring to the fact that victorious Prussian troops had not been allowed to occupy Paris on its fall at the end of the 1814 campaign.

to enter Paris]… Thus, the army will be satisfied and Paris will have only a short, friendly visit.[18]

Blücher got his way.

The Prussian Army Enters Paris

On 7 July the honour of entering the enemy's capital fell to Zieten's I Army Corps. Zieten had suffered the first casualties in this war when hostilities opened on 15 June; Zieten had suffered the heaviest casualties at Ligny on 16 June; Zieten's arrival on Wellington's left at Waterloo allowed the Duke to move men from that flank to save his centre from crumbling; Zieten had marched the hardest to Paris; thus, it was appropriate he be rewarded in such a way. His brigades marched into Paris as follows:

1st Brigade – all bridges and islands on the Seine from the Pont Neuf up to the Pont du Jardin du Roi (otherwise known as the Pont d'Austerlitz) and the 9th Arrondissement.
2nd Brigade – the Palais Luxembourg.
3rd Brigade – the Champ de Mars and les Invalides along with the bridges down from the Pont Neuf to the Pont des Invalides.
4th Brigade – the Place de la Concorde, the Tuileries and the Louvre.
Reserve Cavalry and Artillery – bivouacked on the Champs-Élysées, the baggage trains on the Champ de Mars. Two loaded cannon were positioned on each of the bridges near the Palais de Luxembourg, the Tuileries and the Louvre.

Wellington did not move any significant bodies of troops into Paris itself, but did have 20,000 men set up camp in the Bois de Boulogne on 7 July. One detachment camped on the Champs-Élysées, where it remained until 30 October.

Blücher intended to have Zieten appointed Governor of Paris, but Wellington preferred a candidate less sympathetic to Gneisenau, and suggested Müffling instead. Blücher agreed to this, and one Prussian and one British colonel were made commandants of their respective sides of the Seine. Blücher's most obvious attempts at retribution – the unsuccessful effort to blow up the Pont d'Iéna and the unfulfilled demand for reparations of 100 million Francs – achieved little.

The III Army Corps entered Paris on 8 July, the IV Army Corps following the next day. With the exception of their cavalry, all of the men of these two corps were billeted on the citizens of Paris, as were those parts of the I Army Corps that were not bivouacked in the great squares of the city. Honour was thus satisfied and as early as 9 July Blücher had the III Army Corps begin to leave. It marched to the area of Fontainebleau, Malesherbes and Nemours. The vanguard went on to Pithiviers and Neuville-aux-Bois, detachments being sent to Orléans and Gien. The IV Army Corps moved to the Versailles area on 12 July, spreading out as far as Rambouillet and Houdan the next day. The Reserve Cavalry went to Chartres, the vanguard to Châteaudun,

[18] Voss, p 142.

detachments to Blois, Vendôme, le Mans, Alençon and Évreux. The Reserve Cavalry of the II Army Corps under Generallieutenant von Katzeler moved into the area of Poissy, Mantes and Pontoise.

Of the various detachments from the main army, the Queen's Dragoons under Oberstlieutenant von Kamecke had followed up the French cavalry withdrawing from around Coucy to Soissons. According to Blücher's orders of 27 June, Kamecke was then to cross the Aisne below Soissons to keep a close eye on the French. As the bridges there were destroyed, he could only cross the river at Choisy-au-Bac (near Compiègne), before returning via Breuil to the main road from Soissons to Paris. Thus, Kamecke came up behind the I Army Corps and then moved to Pontoise on the other flank of the army. Here, he received the orders quoted above that Gneisenau had sent on 30 June from Gonesse. He then rode through the night via Dammartin to Lizy-sur-Ourcq, a distance of over 70 km. On 1 July, after a short rest, he rode on to Montreuil, 10 km north-east of la Ferté-sous-Jouarre. He sent patrols to Meaux, la Ferté and Château-Thierry. His destruction of the Marne bridges was therefore somewhat late. On 2 July Kamecke moved on, hoping in vain for the arrival of Oberstlieutenant von Schmiedeberg. He was in the area north of Meaux on 4 and 5 July, and on the 6th went back to 10 km east of Dammartin, where Blücher ordered him to rest the regiment. Kamecke had often met with armed resistance from the local farmers, but on 4 July had also made contact with a detachment of Cossacks from Czernitscheff's corps of the advancing Austro-Russian army.

Oberstlieutenant von Schmiedeberg remained with his Silesian Uhlans in the area of Festieux, south-east of Laon, until 28 June. On 29 and 30 June, he moved via Compiègne to Verberie where he received his new orders. On 1 July he moved via Villers-Cotterêts towards Fère-en-Tardenois and on the 3rd he went on to Épernay, where he took several prisoners. He remained there waiting for the vanguard of Wrede's army, which arrived in Châlons nearby on 5 July. He returned to Gonesse via Dammartin on 11 July.

The 12th Hussar Regiment that had been ordered around the south of Paris and along the right bank of the Seine towards Corbeil on 3 July was no longer needed to establish communications with Kamecke and Schmiedeberg after the signing of the Convention of Paris, so it was recalled.

However the fighting was not yet over. The fortress war was to continue for some months more.

Chapter 19

The Fortress War

The Significance of the Fortress War

The French fortresses played a noteworthy role in the campaign of 1815.[1] Although they did little to hinder the Allied advance into France, they caused considerable nuisance to the lines of supply and communication. Furthermore, they were potential bases for a popular uprising, which the Allies considered likely because of the political instability in France. The fortresses accordingly attracted considerable attention.

The fortress commandants were mainly staunch and determined Bonapartists; others were prepared to hand over their forts to the royalists, but were not willing to surrender to the Allies. Prussian policy with regard to the French fortresses was that those surrendering to the Allies should be jointly occupied and the garrison treated in a friendly fashion; those that did not were to suffer the full rigours of a siege.[2]

On 23 June Blücher wrote to Prinz August of Prussia, the supreme commander of the sieges,

> I beseech Your Royal Highness that in the event of the King of France himself sending you French military or civilian commissioners to accept no terms from them, but to send them without delay to my headquarters. It is important that we avoid interference from the French in all matters of military operations or administration without exception. Above all, I ask Your Royal Highness not to allow any Frenchman, whatever his political persuasion, in the presence of your person.[3]

On 29 June Blücher again ordered that only the unconditional surrender of fortresses should be accepted and an order-in-cabinet to this effect was issued on 3 July.

Wellington had a different policy. As seen earlier, he had handed Cambrai and other places over to Louis XVIII, even after having started operations against them, if the commander raised the royal flag. King Louis naturally wished to control as many fortresses as possible for himself, since they had important stocks of war materials. When pressed by the Allies to order a commandant to surrender directly to them, he temporised.

Although the outcome of the war had been decided and, after the signing of the Convention of Paris, peace talks were in hand, the fortress war continued for some time in various parts of France. Two groups of fortresses and

---

[1] Recommended further reading includes the works by Blesson and Ciriacy cited in the Bibliography. Both authors participated in the sieges.

[2] A glossary of technical terms relating to siege warfare can be found on pages 367–9.

[3] Voss, p 191.

sieges are examined in this chapter, namely the group of northern fortresses west of the Sambre, and the fortresses on and east of that river and on the Meuse. Wellington and Blücher had agreed at Catillon on 23 June that the first group would be dealt with by Wellington's army, the second group by the Prussians.

Sieges Conducted by Wellington's Army

As mentioned earlier, Wellington delegated the investment of his allocated targets to Prins Frederik of the Netherlands. For this task the Prince used Stedman's 1st Netherlands Division, the Indian Brigade, the Belgian 5th Light Dragoons and Ghigny's cavalry brigade, the latter reinforced by Gey's half horse battery. These troops were joined by the 12-pounder batteries Du Bois and Severyns and an artillery park of 30 vehicles from the 1st Company of the 1st Line Artillery Regiment under Captain van der Linden. Stevenart's Battery, which had suffered severely at Waterloo, also joined them as did an additional battery just mobilised, the 6-pounder Battery Kaempfer.

After his appointment Prins Frederik took his headquarters to Houdain, just north of Bavay on 21 June and next day, he moved it to Wargnies-le-Petit, 5 km north-east of le Quesnoy, his first objective. Le Quesnoy was a relatively small fortress and was invested by the Netherlands troops. The two Nassau regiments, however, were sent to Valenciennes and, following a reorganisation, marched to the I Corps at le Cateau-Cambrésis. A regiment of Ghigny's cavalry replaced them, moving initially to Curgies, 5 km south-east of Valenciennes.

Several small demonstrations were undertaken against le Quesnoy on 23 June, but these were unsuccessful, as were further operations on 26 June. However, on 27 June, after Wynands' battery and Gey's half battery had bombarded the fortress for a while, the assaults undertaken were more forceful and the commandant entered into negotiations. He then declared the fortress for Louis XVIII. Anthing's brigade occupied it, finding 51 heavy guns there.

That same day, Stedman took the 1st Division from Jenlain towards Valenciennes. He crossed the Scheldt (Escaut) at Trith and invested the western side of the fortress with the 1st Brigade upstream by the cobbled road to Cambrai, and with the 2nd Brigade downstream. The Indian Brigade invested the eastern side and observed the small fort of Condé, 11½ km to the northeast. The 2nd Battalion of the 5th Regiment was left behind in le Quesnoy as its garrison. The main part of the cavalry brigade also remained on the east side, but sent detachments to observe the fortresses of Douai to the west and Bouchain (half way between Valenciennes and Cambrai). The Prince moved his headquarters to Curgies.

On 30 June some of the heavy guns found in le Quesnoy were brought up and placed in two batteries. One, consisting of one 20-pounder, four 16-pounders and one 12-inch mortar, served at first by gunners from the Indian Brigade, was placed on the right bank of the Scheldt, between Marly and Saultain. Later, the crews were replaced by men of Kaempfer's battery, and finally by men of Steenberghe's. The other battery, consisting of six

12-pounders, was placed on a ridge above the cobbled road on the left bank. It was crewed by Wynands' men.

The bombardment began on 1 July and employed heated shot and incendiaries. It continued for three days and nights, burning down part of the town and the suburb of Marly. The commandant, Général Roy, stood firm at first. He put down an uprising of the town's inhabitants, who had even raised the white flag, and expelled 1,500 of them from the town. However, on 4 July, he asked to be allowed to send an officer to Paris to report on the situation. Permission was granted and the bombardment halted but, because Roy did not fulfil the conditions required, fire was reopened on 7 July and continued in varying intensity until the 20th. That day Roy declared for Louis XVIII, but refused to hand over the fortress. Frederik requested Wellington for instructions, but ceased fire and moved his troops to more comfortable quarters in the meantime. The Indian Brigade was billeted in the villages around Condé, Stedman's division in those between Valenciennes and Denain, 10 km to the west, and the cavalry to the south, on both sides of the Brunhild Road. Steenberghe's battery was attached to the 1st Brigade. Wellington replied on 4 August and the capitulation of Valenciennes was agreed on the 12th. The French regulars were dismissed and the National Guard took over the garrison duties.

A similar agreement was made with Général Bonnaire, commandant of the small fort of Condé, which had been observed by part of Frederik's forces and a detachment of Netherlanders sent from Mons. The fortresses of Lille, Douai and Bouchain were not attacked, and had earlier declared for Louis XVIII.

Sieges Conducted by the Prussian II Army Corps

King Friedrich Wilhelm appointed Prinz August of Prussia to carry out the task of commanding the siege operations conducted by the forces under Prussian command. The troops he had available for this were the II Army Corps that, as we have seen, was taken out of the field army for this purpose, the North German Federal Army Corps, and the garrison of the fortress of Luxembourg. These forces conducted most of the siege operations in this war.

Blücher's 'Disposition' for 22 June had designated II Army Corps to conduct siege operations even before the agreement with Wellington was signed at Catillon. After the earlier battles the corps had a little over 20,000 men left under arms. Four cavalry regiments and a horse battery had been placed at the disposal of army headquarters, while numerous smaller detachments had been left behind to secure communications with the rear. The Prussians had no siege equipment at their disposal and the field artillery of the army corps had relatively little ammunition. However, the capture of Avesnes, and later of other forts, provided the Prussians with the necessary equipment and supplies to conduct their operations. Oberst von Roehl took command of the mobile artillery, together with its waggon trains that, after earlier losses, were manned by 39 officers and about 1,500 other ranks.

Oberst von Ploosen, formerly an engineer officer in the French Army, was appointed chief engineer officer for the sieges. He arrived to take up his post on 30 June. Additional engineer officers were made available in dribs and drabs, and two companies of the Mansfeld Pioneer Battalion, whose men were miners, were brought up from Cologne in waggons. By the beginning of July about 26 engineer officers and 600 men were available, including a number of infantry allocated to the Field Pioneer Companies at the beginning of the siege of Maubeuge.

Blücher specified the first deployment of the army corps in the 'Disposition' of 22 June but Prinz August was allowed to determine which fortresses he was to besiege, in what order, and in what manner. Taking over his command on 24 June in Colleret, he decided to tackle Maubeuge and Landrecies first as these fortresses interrupted lines of communication.

Siege of Maubeuge, 24 June–12 July

Maubeuge was the strongest and most significant French fortress on the River Sambre. It lay in a narrow valley on the left bank of the river, was cut by a tributary of the Sambre, and dominated by the heights along the southern bank. The works were built to Vauban's earlier style, the outline forming an almost regular heptagon. The walls had been built high, and the bastions had particularly tall cavaliers which dominated the southern heights. However the outer walls were in a neglected state, and parts had even fallen down. There was a low hornwork in front of the long curtain wall on the southern side, covered by two arms of the river and a marshy hollow and the other sides were covered by ravelins. The fortress had only two gates, one in the south-west corner, the other in the north.

There were two major outworks, one in front of the north-west corner and one on the eastern side. These had ditches, palisades and covered communication trenches linked to the fortress. One of these redoubts, Mont-la-Croix, was also built up on a small mound. The fortified camp of Rousies was outside the fortress to the south, on the plateau along the southern edge of the valley. This camp was about 3 km long, defended by flèches linked by breastworks. Bonaparte had intended to extend these earthworks in the spring of 1815, but little had been accomplished and parts had already fallen down. Only two of these works were ready for defence. The Redoubt la Falaise, a star-fort, was east of the cobbled road to Beaumont. This was a well-built position with palisades and a deep ditch. It did not have a particularly good line of fire, but was a strong defence point that could only be scaled with ladders. There was also a smaller redoubt, de la Tablanière, close to the south-west gate of the fortress, la Port de la France. Both positions were linked to the fortress with communication trenches.

The fortress commandant was Général Latour-Maubourg. He had a garrison of about 3,000 men at his disposal, of whom only a couple of hundred were line troops or customs officers; most were either National Guardsmen or old soldiers, and only 60 were trained gunners. However, there were 80 heavy cannon in the fortress, sufficient quantities of ammunition and supplies were available, and the 5,000 inhabitants of the town stood behind the garrison and its commandant, so Latour-Maubourg was not inclined to surrender readily.

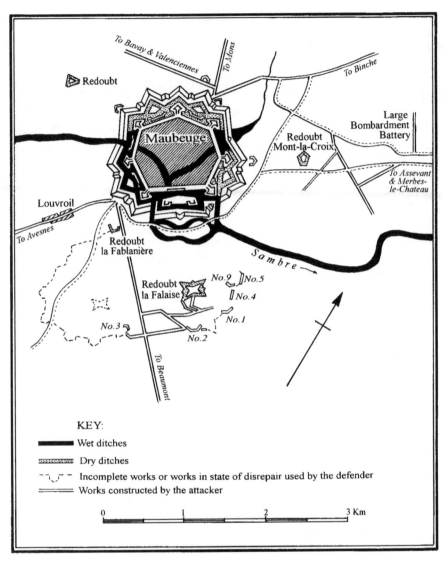

19. Plan of the Fortress of Maubeuge

As mentioned earlier, the Prussian 5th Brigade and a Hanoverian hussar regiment from Estorff's brigade had observed the fortress from 20 June, and on 24 June Generalmajor von Pirch I, commander of the II Army Corps, ordered the investment of Maubeuge. The 7th Brigade, which arrived on 23 June, drew up on the right bank of the Sambre, with its main body at Cerfontaine, 4 km to the south-east. The 5th Brigade, with its headquarters at Boussois, 5 km to the east, covered the left bank. For communications purposes, a bridge was built over the river at Recquignies. The besieging Prussians numbered 7,700 infantrymen, 960 cavalry, 500 artillerymen and 546 engineers. The necessary ordnance was due to come up from Guise and Avesnes and was to consist of three 24-pounders, seven 12- and 16-pounders, three howitzers, three light mortars and two 50-pound mortars, but by 28 June only six of these pieces had arrived.

Not wishing to wait any longer, Prinz August decided to begin the bombardment while the memory of their recent defeat was still fresh in the minds of the French garrison. Thus, on the night of 27/28 June, three battalions of the 7th Brigade were sent against the fortified camp and one battalion of the 25th Regiment against the Louvroil suburb to gain good positions for the batteries. The French did not resist these moves. The ring of investment could now be brought so close that infantry outposts were placed within musket range of the fortress. The garrison mounted a sortie of about 400 men against a supply dump on the afternoon of 29 June along the roads to Avesnes and Beaumont but, warned by these outposts, the Fusilier Battalion of the Elbe Landwehr Regiment easily repelled this.

In the night of 28/29 June, all the 12-pounders and howitzers available were brought up into position. One battery of eight 12-pounders was deployed on the left bank of the Sambre in front of the village of Assevant. Two batteries of 7-pounder howitzers, 14 pieces in all, were placed behind the lines of the old fortified camp on both sides of the road to Beaumont. One battery of four 10-pounder howitzers deployed a little further to the west, just behind the redoubt of the old camp.

This mass of artillery opened fire at 7.30 a.m. on the 29th. The bombardment continued, with an occasional pause, into the night. The town caught fire and the great church was burned down. The French artillery did not reply and the fortress itself was not damaged in the slightest, so the commandant rejected a call to capitulate. Instead, he prepared the outworks for an assault. Six of the Prussian howitzers were also damaged by use, so after 2,900 rounds had been fired, the bombardment ceased. From 3 a.m. on 30 June the guns were slowly withdrawn under the cover of some of the 7-pounder howitzers, though one of the batteries on the left continued to fire until 3 p.m. that day.

Oberst von Ploosen then drew up a plan of attack based on the close investment that was already in hand, deciding to bring the parallels and batteries as near to the fortress works as possible. The point of assault was, as agreed with Prinz August, the Falaise redoubt at the south-east corner of the fortress. The flank and rear of this bastion could be attacked from the east, from the heights of the fortified camp. The ditch was dry on this flank, while the escarpment of the wet ditch on the southern side had several breaches. By opening fire on the southern side, Ploosen hoped the French would be fooled into believing the assault was to come there and would move their guns in anticipation.

While the preparations were going on numerous requests were made to the Duke of Wellington to send his siege train of 38 heavy guns under Colonel Dixon and four engineer officers from Mons. This finally arrived on 8 July and the artillery park was set up at Boussois.

In the night of 8/9 July, the assault on la Falaise began. A parallel about 600 paces long was dug with a communication trench to the old camp and two cross trenches, one only 80 paces from the redoubt. In addition, three batteries were dug for the nine new light mortars Wellington was supplying. The tall crops hid this work from the French who did nothing to stop it. However, at 7 a.m. on 9 July they opened musket fire against the Prussian front line and fired 150-pound mortar bombs from the fortress, but these had no effect. The Allied mortar batteries and a detachment of 28 riflemen in the communication trenches fired into the fort with such effect that the garrison had to take cover. At 11 p.m. they abandoned the position, taking their cannon with them. The Redoubt de la Tablanière was also abandoned.

Also on the night of the 8th/9th a parallel about 1,100 paces long was cut on the other side of the Sambre only about 300 paces from Mont-la-Croix. A communication trench extended to the road to Assevant. The French did not interrupt this work as they were fully occupied in moving their guns to the southern side of the main fortress. This artillery bombarded la Falaise so heavily the next morning that Prinz August reduced the garrison from a full company to 30 men. They took cover behind a solid wall. Only the Prussian battery on the left flank was able to return the fire.

On the night of 10/11 July progress was made in the building of further batteries. Battery Nr. 4 was constructed for six British 24-pounders on the right bank, behind the flank work of the old camp. Next to it, Battery Nr. 5 was built for two 50-pounder mortars, but a third, Nr. 9, for four 24-pounders, could not be completed owing to heavy fire from the French. On the opposite bank, construction began of Batteries Nrs. 6, 7 and 8 for 12 heavy mortars, and an approach sap to Mont-la-Croix. Although the French bombarded these works, this had little effect, but a sortie by about 500 men at 1.30 a.m. caused some disruption. The Prussian outposts and labourers were thrown back into the parallels, but managed to defend the artillery pieces there long enough for the trench guards to double up to the front. Under the personal leadership of Prinz August, the F./22nd Regiment, supported by the 1st Pomeranian Infantry and the 5th Westphalian Landwehr, forced the French to retire. As it was close to daybreak by then, it was not possible to complete the earthworks, so nine British light howitzers were brought up instead of the heavy howitzers that had originally been planned.

Full scale firing commenced at 7 a.m. on the 11th. Oberst von Roehl saw to it personally that the heavy batteries on the right bank came into action, and the 24-pounders opened fire at 7 a.m., the mortars a little earlier. The heavy guns of the fortress artillery replied with great violence. Concentrating on the Allied 24-pounder battery, they almost forced it to cease firing. However, the Allied guns were also effective, blowing up several French pieces. The mortar fire was particularly telling, the heavies shooting against the town, the lights against Mont-la-Croix. After suffering a bombardment of about 500 rounds, the French abandoned the latter redoubt, with only a few officers and gunners keeping up some small arms fire.

Until about 3 p.m. the fire coming from the fortress increased steadily, but then at 4 p.m. the commandant hoisted the white flag, requesting terms for capitulation. These were agreed on the morning of 12 July. Under these terms, the commandant was permitted to leave the fortress with the honours of war and march off to the far side of the Loire, taking along 150 line troops, two cannon and several wagons. The National Guard was dismissed. On the morning of 14 July, the I./1st Pomeranian Infantry Regiment occupied the fortress. The booty included 76 artillery pieces, 5,000–6,000 working muskets, plus 15,000 more in the process of manufacture, a large supply of cartridges and shot and 25 tons of powder, along with a substantial quantity of tools and other materials belonging to the small-arms factory.

Prussian losses were 16 dead and 67 wounded. Some 4,400 rounds of artillery ammunition were expended but only about one third of the attacker's guns were even called on to fire.

Siege of Landrecies, 22 June–21 July

Like Maubeuge, Landrecies blocked the use of the River Sambre for shipping and supplies. The fortress here was also in the Vauban style, an irregular pentagon just 300–400 paces across the inside with narrow bastions, five ravelins and counterguards in front of the two bastions on the eastern side. The suburb on the left bank was surrounded by a large hornwork. The main wall reached to 12 metres above the bottom of the ditch and its masonry was in good condition. The ditches were wet, being fed by the Sambre. As the fortress lay in a hollow, it was covered upstream by flooding on the river side, downstream by the marshy terrain. The only slightly rising ground within artillery range was on the eastern side. There was one gate at the south-east of the fortress, and a second to the north-west in the hornwork. The immediate area was filled with houses, gardens and hedges, blocking the line of sight, while trees were growing on the glacis. The fortress commandant. Colonel Plaige, had been unable to get authorisation to clear these obstructions. The garrison consisted of 2,000 men, mainly National Guardsmen. They were largely Bonapartist in their sympathies, while the residents were largely royalist. There were 45 heavy cannon on the walls and ammunition was plentiful.

We saw earlier that men of the IV Army Corps under Generallieutenant von Hake invested Landrecies on 22 June. They were replaced on 24 June by a force under Oberst von Borcke consisting of the 26th Regiment, two squadrons of the Neumark Dragoons and two cannon. The entire 6th Brigade arrived on 25 June, except for one battalion, the I./Elbe Landwehr, which was left behind to cover Avesnes. Bivouacking at Maroilles, the brigade invested

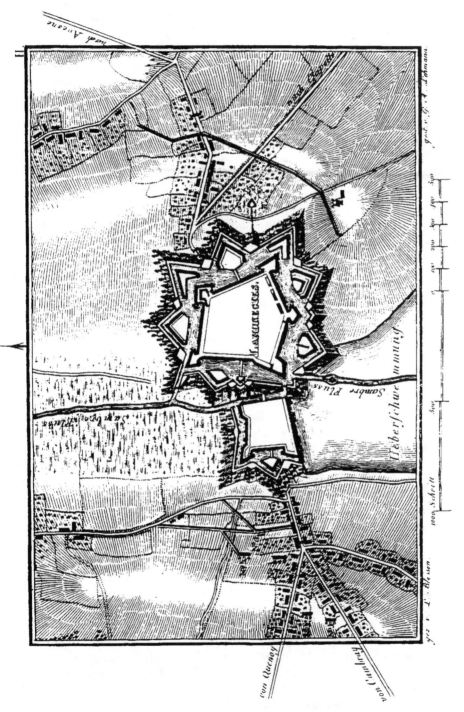

Plan of the Fortress of Landrecies

the fortress on the right bank, while Borcke's detachment covered the left from Fontaine-aux-Bois, 3.5 km north-west of Landrecies. Covered by the terrain, the outposts moved up to the foot of the glacis, and small arms fire was continually exchanged. The howitzers of the 6th Brigade occasionally fired a few shells into the town, but with little perceived effect. Although a new commandant appointed by Louis XVIII arrived on 6 July, Plaige refused to conduct any negotiations, even after the news of the capitulation of Maubeuge arrived and the king had sent a further order on 13 July.

Borcke was sent away to Rocroi on 27 June along with the F./9th Infantry and two battalions of Elbe Landwehr and the II./26th Regiment joined him on 1 July. The I./Elbe Landwehr returned from Avesnes on 29 June, only to be sent on to St Quentin on 13 July. These troop movements made it necessary to change the dispositions around Landrecies. Once the siege of Maubeuge was over, the infantry and artillery there became available for deployment elsewhere. Prinz August sent the vanguard of the 7th Brigade on to Landrecies on the evening of 13 July, the main body following up the next afternoon, along with six cannon, five howitzers and nine mortars taken from those captured at Maubeuge. The 5th Brigade was sent off to be deployed at Rocroi, Mariembourg and Philippeville. Once the 7th Brigade came up from Maubeuge to join the 6th on 15 July, four of its battalions deployed on the right bank, two on the left.

The entire investment corps was placed under the command of Generalmajor von Krafft. It now consisted of 13 battalions and six squadrons (two from the Neumark Dragoons and four from the 4th Kurmark Landwehr Cavalry), and totalled 7,700 infantry, 576 cavalry, 400 gunners and 675 sappers. Generalmajor von Brause commanded the troops on the right bank – nine battalions and five squadrons; Oberst von Schon the left – four battalions and one squadron. A bridge was laid over the Sambre below Ogny, and a second later at Maroilles on the Helpe Mineure.

Ploosen suggested that the eastern side of the fortress be selected as the point of attack. On this side, the terrain favoured the attacker and there were several faults in the construction of the fortress, particularly the large barrack block close to the outer wall. The western hornwork was selected as the target for a feint. The necessary artillery – 26 captured French and 30 British pieces – arrived at Maroilles on 17 July. During the night of 19/20 July, a parallel was dug 300 paces in front of the hornwork. It ran from the cobbled road to le Quesnoy up to the Sambre. The French did not interrupt the work but the next morning, the fortress opened a heavy fire. However, at 11 a.m. the commandant raised the white flag and offered to capitulate to Louis XVIII. The Prussians rejected this offer.

The next night, five batteries were dug behind the parallel and the western suburb on both sides of the road to le Quesnoy. Ten 24-pounders, three heavy and six light mortars were deployed. At the same time, on the right bank, a parallel was opened from the covered road right across the two cobbled roads to Avesnes and la Capelle. The Prussians opened fire at 7 a.m. on 21 July. As the larger part of the garrison was seen at roll call on the right bank, they concentrated on the gate and the bridge between the town and hornwork. The counter-battery fire was ineffective and confusion broke out in the town. The new commandant, appointed by King Louis, marched at the head of the residents and forced Plaige to agree to surrender, although the garrison appeared to want to continue fighting.

The hornwork was handed over that evening, but only after its garrison were persuaded to do this by its second-in-command. That night, a group of French soldiers attempted to blow up the main powder magazine, and the Prussian commissioners, sent to negotiate the capitulation of the fort, had to take refuge in the hornwork. On 22 and 23 July, however, the garrison left Landrecies under the same terms as the garrison of Maubeuge, the commandant marching off to the Loire with 150 infantry of the line and two cannon.

In 1794, during the Revolutionary Wars, this fortress had held out for several months. This time the siege had cost the attacker just seven casualties and 180 rounds of artillery ammunition. For that, 45 guns and a substantial amount of provisions and munitions were gained. Most important was the fact that shipping was now free to move from the Sambre through the Oise to the Seine.

Two battalions of the 22nd Regiment then occupied this important fortress. The diary of Premierlieutenant von Becker of the 22nd Regiment contained some interesting stories of the occupation,

> We were allocated good quarters; the officers ate together in a tavern paid for by the town. We stayed there for three weeks and recovered from our hardships. At daybreak on 2 August all the houses in both the fortress and the surrounding places were examined and the inhabitants disarmed. This was because of a rumour that a mutinous uprising was planned against us in the fortress. From 2 o'clock in the morning, troops occupied every street corner. Nobody was allowed to leave his house and all communication was strictly forbidden. Our officers, each accompanied by four armed sergeants, then went from house to house, while all the inhabitants were still in bed, searching their homes. All firearms, hunting rifles, pistols, sabres and swords were confiscated and deposited in the arsenal.
>
> On 3 August, the birthday of our king, the battalion held a mass in the market square. A French priest had built an altar and celebrated the mass with music. At noon a large feast was arranged for the officers in the town hall to which all officials and local dignitaries were invited. On toasting the health of His Majesty, all captured guns on the walls of the fortress fired three salvoes. There was so much champagne flowing that many were affected. In the suburb towards le Quesnoy, a firework display prepared by the artillery took place that evening. Then everywhere was lit up and this celebration ended late that night.[4]

It would seem that the Prussians ate out Landrecies with such voracity that the inhabitants seriously considered an uprising. Ten days later, Becker and his battalion marched off for Rocroi.

---

[4] Anon, *Infanterie-Regiments Nr. 22*, pp 123–4.

After the fall of Landrecies, only the capture of the fortresses along the Meuse River could better secure the line of communications. However, these fortresses were larger and stronger than the siege equipment to hand could deal with. The Prussian siege train had been moved from Wesel on the Rhine to Namur initially, but Hake was now using most of this equipment in the siege of Mézières, discussed below. For the materials taken from Maubeuge and Landrecies to be used against Givet and Rocroi on the Meuse, then Mariembourg and Philippeville would first have to be taken. Thus, the larger part of the II Army Corps was next allocated to this task.

II Army Corps is Reorganised

Prinz August issued a series of orders on 22 July that resulted in the II Army Corps being reorganised as listed below. Generalmajor von Pirch I took command of the troops investing Philippeville and Mariembourg. Pirch established his headquarters in Senzeille, 6 km south-west of Philippeville on 21 July and when Prinz August moved his headquarters there on the 24th, Pirch transferred his to the nearby village of Villers.

Generalmajor von Tippelskirch took command of the force at Philippeville. It included seven battalions from the 5th Brigade, namely the 1st Pomeranian Regiment, the 25th Regiment (including the Fusilier Battalion at Vervins – see below), the II./5th Westphalian Landwehr and 6-pounder Foot Battery Nr. 10; five battalions from the 6th Brigade, namely the I. and II./Colberg, I. and F./26th, I./1st Elbe Landwehr and 6-pounder Foot Battery Nr. 5; two squadrons of the Neumark Dragoons and one from the 1st Elbe Landwehr Cavalry; six batteries from the Reserve Artillery, namely 6-pounder Foot Battery Nr. 37, 12-pounder Batteries Nrs. 4 and 8, 7-pounder Howitzer Battery Nr. 2 and Horse Batteries Nrs. 5 and 14; 16 officers from the Engineer Brigade with the 6th Field Pioneer Company and the 1st and 2nd Mansfeld Pioneer Companies, a total of seven officers and 500 other ranks.[5]

Major von Roebel took charge of the force at Mariembourg. It included two battalions from the 5th Brigade, namely the I. and F./5th Westphalian Landwehr; one squadron from the 1st Elbe Landwehr Cavalry; and one officer from the Engineer Brigade along with the 7th Field Pioneer Company (two officers, 200 other ranks).

At Givet, Generalmajor von Krafft commanded the following force: the 8th Brigade (nine battalions, one battery); four battalions from the 6th Brigade, namely the F./Colberg, II./26th Regiment, and the II. and F./1st Elbe Landwehr and the 5th Kurmark Landwehr Cavalry Regiment.[6]

At Rocroi, under the orders of General von Braun, Oberst von Hake commanded the following force: the I. and F./14th Regiment from the 7th Brigade and two squadrons from the Neumark Dragoons.[7]

The remainder of the 7th Brigade was placed under the command of Generalmajor von Brause and used to garrison various parts of the occupied

5 Voss, pp 204–5.
6 Voss, p 205.
7 Voss, p 205.

territory as follows: two battalions of the Elbe Landwehr Infantry as the garrison of Maubeuge, replacing the battalions of the 5th Brigade left there earlier that were then sent on to Philippeville on 25 July; Park Column Nr. 14 and Artisan Column Nr. 3 were also sent to Maubeuge; one battalion of the Elbe Landwehr Infantry, with two companies in Bavay, two in Charleroi; two battalions of the 22nd Regiment as the garrison of Landrecies and Berlaimont, the latter being the crossing point over the Sambre between Landrecies and Bavay; one battalion of the 22nd Regiment in Beaumont and Solre-le-Château, as well as between Trélon and Liessies.[8]

The 7th Brigade received the following additional forces: the 4th Kurmark Landwehr Cavalry Regiment, deployed between Laon and Vervins; the 11th Hussar Regiment, observing Laon from posts around Vervins and Marle, supported at first by a battalion of the 8th Brigade that was later replaced by the F./25th Regiment.[9]

Used elsewhere were four regiments of the Reserve Cavalry – Queen's Dragoons, Pomeranian and Brandenburg Hussars, Silesian Uhlans – along with Park Columns Nrs. 4 and 6, all attached to the main army, and two squadrons of the Elbe Landwehr Cavalry in St Quentin.

The horse depot was established in Noyelles-sur-Sambre. The 12-pounder Battery Nr. 10 was still on its way from Wesel, while Park Columns Nrs. 17, 18 and 20 were still in Madgeburg along with Laboratory Column (mobile ammunition workshop) Nr. 2.[10]

Mariembourg, 24 June–30 July

The fort of Mariembourg was a small square-shaped building a little over 400 paces long, surrounded by a wet ditch and a plain wall four metres high and one metre thick with bastion-like cavaliers in the corners. Outside the walls were simple, low earth lunettes dominated by the surrounding heights.

First to invest the fort was Oberst von Reckow with the 8th Brigade on 24 June. When his demand for it to capitulate was rejected, two howitzers from the brigade battery opened fire. The garrison, about 350 men strong, staged a sortie from the entrenched mill that stood in front of the only gate. This attack achieved little. That evening, Reckow moved on to Givet, leaving behind Major von Kwiatkowski with the I./3rd Elbe Landwehr and a small detachment of cavalry. At first, Kwiatkowski observed Mariembourg from a distance but he moved closer to the fort on 7 July after a minor skirmish with the garrison. On 19 July Major von Roebel relieved him with the I./5th Westphalian Landwehr and one squadron of the 1st Elbe Landwehr Cavalry.

On 26 July Oberst von Ploosen personally delivered a further demand for capitulation. The commandant of Mariembourg declared himself prepared to hand over the fort once the ditch had been drained and the walls breached but Ploosen suggested to Prinz August that a mortar bombardment might make the fort capitulate. The following night a parallel 800 paces long was

8 Voss, p 205.
9 Voss, p 206.
10 Voss, p 206.

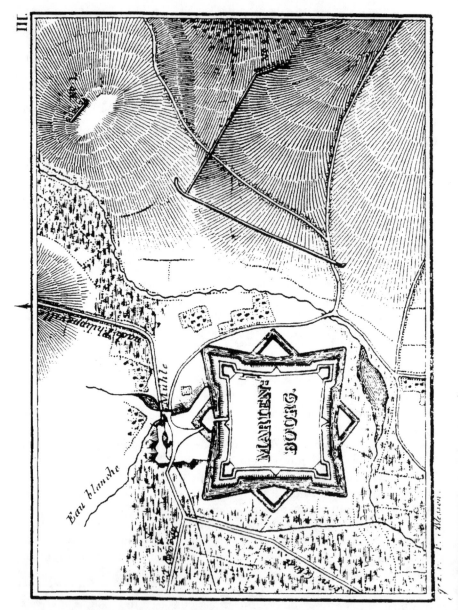

Plan of the Fortress of Mariembourg

constructed for two batteries containing 12 British mortars. The stony ground, made muddy by the heavy rain, made life difficult for the diggers. At daybreak, four guns of the fort's artillery opened fire, making the completion of the batteries and the bringing up of ammunition most difficult. At last, at 7 a.m., the Prussians started to lob shells into the fort, continuing to do so until noon. At first, the shells passed over their small target, but even when they began to strike their mark, the fires they caused were soon put out. The lack of success here led Prinz August to decide to bring up the heavy artillery. Four 16-pounders and six 24-pounders were sent for from the artillery park formed for the siege of Philippeville. They proved to be unnecessary. The bombardment recommenced at 1.30 p.m. and by 3 p.m. the garrison had exhausted its ammunition supply and hoisted the white flag. The garrison was allowed to vacate the fort with the usual terms, taking two cannon with them, and the Prussians occupied it on 30 July. Later, on the orders of Prinz August, they demolished the fortifications. Prussian losses were again minimal.

Philippeville, 24 June–10 August

As this fortress blocked the easiest line of communication between the valleys of the Sambre and Meuse rivers, Philippeville presented more of a problem to the Allies than Mariembourg. Moreover, the fortifications themselves were particularly well sited on a hill which dominated the entire area, and had marshy terrain to the north-west, north, north-east and south. To the south there was a valley about 2 km long, starting at the centre of the west side of the fortress and leading to the village of Neuville, which offered the only cover to an attacker. The fortress itself dated from the 17th century, and had been extended by Vauban into the shape of an almost regular pentagon whose south-west and south-east sides were slightly indented. The five bastions had either high cavaliers or sections in them. In front of the points of the two bastions to the north-west and north-east were flèches along the covered road that formed a counterguard. Ditches with ravelins in front protected the curtain walls. Three of these had redoubts, each of which had simple flèches to the left and right. All the ditches were dry and a system of mines was present. There were nine further flèches along the covered road, all of which were made of masonry. Almost all of the masonry was in good condition and able to withstand direct fire. The garrisons of the outer works greatly hindered the attackers' reconnaissance work. The stony ground made digging difficult and there were too few buildings and hedges in the surrounding area to offer any appreciable cover.

The commandant of the fortress, Général Cassaigne, had 1,200 National Guards, 260 veterans and invalids, 40 customs officers, 100 gunners of the line, and 100 gunners of the National Guard in his garrison. These 1,700 men amounted to just over half of the ideal wartime garrison of 3,000 men, and the 51 available heavy guns were likewise less than the planned wartime complement. There were sufficient supplies of ammunition and provisions and the 1,200 residents largely supported the garrison.

The first Prussian troops to appear at Philippeville were from Sohr's detachment on 23 June, as discussed on page 204. They were followed by the 8th Brigade on the evening of 24 June, which was reinforced in turn, first by two squadrons of the 4th Kurmark Landwehr Cavalry Regiment, later by two of the 5th Regiment. Initially the fortress was only lightly screened but, from 18 July, troops from the 5th Brigade started to arrive from Maubeuge led by the 1st Pomeranian Infantry Regiment along with elements of the Neumark

Plan of the Fortress of Philippeville

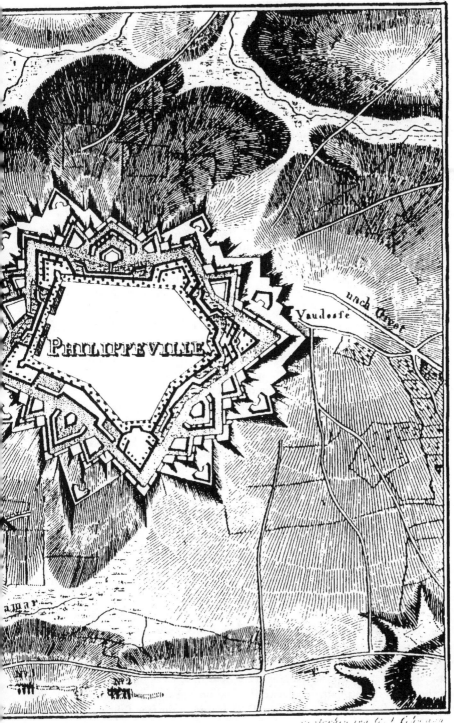

PHILIPPEVILLE

Vaudesse

nach Givet

Dragoons and Elbe Landwehr Cavalry and a horse battery. Part of the 8th Brigade then moved on from Philippeville to Givet. Once all the troops designated to conduct the siege of Philippeville had arrived, the line of investment was tightened as follows. The main body of the 6th Brigade camped near Cerfontaine (8 km west of Philippeville). Its outposts occupied the villages of Neuville, Samart and Sautour around 3 km to the south of the fortress. The 5th Brigade closed up on its left at Villers, 4½ km west of Philippeville, covering the western front over and beyond the road to Beaumont. A special detachment under Major von Dossow of the Neumark Dragoons guarded the northern and eastern fronts. His line of outposts ran from the village of Jamagne, north of the fortress, to the road to Givet. Most of the Prussian forces therefore deployed to the west of Philippeville. The siege equipment coming from Maubeuge and Landrecies was assembled at the village of Daussois, six km to the north-west on the road to Beaumont. The II./5th Westphalian Landwehr guarded it.

Unlike the previous sieges, as the terrain lacked cover, the line of investment here had to be placed at an appreciable distance from the fortress to avoid the fire from the defenders. The troops on outpost duty suffered from the continuously bad weather and a shortage of horses, and the bad weather hindered the movement of the siege equipment. It took until 6 August to bring it all up.

The artillery included 30 British 24-pounder and six French 12- and 16-pounder cannon; six British 25-pounder and six French 6- and 8-inch howitzers; nine British and four French 50-pounder, 13 French 25-pounder and 12 British 7-pounder mortars. There were 41,338 rounds of ammunition available, and 7,400 rounds of British ammunition were due from Mons on 8 or 9 August. The guns of the field artillery are not included in these figures. Of these, all the 12-pounders and some of the 6-pounders had been left behind at Landrecies to free their crews to man the siege artillery; there were some 490 Prussian gunners available. Numerous baskets, fascines and various other siege materials were manufactured.

Ploosen conducted and had had conducted numerous reconnaissances. This led to Prinz August deciding not to assault the bastion on the eastern side, as both the defenders and Ploosen originally anticipated, but to concentrate on the western side, particularly on the southern bastion. The valley from Neuville rose up to the ridge here, which favoured the construction of parallels to the north and south of the marshy valley. This facilitated the bringing up of the siege artillery. The first parallel was planned to come close to the fortress, that is, well in front of the outpost line.

The digging work began on the night of 7/8 August. The 23rd Infantry Regiment had also been ordered up from Givet and, after its arrival early on 8 August, it was set to work immediately. To secure the work, two companies each of the 1st Pomeranian and Colberg Regiments were deployed in the first line. Two of the 1st Pomeranians were held in reserve on the left flank. Two of the F./5th Westphalian Landwehr stood on the right flank from the southern valley, and one company of the F./25th Regiment faced the eastern side of the fortress. About 1,500 men worked in the earlier hours of the night, being relieved by 1,300 others at 5 a.m. By the morning, despite the stony ground, the parallel had been dug only 260 paces from the covered way, attaining a length of 1,800 paces. It crossed the cobbled road from Beaumont, and reached across the valley. A communication trench of a similar length was also dug to link the valley to Neuville. It offered cover from small arms fire.

At the same time, the artillery constructed six batteries. One faced the eastern side of the fortress, on the road to Givet. It contained six 7-pounder mortars. Two more were built, with a total of six 25-pounder howitzers, south of the fortress covering the right flank of the parallels. These flanked the bastion under attack and were to the rear of the barracks at the point of attack. Three were to the west, on both sides of the road to Beaumont. These were the main artillery positions and contained the four 50-pounder mortars and the nine 25-pounder howitzers. It was not possible to deploy the 24-pounder cannon because the rocky terrain could not provide the required cover.

The construction work took place in fog. The fog did not lift until 6 a.m. when the French opened a heavy and effective fire on the attackers, firstly against the parallels, then against the batteries on the east and south sides which opened fire first, later against the batteries on the west side. The Prussian batteries kept up an effective fire until noon when Cassaigne tried to begin negotiations. The talks got nowhere but the Prussians used the cease-fire to repair the damage to the parallels and even improve them.

At 3 p.m. the bombardment restarted, with the fortress catching fire in several places. The largest fire raged in the large barrack block directly behind the bastion under bombardment. The fire, and Prinz August's order for the batteries to concentrate on this bastion, led to the resistance at that point collapsing. An emissary appeared at 7 p.m. and offered the surrender of the fortress. The by now usual terms were offered and the digging of further parallels planned for that night was cancelled. However, the existing parallels were strongly manned that night, leading to consternation in both the garrison of the fortress and the population of the town. The next morning, the Prussians took over the western gate and, on 10 August, the remainder of the town. They disarmed the National Guard and allowed the commandant of the fortress to march off to the Loire with his token 150 men and two guns.

The Prussian losses were one officer and five other ranks dead, and two wounded. They used up 1,800 rounds of artillery ammunition. For that, the war booty consisted of 49 guns and substantial amounts of small arms, flints, ammunition and entrenching tools. Of the artillery, 12 cannon and three mortars were immediately sent to join the artillery park at Givet, along with 20,300 rounds and 35,000 pounds of powder.

As early as 10 August, Prinz August ordered the 7th Brigade, reinforced by the 5th Westphalian Landwehr Regiment, to move to the siege of Rocroi, described next. The remainder of the troops who had invested Philippeville either remained there as its garrison, or were quartered in the districts of Avesnes and Vervins. On 11 August the Prince moved his headquarters to Gué d'Hossus, 3½ km north of Rocroi on the road to Mariembourg.

Rocroi, 29 June–18 August

The fortress of Rocroi caused particular nuisance to the Prussians as it blocked the only direct line of communication between the part of the II Army Corps besieging Givet and the North German Federal Army Corps at Mézières. The heavy rain that summer had restricted the use of the alternative unmade roads through the Ardennes. The fortress lay on the highest point of a ridge generally running from east to west and separating two broad valleys. The road to Mariembourg ran along one of these valleys. The other ran to the south-west, in the general direction of Maubert-Fontaine. The gentle slopes running to the north and north-west were totally dominated from the town. However, to the west and south, along the roads from Maubert-Fontaine and Mézières, there were several farm houses and gardens within musket range of the glacis. The steeper slope to the north-west was also partially obscured.

Rocroi was a Vauban-style fortress built in the shape of an almost regular pentagon. It was small, measuring only about 350 paces across, but it was in good condition. The breastworks had been improved, the covered way palisaded, the entrances to the ditches and all the necessary parts of the counterscarp reinforced. Of the five bastions, the one pointing to the south included a cavalier, while the neck of the north-eastern one was closed off and separated from the town by a ditch, making it into a citadel of sorts. Both these bastions were covered by counterguards and lunettes in front of the glacis. These lunettes, and the one in front of the north-west side, were not defended. In front of the point of the glacis of the west bastion was a flèche with its own glacis, though this did not fully protect the escarpment wall against direct fire, and four of the five ravelins were rather narrow. The ditches were built dry, but contained rainwater in various places. Two gates led out of the town, one to the north-west, one to the west. The garrison of about 1,500 men with 35 guns under Général Projean, although not at full strength, was determined to fight, as was Sub-Prefect Robert. The officers commanding the engineers and artillery were less so, as was the Mayor.

At first, Rocroi was only observed by troops from the 8th Brigade at Philippeville and Givet. On 29 June Oberst von Borcke arrived with the F./9th Infantry, two battalions of Elbe Landwehr and two squadrons of the Neumark Dragoons and was joined on 1 July by the II./26th Regiment. These units moved on to Givet on 19 July, however, being replaced in dribs and drabs thereafter. First to arrive was the F./5th Westphalian Landwehr. followed by the I. and F./14th Regiment on 24 July, and two companies of the F./2nd Elbe Landwehr on the 29th. This small force was kept on its toes as Projean conducted several sorties, often with 500 or more men. From 24 July Borcke was able to place one battalion and one squadron at each gate and this stopped the French sorties for the moment.

Generalmajor von Brause took over the command of the siege on 10 August and the next day Prinz August arrived and inspected the northern side of the fortress personally. He then set up his headquarters opposite it at Maubert-Fontaine. Late that evening, the French staged a sortie to welcome him. About 500 men left via the south-western gate and threw back the weak

Plan of the Fortress of Rocroi

outpost at la Guinguette, at the fork in the road to Chimay and Maubert-Fontaine, 3 km to the west. The French lost several prisoners, however.

An assault on the north-eastern side was the original plan. However, the Prince and Ploosen reconsidered this after a more thorough inspection, deciding to attack from the west, and concentrate on the bastion close to the west gate. An attack here could be made using the cover provided by the houses and gardens on both sides of the steep slopes. The siege park was set up in the village of la Taillette, 2 km west of the town.

The engineer brigade and the first guns arrived from Philippeville on 11 August. By the 14th, all the guns had arrived. These included six 8-inch howitzers and 27 mortars, 15 of which were heavy 25- and 50-pounders, along with 14 officers and 400 gunners. However, only 100 rounds of ammunition were available per gun and the sappers had only managed to obtain limited quantities of entrenching tools and building materials. Brause divided the available troops into three groups. He deployed the F./14th Infantry and F./2nd Elbe Landwehr, I. and II./5th Westphalian Landwehr and one squadron of Neumark Dragoons in Sévigny-la-Forêt and set up his own headquarters there. Oberst von Schon commanded the I. and II./14th Infantry and I. and II./2nd Elbe Landwehr and one squadron of Neumark Dragoons in Gué d'Hossus, and Major von Sack led the 22nd Infantry Regiment and the F./5th Westphalian Landwehr in Grande Chaudière and le Rouilly (3 km north-west and west of Rocroi respectively).

The attack plan called for the construction of parallels and batteries to take place simultaneously. However, providing covered construction sites for the batteries took several days, so the work proper could only be started on the night of 15/16 August.

On the evening of 14 August, the fortress artillery bombarded the area, and again on the evening of the 15th, but on both occasions without interrupting the digging work. On the contrary, a firework display on the target bastion in celebration of Napoleon's birthday on 14 August provided so much illumination that the construction work was facilitated. An approach trench was dug to within 150 paces of the covered way in front of the point of the bastion of the abandoned flèche. The parallel then built was over 800 paces long and its right flank ran through the road to Maubert-Fontaine, while the left rested against a marshy area next to the top of the ridge. There was also a communication trench 650 paces long to this road. All this work was completed in one night by 650 men, protected by 3½ infantry battalions.

Alerted by some careless engineers, the French unsuccessfully attempted to interrupt the work with artillery fire. The 22nd Regiment provided some of the guards for the digging work. Its history described what happened,

> Our skirmishers hid behind hedges and garden fences. We had got so close to the walls that we could hear the sentries calling to each other every quarter of an hour, 'Sentinelle, prenez garde à vous!' Two hours after midnight, the rattling of some passing cannon alerted them and they fired off in all directions, but over our heads, as they did not realise how close the digging was to them.[11]

At the same time, the artillery constructed five batteries. Three of these, containing six 50-pounder and six 25-pounder mortars, stood just behind the parallel. Their designated targets were the bastion close to the west gate and the ravelin next to it. The other two batteries, containing the three remaining

---

[11] Anon, *Infanterie-Regiments Nr. 22*, p 126.

25-pounder mortars and four 25-pounder howitzers, stood north of the town to the flank and rear of the works being attacked. At 7 a.m. on 16 August, as the fog cleared, the batteries opened fire. At the same time, led by two British engineer officers, the Prussians dug a sap from the parallel towards the flèche through what was, in places, marshy terrain.

The fortress artillery replied with effective fire. On the western side of the fortress, Battery Nr. 3, furthest to the north, was totally destroyed after having fired only 16 times, and several bombs landed on the howitzer battery. Under the personal supervision of the Prince, the three other batteries bombarded the walls and houses of the town so effectively that the magazine at the western gate of the fortress was in danger of collapse. As early as 9 a.m. the fortress artillery and engineer officers appeared offering negotiations. The Prussians used the time gained by the talks to get to the top of the glacis in front of the flèche under attack and to place the British light mortars in the parallels.

At noon, the capitulation was agreed with the usual terms and on condition that the west gate be handed over that evening. This outraged the town's population, and even the garrison, led by a battalion commander, staged a protest. The commandant, in the bastion used as a citadel, lost control of the situation. However, the appearance of three Prussian battalions at the gate pacified the rebels. The I./14th Regiment took control of the gate and on 18 August the total capitulation agreed indeed took place without any further disturbance. Eleven light guns were left in the fortress, while 13 heavy pieces, three howitzers and six mortars were made ready to be used at Givet. A substantial quantity of small arms and ammunition was taken. Prussian casualties in the siege were 12 wounded. Only 746 artillery rounds had been fired.

Givet-Charlemont, 25 June–30 November

The Prussian siege corps now faced its hardest task. The fortress of Givet obstructed both any shipping attempting to use the Meuse and the shortest land route to Northern France from Luxembourg and the Prussian Rhine Province. Its possession would facilitate the Prussian Army's communications with Germany which, until now, had run via Liège and Namur, the long way round. The routes to the south of Luxembourg had been allocated to the Austro-Russian army, so Blücher's need was urgent. He acted accordingly.

Givet-Charlemont comprised a series of fortifications running for around 12,000 paces along both sides of the River Meuse but its core was on the northern bank at Charlemont. The Emperor Charles V had started to build this stronghold and Vauban had extended it; indeed, the fortifications at Charlemont are often regarded as his masterpiece. They stood on a wedge-shaped ridge running roughly west to east and rising to about 120 metres above the Meuse valley. The southern face ran down towards the river, the eastern end was a sheer cliff, and the northern side was very steep. The western side grew wider as it approached the village of Foisches below the fortress and 2½ km away. Here, the ridge dropped steeply into the valley of a tributary of the Meuse coming from the north. The terrain in this direction was bare and rocky, so any siege work here was impossible. The ditches were cut in natural rock, except those towards Foisches. The glacis were mostly inclined at 45 degrees and were built on a natural hillside. Masonry and ditches forming flèches and lunettes covered the few gentler slopes. A crenellated flanking wall closed the rock face on the Meuse. These numerous Vauban works made this fortress virtually impregnable.

On the north-western side, an isolated rocky hilltop was used as a basis for the Condé fort. The hollowed-out mass of rock was used as a redoubt and contained a system of mines. The covered connecting way to the Condé fort was a little over 400 paces long, and thus not easy to cut off. The crown of the wall of the main fortress was almost hidden from the fort because of the steepness of the glacis. The fortress contained numerous underground storage rooms.

On the eastern peak of the hill, filling the bend in the Meuse, stood the town of Grand Givet. It was protected by two bastions with a low profile and half a bastion reinforced with two ravelins, the eastern one of which contained a separate redoubt. Broad, deep, wet ditches surrounded all these works.

The broad back of the Mont d'Haurs rose on the southern bank of the Meuse. Its peak, about 1½ km from the river, was about 10 metres above Charlemont. To the north-east and east its steep, rocky face descended into the valley of the River Houille, a tributary of the Meuse. To the south-west the valley of the Houille was also steep and rocky. On the Mont d'Haurs was an entrenched camp about 1,800 paces long and 800 wide. To the south, running along the gentle slope on its main front, were three bastions each with an orillon, two ravelins and two flèches. To the west, a high wall with breastworks ran along the edge of the hill, taking the fortifications up to the river. The only road to the camp was on its northern side, running from the Meuse valley.

The town of Petit Givet lay at the foot of the rocky face of the Mont d'Haurs. The Houille ran through it and a stone bridge linked it to Grand Givet. Its fortifications consisted of three bastions with broad, deep, wet ditches, but no other outer works. The fort of Vignes stood on a dominating hill to the north-west, where it covered the roads to Dinant and Luxembourg. Although it was built of earth, it was in a good condition, with the necks of the bastions being protected by loop-holed walls more than a metre thick. Further away from the town and nearer to the Meuse was a quickly repaired old earth redoubt that the garrison only occupied by daylight. An entrenched outpost stood on a small hilltop on the far side of the brook to the west. In general, the fortifications at Petit Givet were weaker and less well covered than those at Grand Givet but the only entrance to the town was through a narrow rocky passage that was blocked by a wall and an old tower.

The necessary garrison on a war footing was reckoned at 11,000 men with 148 guns. However, the strong position and fortifications meant that a smaller force could conduct a determined defence. On the other hand, the fortress could give cover and accommodation to 20,000–25,000 men. At this time, the garrison consisted of:

4 battalions of National Guards	1,331 men
from the Ardennes, Cher and Marne	
1 marching company of line infantry	158 men

Old soldiers recalled to the colours	360 men
Customs officers	163 men
One company of line artillery	130 men
Other gunners	250 men
Sappers	69 men
Town National Guard	600 men
Total	3,061 men

In addition to this there were some officers who had fled to the fortress after Waterloo.

The commandant of the fortress was Général Comte Burke and the chief of the fortress engineers was Colonel Flayel. Burke had kept himself well informed of the events elsewhere in France and declared himself for Louis XVIII, hoisting the white flag over the fortress and demanding to be treated as an ally. The Prussians did not accept that, but were put in a difficult situation since Wellington had forbidden the Prussians to use any of the siege equipment he had loaned them against fortresses which had declared for the king. Blücher had already informed Prinz August of this on 17 July and repeated the instruction not to do so on 12 August, ordering the British artillery to be returned once Rocroi had fallen. The Prussians would find it difficult to assemble the necessary resources to take Givet.

The first Prussian forces to arrive in the area were parts of the 8th Brigade which reached Givet on 25 June. Initially these could only observe the fortress. On 19 July, after the fall of Philippeville and Rocroi, the brigade was reunited, with the exception of the F./25th Regiment. The F./25th came up only on 24 July, via Vervins, along with the battalions of the 6th Brigade that had been at Rocroi. Generalmajor von Bose took command of the investing force. On the evening of 10 August, the remainder of the 6th Brigade arrived. Only then was a closer investment of the fortress begun.

Blücher issued a 'Disposition on the Besieging of Fortresses' on 20 August. This arrived in Prinz August's headquarters on the 23rd and read,

So that the sieges are co-ordinated, HRH Prinz August is to take command of all the troops and materials being used for this purpose. These troops consist of the II Army Corps and the Corps of the North German princes under the orders of Generallieutenant von Hake, and of that part of the garrison of Luxembourg under the orders of the Prince of Hesse-Homburg which has moved to Longwy.

The fortresses that now must be attacked are:

1. Givet and Charlemont. For this siege, three brigades of the II Army Corps and the two brigades of the Electorate of Hesse from the [North] German Army Corps are to be used.

2. The citadel of Mézières. Here, a Prussian brigade and all [the North German] troops under the orders of Generallieutenant von Hake, except the Hessians and Mecklenburgers, are to be employed. These troops are also to be used to blockade the citadels of Sedan and Montmédy.

3. Longwy. The troops from Luxembourg and the Grand Duchy of Mecklenburg are to be used.

As many guns as necessary are to remain at Mézières to force the citadel to surrender, if it continues to offer resistance. HRH will then decide which guns and troops are to be used against Givet and Montmédy. The deployment of troops, guns and supplies is to be left entirely to HRH, so long as these objectives are attained.[12]

This wording of this disposition was slightly misleading since Prinz August had already been placed in command of the Siege Corps on 23 June and it was flawed in that it did not take into account the need to protect the long lines of communication from a rebellious local population. The mixing of Prussian and other German troops was a deliberate attempt to make the lesser princes dependent on the Prussians. This was opposed particularly by the Hessians, who felt the claim to independence they had established at Sedan and Mézières (*see below*) was being compromised.

Once the 7th Brigade replaced the 8th at the end of August, the following troops were deployed:

On the left bank of the Meuse facing Charlemont:
7th Brigade, plus three battalions and the brigade battery of the 6th Brigade and a cavalry regiment. Four battalions were on outpost duty; one guarded the siege train at Agimont, 3½ km north-west of Charlemont; and the main body camped at Doische, 5½ km west of Charlemont.

On the right bank, facing Petit Givet and the Mont d'Haurs:
Six battalions of the 6th Brigade and a cavalry regiment.[13]

Prinz August established his headquarters at Romedenne, 9 km north-west of Charlemont on the road to Philippeville. From here, he conducted a thorough survey of the fortifications. In his report to Blücher, the Prince informed the Field Marshal that because of the shortage of cannon, ammunition and entrenching tools, there was no foreseeable possibility of successfully attacking Charlemont. Prinz August then suggested to Blücher that he attempt to negotiate free passage of the Meuse and use the II Army Corps elsewhere. This was particularly necessary as the Prussians and North Germans were already consuming all the available food in the area they occupied. Furthermore, the Netherlanders, as always, were turning down almost all requests for supplies and the Russians were encroaching on the supply area of the North Germans.

Blücher rejected the Prince's suggestion, instead insisting that the fortress be stormed immediately. The one advantage the Prussians had was their superior numbers, which meant that the defender would have difficulty in covering all points at once. Prinz August decided first to take the Vignes Fort while bombarding both towns and the entrenched camp and then to attempt to seize Givet and the Mont d'Haurs.

Strenuous efforts were made to acquire the necessary equipment. The men and horses of all of the field batteries of the II Army Corps were used to transport it. At first, the siege train was set up at Gimnée, 6½ km west of

---

[12] Voss, pp 217–8.
[13] Voss, p 221.

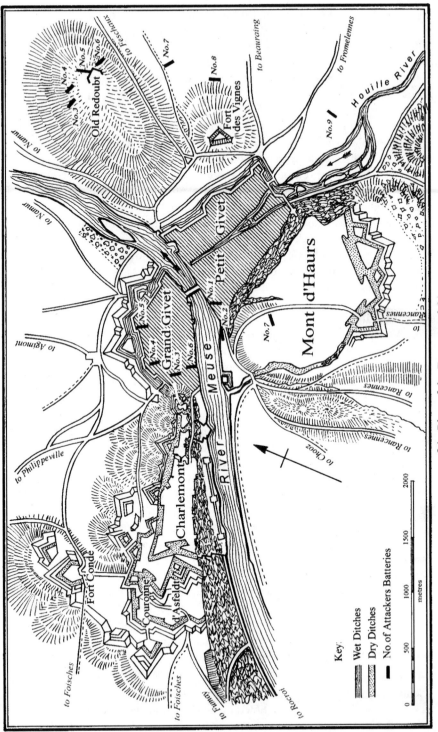

24. Plan of the Fortress of Givet

Charlemont, between the roads to Philippeville and Rocroi, but at the beginning of September the Prince had it briefly moved to Agimont. The artillery,
ammunition and entrenching equipment from Philippeville and Rocroi were
moved up in waggons over the country lanes. Items from Maubeuge,
Landrecies and Avesnes were transported by ship to Namur then, along with
the materials coming from Wesel and Jülich, down the Meuse to Hastière, half
way between Dinant and Givet. Here, everything was loaded onto waggons
for the final stage of its journey. Prussian artillery ammunition was obtained
from the North German Army Corps and brought to Vireux, 10 km above
Givet. Later all these guns were parked at Fromelennes, 2½ km south-east of
Petit Givet. By 6 September, 66 heavy cannon, seven 10- and seven
25-pounder howitzers, 49 mortars (10-, 25- and 50-pounders) and the materials for 16,000 round-shot and 10,000 shells had been assembled. Several
artillery marching companies, an artisan company and a mobile ammunition
workshop designated for the III Army Corps were diverted there and Park
Columns Nrs. 4, 6 and 11 were transferred from the I Army Corps. This was
enough to make a serious attempt at taking Givet.

The sapper companies started work preparing the required materials
immediately after their arrival on 21 August. Some equipment was purchased
in the Netherlands. Temporary bridges were built over the Meuse upstream at
Chooz, 3½ km above Charlemont, and at Ham, closer to Charlemont by land
but further away by water, and later, a third downstream at Heer, 2½ km below
Grand Givet. Other than taking pot-shots at scouts, the garrison of the fortress
undertook little. A small sortie in the direction of Foisches on 2 September
was easily brushed off by the F./22nd Regiment.

On the night of 2/3 September, in preparation for the assault on Petit
Givet a detachment of one officer and 60 fusiliers of the Colberg Regiment
was ordered to take the old redoubt to the north-west and prepare it for
defence. This operation was a total success. The next morning the returning
French garrison was surprised and thrown back in confusion. The garrison first
tried to eject the Colbergers with a bombardment but the earthworks provided
them with sufficient cover. A company of the 14th Regiment moved up in
support, just in time to help hold off a sortie by 600 men and two cannon. The
fighting lasted for two hours, the Prussians losing six dead, and one officer and
20 other ranks wounded. The French appear to have lost more. A further
sortie by 150 men on 5 September in the direction of Charnois, 2 km south of
the Mont d'Haurs, was also thrown back with minimal Prussian losses.

The arrival of the Hessian troops on 4 and 5 September led to a redeploy-
ment of the besieging forces. Of the 22 battalions, eight squadrons and two
batteries now forming the assault force, most were transferred to the right
bank of the Meuse. They were deployed as follows:

Forces on the right bank
  Commanded by Generalmajor von Brause, headquarters, at Baronville,
  8 km east of Givet, near the cobbled road to Luxembourg.
  Right flank: commanded by Major von Mirbach, the F./Colberg, F./14th
  Regiment and the I./2nd Elbe Landwehr Regiment, bivouacking at

Massembre, 2½ km north-east of Petit Givet. In reserve to the rear, the 2nd Electoral Hessian Brigade under Generalmajor von Müller, on the heights behind the village.

Centre: commanded by Major von Schmidt, the I./Colberg and the I. and II./1st Elbe Landwehr, at Dion, 4 km south-east of Petit Givet.

Left flank: facing the Mont d'Haurs, commanded by Oberst von Reuss, the I. and II./26th Regiment and the II./Colberg, at Charnois and at Flohimont, in the Houille valley east of Charnois.

Cavalry: the 10th Hussars cantoned in the villages east of Petit Givet, sending detachments to both flanks as well as to the bridge at Heer.

Forces on the left bank

Commanded by Oberst von Schon.

Right flank: the II. and F./22nd Regiment, from the cobbled road to Fumay, including the bridge at Chooz, to the cobbled road to Philippe-ville, with the I./22nd in reserve at Foisches.

Left flank: the II./14th Regiment, from the road to Philippeville to the Meuse downstream of the town; the II./2nd Elbe Landwehr at Agimont, covering the siege train.

Reserve: the F./26th Regiment and F./1st Elbe Landwehr with the two batteries and two squadrons of the Elbe Landwehr Cavalry, camping at Doische, with two more squadrons to the rear.

The 1st Electoral Hessian Brigade under Generalmajor Prinz Solms did not remain with the besieging forces but was transferred to quarters around Chimay and Signy-le-Petit, well away to the south-west. The I./14th Regiment and F./2nd Elbe Landwehr were sent further on still.[14]

The planned opening of the parallels against the Fort des Vignes on 4 September was delayed because Oberst von Ploosen was suspected of being in communication with Louis XVIII and was removed from his post. His replacement was Kapitain von Vigny. Twenty-four cannon, 12 howitzers and 26 mortars were allocated to the attack. They were to be deployed in nine batteries in an arc running from the eastern bank of the Meuse downstream of the town round to as far as the Houille. The first four of these batteries were built on both sides of the old redoubt during the night of 8/9 September.

However, by the afternoon of 8 September, the commandant of the fortress had already concluded that his forces could not hold all four major sections of the works. Thus, he commenced negotiations, and on 11 September, personally handed over the two towns and the Mont d'Haurs along with 11 guns to Prinz August, having agreed a cease-fire with 24 hours' notice to be given of renewed hostilities. One battalion of Prussians occupied Grand Givet and three more set up camp to the south-east of Petit Givet, placing pickets in that town and on the Mont d'Haurs.

To comply fully with Blücher's orders, the works preparatory to an assault on Charlemont were continued and in fact only ceased after the first October frosts made a formal attack impossible. The construction of six batteries containing a total of 23 cannon, howitzers and mortars was commenced in Grand

14 Voss, p 224.

and Petit Givet, though only indirect fire would be effective against Charlemont. Work on a further battery on the Mont d'Haurs for eight 24-pounders began on 16 September and a mine from Grand Givet under the main wall of Charlemont was started at the same time. It was estimated that this work would take five to six weeks to complete. On 20 September Burke told the Prussians that he would try to hinder this work with a bombardment, but the same day provisional orders for a general cease-fire arrived from Paris, being confirmed four days later. Charlemont continued to be besieged formally until 30 November, after the declaration of peace, and was handed over to Russian troops of occupation.

The North German Federal Army Corps[15]

In Chapter 12 (pages 173–83) we saw that this corps was very much a mixed bag. Some troops were well trained and motivated, others lacked discipline. Supplies were irregular and many of the smaller contingents lacked various necessities. The Oldenburgers did not even have sufficient ammunition. The strength of the corps, without the Mecklenburgers who had yet to arrive, was listed at 416 officers, 17,040 other ranks and 1,042 cavalry. The artillery consisted of two batteries of 6-pounders with a Hessian waggon train.

As we also saw earlier, the corps received the news of the opening of hostilities on 16 June, and was ordered to march to Namur. Generallieutenant von Engelhardt had taken over command. On 22 June Engelhardt marched to Neufchâteau, sending Oberst von Egloffstein's Anhalt-Thuringian brigade from there with a squadron of Hessian dragoons and two guns to Bouillon. The next day, the Hessian brigades reached a bivouac at Florenville, and on the 24th, the main body bivouacked at Bazeilles, while the vanguard took the Meuse crossing at Mouzon.

Investment of Bouillon

Since 1814 the town of Bouillon had supposedly been a sovereign duchy, but the French still occupied it. It lay in the Semois valley, protected by a hilltop castle. Its commandant, Général Bonnichon, rejected calls for capitulation and replied to the ineffective howitzer fire that was all Egloffstein's men could bring to bear. Local conditions prevented a direct assault, so Egloffstein marched off to Sedan, arriving there on 26 June. He left the Lippe-Waldeck Regiment at Bouillon to blockade it.

On 21 July Bonnichon offered to surrender to Louis XVIII. However, the Allies were planning to incorporate this area in the Kingdom of the Netherlands, so he was told simply to hand over the castle. He refused, and on 14 August a contingent of Netherlands troops moved up to replace the besieging forces. Bonnichon finally surrendered to the Netherlanders on 23 August.[16]

---

[15] Recommended further reading is Renouard, *op cit.*
[16] De Bas, *Prins Frederik*, p 921.

Bombardment and Occupation of Sedan, 26–27 June

On 24 June Engelhardt was approaching Vandamme's line of retreat. However, despite every effort, his forces had only covered 40 km in the previous three days, so they were unable to intervene. The Hessian cavalry did encounter several bodies of French horsemen at this time, particularly at Stenay. However, it is unlikely they were from Vandamme's corps, but were possibly either mounted National Guards, men separated from their units, or patrols sent from the fortress of Montmédy.

On 26 June Engelhardt had the fortress of Sedan fired upon by his Hessian Jäger and field artillery, which by now were advancing down both sides of the Meuse valley. The commandant, Baron Choisy, offered negotiations at 5 p.m., the result of which was the handing over of the town and its considerable supplies of provisions. Two Hessian battalions occupied the town, while its garrison – two battalions of National Guard of the Marne and Meuse, a number of National Guard artillerymen, plus some customs officers and gendarmes – withdrew into the castle with 30 guns, promising to remain neutral. Further negotiations resulted in the surrender of the castle along with 29 guns and a substantial amount of ammunition on 20 August. The defending troops were dismissed.

Siege of Mézières, 28 June–10 August

On 28 June, by moving up the 3rd Brigade, the corps could now close up on the fortress of Mézières. This fortress housed extensive weapon and ammunition supplies, two gunmakers' workshops, a powder mill in Charleville and an ammunition factory.

The fortress stood across a promontory some 300 metres wide formed by a bend in the Meuse. It consisted of five individual parts: the old town fortifications, a pentagon running from east to west from which the bridges to the north and south over the Meuse ran; the fortifications of St Julien on the peninsula to the west, a hexagonal redoubt with a hornwork and glacis; the citadel to the east, an irregularly shaped work with bastions, a ravelin and glacis and, in front of this, a flèche built of rocks and covered with earth to protect the wells supplying water to Mézières, this flèche being connected to the citadel by means of a covered way; and finally the two fortification systems covering the bridges over the Meuse, to the north a hornwork with a ravelin, and to the south, a crown-work without any outworks, these last two sections being dominated by higher works in the town and citadel. The Meuse flowed around all five parts, providing the ditches with water.

The town of Charleville stood on the left bank of the Meuse, only 800 metres from the northern bridge. The Meuse protected it to the east. Running around the other three sides of the town was a strong, high wall reinforced by abatis and palisades and with solid gatehouses. A row of houses stood along both sides of the road between Charleville and Mézières.

To the west of Mézières was the village of St Julien. The market gardens surrounding it reached to the foot of the glacis but this was palisaded and well prepared for the defence. The heights to the south at Mohon and east of the

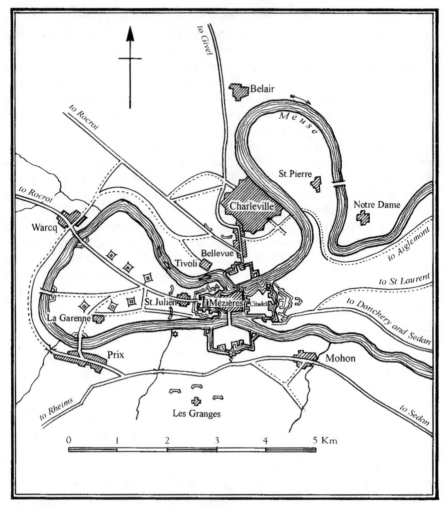

25. Sketch of the Siege of Mézières

citadel towards St Laurent gave observation over the hollow in which the fortress lay but were out of artillery range.

The commandant, Général Lemoine, had commanded a division in Vandamme's corps until 11 June. On arriving here, he found two battalions of National Guards of the Meuse, 900 men. Davout then ordered them elsewhere for a time, and on their return, there were only 400 men left – the rest had deserted. Lemoine was, however, an energetic and determined man. By gathering together stragglers and lightly wounded men, particularly officers, escaping from Waterloo, by taking command of 350 customs officers and by mobilising the town's National Guard, he was able to bring the garrison almost up to its wartime strength of 3,000 men and man the 60 fortress guns. The garrison of roughly another 1,000 National Guards in Charleville was under the command of Général Laplanche.

Generallieutenant von Hake took command of the German forces here on 28 June. He ordered a close investment of the fortifications, with the Thuringian brigade deployed on the right bank and the Hessians on the left. He then requested Prinz August to have him sent siege artillery, a request he had to repeat several times as the few guns available were all being used elsewhere.

Storming of Charleville, 29 June

Engelhardt had already prepared an assault on Charleville which now began on 29 June. Oberstlieutenant Scheffer led the attack by the F./Regiment Kurfürst, F./Regiment Prinz Solms, two companies of Jäger, two squadrons of hussars, three guns and a Prussian sapper company. Scheffer managed to find places near the west gate where he could deploy his men in cover. The houses and gardens near the town protected his men from musket fire from Charleville, while a low ridge covered them from fire from Mézières.

At 4 p.m., after two calls for the fortress to surrender had been rejected, the North Germans opened both small arms and artillery fire. This had little effect, and the fire returned from the fortress caused more problems to the attackers. Rapid action was needed, so Major Bödicker had the Hessian Jäger and Prussian sappers climb parts of the palisades and cut others down. Once the gate had been blown up, the infantry advanced into the town followed by the hussars. Resistance collapsed quickly and Laplanche surrendered along with 18 other officers and all but 50 or 60 of their men who managed to get to Mézières. The assault on Charleville had cost the North Germans one officer and two other ranks dead, one officer and 33 other ranks wounded.

At first, only the Jäger companies occupied Charleville, but from 30 June, Scheffer's entire detachment moved into the town. Some of his men spent their nights under the arches of the buildings around the market place, while others bivouacked to the south-west of the town, spending the days inside the town itself. To provide additional security Scheffer had pickets deploy on the glacis of the hornwork and at Tivoli on the Meuse. Some 600 of Scheffer's men were fortunate enough to get brand new muskets from the factory at Charleville.

A pontoon bridge was laid from Charleville to St Pierre, another above Mohon, and a third downstream at Aiglemont and the besieging troops were redeployed on 1 July. The 1st and part of the 2nd Brigade now stood on the left bank of the Meuse, while most of the 2nd and all of the 3rd were on the right bank. A detachment of men from both Hessian brigades occupied Charleville. Three detachments were deployed, each consisting of one infantry battalion, a division of Jäger and one cavalry squadron. One was placed in Mouzon to observe Montmédy; one in Launois, halfway between Mézières and Rethel, to observe the road to Rheims; and the third went to le Chesne, 30 km east of Rethel, to observe the road running via Vouziers to Châlons-sur-Marne.

Deployment of the North German Corps, 1 July[17]

Headquarters of Generallieutenant von Hake: Sedan
Headquarters of Generallieutenant Engelhardt: Donchery

1st Brigade
Brigade Headquarters: Flize
F./Prinz Solms, Grenadier Battalion von Lossberg: in Charleville under the command of Oberstlieutenant Scheffer
F./Landgraf Karl: Launois
I./Landgraf Karl: bivouacking between la Francheville and St Marceau
I./Prinz Solms: les Petits Ayvelles and Chalandry
½ Battery Nr. 1: Charleville
½ Battery Nr. 1: les Petits Ayvelles
Cavalry: les Grandes Ayvelles
Field Hospital: Dom-le-Mesnil

2nd Brigade
Brigade Headquarters: Vivier-au-Court on the right side of the Meuse
F./Kurfürst: Charleville, under Oberstlieutenant Scheffer
F./Kurprinz: le Chesne
I. & II./Kurfürst: Lumes and Nouvion-sur-Meuse
I./Kurprinz: 1 coy on outpost duty at Mohon; 3 coys at Villers, near Mézières
Grenadier Battalion von Haller: Donchery
Battery Nr. 2: Vrigne-Meuse
Field Hospital: le Dancourt
Jäger Battalion
    ½ coy in Charleville
    ¼ coy in Launois
    ½ coy in le Chesne
    ¼ coy in Mouzon
    ¼ coy bivouacking at la Francheville
    ¼ coy bivouacking at Mohon
    ½ coy at St Laurent
    1½ coys in Rumel and Issancourt

---

[17] Renouard, pp 116–8.

Cavalry Brigade
Life Dragoon Regiment
  1 squadron in le Chesne
  1 squadron in Mouzon
  2 squadrons in Glaire and Wadlincourt
  – less a detachment of 40 troopers in headquarters in Sedan
Hussar Regiment
  1 squadron in Charleville
  1 squadron in Launois
  1 squadron in la Francheville and Mohon
  1 squadron in Aucourt, Maraucourt and Tendrecourt, pickets at St Laurent
Park Column in Frenoy

3rd (Anhalt-Thuringian) Brigade
Brigade Headquarters: Gernelle
2 Weimar battalions: Mouzon
2 Gotha battalions: St Laurent, on outpost duty
Schwarzburg Battalion: Montcy-St Pierre
2 Anhalt battalions: Cons and Aiglemont
Waldeck Battalion: Sedan
Lippe Battalion: at the blockade of Bouillon
2 Oldenburg battalions: Sedan

Occupation of Rheims, 8 July

On orders received from Blücher during the night of 4/5 July, patrols were sent towards Laon and Rheims to establish contact with the Austro-Russian army and to prevent French raiding parties from gathering in the hills. Hearing from Major von Falkenhausen, commander of a cavalry detachment from the main army, on 30 June that, 'The commandant [of Rheims] will capitulate as soon as he sees artillery',[18] Major Bödicker took the detachment at Launois there. A convention was signed on 8 July, allowing the garrison of Rheims to withdraw to Soissons in return for the supplies in the town being left for the Prussians.

Scheffer took another detachment to Rozoy, in the direction of Laon. Awaiting further orders from Hake, he left one battalion and one squadron observing Laon and then went on to Rheims. On 15 July, a third detachment, moving on via Stenay, clashed with a party of 200 Frenchmen coming from Montmédy at Chauvency-le-Château, 4 km west of Montmédy. A determined attack by a squadron of Hessian dragoons drove them off.

Bombardment of Mézières

After the fall of Charleville, disturbances broke out in Mézières which the commandant put down with some force. However, the besiegers noticed that, for a time, neither the tricolour nor the royal standard flew from the flagpole. This led to a bombardment to break civilian morale being considered.

The limited artillery and ammunition available hindered this, so Prinz

---

[18] Voss, p 233 fn.

August had 57 heavy guns brought up from Wesel via Venlo. More came from Jülich by water via Liège to Namur and from there on land via Ciney to Mézières. The Prussian artillery officer stationed in Namur sent on nine French howitzers and 25 cannon that had been assembled there, but transporting them caused great difficulty and took a long time. Despite the very greatest efforts, by 20 July Hake only had at his disposal six 12-pounder cannon, four 10-pounder howitzers and six 20-pounder mortars, each with 200 rounds of ammunition. Nevertheless, during the night of 23/24 July he had a howitzer battery built in the gardens of Mohon and the next night a howitzer, a mortar and a 12-pounder battery in gardens in Charleville. In the meantime ten men from each Hessian infantry battalion had been trained as gunners.

Sortie Against Mohon, 25 July

The garrison did not fail to notice the construction work and subjected it to a heavy bombardment. During the day on 24 July it undertook a sortie against the outposts at Bellevue and Tivoli, but a detachment from the Oldenburg Regiment drove this back with minimal losses to themselves. The next day, between 9 a.m. and 10 a.m., Lemoine staged a break-out from the fortress with about 1,200 men and two limbered guns in three columns. The two weaker detachments moved against Charleville and St Laurent, the main column against Mohon. The men of the F./Kurfürst at Mohon did not notice the French advancing towards them – the attackers were hidden by the tall crops – and were surprised and thrown back. Although the battalion commander was wounded, the Hessians held on to the village and defended the battery, supported by a young engineer officer and a few gunners until reinforcements arrived. Oberst Zincke with the I./Solms moved forward from the rear, as did Major von Bardeleben with the F./Landgraf Karl and a detachment of Jäger, attacking the flank of the sortie. The French fell back to the wall of the crownwork under the weight of superior numbers, losing 16 dead, over 50 wounded and 13 prisoners. A detachment of Oldenburgers drove back the 400 Frenchmen attacking St Laurent.

At daybreak on 26 July, Hake began a bombardment which continued until the morning of the 27th. Fire broke out in several parts of the town, but it was always extinguished. The only real success was burning down one magazine, and in reply the fortress artillery caused substantial losses to the attackers – 49 men – and buildings in Charleville caught fire several times.

An envoy sent by Louis XVIII held talks with Lemoine on 28 July but achieved nothing, so the Prussians decided to stage a formal assault. By 4 August an artillery park had been assembled at Warcq, consisting of 50 cannon, of which 13 were light pieces, six light and five heavy howitzers, and 12 light and 16 heavy mortars. The attack was to be made over peninsula of St Julien and two bridges were built, one at Prix, the other at Warcq later, and these were protected with earthworks. On the eastern side, the flèche in front of the citadel, occupied only by infantry, was earmarked for a preliminary attack. At 11 p.m. on 31 July a company of the 1st Oldenburg Battalion assaulted and captured it, but the artillery fire from the citadel that opened the next morning, drove the attackers back. Three companies of the Oldenburgers repeated the attack twice on the night of 1/2 August, but again the artillery fire forced them to retreat. Losses were 28 men dead and wounded.

An attempt to seize St Julien itself during the night of 6/7 August failed but by the end of that night the besiegers had taken control of the St Julien peninsula. The bridges were secured with earthworks that were gradually extended to redoubts. Two batteries were then built south-west of Charleville, containing five howitzers and one 6-pounder. A further three were built for a total of six howitzers and four mortars at les Granges on the southern bank of the Meuse, but these were never used. In the night of the 8th/9th, 1,400 labourers, covered by one battalion, dug a parallel 500 paces from the glacis of the western hornwork. Both its flanks rested on the banks of the Meuse. Two batteries, one for 12-pounders, one for mortars, were also begun and, despite heavy fire from the defenders, were completed by the morning. At 5.30 a.m. on the 9th, five of the batteries opened fire – two of those south-west of Charleville, two from the St Julien peninsula and one at les Granges. The defenders replied with a lively but largely ineffective counter-fire, abandoning the burning village of St Julien at 4 p.m., and finally offering negotiations at 6 p.m. An agreement was reached on 10 August, and the town and 30 guns was handed over on the 13th. Some of the National Guard were dismissed and the commandant withdrew into the citadel with 800 men to consider handing that over as well, for which he was given until 1 September. Until then, there was to be a cease-fire.

Preparations Against the Citadel of Mézières

The agreement annoyed Blücher considerably because the first clause specified that, on the conclusion of peace, the fortress of Mézières would be handed over to the King of France in the condition it was when it was captured. This conflicted with an instruction Blücher had issued on 9 August for all fortresses to be blown up on being evacuated. When he received this order Hake wanted to abrogate the agreement, but Prinz August decided to accept it, while at the same time preparing for a later assault on the citadel.

Consequently, Hake had a number of hidden batteries built, including some actually within the town of Mézières, at Couronne de Champagne and Corne d'Arches. Work was also started on a mine leading from a cellar in the town to the escarp of the citadel. By the evening of 25 August this was less than 5 metres from the wall and was due to be ready for detonation on the 31st. On 26 August Hake ordered six battalions and two squadrons resting outside the town to join the five and a half battalions in Mézières. By 31 August five batteries with 28 mortars and two howitzers were ready to start the bombardment and two breaching batteries with 12 cannon stood only 12 metres from the front wall of the citadel, concealed in houses. Lemoine protested about this, but was unable to offer resistance, so on 3 September, he agreed the conditions for surrendering the citadel, and withdrew to the Loire with the garrison and four guns. The Prussian 8th Brigade occupied it, finding 31 guns and substantial quantities of ammunition there.

Siege of Montmédy

By now, all that remained on the northern French frontier were the two small fortresses of Montmédy and Longwy which blocked important roads from Luxembourg through the Ardennes. Prinz August's original intention was to take Longwy first, but news of the forthcoming peace from Paris led him to designate the weaker Montmédy as his main priority. He assembled the necessary materials and equipment.

The fortress of Montmédy was in the shape of an irregular triangle with bastions standing on a pillar of rock rising from the Chiers valley. Meadows and fields surrounded it to the west, south and east; to the north was a hollow with vineyards on the opposite rise. On the crown of the hill in the valley to the north-east stood the town of Médy. A strong wall 7 metres high and 1½ metres thick surrounded it. Two branches of this wall ran down the hill, securing the road from the town to the fortress. Several outworks came up to 200 paces from the town wall. The town had three gates, the southern one linking to the bridge over the Chiers. The fortress drew its water from the town's wells and water-pipes. Général Laurent commanded the garrison which consisted of 150 men of the 56e de Ligne, two battalions of the National Guard of the Ardennes, 700 old soldiers and a number of customs officers and gendarmes.

During his earlier march to Mézières, Engelhardt had detached the two Weimar battalions, a division of Jäger and one squadron under Major von Lynker to observe the fortress from Stenay 12 km to the west. The Mecklenburg brigade finally arrived to join the North German Army Corps on 15 August, having left home on 4 July. Reinforced by two companies of Hessian Jäger and two squadrons of Hessian dragoons, it now began a closer investment of Montmédy. Four battalions drew up on the northern bank of the Chiers, two on the south. On 4 September, however, Hake had them move off to join the siege of Longwy, replacing them with a force under General von Warburg consisting of the Oldenburg battalions, the Lippe-Waldeck Regiment, a detachment of Hessian Jäger and the Mecklenburg Hussar Regiment. Preparations for the attack commenced with the occupation of three villages close to the fortress under the cover of heavy infantry fire – there was no siege artillery available. The Jäger used rifle rests for sniping and undertook many small raids. In the night of 4/5 September, the besiegers took the heights north of Chiers from which the town drew its drinking water. The garrison counter-attacked the next morning, but without success.

Hake then took charge of the siege personally, moving his headquarters to Stenay. He had the 21st Regiment, from the 8th Brigade, and a Weimar battalion move up. Close and detailed reconnaissance by the Prussian artillery and engineer officers on his staff confirmed that the available means were insufficient to undertake a formal assault against the fortress. Only a bombardment could succeed. In the night of 11/12 September, the besiegers took a large reservoir used by the town and built a number of batteries there in the following nights. Hake, knowing that both Blücher and Prinz August wanted a rapid end to this matter, decided to attempt to take the town of Médy, thereby completely cutting off the water supply to the fortress. Both Warburg and the commander of the Oldenburgers expressed their opposition to this, as such a venture was very difficult. The Oldenburg battalions, the Mecklenburg hussars and the Hessian dragoons were therefore sent to secure Metz, Thionville and Verdun and the Anhalt-Thuringian brigade replaced them.

Storming of Médy-bas, 12–13 September

As soon as the following night, Hake had two assault columns move up. The Prussian Kapitain von Restorf and the Hessian Kapitain Schneidt led the first. It consisted of 200 men from the 21st Regiment, 200 of the Lippe-Waldeck Regiment, 25 Hessian Jäger and 25 Prussian sappers. There were to advance from the village of Fresnois to the north-east of the town against the north-west gate (Porte de France) and the north-east gate (Porte de Luxembourg). The Hessian Kapitain Schnöddel and the Prussian Kapitain von Tuckermann led the second column. It consisted of 200 men of the 21st, 100 each from the Weimar and Lippe-Waldeck Regiments, 25 Jäger and 12 sappers. They were to cross the Chiers over a plank bridge at the village of Iré-lès-Près, to the south-east of the town. They were then to move upstream along the river towards the southern side of the town and the south-east gate (Porte de Champagne). The troops were to carry scaling ladders and other equipment.

Both columns were to assemble at 11 p.m. and deploy precisely at the best places to climb which also offered cover from the fortress. The assault was to commence at 2 a.m. Although the weight of the ladders delayed the advance by half an hour, the attack was totally successful. The surprised garrison, about 350 men strong, was forced to fall back to the fortress after a short struggle, but once there they opened a heavy fire. Nevertheless, the Germans were able to destroy the two wells, after which 550 men remained in the town while the others fell back. At daybreak, the men in the town were again subjected to concentrated fire but fortunately one of the residents brokered an agreement with the commandant at 9 a.m. to allow the town to be evacuated. Total losses to the attackers were two officers and nine other ranks dead, four officers and 94 other ranks wounded.

Five batteries were set up the following night and protected by fascines since the ground was too stony to dig. The commandant offered talks on 16 September, and on the 19th capitulation with the usual terms was agreed. The fortress was handed over on 22 September along with 53 guns and a substantial amount of ammunition.

Actions of the Garrison of Luxembourg

As we saw earlier, Blücher had ordered the Prussian garrison of Luxembourg to move to Longwy on 20 June. This fortress stood on the right (west) side of the Chiers valley. It was in the shape of a regular hexagon with bastions built in the Vauban style. In front of the north-east side was a hornwork with a lunette, to the south, a simple lunette with a blockhouse. The lower town stood about one km south of the centre of the fortress, in a valley 100–130 metres below it. East of the fortress was a wooded ridge, the Mont du Chat, which formed the crest of that side of the valley. This line of heights and the overlooking hilltop to the west were about one km away, at extreme artillery range.

The commandant, Général Ducos, had at his disposal three battalions of National Guards of the Vosges and the Meurthe, a battalion of old officers and soldiers, and about 100 customs officers, nearly 2,000 men. The residents of the town also took an active part in its defence. However, Ducos had only 17 trained artillerymen to man his 65 guns.

First Attempt on Longwy, 1–12 July

In late June the garrison of Luxembourg, under Generallieutenant Prinz von Hessen-Homburg and the commandant Major du Moulin was only about 3,000 men strong. It consisted of two Landwehr regiments, two separate Landwehr battalions, four garrison battalions, one squadron of uhlans, three provisional artillery companies and a sapper company formed from men taken from the infantry. The Landwehr battalions were weak in numbers, inade-quately clothed and poorly equipped.

Hesse-Homburg moved off to Longwy with 2,500 men and 12 guns (four cannon, eight howitzers and mortars). This force consisted of the 4th Elbe and the 6th Westphalian Landwehr Regiments, the I./7th and I./10th Westphalian Landwehr, Garrison Battalions Nrs. 6 and 24, the 5./8th Uhlans, the sapper company and a detachment of artillery. During the night of 1/2 July, they arrived at their destination. The main body drew up to the north-east of this fortress, west of the cobbled road from Luxembourg, commencing a bombardment immediately. At the same time, Hesse-Homburg's men stormed the southern flèche but, supported by artillery fire, the garrison recaptured it.

Eight more guns arrived from Luxembourg on 3 July, and on the 4th the bombardment was renewed. A battery was begun on the Mont du Chat and completed by 9 July. From then until the 12th it conducted an effective fire on the fortress. In the meantime, a parallel was opened on the north side.

By then the commandant of the fortress had sent for help and Général Mériage marched from Metz and Thionville with a relief force of 2,000 infantry and 60 cavalry. They arrived on the night of 11/12 July, getting close to Longwy late in the evening before the Prussian cavalry outpost at Haucourt noticed their approach. Mériage marched north through wooded terrain from there via Herserange and Longlaville, then around towards the east of the town. He crossed the Chiers at Longlaville, then attacked the village of Mont-St Martin on the cobbled road from Luxembourg, the site of Hesse-Homburg's headquarters. This surprise attack dispersed the I./6th Westphalian Landwehr, a whole company of which was taken prisoner. At the same time, more of Mériage's men attacked the II./4th Elbe Landwehr at Réhon, to the south of the town and on the Mont du Chat, and a sortie from the fortress moved against the 6th Garrison Battalion, which was drawn up in the parallel. Both these last assaults were carried out and resisted with such determination that hand-to-hand fighting resulted. The French move cut off the battery on the Mont du Chat, but the Landwehr were able to fight their way out, taking all but one mortar with them.

Hesse-Homburg rallied some of the troops at la Colombe, north of the fortress, while du Moulin rallied others further to the west at Piedmont. In the darkness neither commander knew the whereabouts of the other. Uncertain of the situation Hesse-Homburg ordered the siege artillery to move off to the north-west to Musson and Halanzy and had the parallels evacuated. Du Moulin, after having retaken Mont-St Martin at 11 p.m., then found the parallels empty and so withdrew to the north-east down the main road to Arlon. The next day, the entire besieging force gathered at Dippach, about 18 km north-east of Longwy. It had lost 3 officers and 77 other ranks dead and wounded, 3 officers, 206 men and 3 guns captured.

On 23 July Blücher replied to the news of this setback with a promise to send Hake reinforcements as soon as possible. The approach of the vanguard of the Prussian VI Army Corps marching from Trier to France allowed Hesse-Homburg to advance again and on 24 July he moved to Aubange, about 4 km north of Longwy. At the beginning of August he moved to invest the fortress again, this time setting up a camp at Tellancourt, 10 km to the west on the road to Longuyon, but also leaving three battalions at Aubange to cover the Luxembourg road. Meanwhile, Garrison Battalions Nrs. 7 and 19 and a number of men recovered from their wounds had joined him, along with two squadrons of Hessian dragoons from Mézières. On 27 August 1,500 replacements arrived for the Landwehr battalions, and on 7 September the Mecklenburg brigade, half of which was immediately sent to Thionville. On 9 September two half companies of sappers of the North German Army Corps and three companies of artillery came up from Luxembourg. Finally, one company of Mansfeld Pioneers from the Prussian II Army Corps joined them, and on 12 September, the 23rd Regiment from the 8th Brigade arrived. The number of siege guns was brought up to 26. A further 30 arrived from 10 September, but did not come into action.

Siege of Longwy, to 18 September

During the night of 10/11 August, the lines of investment of Longwy closed up to 800–1,000 paces from the fortress. The three I. Battalions of the Westphalian Landwehr Regiments took up positions on the Mont du Chat. Two battalions of the 4th Elbe Landwehr deployed in the valley at Réhon to the south, and on both sides of the cobbled road to Longuyon. The remaining battalion of this regiment and the four garrison battalions moved to the area of Warnimont, north-west of the town. A parallel was opened 950 paces from the glacis.

The commandant, who had earlier rejected calls for surrender asked on 11 August for permission to send an officer to Paris to get orders from the King, with a cease-fire to begin in the meantime. The officer returned on 21 August with instructions for the commandant to dismiss the National Guard, about 400 men, if they so wished – which the besiegers permitted – but to continue to hold the fortress. The cease-fire was then ended and on the night of 9/10 September 13 guns began a bombardment from the north and west, three from the south and seven from the Mont du Chat. At the same time, another parallel was opened on the west side. The fortress artillery replied with great effect until the besiegers were able to disable an observation post in the church tower in the town from which the French fire was being directed via a voice tube.

In the night of 13/14 September, a parallel was to be dug at the foot of the lunette on the glacis on the south side, which was then to be stormed by men of the 23rd Regiment. Despite the heavy canister fire, the Prussians largely succeeded, but 25 French officers held on to the blockhouse. A detachment of eight gunners and infantrymen managed to set it alight with grenades and tar baskets, forcing the defenders to surrender, but only after six of the attackers were killed.[19] Lieutenant Gärtner of the artillery, leading the attack, was wounded, seven of the ten gunners and most of the infantry were killed or wounded. French losses were one officer and 47 other ranks dead, seven officers and 212 other ranks wounded.

However, the attack broke the will of the commandant to continue the fight. That evening, he offered to surrender the fortress if the garrison could go to Metz. Prinz August agreed to this the next day, and on 18 September the fortress was handed over, along with 65 guns and large stocks of ammunition.

The fortress war then ended with Blücher having taken ten French fortresses – 12 including Avesnes and Guise which were captured by the field army – 500 guns and large quantities of supplies. Any possible attempt by the French to continue the war using these fortresses as a base or to use them to supply any uprising was thus thwarted. The breaking of the French will to resist in the northern fortress belt was almost entirely a German and largely a Prussian achievement with Wellington's forces only having played a minor role. The war was coming to its end.

[19] Anon, *MWBl.* Nr. 18, 1816.

Chapter 20

Wellington and the Prussians

"The battle of Waterloo is undoubtedly one of the most interesting events of modern times but the Duke entertains no hopes of ever seeing an account of all its details which shall be true."
WSD, vol X, p 507. Letter from Wellington to Sir John Sinclair, 13 April 1816.

Unfriendly Allies

During the Napoleonic Wars Britain was the wealthiest country in a Europe becoming more and more exhausted by over two decades of almost uninterrupted warfare. In the peace negotiations that took place in Vienna after Napoleon's first abdication in 1814 Britain's representatives were therefore well able to pursue the traditional British policy of establishing a balance of power between the continental European nations. To this end the British developed an alliance with Austria to oppose the Prussians and Russians. France, with the monarchy restored, joined the Anglo-Austrian camp. One of the chief architects of this arrangement had been the Duke of Wellington, who had been appointed British ambassador to France after Napoleon's fall. Later, he went to Vienna to participate in the Congress. Wellington was one of the leaders of the anti-Prussian party in British politics, and had been instrumental in blocking Prussian aims. During the negotiations over the shape of post-Napoleonic Europe at the Congress of Vienna, Britain, Austria and France even went so far as to sign a secret treaty to oppose with force if necessary what they saw as Prusso-Russian expansionism. For a time, Europe teetered on the brink of a new war, one amongst erstwhile allies. However, the deadlock at Vienna eventually broke, and the talks progressed.

During the long years of French occupation following the catastrophic defeat of the much vaunted Prussian Army at the battles of Jena and Auerstedt in 1806, German patriots drew much of their inspiration from Wellington's military successes against the French in Spain and Portugal. For some years he was a popular figure in Prussia, but the perception of the Great Duke changed in Prussian ruling circles during the Congress of Vienna, when Wellington did much to thwart Prussia's aims with behind-the-scenes manoeuvring. While some Prussian leaders, notably Blücher, continued to regard the Duke as an honourable man, Gneisenau, Grolman and others grew suspicious of him.

These suspicions deepened after Napoleon's return and Wellington's and Blücher's appointment to command armies against him. The major cause of disagreement between Wellington and his Prussian allies in that spring of 1815 was over who should control the military contingents of the minor German states. Both Wellington and Blücher were suffering from a shortage of man-power and needed every recruit they could get. Moreover, there were strong political overtones: gaining control over the military contingent of a German state was perceived as gaining its political allegiance. Being the more astute politician and having ready cash at hand, Wellington usually outmanoeuvred his Prussian allies in these negotiations. By the outbreak of hostilities in June 1815, the only non-Prussian soldiers who remained with Blücher's army were a handful of Saxons, the remnants of a contingent which had rebelled against its Prussian commanders. On the other hand, the largest single nationality in the Duke's army was German, many of them from territories that Prussia was hoping to include in its sphere of influence.

All this meant that, by June 1815, most of the leading Prussian command-ers had ceased to regard the Duke of Wellington as a friend. Some of the Duke's actions in the Waterloo campaign, particularly his failure to support the Prussian forces actively and directly in the Battle of Ligny on 16 June 1815, only served to increase suspicions of his motives.

Wellington's Report and his Waterloo Myths

On the morning after the battle, the Duke of Wellington sat down in his head-quarters in the Inn of Jean de Nivelles at Waterloo to write his official report on the events of the previous days to Earl Bathurst, the Secretary of State for War and the Colonies, in London. This document, dated 19 June 1815, was the first communication the Duke had sent to London since the outbreak of hostilities in the Netherlands on 15 June. In it, he gave his version of those dramatic events of the previous few days. As with all accounts given by the leading figures of this campaign, there is a certain amount of self-justification, and glossing over of errors. Few have looked at this report in any detail, let alone compared its claims with the documentary record, but it has proved to be the source of several lasting and important myths about the campaign. Here, we will examine some of the claims made by the Duke when still flushed with victory, and before other records of the campaign became avail-able. This document was first published in *The Times* on 22 June 1815 and later included in Volume XII of the *Dispatches*.[1]

It would seem that Wellington first began to pen this despatch in the early hours of the 19th. The Duke later left for Brussels where he continued to write his report, finishing it by noon. Wellington then selected Major Henry Percy of the 14th Light Dragoons for the honour of taking it to London. Percy arrived at his destination on 21 June.

The first volume of this work examined several dubious claims made in this report concerning Wellington's actions and the orders he sent to his army, the positions of his troops and his contacts with his Prussian allies. He stated first of all that 'I did not hear of these events [the beginning of Napoleon's advance] till in the evening of the 15th' and secondly that 'I immediately ordered the troops the troops to prepare to march'. The reasons why these claims cannot be taken at face value are given fully in the first volume.

[1] *WD*, vol XII, pp 478–84.

The evident inconsistency between Wellington's account and the records he would have had available when writing the report deserves closer examination and explanation. It is possible that in the four days since the outbreak of hostilities, the Duke's recollection had been blurred by the events that had taken place in the meantime. For a man of Wellington's intellect and with his reputation for attention to detail, that seems unlikely. Moreover, as it took the Duke several hours to complete the writing of this report, he had every opportunity of considering how to phrase his points. Thus, it would seem more probable that Wellington had another reason for making such claims.

Wellington knew he had been slow in reacting to the situation. Mulling over the events of the previous days, the Duke was no doubt aware that he should have at least ordered his troops to concentrate in their assembly points when he heard the news of the outbreak of hostilities at 9 a.m. on the 15th. That done, he could have reacted to the various additional reports that came into his headquarters at 3 p.m. by ordering at least part of his forces to the front, and his Reserve in and around Brussels could have marched for several hours that day, closing the gap between Wellington's and Blücher's forces that Napoleon was intent on penetrating. Was a man as proud and ambitious as the first Duke of Wellington going freely to admit his error? All that was on record on 19 June 1815 was the time at which Wellington issued his orders, between 6 p.m. and 7 p.m., so it would seem probable that an embarrassed Wellington glossed over his error with a likely sounding story that accorded with that fact.

Wellington's report next failed to point out that the Allied efforts to oppose the French at Quatre Bras would not even have got started if the local Netherlands commanders had not disobeyed his specific orders to move away and 'collect at Nivelles'.[2]

Perhaps more significantly the report then continued, 'In the mean time, I had directed the whole army to march upon Les Quatre Bras.' However, his own records show that before leaving Brussels for the front on the morning of 16 June, he had yet to order a single unit to Quatre Bras. Various units had indeed been ordered to move from Brussels to the point where the Brussels *chaussée* divided into two roads, one leading to Quatre Bras, and one to Nivelles. It is, however, questionable whether, at this stage, Wellington had finally decided to move any, let alone all, of his forces to Quatre Bras. Various soldiers' memoirs record their units stopping on the way south from Brussels, to eat and rest near what would be the Waterloo battlefield, on the morning of the 16th and only being ordered to move forward from there around midday, well after Wellington himself had ridden past them to the front. The record relating to other units which eventually reached Quatre Bras by other routes via Braine le Comte and Nivelles tells a similar story. Some only received orders to go to Quatre Bras in the afternoon of the 16th, others only arrived at all by moving on their own initiative.

Unfortunately, even though Wellington had not 'directed the whole army to march to Quatre Bras', there are several indications that he told various people at the time that this is what he had done. Müffling wrote to Blücher on the evening of 15 June that Wellington would be 'at Nivelles with his entire force' on the 16th and later, after midnight, that Wellington would have 20,000 men at Quatre Bras by 10 a.m. on the 16th.[3] The Prince of Orange seems to have been given similar information for, at 6 a.m. on 16 June, he told a Prussian officer that, 'within the next three hours the entire Belgian army and the bulk of the English army can be concentrated at Nivelles',[4] from where it could readily move via Quatre Bras to support the Prussians that day. That may indeed have been what Wellington said to the Prince and Müffling, but the Duke's actions and the movements of his troops tell a different story, as we have seen. Wellington misinformed his Prussian allies as to his movements and intentions, repeated this false information to the Prince of Orange and also misled Bathurst as to his true actions.

The report also glossed over an even more significant failure. As early as 3 May 1815, at a conference held in Tirlemont, Wellington and Blücher had agreed to move rapidly and in force to support each other in the event of one of their armies being attacked by Bonaparte. In case of a French assault via Charleroi, the Prussians planned to fall back to the Sombreffe position to fight a major rearguard action, in which they would be supported by Wellington's forces.[5] Müffling's letters, the so-called Frasnes Letter written by the Duke on the morning of the 16th, and the promises he made during his meeting with Blücher that afternoon all amounted to a reiteration of this very firm commitment to support the Prussians at Ligny. Even worse, the Duke allowed this promise to stand during the 16th in the knowledge that it was unlikely he would be able to do more than meet part, if any, of what he had undertaken and when it came to his report for Bathurst he only included the rather milder 'I was not able to assist them as I wished'.

Despite the Duke's efforts to have his actions viewed in the best light, his generalship in the first days of the campaign has often been criticised. His activities on 18 June, however, are usually seen more favourably, but in fact the misrepresentation of events in his report also continued into the sections of it dealing with the Battle of Waterloo.

The 'late' arrival of the Prussians at the Battle of Waterloo has been the subject of much discussion in English-language histories of the campaign. One can understand the hard-pressed infantryman on the ground perceiving any aid as being too little, too late, but when the Duke wrote that, 'about seven in the evening... the march of General Bülow's corps... had begun to take effect' he was being less than frank. Wellington was kept well versed in every aspect of the Prussian movements that day. While it is true that he accepted battle expecting the Prussians to arrive at 11 a.m., he and Blücher remained in close contact throughout.[6] A line of communication was established at 10 a.m. and the Duke became aware that the Prussians had suffered delays during their march. Through Müffling, Wellington learned that two brigades of Bülow's

---

[3] Nostitz, p 22 fn.
[4] Lettow-Vorbeck, p 298.
[5] To gain an outline of the contents of this meeting and the decisions made, see *WD*, Vol XII, pp 345–6; Nostitz, p 11; Ollech, p 44; Thurn und Taxis, p 313.
[6] Müffling, *Leben*, p 246.

corps had reached St Lambert by 11.30 a.m., and that from 4 p.m., he could expect the IV Army Corps to engage the French.[7]

As we saw earlier, Napoleon had observed the Prussian movements at St Lambert at 1 p.m., and was forced to adopt countermeasures that tied down large numbers of his troops. By shortly after 3 p.m. the Prussians were assembling in the Fichermont wood, causing Bonaparte considerable anxiety. The respite this move brought allowed Wellington to reform his centre after the battering it had received earlier. If he had been uncertain of the Prussian movements before then, which is unlikely, he was certainly aware of them by about 3 p.m., when, to confirm his earlier information, he himself saw Prussian movements in front of St Lambert. Finally, at 4.30 p.m., the Prussian intervention began in earnest, relieving the pressure on Wellington's forces further, a fact of which the Duke must have been aware. To say that the Prussian intervention only became effective at 7 p.m. was clearly an attempt to play down the role of his ally and great rival in the battle. This distortion continues to be repeated even today.

Before accepting primary source material and eyewitness statements at face value, the historian should cross-reference such accounts with the record and other such material to establish its accuracy and veracity. The parts of Wellington's report examined above make it clear that the Great Duke was just as circumspect with the truth as others of his contemporaries. In fact Wellington misled his superiors as much as he misled his allies. His report cannot be taken as an accurate account of the events of the days in question.

A Growing Controversy

In the decades following the victorious campaign of 1815, the former allies continued their dispute. There were various acrimonious exchanges between the Duke of Wellington and members of the Prussian General Staff, such as one between General von Grolman and the Duke. In a memorandum dated 22 April 1829, Wellington made certain comments about the role of the Prussian Army in the 1815 campaign that Grolman objected to.[8] Grolman therefore wrote a bitter reply which was published in the *Militair-Wochenblatt*, the official journal of the Prussian General Staff.[9] This background of conflict may explain the tone and content of certain of Wellington's subsequent comments.

Wellington and Clausewitz

General Carl von Clausewitz had been chief-of-staff of the Prussian III Army Corps that had fought at Ligny and Wavre in 1815 and by the mid-nineteenth century, thanks to his widow's posthumous publication of his papers, Clausewitz, who had died in 1831, had become known as an important military historian and theorist. His book on the Waterloo campaign, published in 1835, was the eighth of his works on war and military leadership. However, unlike other works by the Prussian soldier-philosopher, even now this particular

---

[7] Pflugk-Harttung, *Wavre*, p 621.
[8] *WCD*, vol V, pp 592–7.
[9] Anon, *MWBl*, vol. XXI, No. 22, pp. 90–4. See also Conrady, vol 2, pp. 278, 368–9.

volume has yet to be published in English, though a French edition was first published as long ago as 1900.

On 10 September 1840 the Earl of Liverpool wrote to Colonel Gurwood, the editor of Wellington's *Dispatches*, informing him that he had been working on a translation of Clausewitz's book.[10] Having been a British attaché in Vienna and a volunteer in the Austrian Army at Austerlitz in 1805, Liverpool had some expertise in the German language and background knowledge of the events of the time. At Liverpool's request, Gurwood forwarded his letter to the Duke who immediately asked to see a copy of the manuscript.[11] This was duly forwarded to Wellington, and there the matter rested for nearly two years.[12] However, in 1842 the volume of Archibald Alison's *History of Europe* covering 1815 was published.[13] This led to a discussion between Wellington and certain of his associates, particularly Charles Arbuthnot and Francis Egerton (better known by his later title of Earl of Ellesmere).

Arbuthnot lived in Apsley House, Wellington's residence in London and was a close confidant of the Duke. E.A. Smith, Arbuthnot's biographer, described him in earlier life as

> the eyes and ears of Castlereagh and Wellington, and in a real sense the polit-
> ical agent of each, protecting their interests and serving their advantage when-
> ever he could... He identified himself so closely with Wellington in the 1820s
> that he was considered to have no views of his own. Greville alleged that he
> 'is weak, but knows everything; his sentiments are the Duke's'.[14]

Ellesmere was widely travelled and a man of many talents. Among other writings, he translated Clausewitz's history of the 1812 campaign into English, a work which appeared in 1843. As a young man he had come to know the Duke of Wellington, and in later years spent much time with the Duke. He kept regular notes of their discussions and of other events, which were published by his daughter in 1903, under the title *Personal Reminiscences of the Duke of Wellington by Francis, the First Earl of Ellesmere*. As well as translating Clausewitz's 1812 volume, Ellesmere also wrote reviews of certain works on the Waterloo campaign by senior Prussian officers, and informed Wellington, who did not speak German, of the contents of these works. Respecting his knowledge and ability, Wellington had Ellesmere assess Liverpool's transla-tion of Clausewitz,[15] which was duly confirmed as accurate.[16] Despite that, or perhaps because of it, this manuscript, parts of which were embarrassing to

---

[10] BL Add MS 38,303 fols 82–83 contain Liverpool's file copy, the copy received by
   Wellington is in WP 2/71/28. Clausewitz's work, *Der Feldzug von 1815 in Frankreich*
   was published in Berlin in 1835 by Ferdinand Dümmler, a former member of
   Lützow's Freikorps.
[11] See WP 2/71/36/37 and BL Add MS 38,196 fol 143 for the details.
[12] WP 2/71/72.
[13] Sir Archibald Alison (1792–1867) was the author of a multi-volume *History of Europe*,
   a most popular work in its time.
[14] Smith, p 159.
[15] WP 8/3/2.
[16] WP 2/91/148.

Wellington, sits, gathering dust, as part of the Wellington Papers in the Hartley Library at the University of Southampton.[17]

Arbuthnot and Ellesmere suggested that Wellington write a *Memorandum on the Battle of Waterloo*, which would be forwarded to Ellesmere so that he could use the information to answer various of the points made by Clausewitz and Alison,[18] as well as for a review Ellesmere was writing on Rauschnick's biography of Blücher.[19] Ellesmere worked on a draft of the memorandum in August 1842 and returned it to Gurwood, who passed it on to Wellington, who then discussed it with Arbuthnot. In a letter dated 28 August Wellington commented to Gurwood that, 'Lord Francis' design has been carried into execution very ably.'[20] Thus, it is very clear who was involved in producing this account and who led this group.

Wellington seemed to have taken particular exception to some of Clausewitz's comments, writing to Gurwood on 17 September 1842, 'I am trying to finish the memorandum on Clausewitz for Lord Francis [Ellesmere]. I will send it to you as soon as it will be finished. But I am really too hard worked to become an author and to review these lying works called histories.'[21]

The Memorandum

The Duke of Wellington finished his *Memorandum on the Battle of Waterloo* on 24 September 1842.[22] The *Memorandum* was one of only a very few written comments the Duke made on the campaign and as he made a particular issue of criticising Clausewitz in it, then the two accounts deserve further consideration. The *Memorandum* began with an outline of the political background to the campaign, then continued with a short discussion of the overall military situation and the subsequent allied deployment before moving on to deal with Clausewitz's criticisms – real or perceived.

It should be noted that, after having finished with this document, Ellesmere returned it to the Duke. Wellington did not want it to be circulated, writing to Gurwood on 8 October 1842 that, 'I don't mean that this paper should be published! I have written it for Lord Francis Egerton's [Ellesmere's] information, to enable him to review Clausewitz's history! I don't propose to give mine enemy the gratification of writing a book!'[23] However, his son later published it after Wellington's death as part of the *Supplementary Despatches*.[24]

The 'Line of Battle'

The first of Clausewitz's criticisms the Duke referred to, related to the 'line of battle', that is the structure, organisation and dispositions of Wellington's

---

[17] It is contained in file no. WP 8/1/2.

[18] Strafford, p 236; BL Add MS 38,303 fols 191–2.

[19] Strafford, p 235. Gottfried Peter Rauschnick's *Marshal Vorwärts!* was a popular biography that had just been published in Germany.

[20] WP 8/3/1.

[21] WP 8/3/10.

[22] Strafford, p 235.

[23] WP 2/93/17.

[24] See *WSD*, vol X, pp 513–31.

army. This came in the section of Clausewitz's work entitled 'Comments on Wellington's Deployment'.[25] Wellington took this criticism personally, considered it unfounded and felt that it set 'the general temper and tone of this History'. He devoted an entire paragraph to complaining about the way that 'historians… [are] too ready to criticise the acts and operations not only of their own Generals and armies, but likewise of those of their best friends and allies of their nation, and even those acting in co-operation with its armies.'[26] The Duke then concluded this paragraph with a warning about accepting Clausewitz's criticisms.

However, reference to the original German text indicates that Clausewitz was not making any personal criticism of the Duke or of his dispositions. Rather, he was saying that the records available to him at the time of writing were so imprecise that it was difficult for the historian writing on these events to establish the exact positions and movements of Wellington's troops.[27] Wellington's annoyance was entirely unjustified; after all, the relevant volume of Wellington's *Dispatches* had not been published until 1838, seven years after Clausewitz's death, and three after the posthumous publication of his volume covering 1815.

The Deployment of Wellington's Army

The next point Clausewitz examined was the deployment of Wellington's army. Clausewitz explained why the allies had spread their troops over a large area before the outbreak of hostilities, and what their plans were in the event of a French invasion along any of the several possible routes. Clausewitz's view was that with this dispersal of his forces Wellington could not keep the promises he had made to support Blücher promptly,

> It was simply impossible for Wellington's army, spread over a distance of 20 miles [20 German miles, approximately 150 km], to concentrate on its far left flank either at Nivelles or Quatre Bras… [28]

Wellington was very much aware that he had not discerned Napoleon's intentions correctly. The Duke had feared the French would make their main move around his right flank at Mons but the Prussians correctly considered the Charleroi to Brussels route to be the one most likely to be chosen by Napoleon as this was the vulnerable hinge between the two allied armies. The Duke knew of his error of judgement, and would make efforts to ensure that later commentators did not dwell on the point.

Clausewitz's continued by describing the events immediately preceding the outbreak of hostilities on 15 June, and the responses of the two allied senior commanders to this,

> The reports Field Marshal Blücher received on 14th June that led him to order the concentration of his army during the night of the 14th to 15th, appear not to have caused the Duke of Wellington to make a decisive move. Even when, on the evening of the 15th, he received reports that General Zieten had been

25 Clausewitz, pp 27–33.
26 *WSD*, vol X, p 517.
27 Clausewitz, pp 27–33.
28 Clausewitz, p 32.

attacked at Charleroi and driven back by the main French army, he still considered it unwise to have the reserve march off to his left flank, and even less advisable to weaken his right flank. Rather, he believed that Bonaparte was going to advance along the road from Mons and considered the action at Charleroi a feint, so he merely ordered his troops to make ready. Only after the arrival of the report at midnight from General Dörnberg, the commander of the outpost at Mons, that he had not been attacked and the enemy appeared to be moving more to their right, did Wellington order the reserve to march off. It passed the Forest of Soignes, according to General von Müffling's account, by 10 a.m. From there to the battlefield at Sombreffe was only three [German] miles [about 22 km]. The Duke's reserve could still have arrived on time, but much time was lost when the Duke first rode to his left flank at Quatre Bras, reconnoitring the enemy at Frasnes, then to Prince Blücher in Sombreffe. He arrived there at 1 p.m., needing to convince himself that the enemy was really attacking with his main force there, as well as to have discussions with the Prince. While this was happening, it appears that the reserve awaited further orders at the exit from the Soignes Wood, that is on the crossroads from Nivelles to Quatre Bras. Even then, he still had enough time, but the Duke had divided his forces because he always wanted to be in a position to react according to circumstances. Because of this intention, he had not wanted to move the Prince of Orange's right flank earlier, and was thus too weak to support Blücher [29]

Clausewitz's version is supported by the documentary record, and is a clear and fair outline of those events, even accepting that Wellington did not hear of the French attack until the evening of the 15th. In fact, as discussed in the first volume of this work, Wellington heard this news at 9 a.m. that day, but chose not to react, a serious error of judgement, one that could have had disastrous consequences for the outcome of the campaign. It would appear that the Duke, rather than admit his failure to react promptly to the news of the outbreak of hostilities, a point which Clausewitz did not labour, tried to explain it away by claiming that he heard it later than was actually the case. His version in the *Memorandum* was,

> ... having received the intelligence of that attack [on the Prussian positions on the morning of 15th June] only at three o'clock in the afternoon of the 15th, he [Wellington] was at Quatre Bras before the same hour on the morning of the 16th, with a sufficient force to engage the left of the French army.[30]

Wellington then went into the matter in more detail,

> The first account received by the Duke of Wellington was from the Prince of Orange, who had come in from the out-posts of the army of the Netherlands to dine with the Duke at three o'clock in the afternoon.[31]

As this was the second occasion in the *Memorandum* that the Duke mentioned this time as being 3 p.m., it would seem he was certain of this. This

[29] Clausewitz, pp 50–1.
[30] WSD, vol X, p 523.
[31] WSD, vol X, p 524.

claim should be compared with his own contemporary account in his letter to the Duc de Feltre[32] of having received the news by 9 a.m. and with his official report to Earl Bathurst in which he stated, 'I did not hear of these events till the evening of the 15th.'[33] This triple inconsistency in the Duke's statements and records makes it difficult to rely on any of his testimony on this issue.

The Memorandum continued,

> While the Prince was with the Duke, the staff officer employed by Prince Blücher at the Duke's headquarters, General Müffling, came to the Duke to inform him that he had just received intelligence of the movement of the French army and their attack upon the Prussian troops at Thuin.[34]

Zieten's records show that he sent a message to Müffling from Charleroi about 11 a.m.,[35] which would have taken about four hours to arrive. Müffling's account confirmed receipt of a message from Zieten at 3 p.m., but it does not support Wellington's claim that this despatch bore news of the French assault on the Prussian outposts at Thuin.[36] As Charleroi fell to the French shortly before 11 a.m., then logically Zieten would have been informing Müffling of the latest event of significance, and not what had happened seven hours previously. Indeed, about the same time, Zieten sent Blücher a message reporting the town's fall.[37] Perhaps in the general excitement that interrupted Wellington's dinner at 3 p.m. Müffling did not pass on all the news he had received, particularly that of the fall of Charleroi.

What could explain the disparities in Wellington's versions of these events? By 1842 various accounts of the campaign had been published, so did Wellington consider the false statement in his official report no longer to be tenable? As both the Prince of Orange and Müffling had witnessed the events at 3 p.m., did the Duke feel that he could safely plump for that time now?

'Sufficient Force' at Quatre Bras?

What strength did Wellington actually have available at Quatre Bras on the morning of 16 June 1815? Was it 'a sufficient force to engage the left of the French army' as the Duke claimed in the *Memorandum*?[38] That morning, the only allied troops deployed at Quatre Bras were eight battalions and two batteries of the Netherlands army.[39] At 2 p.m. when Ney and his men began their attack on this position the French force included parts of Reille's II Corps (19,000 men), the Guard Light Cavalry Division (2,000 men), and the 3rd Cavalry Corps (3,000 men).[40] Were less than 8,000 rather nervous Netherlanders really 'a sufficient force'? As Chesney pointed out in his *Waterloo Lectures*, Wellington, 'had only present at Quatre Bras three-eighths of his infantry, one-third of his guns, and one-seventh of his cavalry. Truly, in holding his own, the great Englishman owed something that day to Fortune.'[41]

[32] *WD*, vol XII, p 473.
[33] *WD*, vol XII, p 478.
[34] *WSD*, vol X, p 524.
[35] Hafner, *Militärisches*, p. 253.
[36] Müffling, p 228.
[37] Hafner, *Militärisches*, p. 253.
[38] *WSD*, vol X, p 523.
[39] De Bas & T'Serclaes de Wommersom, vol. III, pp 96–7.
[40] Delhaize & Aerts, pp 76–7.
[41] Chesney, p 129.

When Did Wellington Issue Orders?

The next paragraph in the *Memorandum* repeated Wellington's misleading claim to have first heard the news of the outbreak of hostilities at 3 p.m. rather than 9 a.m. and led up to the assertion that,

> Orders were forthwith sent [i.e. at 3 p.m.] for the march of the whole army to its left.
>
> The whole moved on that evening and in the night, each division and portion separately, but unmolested... [42]

In fact Wellington's first orders that day were issued from 6 p.m. and were not for the army to march anywhere, let alone to its left, but rather for it to concentrate at its assembly points.[43] The first movement orders were issued at 10 p.m.,[44] and in view of the time of day, and the distance these orders had to be carried, then the very earliest they could be implemented would be at daybreak on 16 June, so 'the whole' certainly did not move 'that evening and in the night', as Wellington claimed. As Wellington's own papers indicating this were published in 1838, four years before he composed the *Memorandum*, it is surprising that he made such statements, particularly as he referred to these papers when writing the *Memorandum*.[45] Arbuthnot, in a letter to Ellesmere of 22 July 1842 noted, 'He [Wellington] stayed with me for some time, and read to me various parts from page 375 to 476 [of Volume XII of the *Dispatches*].'[46] These pages cover Wellington's outgoing correspondence from 11 May to 17 June 1815, including the orders issued on 15 June.

Quatre Bras

The *Memorandum* continued by giving an accurate outline of Wellington's own movements on the morning of 16 June, however, the Duke next made a number of statements about his troop positions and movements that day, which warrant further examination. These statements read as follows,

> In the mean time [i.e. between 1 p.m. and 3 p.m.] the reserve of the Allied army under the command of the Duke of Wellington had arrived at Quatre Bras. The historian [Clausewitz] asserts that the Duke of Wellington had ordered these troops to halt at the point at which they quitted the Forêt de Soignies [sic]. He can have no proof of this fact, of which there is no evidence; and in point of fact the two armies were united about mid-day of the 16th of June, on the left of the position of the Allied army under the command of the Duke of Wellington. These troops, forming the reserve, and having arrived from Bruxelles, were now joined by those of the 1st division of infantry, and the cavalry† [footnote in the original]
>
> †The Duke of Wellington was at Quatre Bras about 3 o'clock, on his return from Ligny.[47]

Each of these claims needs to be examined in turn.

[42] *WSD*, vol X, p 524.
[43] *WD*, vol XII, p. 474.
[44] *WD*, vol XII, p. 474.
[45] Strafford, pp 235–7.
[46] Strafford, p 236.
[47] *WSD*, vol X, p 525.

Firstly, the record shows that only part of the Reserve arrived at Quatre Bras by 3 p.m., namely Picton's 5th Division, followed shortly by the Brunswickers.[48] The 6th Division was partly in Ghent; the Nassauers arrived about 8 p.m.;[49] and the 5th Hanoverian Brigade only reached Genappe by 11 p.m.[50] Thus Wellington's statement is not the entire story.

Wellington was well aware that Picton's men had indeed halted south of the forest, since he had passed them on his way to the front, nor did he order them to move on immediately. Clausewitz's criticism of Wellington on this point was justified and the Duke's assertion to the contrary unfounded. Likewise, as allied reinforcements only started arriving at the front at Quatre Bras after 2 p.m., then Wellington's claim that, 'the two armies were united about mid-day' was equally misleading. Particularly so as Picton's men only received the order to march on to that point at noon, and, as it would seem that the Duke issued that instruction, his assertion to the contrary is also untrue. Furthermore, Wellington's claims that the 1st Division of infantry and the cavalry joined him at Quatre Bras about 3 p.m. were incorrect as well. The 1st Division seems to arrived at Quatre Bras about 5 p.m. and the cavalry did not see action at Quatre Bras that day because it only arrived after dark.

When did Wellington Order his Troops to Quatre Bras?

In the 'after orders', issued by Wellington at 10 p.m. on 15 June, not a single unit was instructed to move to Quatre Bras.[51] Yet at midnight, Wellington had Müffling inform Blücher that he would have 20,000 men at Quatre Bras by 10 a.m. the next day.[52] In fact, the only formations the Duke had ordered to move by then were sent to Nivelles and Enghien, from where they could counter any French move via Mons. The next news from the front arrived about midnight. This was the report that the French had advanced as far as Quatre Bras that evening, apparently the first time that this place was mentioned that day. The Prince of Orange told Constant Rebecque, his chief-of-staff, 'At first, the Duke believed that the attack on Charleroi was a feint; only when the report of the appearance of the enemy at Frasnes arrived, did he decide to move all his forces to Quatre Bras.'[53] However, Wellington's records show that, before leaving Brussels for the front on the morning of 16 June, he had yet to order a single unit to Quatre Bras, only taking that decision during the course of 16 June, not before. The issue of which troops Wellington actually ordered to which place and when is covered in more detail in the first volume of this work.

Wellington had evidently promised the Prussians to come to their aid on 16 June with 20,000 men, but in the early afternoon only the 8,000 men of the 2nd Netherlands Division were present at Quatre Bras, and all that had been definitely ordered to go there was the 5th British Division, some 5,000 men more. Even if the French did not attack, a detachment would need to be left to guard this vital cross-roads, so the Duke would have been unlikely to have

---

[48] See, for instance, Costello, p 151.
[49] Pflugk-Harttung, *Vorgeschichte*, pp 305–6.
[50] Pflugk-Harttung, *Vorgeschichte*, p 307.

[51] *WSD*, vol X, p 474.
[52] Nostitz, p 22 fn.
[53] *Journal* of Constant Rebecque.

been able to move half the promised number of men to support the Prussians at Ligny within the time specified.

Clausewitz's point that 'the Duke... was thus too weak to support Blücher', is supported by the record, whereas Wellington's rebuttal of the Prussian and warning not to accept his criticisms are unfounded. Does the incompatibility of Wellington's claims in the *Memorandum* with the record, and particularly the Duke's own papers, explain his evident sensitivity about the issue and his unfounded accusations?

Subsequent Histories and the 3 p.m. Myth

Using the information provided by the Duke, Ellesmere went on to write his review of Rauschnick's life of Blücher, this being published in 1842 in Volume LXX of the *Quarterly Review*. Following the line given by the Duke, Ellesmere explained,

> As Buonaparte's first attack was on the Prussian outposts at Thuin, it was natural that the first intelligence of hostilities should come from the Prussians, but their officer met with some delay, and the news was, in fact, brought by the Prince of Orange. He found the Duke, not at half-past seven, but soon after three o'clock, at dinner at his hotel...[54]

It did not stop there. In Volume LXXVI of the *Quarterly Review*, Ellesmere erroneously accused the Prussians of having failed in their duty to inform Wellington of the outbreak of hostilities, writing,

> At five o'clock in the morning of the 15th it was apparent to the Prussians that the attack upon the advanced corps of General Ziethen was a serious one, a *bona fide* movement of Napoleon by Charleroi. This was the one thing needful in the eyes of the Duke of Wellington; with it his course was clear, and without it, as we have seen, determined not to move a regiment from its cantonments. We cannot explain how it happened, but we are certain that it was no fault of the British commander-in-chief, that no Prussian report of the transaction reached Brussels till five in the afternoon. The distance being about forty miles, there can be no question that the intelligence on which he acted might and ought to have reached him by 10 A.M.[55]

It is interesting to note that, though Ellesmere was effectively acting as a mouthpiece for Wellington, he wrote anonymously for the *Quarterly Review*. Should Ellesmere's writings have been challenged for their accuracy, then the Duke himself would not have been directly implicated.

This version of events, incorrect though it was, found its way into numerous subsequent accounts. The first edition of William Siborne's great classic *History of the War in France and Belgium in 1815*, published in 1844, just two years after Ellesmere's review, repeated this item of misinformation, stating, 'It was between three and four o'clock in the afternoon of the 15th that the Duke of Wellington received information of the advance of the French

[54] *Quarterly Review*, vol LXX, p 470.
[55] *Quarterly Review*, vol LXXVI, p 216.

Army.'[56] Fortunately, Siborne later conducted a thorough investigation of the issue[57] and in the third edition of his work, published in 1848, he confirmed that Zieten's 'report to the Duke of Wellington arrived in Brussels at 9 o'clock in the morning'.[58] Despite this, many later accounts ignored Siborne's correction and continued to follow Wellington's line, as a glance through English-language Waterloo literature will show.

Between them, Wellington and Ellesmere succeeded in misleading most historians on this important question. Siborne was one of the few British Waterloo historians who took so much effort to establish the facts. He was one of the few British Waterloo historians of his and later generations who could read German and troubled to refer to German-language sources.

German Waterloo historians, on the other hand, have always considered that Zieten's news arrived in Brussels much earlier than Wellington's version as given in 1842. When asked by General Grolman to confirm that he had informed Wellington of the outbreak of hostilities early that morning, Zieten did so in a letter of 21 January 1819. Major von Damitz, in his history of the campaign written in 1837 on behalf of Grolman, believed that the news arrived in Brussels at 11 a.m.[59]. Later historians, such as Ollech, writing in 1876, found it hard to reconcile the time of Zieten's despatch with both Wellington's and indeed Müffling's claim that the news first arrived in Brussels at 3 p.m.[60] Pflugk-Harttung conducted a more detailed examination of the issue in his *Vorgeschichte der Schlacht bei Belle-Alliance – Wellington*, published in 1903.[61] Pflugk-Harttung examined all the available evidence and tried to make sense of conflicting accounts. He concluded that Wellington received Zieten's message by 9 a.m., but did not react until confirmation of its contents was received from elsewhere. Lettow-Vorbeck, who wrote the German General Staff history of the campaign a year later, came to a similar conclusion, believing that Wellington simply did not attach particular importance to the report.[62]

The version of events established by German historians, and supported by Siborne, was that Zieten did indeed send the news to Wellington, and that the Duke received it by 9 a.m. However, Wellington did not take it seriously, which later turned out to be a major error of judgement, and one that he evidently did not want to admit.

As Clausewitz was dead by the time the Duke of Wellington made the criticisms discussed here, he could not reply to them. Many historians have

---

[56] Siborne, *History*, pp 76–7.
[57] See BL Add MS 34,708 fols 265–72, 280–7.
[58] Siborne, *History*, p 36.
[59] Vol I, p 106.
[60] Müffling, *Leben*, p 115. The probable explanation for Müffling's apparent ignorance of the events at the border is that while, shortly before 5 a.m. on 15 June, Zieten sent Wellington the message informing him of the outbreak of hostilities which arrived in Brussels at 9 a.m., the Duke, considering the message unimportant, did not inform Müffling of its arrival. Zieten sent a further message at 11 a.m. directly to Müffling, informing him of the fall of Charleroi to the advancing French. This message would have arrived about 3 p.m., and was the first Müffling heard of the events.
[61] Pflugk-Harttung, *Vorgeschichte*, pp 44–79.
[62] Lettow-Vorbeck, p 282.

accepted Wellington's version of particular events rather than Clausewitz's correct assessment. The Duke of Wellington's riposte was merely a reaction to having his errors of judgement brought to light and discussed. Because Clausewitz's history has yet to be published in English, non-German historians writing on this campaign have often followed Wellington's version without question. However, the inconsistencies in the Duke's various accounts should at least have induced these historians to look as his testimony in more detail to establish its reliability. Histories based on claims made in the *Memorandum* are as unreliable as the *Memorandum* itself.

Chapter 21

Waterloo – A German Victory

In the Preface to the first volume of this work, I made clear what was to be its central theme. It was to demonstrate by reference to source material in the German language the full role of the German nation in this the final act in the overthrow of Napoleon Bonaparte, a role often underplayed in English-language literature. This theme has been continued throughout this second volume.

In the theatre in the Low Countries, where most of the fighting of this campaign took place, the overwhelming majority of the allied troops engaged spoke German as their native language. Of the 209,000 Allied soldiers in this theatre, 30,000 were English-speakers, 24,000 were Netherlanders, some of them Dutch- and some French-speaking; the remaining 155,000 were Germans. Not only did the Germans form the largest national contingent in Wellington's army, Blücher's Prussians also provided the largest army in the theatre. In the four crucial days of this campaign, 15–19 June, it was German troops, particularly Blücher's Prussians who were most heavily engaged, did the most marching and suffered the most casualties.

The subsequent race to Paris was also largely a one-sided matter, with Blücher's men, by means of several forced marches, reaching the gates of Paris first, then circumventing its northern defences, before forcing the surrender of that great city from the south. The Duke of Wellington followed in the trail the Prussians had blazed, his army only providing cover to the Prussian move around the south of the city. The role of the Duke's army in the difficult, and largely successful, capture of the fortress belt in Northern France was also minimal. This important achievement was accomplished in the main by Prussian forces supported by various German contingents, and did much to ensure that prolonged resistance to the Allies did not occur. It also secured the lines of communication of the forces in the field in and around Paris and, without it, the successes the Allies had gained might not have been guaranteed.

History, particularly that written in the English language, regards the Duke of Wellington as the victor of Waterloo. However, if that victory is to be attributed to any one man, then surely it has to be to Field Marshal Blücher. His army was the first to engage the French, suffered a significant defeat, then held itself together in the difficult circumstances of a retreat before arriving to tip the balance on the fateful field of Waterloo. Moreover, it was Blücher's determination that did not allow Bonaparte the opportunity to rally his defeated forces and contest every inch of the way to Paris as he had done the previous year. By taking the burden of the fighting on his shoulders, Blücher shortened the war, thereby probably saving many lives. This contrasts with the hesitation of the Duke of Wellington on 15 and 16 June, examined in the first part of this work, that led to many lives being lost unnecessarily.

Falling victim to a deception by Napoleon is the most probable reason why, on 15 June 1815, Wellington delayed the concentration of his forces. This issue, along with the Duke's consequent misleading of Blücher as to his positions, movements and intentions on 16 June, was discussed in the first part of this work. The examination of Wellington's subsequent falsification of part of the record, begun in part one, has been carried on in more detail in this volume. Like most leading figures in politics, it seems that Wellington was reluctant to leave anything but the best impressions of his activities for posterity. The conflicts in his own published records should have led historians to question more closely the validity of the Duke's testimony. However, most writers have either ignored their hero's unreliability or made implausible excuses as to the meanings or origins of certain texts and documents. An open, questioning mind would have resolved this issue long ago, and one can only blame sycophantic historians for the false impression of these events they have done much to convey. Wellington's circumspection when dealing with his own errors is understandable and was certainly no worse and probably much less than certain of his contemporaries. Nevertheless, he was the last person to express any opposition to an exaggeration of his role in this campaign or a glossing over of his errors. The Duke gained from the attribution of the victory of Waterloo both in prestige and power. Can one in fairness have expected him to have acted otherwise?

The performance of the commanders of the two wings of the Allied forces in the Low Countries is also worthy of comparison. If we are to judge the two commanders' relative performances by means of the crude rule of 'getting there the firstest with the mostest', then for the fighting of 16 June, in which both Wellington and Blücher had planned to stage the decisive battle of the campaign, having failed to ensure the timely arrival of Bülow's forces, Blücher got 75% of his men to the right place at the right time. Wellington, by contrast, only managed to bring three-eighths of his infantry, one-third of his guns and one-seventh of his cavalry, that is 33% of his total forces, to the right place at the right time. The contrast in the level of their respective performances is striking. Two days later, at Waterloo, Wellington only committed 66% of his army to the decisive battle, while Blücher managed to bring up about 50% of his surviving troops, with another 25% engaging the French in the rear of his advance. The remainder of his men – all were committed to this fight – were struggling to make their way through the treacherous mud on the narrow, hilly lanes leading from Wavre to Plancenoit. Wellington, by contrast, had decided not to use all of his forces in that day's battle. Thus, by these criteria Wellington's performance averaged out to a mere 50%, while Blücher's remained at a consistent 75%.

There are other criteria by which one can make judgements of performance and exertions. Even leaving those parts of Wellington's army furthest from the front out of the reckoning, the burden of the operations of 15-19 June still fell on the Prussians. The Prussian army corps as a whole marched a good deal further in those crucial days of this campaign and fought more actions. In the campaign after the Battle of Waterloo, the Prussians marched further and fought more often than Wellington's forces, as reference to the relevant tables in the appendices show. These facts are indisputable and show on which nation the bulk of the effort to secure a lasting peace in Europe actually fell. These observations and the information given in the tables below are not intended to be invidious or to play down the role of the remainder of the Allied forces in this campaign. Rather, they serve to underline the historiographical point that is the theme of this work.

The most convincing evidence in support of the case that it was the German nation that contributed the most to the Allied victory in 1815 is the analysis of casualties given in this work. Three-quarters of the Allied dead, wounded and missing in this campaign were Germans, the remainder being divided between the other contingents of Wellington's army. To regard the Duke of Wellington, as most British historians have done, as the sole or even the prime victor of Waterloo is to fail to consider the factual evidence fully. Waterloo was, in fact, primarily a German victory in which both the British Army and the Duke of Wellington played a secondary, supporting role.

Appendices

Losses of the Allied Forces, 15–19 June 1815[1]

Wellington's Army

	Starting Strength	Total lost	%age
German	36,299	5,956	16%
British	32,418	8,360	26%
Netherlanders	24,501	4,114	17%
Total	93,218	18,430	20%

Blücher's Army

	Starting Strength	Total lost	%age
Prussians	117,672	32,367	28%

By Nationality

	Starting Strength	%age of Total Allied Forces	Total Casualties	%age of Contingent	%age of Total Allied Casualties
German	153,971	73%	38,323	25%	75%
British	32,418	15%	8,360	26%	17%
Netherlanders	24,501	12%	4,114	17%	8%
Total	210,890	100%	50,797	24%	100%

[1] Based on Lettow-Vorbeck, p 480. All strength figures are for other ranks only and all casualties are the total of dead, wounded and missing. The Prussian figures come originally from Plotho's work, while De Bas & T'Serclaes de Wommerson was consulted for the Netherlanders, and various regimental and contingent histories for the German forces.

Who Marched Furthest and Fought Hardest, 15–19 June 1815?

	Distance marched (km)	Km/day	Battles fought
British (incl. KGL & Hanoverians)			
1st Division	59	12	2
2nd Division	77	15	1
3rd Division	49	10	2
4th Division	106	21	1
5th Division	47	9	2
6th Division	47	9	2
Reserve Cavalry	76	15	1
Netherlanders			
2nd Division	14	3	2
3rd Division	26	5	2
Cavalry Division	26	5	2
German			
Brunswick Corps	52	10	2
Nassauers	47	9	2
Prussian			
I Army Corps	105	21	3
II Army Corps	85	17	2
III Army Corps	115	23	2
IV Army Corps	157	31	1

The Race to Paris
Places and Distances, 19 June–4 July 1815

Date	I Army Corps	IV Army Corps	III Army Corps	Wellington's Army
19 June	Charleroi 20 km	Fontaine l'Evêque 34 km	St Agatha-Rode 27 km	Nivelles 26 km
20 June	Beaumont 28 km	Colleret, near Maubeuge 40 km	Gembloux (Combat at Namur) 25 km	Binche 25 km
21 June	Avesnes (Combat at Avesnes) 7 km	Landrecies 10 km	Charleroi 28 km	Malplaquet 34 km
22 June	Etrœungt –	Fesmy –	Beaumont 26 km	Le Cateau-Cambrésis –
23 June	Etrœungt 32 km	Fesmy 26 km	Avesnes 20 km	Le Cateau-Cambrésis –
24 June	Guise 31 km	Bernoville 22 km	Nouvion 42 km	Le Cateau-Cambrésis 22 km
25 June	Cerizy 22 km	St Quentin 52 km	Homblières –	Cambrai 37 km
26 June	Chauny 56 km	Lassigny 43 km	Homblières 66 km	Péronne 48 km
27 June	Gilocourt (Combat at Compiègne) 21 km	Pont-Ste Maxence (Combat at Senlis) 34 km	Compiègne 23 km	Nesle 27 km

Date	I Army Corps	IV Army Corps	III Army Corps	Wellington's Army
28 June	Nanteuil (Combat at Villers-Cotterêts) 32 km	Marly-la-Ville 18 km	Crépy 27 km	Orvillers 28 km
29 June	Aulnay —	le Bourget 6 km	Dammartin —	St-Martin-Langueau 43 km
30 June	Aulnay 2 km	(Combats at Aubervillers and St Denis) 28 km	Marching to St Germain 58 km	Louvres 12 km
1 July	Le Mesnil 32 km	Marching to St Germain 18 km	(Combats at Versailles and Marly) 28 km	Gonesse
2 July	Meudon (Combats at Sèvres and Issy) 6 km	Versailles	le Plessis Piquet	
3 July	Combat at Issy			
4 July			Convention for the evacuation of Paris	
Total distance marched and combats fought	289 km 5 combats	331 km 2 combats	370 km 2 combats	302 km 0 combats

Orders of Battle

Prussian Army at Waterloo
18 June 1815

Commander in Chief   *Generalfeldmarschall Fürst Blücher von Wahlstatt*
Chief-of-staff   *Generallieutenant Graf von Gneisenau*

I Army Corps   *Generallieutenant von Zieten*

1. Brigade   *Generalmajor von Steinmetz*
12th Infantry Regiment	(3 battalions)
24th Infantry Regiment	(3 battalions)
1st Westphalian Landwehr Infantry Regiment	(3 battalions)
3. and 4. Companies/Silesian Schützen Battalion	(2 companies)
1st Silesian Hussar Regiment Nr. 4	(4 squadrons)
6-pounder Foot Battery Nr. 7	(6 6-pounders, 2 howitzers)

2. Brigade   *Generalmajor von Pirch II*
6th (1st West Prussian) Infantry Regiment	(3 battalions)
28th Infantry Regiment	(3 battalions)
2nd Westphalian Landwehr Infantry Regiment	(3 battalions)
1st Westphalian Landwehr Cavalry Regiment	(4 squadrons)
6-pounder Foot Battery Nr. 3	(5 6-pounders, 2 howitzers)

3. Brigade   *Generalmajor von Jagow*
7th (2nd West Prussian) Infantry Regiment	(3 battalions)
29th Infantry Regiment	(3 battalions)
3rd Westphalian Landwehr Infantry Regiment	(3 battalions)
1. and 2. Companies/Silesian Schützen Battalion	(2 companies)
6-pounder Battery Nr. 8	(6 6-pounders, 2 howitzers)

4. Brigade   *Generalmajor Graf Henckel von Donnersmarck*
19th Infantry Regiment	(3 battalions)
4th Westphalian Landwehr Infantry Regiment	(3 battalions)
6-pounder Foot Battery Nr. 15	(6 6-pounders, 2 howitzers)

Reserve Cavalry   *Generalmajor von Roeder*
1. Brigade   *Generalmajor von Treskow*
5th Dragoon Regiment	(4 squadrons)
2nd (1st West Prussian) Dragoon Regiment	(4 squadrons)
3rd (Brandenburg) Uhlan Regiment	(4 squadrons)
6-pounder Horse Battery Nr. 2	(6 6-pounders, 2 howitzers)

2. Brigade   *Oberstlieutenant von Lützow*
6th Uhlan Regiment	(4 squadrons)
1st Kurmark Landwehr Cavalry	(4 squadrons)
2nd Kurmark Landwehr Cavalry	(4 squadrons)
6-pounder Horse Battery Nr. 7	(6 6-pounders, 2 howitzers)

Reserve Artillery   *Oberstlieutenant von Rentzell*
   12-pounder Foot Battery Nr. 2   (6 12-pounders, 2 howitzers)
   12-pounder Foot Battery Nr. 6   (6 12-pounders, 1 howitzer)
   6-pounder Foot Battery Nr. 1   (6 6-pounders, 2 howitzers)
   6-pounder Horse Battery Nr. 10   (6 6-pounders, 2 howitzers)
   7-pounder Howitzer Battery Nr. 1   (8 howitzers)
   Pioneer Company Nr. 1

II Army Corps   *Generalmajor von Pirch 1*
(promoted to Generallieutenant 11 July 1815)

5. Brigade   *Generalmajor von Tippelskirch*
   2nd (1st Pomeranian) Infantry Regiment   (3 battalions)
   25th Infantry Regiment   (3 battalions)
   5th Westphalian Landwehr Infantry Regiment   (3 battalions)
   Feldjäger Company   (1 company)
   1. and 2./11th Hussar Regiment   (2 squadrons)
   6-pounder Foot Battery Nr. 10   (6 6-pounders, 2 howitzers)

6. Brigade   *Generalmajor von Krafft*
   9th (Colberg) Infantry Regiment   (3 battalions)
   26th Infantry Regiment   (3 battalions)
   1st Elbe Landwehr Infantry Regiment   (3 battalions)
   3. and 4./11th Hussar Regiment   (2 squadrons)
   6-pounder Foot Battery Nr. 5   (6 6-pounders, 2 howitzers)

7. Brigade   *Generalmajor von Brause*
   14th Infantry Regiment   (3 battalions)
   22nd Infantry Regiment   (3 battalions)
   2nd Elbe Landwehr Infantry Regiment   (3 battalions)
   1. and 3./Elbe Landwehr Cavalry Regiment   (2 squadrons)
   6-pounder Foot Battery Nr. 34   (6 6-pounders, 2 howitzers)
                                 (British guns)

8. Brigade   *Generalmajor von Bose*
   21st Infantry Regiment   (3 battalions)
   23rd Infantry Regiment   (3 battalions)
   3rd Elbe Landwehr Infantry Regiment   (3 battalions)
   2. and 4./Elbe Landwehr Cavalry Regiment   (2 squadrons)
   6-pounder Foot Battery Nr. 12   (6 6-pounders, 1 howitzer)

Reserve Cavalry   *Generalmajor von Wahlen-Jürgass*
1. Brigade   *Generalmajor von Thümen*
   1st (Queen's) Dragoon Regiment   (4 squadrons)
   6th (Neumark) Dragoon Regiment   (4 squadrons)
   2nd (Silesian) Uhlan Regiment   (4 squadrons)
   6-pounder Horse Battery Nr. 6   (6 6-pounders, 2 howitzers)

2. Brigade   *Oberstlieutenant von Sohr*
   3rd (Brandenburg) Hussar Regiment   (4 squadrons)
   5th (Pomeranian) Hussar Regiment   (4 squadrons)

3. Brigade   *Oberst von der Schulenburg*
   4th Kurmark Landwehr Cavalry Regiment   (4 squadrons)
   5th Kurmark Landwehr Cavalry Regiment   (4 squadrons)

Reserve Artillery   *Major Lehmann*
   12-pounder Foot Battery Nr. 4   (6 12-pounders, 2 howitzers)
   12-pounder Foot Battery Nr. 8   (6 12-pounders, 2 howitzers)
   6-pounder Foot Battery Nr. 37   (6 6-pounders, 2 howitzers)
   6-pounder Horse Battery Nr. 5   (6 6-pounders, 2 howitzers)
   6-pounder Horse Battery Nr. 14   (6 6-pounders, 2 howitzers)
   Pioneer Company Nr. 7

IV Army Corps   *Generallieutenant Graf Bülow von Dennewitz*

13. Brigade   *Generallieutenant von Hake*
   10th (1st Silesian) Infantry Regiment   (3 battalions)
   2nd Neumark Landwehr Infantry Regiment (3 battalions)
   3rd Neumark Landwehr Infantry Regiment (3 battalions)
   1. and 2./2nd Silesian Landwehr Cavalry Regiment (2 squadrons)
   6-pounder Foot Battery Nr. 21   (6 6-pounders, 2 howitzers)

14. Brigade   *Generalmajor von Ryssel*
   11th (2nd Silesian) Infantry Regiment   (3 battalions)
   1st Pomeranian Landwehr Infantry Regiment (3 battalions)
   2nd Pomeranian Landwehr Infantry Regiment (3 battalions)
   3. and 4./2nd Silesian Landwehr Cavalry Regiment (2 squadrons)
   6-pounder Foot Battery Nr. 13   (6 6-pounders, 2 howitzers)

15. Brigade   *Generalmajor von Losthin*
   18th Infantry Regiment   (3 battalions)
   3rd Silesian Landwehr Infantry Regiment   (3 battalions)
   4th Silesian Landwehr Infantry Regiment   (3 battalions)
   1. and 2./3rd Silesian Landwehr Cavalry Regiment (2 squadrons)
   6-pounder Foot Battery Nr. 14   (6 6-pounders, 2 howitzers)

16. Brigade   *Oberst von Hiller*
   15th Infantry Regiment   (3 battalions)
   1st Silesian Landwehr Infantry Regiment   (3 battalions)
   2nd Silesian Landwehr Infantry Regiment (3 battalions)
   3. and 4./3rd Silesian Landwehr Cavalry Regiment (2 squadrons)
   6-pounder Foot Battery Nr. 2   (6 6-pounders, 2 howitzers)

Reserve Cavalry   *Generalmajor Prinz Wilhelm von Preussen*

1. Brigade   *Oberst Graf von Schwerin*
   6th (2nd Silesian) Hussar Regiment   (4 squadrons)
   10th Hussar Regiment   (4 squadrons)
   1st (West Prussian) Uhlan Regiment   (4 squadrons)
   6-pounder Horse Battery Nr. 1   (6 6-pounders, 2 howitzers)

2. Brigade   *Generalmajor von Watzdorff*
   8th Hussar Regiment   (3 squadrons)
   6-pounder Horse Battery Nr. 12   (6 6-pounders, 2 howitzers)

3. Brigade   *Oberstlieutenant von Sydow*
   1st Neumark Landwehr Cavalry Regiment (4 squadrons)
   2nd Neumark Landwehr Cavalry Regiment (4 squadrons)
   1st Pomeranian Landwehr Cavalry Regiment (4 squadrons)
   2nd Pomeranian Landwehr Cavalry Regiment (4 squadrons)
   1st Silesian Landwehr Cavalry Regiment   (4 squadrons)

Corps Reserve Artillery   *Major von Bardeleben*
   12-pounder Foot Battery Nr. 3   (6 12-pounders, 2 howitzers)
   12-pounder Foot Battery Nr. 5   (6 12-pounders, 2 howitzers)
   12-pounder Foot Battery Nr. 13   (6 12-pounders, 2 howitzers)
   6-pounder Foot Battery Nr. 11   (6 6-pounders, 2 howitzers)
   6-pounder Horse Battery Nr. 11   (6 6-pounders, 2 howitzers)
                                        (British guns)

   Pioneer Company Nr. 5

Strength

Approximately 75,000 Prussian troops marched to Waterloo. Of these, about 47,000 reached the battlefield during the fighting, and about 28,000 were effectively engaged.

Anglo-Dutch-German Army
18 June 1815

Commander-in-Chief   Field Marshal the Duke of Wellington

Cavalry   *Lieutenant General the Earl of Uxbridge*

Household Brigade   *Major-General Lord Somerset*
   1st Life Guard Regiment   (3 squadrons)
   2nd Life Guard Regiment   (3 squadrons)
   Royal Horse Guard Regiment (Blues)   (3 squadrons)
   1st (King's) Dragoon Guard Regiment   (4 squadrons)

2nd (Union) Brigade   *Major-General Sir Wm. Ponsonby*
   1st (Royal) Dragoon Regiment   (3 squadrons)
   2nd (Royal North British) Dragoon Regiment (3 squadrons)
   6th (Inniskilling) Dragoon Regiment   (3 squadrons)

3rd Brigade   *Major-General Sir Wm. Dörnberg*
   23rd Light Dragoon Regiment   (3 squadrons)
   1st Light Dragoon Regiment   (4 squadrons)
   1st KGL Light Dragoon Regiment   (4 squadrons)

4th Brigade   *Major-General Sir John Vandeleur*
   11th Light Dragoon Regiment   (3 squadrons)
   12th (Price of Wales') Light Dragoon Regiment (3 squadrons)
   16th (Queen's) Light Dragoon Regiment (3 squadrons)

5th Brigade   *Major-General Sir Colquhoun Grant*
   7th (Queen's Own) Hussar Regiment   (3 squadrons)
   15th (King's) Hussar Regiment   (3 squadrons)
   13th Light Dragoon Regiment   (3 squadrons)
   2nd KGL Hussar Regiment   *(detached)*

6th Brigade   *Major-General Sir Hussey Vivian*
   10th (Prince of Wales' Own) Hussar Regiment (3 squadrons)
   18th Hussar Regiment   (3 squadrons)
   1st KGL Hussar Regiment   (4 squadrons)

7th Brigade   *Colonel von Arentsschildt*
   3rd KGL Hussar Regiment   (4 squadrons)

Hanoverian Cavalry Brigade   *Colonel von Estorff*
   Cumberland Hussar Regiment   (4 squadrons)
   Prince Regent's Hussar Regiment   (4 squadrons)
   Bremen & Verden Hussar Regiment   (4 squadrons)

Netherlands Cavalry Division   *Lieutenant-General Baron de Collaert*
Netherlands Heavy Cavalry Brigade   *Major-General Baron Trip van Zoutelande*
   1st Carabineers   (3 squadrons)
   2nd (South Netherlands) Carabineers   (3 squadrons)
   3rd Carabineers   (3 squadrons)

1st Netherlands Light Cavalry Brigade *Major-General van Ghigny*
   4th Light Dragoons   (4 squadrons)
   8th (South Netherlands) Hussars   (3 squadrons)

2nd Netherlands Light Cavalry Brigade   Major-General van Merlen

5th (South Netherlands) Light Dragoons	(3 squadrons)
6th Hussars	(4 squadrons)

Brunswick Cavalry

Hussar Regiment	(3 squadrons)
Uhlan Squadron	(I squadron)

Artillery attached to the cavalry   Lieutenant-Colonel Sir Augustus Frazer

Bull's Troop, Royal Horse Artillery (RHA)	(5 6-pounders & I howitzer)
Gardiner's Troop RHA	(5 6-pounders & I howitzer)
Mercer's Troop RHA	(5 9-pounders & I howitzer)
Ramsay's Troop RHA	(5 9-pounders & I howitzer)
Webber-Smith's Troop RHA	(5 6-pounders & I howitzer)
Whinyates Troop RHA	(5 6-pounders & 2nd Rocket Troop)
½ Petter (Netherlands) Horse Battery	(4 guns)
½ Gey van Pittius (Neth.) Horse Battery	(4 guns)

Infantry

1st (British) Division   Major-General George Cooke

1st (British) Brigade   Major-General Peregrine Maitland
   2nd/1st Guards Regiment
   3rd/1st Guards Regiment

2nd (British) Brigade   Major-General Sir John Byng
   2nd/Coldstream Guards Regiment
   2nd/3rd Guards Regiment

Artillery

Sandham's Battery, Royal Artillery (RA)	(5 9-pounders & I howitzer)
Kuhlmann's Battery, KGL	(5 9-pounders & I howitzer)

2nd (Anglo-Hanoverian) Division   Lieutenant-General Sir Henry Clinton

3rd (British) Brigade   Major-General Frederick Adam
   1st/52nd (Oxfordshire) Light Infantry Regiment
   71st (Highland) Light Infantry Regiment
   Prov/95th Rifles (2 companies)
   2nd/95th Rifles (6 companies)

1st (KGL) Brigade   Colonel du Plat
   1st Line Battalion, KGL
   2nd Line Battalion, KGL
   3rd Line Battalion, KGL
   4th Line Battalion, KGL

3rd (Hanoverian) Brigade   Colonel Hugh Halkett
   Bremervörde Landwehr Battalion
   Osnabrück Landwehr Battalion
   Quakenbrück Landwehr Battalion
   Salzgitter Landwehr Battalion

Artillery

Bolton's Battery, RA	(5 9-pounders & I howitzer)
Sympher's Battery, KGL	(5 9-pounders & I howitzer)

3rd (Anglo-Hanoverian) Division   *Major-General Sir Charles Alten*

5th (British) Brigade   *Major-General Sir Colin Halkett*
  2nd/30th (Cambridgeshire) Regiment
  33rd (1st West Riding) Regiment
  2nd/69th (South Lincoln) Regiment
  2nd/73rd (Highland) Regiment

2nd (KGL) Brigade   *Colonel Christian von Ompteda*
  1st Light Battalion KGL
  2nd Light Battalion KGL
  5th Line Battalion KGL
  8th Line Battalion KGL

1st (Hanoverian) Brigade   *Major-General Count von Kielmansegge*
  Bremen Field Battalion
  Verden Field Battalion
  York Light Battalion
  Lüneburg Field Battalion
  Grubenhagen Jäger Battalion
  Kielmansegge Feldjäger-Korps

Artillery
  Lloyd's Battery, RA   (5 9-pounders & 1 howitzer)
  Cleeves' Battery, KGL   (5 9-pounders & 1 howitzer)

4th (Anglo-Hanoverian) Division   *Lieutenant-General Sir Charles Colville*

4th (British) Brigade   *Colonel Hugh Mitchell*
  3/14th (Buckinghamshire) Regiment
  1st/23rd (Royal Welsh Fusiliers) Regiment
  51st (2nd West Riding) Regiment

6th (British) Brigade   *Major-General George Johnstone*   *(detached)*
  2nd/35th (Sussex) Regiment
  1st/54th (West Norfolk) Regiment
  59th (2nd Nottinghamshire) Regiment
  1st/91st Regiment

6th (Hanoverian) Brigade   *Major-General Sir James Lyon*   *(detached)*
  Lauenburg Field Battalion
  Calenberg Field Battalion
  Nienburg Landwehr Battalion
  Hoya Landwehr Battalion
  Bentheim Landwehr Battalion

Artillery
  Broome's Battery, RA   *(detached)*
  Rettberg's Battery, KGL   (5 9-pounders & 1 howitzer)

5th (Anglo-Hanoverian) Division   *Lieutenant-General Sir Thomas Picton*

8th (British) Brigade   *Major-General Sir James Kempt*
  1st/28th (North Gloucester) Regiment
  1st/32nd (Cornwall) Regiment
  1st/79th Regiment (Cameron Highlanders)
  1st/95th (Rifle) Regiment

9th (British) Brigade   *Major-General Sir Dennis Pack*
  3rd/lst (Royal Scots) Regiment
  1st/42nd (Royal Highland) Regiment
  1st/44th (East Essex) Regiment
  1st/92nd Regiment (Gordon Highlanders)

5th (Hanoverian) Brigade   *Major-General von Vincke*
  Hameln Landwehr Battalion
  Hildesheim Landwehr Battalion
  Peine Landwehr Battalion
  Gifhorn Landwehr Battalion

Artillery   *Major Heise*
  Rogers' Battery, RA   **(5 9-pounders & 1 howitzer)**
  Braun's Battery, Hanoverian   **(5 9-pounders & 1 howitzer)**

6th (Anglo-Hanoverian) Division   **(no commander)**

10th (British) Brigade   *Major-General Sir John Lambert*
  1st/4th (King's Own) Regiment
  1st/27th (Inniskilling) Regiment
  1st/40th (Somerset) Regiment
  2nd/81st Regiment   *(detached)*

4th (Hanoverian) Brigade   *Colonel Best*
  Verden Landwehr Battalion
  Lüneburg Landwehr Battalion
  Osterode Landwehr Battalion
  Münden Landwehr Battalion

Artillery
  Unett's Battery, RA   *(detached)*
  Sinclair's Battery, RA   **(5 9-pounders & 1 howitzer)**

Reserve of British Artillery
  Ross' Troop, RHA   **(5 9-pounders & 1 howitzer)**
  Bean's Troop, RHA   **(5 9-pounders & 1 howitzer)**
  Morrison's Battery, RA   *(at Vilvoorde)*
  Hutchesson's Battery, RA *(at Ostende)*
  Ilbert's Battery, RA   *(at Ostende)*

Netherlands Reserve
  12pdr Battery Bois   *(at Braine-le-Comte)*

Netherlands Reserve Park
  3/2nd Artillery Battalion   *(at Louvain)*
  Kaempfer's Foot Battery   *(at Zottegem)*

1st Netherlands Division   *Lieutenant-General Stedman* *(detached)*

1st Brigade   *Major-General d'Hauw*
  4th (South Netherlands) Line **(1 battalion)**
  16th Jager   **(1 battalion)**
  6th Militia Battalion
  9th Militia Battalion
  14th Militia Battalion
  15th Militia Battalion

2nd Brigade   *Major-General de Eerens*
  1st (South Netherlands) Line   (1 battalion)
  18th Jager   (1 battalion)
  1st Militia Battalion
  2nd Militia Battalion
  18th Militia Battalion

Artillery
  Wynand's Foot Battery   (8 6-pounders)

2nd Netherlands Division   **Lieutenant-General de Perponcher-Sedlnitzky**

1st Brigade   *Major-General Bijlandt*
  7th (South Netherlands) Line   (1 battalion)
  27th Jager   (1 battalion)
  5th Militia Battalion
  7th Militia Battalion
  8th Militia Battalion

2nd Brigade   *Major-General Prinz Bernard von Sachsen-Weimar*
  2nd Nassau Regiment   (3 battalions)
  Orange-Nassau Regiment   (2 battalions)
  Nassau Jäger   (1 company)

Artillery
  Byleveld's Battery   (6 6-pounders & 2 howitzers)
  Stevenart's (South Netherlands) Battery   (8 guns)

3rd Netherlands Division   **Lieutenant-General Baron Chassé**

1st Brigade   *Major-General Detmers*
  2nd Line   (1 battalion)
  35th (South Netherlands) Jager   (1 battalion)
  4th Militia Battalion
  6th Militia Battalion
  17th Militia Battalion
  19th Militia Battalion

2nd Brigade   *Major-General d'Aubremé*
  12th Line   (1 battalion)
  3rd (South Netherlands) Line   (1 battalion)
  13th Line   (1 battalion)
  36th (South Netherlands) Jager   (1 battalion)
  3rd Militia Battalion
  10th Militia Battalion

Artillery
  De Bichin Horse Battery   (8 guns)
  Lux Battery   (8 guns)

Netherlands Indian Contingent   **Lieutenant-General Anthing**   *(detached)*
  5th East Indian Regiment   (3 battalions)
  10th West Indian Jager   (1 battalion)
  11th West Indian Jager   (1 battalion)
  Flank Companies of 19th and 20th Line
  Riesz's Battery   *(detached)*

Brunswick Contingent	*Oberst von Olfermann*

Advanced Guard — *Major von Rauschenplat*
  Avantgarde Battalion

1st Brigade — *Oberstlieutenant von Buttlar*
  Leib-Bataillon (Garde)
  1st Light Infantry
  2nd Light Infantry
  3rd Light Infantry

2nd Brigade — *Major von Wolffradt*
  1st Line Infantry
  2nd Line Infantry
  3rd Line Infantry

Artillery
  Heinemann's Horse Battery   (8 guns)
  Moll's Foot Battery   (8 guns)

Nassau Contingent	*General von Kruse*
1st Regiment	(3 battalions)

Strength

Approximate strength of the forces at the Battle of Waterloo
(excluding detachments):

British	24,000
King's German Legion	6,000
German Contingents	20,000
Netherlanders	18,000
Total	68,000 men and 155 pieces of artillery

French Forces
Armée du Nord

At the time of the Battle of Waterloo the French forces in the campaign had the following overall organisation:

Commander-in-Chief *Emperor Napoleon I*

Right Wing *Maréchal Count Grouchy*
III Corps   (less Domon's Division)
IV Corps
1st Cavalry Corps (less Subervie's Division)
2nd Cavalry Corps
Teste's Division

Left Wing   *Maréchal Ney, Prince de la Moskowa*
I Corps
II Corps   (less Girard's Division)
VI Corps   (less Teste's Division)
3rd Cavalry Corps
4th Cavalry Corps
Domon's Division
Subervie's Division

Reserve
Imperial Guard
Girard's Division (at Quatre Bras)

The French Army at Waterloo
18 June 1815

Imperial Guard *Maréchal Mortier, Duke of Treviso* (absent)

Old Guard   *Général de division Count Friant*
  1st Grenadiers à Pied   (2 battalions)
  2nd Grenadiers à Pied   (2 battalions)
  1st Chasseurs à Pied   (2 battalions)
  2nd Chasseurs à Pied   (2 battalions)

                    Général de division Count Morand
  3rd Grenadiers à Pied   (2 battalions)
  4th Grenadiers à Pied   (1 battalion)
  3rd Chasseurs à Pied   (2 battalions)
  4th Chasseurs à Pied   (2 battalions)

Young Guard   *Général de division Count Duhesme*
  1st Tirailleur Regiment   (2 battalions)
  1st Voltigeur Regiment   (2 battalions)
  3rd Tirailleur Regiment   (2 battalions)
  3rd Voltigeur Regiment   (2 battalions)

Guard Cavalry

Light Cavalry   *Général de division Count Lefèbvre-Desnoëttes*
  1st Regiment de chevauleger-lanciers   (1 squadron)
  2nd Regiment de chevauleger-lanciers   (4 squadrons)
  Chasseurs à Cheval de la Garde   (5 squadrons)

Heavy Cavalry   *Général de division Count Guyot*
  Grenadiers à Cheval de la Garde   (4 squadrons)
  Empress Dragoon Regiment   (4 squadrons)

Artillery of the Guard   *Général de division Desvaux de St Maurice*
  6 Old Guard Foot Batteries   (48 guns)
  4 Old Guard Horse Batteries   (24 6-pounders)
  4 Line Foot Batteries   (6 6-pounders & 2 howitzers each)
  1 Line Horse Battery   (4 6-pounders & 2 howitzers)
  1 Young Guard Foot Battery   (8 guns)

I Corps   *Général de division Drouot d'Erlon*

1st Division   *Général de division Allix*

Brigade   *Général de brigade Quiot*
  54th Line Regiment   (2 battalions)
  55th Line Regiment   (2 battalions)

Brigade   *Général de brigade Bourgeois*
  28th Line Regiment   (2 battalions)
  105th Line Regiment   (2 battalions)

Artillery   *Capitaine Hamelin*
  20/6th Foot Artillery   (6 6-pounders, 2 howitzers)

2nd Division   *Général de division Donzelot*

Brigade   *Général de brigade Schmitz*
  13th Light Regiment   (3 battalions)
  17th Line Regiment   (2 battalions)

Brigade   *Général de brigade Aulard*
  19th Line Regiment   (2 battalions)
  51st Line Regiment   (2 battalions)

Artillery   *Capitaine Cantin*
  10/6th Foot Artillery   (6 6-pounders, 2 howitzers)

3rd Division   *Général de division Marcognet*

Brigade   *Général de brigade Nogues*
  21st Line Regiment   (2 battalions)
  46th Line Regiment   (2 battalions)

Brigade   *Général de brigade Grenier*
  25th Line Regiment   (2 battalions)
  45th Line Regiment   (2 battalions)

Artillery   *Capitaine Emom*
  19/6th Foot Artillery   (6 6-pounders, 2 howitzers)

4th Division   *Général de division Durutte*

Brigade   *Général de brigade Pegot*
 8th Line Regiment   (2 battalions)
 29th Line Regiment   (2 battalions)

Brigade   *Général de brigade Brue*
 85th Line Regiment   (2 battalions)
 95th Line Regiment   (2 battalions)

Artillery   *Capitaine Bourgeois*
 9/6th Foot Artillery   (6 6-pounders, 2 howitzers)

1st Cavalry Division *Général de division Jacquinot*

Brigade   *Général de brigade Bruno*
 7th Hussar Regiment   (3 squadrons)
 3rd Chasseurs à Cheval Regiment (3 squadrons)

Brigade   *Général de brigade Gobrecht*
 3rd Chevauleger-lanciers Regiment (3 squadrons)
 4th Chevauleger-lanciers Regiment (2 squadrons)

Artillery   *Capitaine Bourgeois*
 2/1st Horse Artillery   (4 6-pounders, 2 howitzers)

Reserve Artillery   *Capitaine Charlet*
 11/6th Foot Artillery (6 12-pounders, 2 6-inch howitzers)

II Corps   **Général de division Reille**

5th Division   *Général de division Bachlu*

Brigade   *Général de brigade Husson*
 2nd Light Regiment   (4 battalions)
 61st Line Regiment   (2 battalions)

Brigade   *Général de brigade Campy*
 72nd Line Regiment   (2 battalions)
 108th Line Regiment   (3 battalions)

Artillery   *Capitaine Deshailles*
 18/6th Foot Artillery   (6 6-pounders, 2 howitzers)

6th Division   *Général de division Jérôme Bonaparte*

Brigade   *Général de brigade Baudin*
 1st Light Regiment   (3 battalions)
 3rd Line Regiment   (2 battalions)

Brigade   *Général de brigade Soye*
 1st Line Regiment   (3 battalions)
 2nd Line Regiment   (3 battalions)

Artillery   *Capitaine Meunier*
 2/2nd Foot Artillery   (6 6-pounders, 2 howitzers)

7th Division   *Général de division Girard*

Brigade   *Général de brigade Devilliers*
 11th Light Regiment   (2 battalions)
 82nd Line Regiment   (1 battalion)

Brigade	Général de brigade Pait	
12th Light Regiment		(3 battalions)
4th Line Regiment		(2 battalions)
Artillery	Capitaine Barbaux	
3/2nd Foot Artillery		(6 6-pounders, 2 howitzers)

9th Division — Général de division Count Foy

Brigade	Général de brigade Marbais	
92nd Line Regiment		(2 battalions)
93rd Line Regiment		(2 battalions)
Brigade	Général de brigade Jamin	
100th Line Regiment		(3 battalions)
4th Line Regiment		(3 battalions)
Artillery	Capitaine Tacon	
1/6th Foot Artillery		(6 6-pounders, 2 howitzers)

2nd Cavalry Division — Général de division Piré

Brigade	Général de brigade Baron Hubert	
1st Chasseurs à Cheval Regiment		(4 squadrons)
6th Chasseurs à Cheval Regiment		(4 squadrons)
Brigade	Général de brigade Gauthier	
5th Chevauleger-lanciers Regiment		(3 squadrons)
6th Chevauleger-lanciers Regiment		(4 squadrons)
Artillery	Capitaine Gronnier	
2/4th Horse Artillery		(4 6-pounders, 2 howitzers)
Reserve Artillery	Général de brigade Le Pelletier	
7/2nd Foot Artillery		(6 12-pounders, 2 6-inch howitzers)
1/1st Horse Artillery		(detached)
4/1st Horse Artillery		(detached)

3rd Cavalry Division — Général de division Domon

Brigade	Général de brigade Dommagnet	
4th Chasseurs à Cheval Regiment		(3 squadrons)
9th Chasseurs à Cheval Regiment		(3 squadrons)
Brigade	Général de brigade Vinot	
12th Chasseurs à Cheval Regiment		(3 squadrons)
Artillery	Capitaine Dumont	
4/2nd Horse Artillery		(4 6-pounders, 2 howitzers)

VI Corps — Général de division Mouton, Count de Lobau

19th Division — Général de division Baron Zimmer

Brigade	Général de brigade Baron de Bellair	
5th Line Regiment		(2 battalions)
11th Line Regiment		(3 battalions)
Brigade	Général de brigade Jamin	
27th Line Regiment		(2 battalions)
84th Line Regiment		(2 battalions)
Artillery	Capitaine Parisot	
1/8th Foot Artillery		(6 6-pounders, 2 howitzers)

20th Division   *Général de division Jeannin*

Brigade   *Général de brigade Bony*
  5th Light Regiment   (2 battalions)
  10th Line Regiment   (2 battalions)

Brigade   *Général de brigade Tromelin*
  47th Line Regiment   (1 battalion)
  107th Line Regiment   (2 battalions)

Artillery   *Capitaine Paquet*
  2/8th Foot Artillery   (6 6-pounders, 2 howitzers)

21st Division   **Général de division Baron Teste**

Brigade   *Général de brigade Lafitte*
  8th Light Regiment   (2 battalions)
  40th Line Regiment   (2 battalions)

Brigade   *Général de brigade Penne*
  65th Line Regiment   (1 battalion)
  75th Line Regiment   (2 battalions)

Artillery   *Capitaine Duverrey*
  3/8th Foot Artillery   (4 6-pounders, 2 howitzers)

Reserve Artillery
  4/8th Foot Artillery   (6 12-pounders, 2 howitzers)
  ? Horse Artillery   (6 6-pounders, 2 howitzers)
  1/3rd Engineers   (2 companies)

Reserve Cavalry

1st Cavalry Corps   *Général de division Count Pajol*

4th Cavalry Division   **Général de division Soult**   (with Grouchy)

5th Cavalry Division   **Général de division Subervie**

Brigade   *Général de brigade de Colbert*
  1st Chevauleger-lanciers Regiment   (4 squadrons)
  2nd Chevauleger-lanciers Regiment   (4 squadrons)

Brigade   *Général de brigade Merlin*
  11th Chasseurs à Cheval Regiment   (3 squadrons)

Artillery   *Capitaine Duchemin*
  3/1st Horse Artillery   (4 6-pounders, 2 howitzers)

3rd Cavalry Corps   **Général de division Kellermann**

11th Cavalry Division   **Général de division l'Héritier**

Brigade   *Général de brigade Picquet*
  2nd Dragoon Regiment   (4 squadrons)
  7th Dragoon Regiment   (3 squadrons)

Brigade   *Général de brigade Guiton*
  8th Cuirassier Regiment   (3 squadrons)
  11th Cuirassier Regiment   (2 squadrons)

| *Artillery* | *Capitaine Marcillac* | |
| 3/2nd Horse Artillery | | (4 6-pounders, 2 howitzers) |

12th Cavalry Division — Général de division d'Hurbal

Brigade	*Général de brigade Blanchard*	
1st Carabinier Regiment		(3 squadrons)
2nd Carabinier Regiment		(3 squadrons)
Brigade	*Général de brigade Donop*	
2nd Cuirassier Regiment		(2 squadrons)
3rd Cuirassier Regiment		(4 squadrons)
Artillery	*Capitaine Lebeau*	
2/2nd Horse Artillery		(4 6-pounders, 2 howitzers)

4th Cavalry Corps — Général de division Count Milhaud

13th Cavalry Division — Général de division Wathier

Brigade	*Général de brigade Dubois*	
1st Cuirassier Regiment		(4 squadrons)
4th Cuirassier Regiment		(3 squadrons)
Brigade	*Général de brigade Travers*	
7th Cuirassier Regiment		(2 squadrons)
12th Cuirassier Regiment		(2 squadrons)
Artillery	*Capitaine Duchet*	
5/1st Horse Artillery		(4 6-pounders, 2 howitzers)

14th Cavalry Division — Général de division Delort

Brigade	*Général de brigade Farine*	
5th Cuirassier Regiment		(3 squadrons)
10th Cuirassier Regiment		(3 squadrons)
Brigade	*Général de brigade Vail*	
6th Cuirassier Regiment		(4 squadrons)
9th Cuirassier Regiment		(3 squadrons)
Artillery		
4/3rd Horse Artillery		(4 6-pounders, 2 howitzers)

Strength

Approximate strength of Napoleon's forces at Waterloo:

  73,140 men and 252 pieces of artillery.

Prussian Forces at Wavre
18–19 June 1815

III Army Corps *Generallieutenant von Thielemann*

9. Brigade *Generalmajor von Borcke*
8th (Life) Infantry Regiment	(3 battalions)
30th Infantry Regiment	(3 battalions)
1st Kurmark Landwehr Infantry Regiment	(3 battalions)
1. and 2./3rd Kurmark Landwehr Cavalry	(2 squadrons)
6-pounder Foot Battery Nr. 18	(6 6-pounders, 2 howitzers)

10. Brigade *Oberst von Kemphen*
27th Infantry Regiment	(3 battalions)
2nd Kurmark Landwehr Infantry Regiment	(3 battalions)
3. and 4./3rd Kurmark Landwehr Cavalry	(2 squadrons)
6-pounder Foot Battery Nr. 35	(6 6-pounders, 2 howitzers)

11. Brigade *Oberst von Luck*
3rd Kurmark Landwehr Infantry Regiment	(3 battalions)
4th Kurmark Landwehr Infantry Regiment	(3 battalions)
1. and 2./6th Kurmark Landwehr Cavalry	(2 squadrons)

12. Brigade *Oberst von Stülpnagel*
31st Infantry Regiment	(3 battalions)
5th Kurmark Landwehr Infantry Regiment	(3 battalions)
6th Kurmark Landwehr Infantry Regiment	(3 battalions)
3. and 4./6th Kurmark Landwehr Cavalry	(2 squadrons)

Reserve Cavalry *Generalmajor von Hobe*

1. Brigade *Oberst von der Marwitz*
7th Uhlan Regiment	(4 squadrons)
8th Uhlan Regiment	(4 squadrons)
12th Hussar Regiment	(4 squadrons)

2. Brigade *Oberst Graf von Lottum*
5th Uhlan Regiment	(3 squadrons)
7th Dragoon Regiment	(3 squadrons)
9th Hussar Regiment	(3 squadrons)
Horse Battery Nr. 20	(6 6-pounders, 2 howitzers)

Reserve Artillery *Major von Grevenitz*
12-pounder Foot Battery Nr. 7	(6 12-pounders, 2 howitzers)
12-pounder Foot Battery Nr. 12	(6 12-pounders, 2 howitzers)
Horse Battery Nr. 18	(6 6-pounders, 2 howitzers)
Horse Battery Nr. 19	(1 6-pounder, 2 howitzers)
Pioneer Companies Nr. 4 and Nr. 5	

Notes

The 20th Infantry Regiment, allocated to the 10. Brigade, was in Mainz and later marched to take part in the siege of Landau. The 6-pounder Foot Battery Nr. 36 joined the 11. Brigade on 30 June, and the 6-pounder Foot Battery Nr. 24 joined the 12. Brigade at Paris on 6 July. The 12th Hussars were formed from two squadrons of Saxon uhlans and two of Saxon hussars on 18 June. They first fought at Namur on 20 June. The Reserve Artillery was joined by 12-pounder Foot Battery Nr. 11 at the beginning of August, by 6-pounder Foot Battery Nr. 30 on 7 July, and by 7-pounder Howitzer Battery Nr. 3 at the end of August.

French Forces at Wavre
18–19 June 1815

Commander	*Maréchal Count Grouchy*

III Corps — *Général de division Vandamme*

8th Division — *Général de division Lefol*

Brigade — *Général de brigade Bellard*
- 15th Light Regiment — (3 battalions)
- 23rd Line Regiment — (3 battalions)

Brigade — *Général de brigade Corsin*
- 37th Line Regiment — (3 battalions)
- 64th Line Regiment — (2 battalions)

10th Division — *Général de division Habert*

Brigade — *Général de brigade Gengoult*
- 11th Line Regiment — (3 battalions)
- 34th Line Regiment — (3 battalions)

Brigade — *Général de brigade Dapreyroux*
- 70th Line Regiment — (2 battalions)
- 22nd Line Regiment — (3 battalions)
- 2nd Swiss Infantry Regiment — (1 battalion)

11th Division — *Général de division Berthezène*

Brigade — *Général de brigade Dufour*
- 12th Line Regiment — (2 battalions)
- 56th Line Regiment — (2 battalions)

Brigade — *Général de brigade Lagarde*
- 33rd Line Regiment — (2 battalions)
- 86th Line Regiment — (2 battalions)

Artillery
- 17/2nd Foot Artillery — (6 6-pounders & 2 howitzers)
- 2 Foot Batteries — (6 6-pounders & 2 howitzers each)
- 1 Foot Battery — (6 12-pounders & 2 howitzers)

IV Corps — *Général de division Gérard*

12th Division — *Général de division Pêcheux*

Brigade — *Général de brigade Rome*
- 30th Line Regiment — (2 battalions)
- 96th Line Regiment — (2 battalions)

Brigade — *Général de brigade Schaeffer*
- 63rd Line Regiment — (2 battalions)

13th Division — *Général de division Vichery*

Brigade — *Général de brigade Le Capitaine*
- 48th Line Regiment — (2 battalions)
- 69th Line Regiment — (2 battalions)

Brigade *Général de brigade Desprez*
  59th Line Regiment (2 battalions)
  76th Line Regiment (2 battalions)

14th Division *Général de brigade Hulot*
Brigade *Général de brigade Hulot*
  9th Light Regiment (2 battalions)
  11th Line Regiment (2 battalions)
Brigade *Général de brigade Toussaint*
  50th Line Regiment (2 battalions)
  44th Line Regiment (2 battalions)

7th Cavalry Division *Général de division Vallin*
  6th Hussar Regiment (3 squadrons)
  8th Chasseurs à Cheval Regiment (3 squadrons)

Artillery
  3 Foot Batteries (6 6-pounders & 2 howitzers each)
  1 Foot Battery (6 12-pounders & 2 howitzers)
  1 Horse Battery (4 6-pounders & 2 howitzers)

From VI Corps:

21st Division *Général de division Teste*
  8th Light Infantry Regiment
  40th Line Infantry Regiment
  65th Line Infantry Regiment
  75th Line Infantry Regiment (total 5 Battalions)

Artillery
  1 Foot Battery (6 6-pounders & 2 howitzers)

From 1st Cavalry Corps:

4th Cavalry Division *Général de division Pajol*
  1st Hussar Regiment (4 squadrons)
  4th Hussar Regiment (4 squadrons)
  5th Hussar Regiment (4 squadrons)

Artillery
  1 Horse Battery (4 6-pounders & 2 howitzers)

2nd Cavalry Corps *Général de division Exelmans*

9th Cavalry Division *Général de division Strolz*
  5th Dragoon Regiment (4 squadrons)
  13th Dragoon Regiment (4 squadrons)
  15th Dragoon Regiment (4 squadrons)
  20th Dragoon Regiment (4 squadrons)

10th Cavalry Division *Général de division Chastel*
  4th Dragoon Regiment (4 squadrons)
  12th Dragoon Regiment (4 squadrons)
  14th Dragoon Regiment (4 squadrons)
  17th Dragoon Regiment (4 squadrons)
Artillery
  2 Horse Batteries (4 6-pounders & 2 howitzers each)

The Anglo-Dutch-German Forces
from 23 June 1815

Vanguard

6th Brigade   *Major-General Sir Hussey Vivian*
    10th (Prince of Wales' Own) Hussar Regiment
    18th Hussar Regiment
    1st KGL Hussar Regiment

I Corps   Major-General Sir John Byng

1st (British) Division   *Major-General Cooke*

1st (British) Brigade   *Major-General Maitland*
    2nd/1st Guards Regiment
    3rd/1st Guards Regiment

2nd (British) Brigade   *Major-General Sir John Byng*
    2nd/Coldstream Guards Regiment
    2nd/3rd Guards Regiment

Artillery   *Lieutenant-Colonel S.G. Adye*
    Sandham's Battery, RA,   **(5 9-pounders & 1 howitzer)**
    Kuhlmann's Battery, KGL   **(5 6-pounders & 1 howitzer)**

3rd (British) Division   *Lieutenant-General Sir Charles Alten*

5th (British) Brigade   *Major-General Sir Colin Halkett*
    2nd/30th (Cambridgeshire) Regiment
    33rd (1st West Riding) Regiment
    2nd/69th (South Lincolnshire) Regiment
    2nd/73rd (Highland) Regiment

2nd (KGL) Brigade
    1st Light Battalion, KGL
    2nd Light Battalion, KGL

1st (Hanoverian) Brigade   *Major-General Graf von Kielmansegge*
    Bremen Battalion
    Verden Battalion
    York Battalion
    Lüneburg Battalion
    Grubenhagen Battalion
    2 Jäger Coys.

Artillery   *Lieutenant-Colonel J.S. Williamson*
    Lloyd's Battery, RA
    Cleeves' Battery, KGL

Under the command of Lieutenant-General Baron Chassé (from 16 July, the Prince of Orange, from 16 August Prins Frederik of the Netherlands):

2nd (Netherlands) Division   *Lieutenant-General Baron de Perponcher-Sedlnitzky*

1st Brigade   *Major-General Count van Bijlandt*
    7th (South Netherlands) Line Regiment   (1 battalion)
    27th Jager Battalion
    5th Militia Battalion
    7th Militia Battalion

8th Militia Battalion
Horse Battery Bijleveld   (8 6-pounders)

2nd Brigade   *Major-General Prinz Bernard von Sachsen-Weimar*
  2nd Line Regiment   (1 battalion)
  10th Militia Battalion
  Orange-Nassau Regiment   (2 battalions)
  Nassau Freiwillige Jäger Detachment   (1 company)

Artillery
  Kaempfer's Battery   (6 6-pounders, 2 howitzers)
  [first in action during the siege of Valenciennes, arrived 19 July]
  Stevenart's Battery   (6 6-pounders, 2 howitzers)
  Byleveld's Horse Battery   (6 6-pounders, 2 howitzers)

3rd Netherlands Division   Lieutenant-General Baron Chassé

1st Brigade   *Major-General Detmers*
  35th (South Netherlands) Jager Battalion
  4th Militia Battalion
  6th Militia Battalion
  17th Militia Battalion
  19th Militia Battalion

2nd Brigade   *Major-General d'Aubremé*
  12th Line Regiment   (1 battalion)
  3rd (South Netherlands) Line   (1 battalion)
  13th Line   (1 battalion)
  36th (South Netherlands) Jager Battalion
  3rd Militia Battalion

Heavy Cavalry Brigade   *Major-General Trip*
  1st Carabineer Regiment   (3 squadrons)
  3rd Carabineer Regiment   (3 squadrons)
  2nd (South Netherlands) Carabineer Regiment (3 squadrons)
  6th Hussar Regiment   (4 squadrons)
  ½ Horse Battery Gey   (3 6-pounders, 1 howitzer)

Nassau Division   General von Kruse

  (from 28 June, with II Corps)
  1st Regiment   (3 battalions)
  2nd Regiment   (3 battalions)

II Corps   Lieutenant-General Lord Hill

2nd (Anglo-Hanoverian) Division   Lieutenant-General Sir Henry Clinton

3rd (British) Brigade   *Major-General Frederick Adam*
  1st/52nd (Oxfordshire) Regiment
  71st (Highland) Light Infantry Regiment
  2nd/95th Rifles
  3rd/95th Rifles   (2 companies)

1st (KGL) Brigade   *Colonel du Plat*
  1st Line Battalion, KGL
  2nd Line Battalion, KGL
  3rd Line Battalion, KGL
  4th Line Battalion, KGL

3rd (Hanoverian) Brigade　　　　　*Colonel Hugh Halkett*
　Bremervörde Landwehr Battalion
　Osnabrück Landwehr Battalion
　Quakenbrück Landwehr Battalion
　Salzgitter Landwehr Battalion
Artillery
　Bolton's Battery, RA　　　　　　　(5 9-pounders & I howitzer)
　Sympher's Battery, KGL　　　　　　(5 9-pounders & I howitzer)

4th (Anglo-Hanoverian) Division　*Lieutenant-General Sir Charles Colville*

4th (British) Brigade　　　　　　*Colonel Hugh Mitchell*
　3rd/14th (Buckinghamshire) Regiment
　1st/23rd (Royal Welsh Fusiliers) Regiment
　51st (2nd West Riding) Regiment

6th (British) Brigade　　　　　　*Major-General George Johnstone*
　2nd/35th (Sussex) Regiment
　1st/54th (West Norfolk) Regiment
　59th (2nd Nottinghamshire) Regiment
　1st/91st Regiment

6th (Hanoverian) Brigade　　　　*Major General Sir James Lyon*
　Lauenburg Field Battalion
　Calenberg Field Battalion
　Nienburg Landwehr Battalion
　Hoya Landwehr Battalion
　Bentheim Landwehr Battalion
Artillery
　Broome's Battery, RA,　　　　　　(5 9-pounders & I howitzer)
　Rettberg's Battery, KGL　　　　　(5 9-pounders & I howitzer)

5th (Anglo-Hanoverian) Division

8th (British) Brigade　　　　　　*Major-General Sir James Kempt*
　1st/28th (North Gloucester) Regiment
　1st/32nd (Cornwall) Regiment
　1st/79th Regiment (Cameron Highlanders)
　1st/95th (Rifle) Regiment

9th (British) Brigade　　　　　　*Major-General Sir Dennis Pack*
　3rd/1st (Royal Scots) Regiment
　1st/42nd (Royal Highland) Regiment
　1st/44th (East Essex) Regiment
　1st/92nd Regiment (Gordon Highlanders)

5th (Hanoverian) Brigade　　　　*Major-General von Vincke*
　Hameln Landwehr Battalion
　Hildesheim Landwehr Battalion)
　Peine Landwehr Battalion
　Gifhorn Landwehr Battalion
Artillery
　Rogers' Battery, RA　　　　　　　(5 9-pounders & I howitzer)
　Braun's Battery, Hanoverian　　　(5 9-pounders & I howitzer)

6th (Anglo-Hanoverian) Division   *(no commander)*

10th (British) Brigade   *Major-General Sir John Lambert*
 1st/4th (King's Own) Regiment
 1st/27th (Inniskilling) Regiment
 1st/40th (Somerset) Regiment
 2nd/81st Regiment

4th (Hanoverian) Brigade   *Colonel Best*
 Verden Landwehr Battalion
 Lüneburg Landwehr Battalion
 Osterode Landwehr Battalion
 Münden Landwehr Battalion

Artillery
 Unett's Battery, RA   **(5 9-pounders & 1 howitzer)**
 Sinclair's Battery, RA   **(5 9-pounders & 1 howitzer)**

Brunswick Contingent   *Oberst von Olfermann*

Advanced Guard   *Major von Rauschenplat*
 Uhlan Detachment
 Avantgarde Battalion

1st Brigade   *Oberstlieutenant von Buttlar*
 Leib-Bataillon (Garde)
 1st Light Infantry
 2nd Light Infantry
 3rd Light Infantry

2nd Brigade   *Oberstlieutenant von Specht*
 1st Line Infantry
 2nd Line Infantry
 3rd Line Infantry

Artillery
 Heinemann's Horse Battery   **(8 guns)**
 Moll's Foot Battery   **(8 guns)**

Cavalry

Household Brigade   *Major-General Lord Somerset*
 1st Life Guard Regiment
 2nd Life Guard Regiment
 Royal Horse Guard Regiment (Blues)
 1st (King's) Dragoon Guard Regiment

2nd (Union) Brigade   *Major General Sir Wm. Ponsonby*
 1st (Royal) Dragoon Regiment
 2nd (Royal North British) Dragoon Regiment
 6th (Inniskilling) Dragoon Regiment

3rd Brigade   *Major General Sir Wm. Dörnberg*
 23rd Light Dragoon Regiment
 1st Light Dragoon Regiment
 1st KGL Light Dragoon Regiment

4th Brigade   *Major General Sir John Vandeleur*
 11th Light Dragoon Regiment
 12th (Price of Wales') Light Dragoon Regiment
 16th (Queen's) Light Dragoon Regiment

5th Brigade	Major General Sir Colquhoun Grant

7th (Queen's Own) Hussar Regiment
15th (King's) Hussar Regiment
2nd KGL Hussar Regiment

7th Brigade	Colonel von Arentsschildt

13th Light Dragoon Regiment
3rd KGL Hussar Regiment

1st Netherlands Light Cavalry Brigade	Major-General van Ghigny

4th Light Dragoons
8th (South Netherlands) Hussars

2nd Netherlands Light Cavalry Brigade	Major-General van Merlen

5th (South Netherlands) Light Dragoons
6th Hussars

Brunswick Cavalry
Hussar Regiment
Uhlan Squadron

Siege Corps

1st Netherlands Division	*Lieutenant-General Stedman*

1st Brigade	*Major-General d'Hauw*	
4th (South Netherlands) Line	(1 battalion)
16th Jager	(1 battalion)
6th Militia Battalion	
9th Militia Battalion	
14th Militia Battalion	
15th Militia Battalion	

2nd Brigade	*Major-General de Eerens*	
1st (South Netherlands) Line	(1 battalion)
18th Jager	(1 battalion)
1st Militia Battalion	
2nd Militia Battalion	
18th Militia Battalion	

Netherlands Indian Contingent	*Lieutenant-General Anthing*
5th East Indian Regiment	(3 battalions)
10th West Indian Jager	(1 battalion
11th West Indian Jager	(1 battalion
Flank Companies of 19th and 20th Line	
Riesz's Battery	(8 6-pounders)

1st Netherlands Light Cavalry Brigade	*Major-General van Ghigny*
4th Light Dragoons	(4 squadrons)
5th (South Netherlands) Light Dragoons	(3 squadrons)
8th (South Netherlands) Hussars	(3 squadrons)
½ Horse Battery Gey van Pittius	(3 6-pounders, 1 howitzer)

Later joined by:
12-pounder Battery Du Bois
12-pounder Battery Severyns

Siege Warfare Glossary

As the reader may not always be familiar with the technical terms used to describe various parts of fortress buildings and for aspects of siege warfare, it is hoped that the small glossary here will assist in ensuring the clarity of Chapter 19.[1] Cross references to other glossary entries are shown in *italic type*.

Bastion   Part of the inner enclosure of a fortification, making an angle towards the outside, and consisting of two faces, two flanks and an opening to the centre of the place called a *gorge*, usually made of earth, faced sometimes with brick, but rarely with stone.

Casemate   A work made under the *rampart*, like a cellar or cave, with loopholes to place guns in it.

Cavalier   A work raised generally within the body of a fortress, perhaps three of four metres higher than the rest of the works. Most commonly situated within a *bastion*, being made in much the same form. Sometimes placed in the *gorges* or on the centre of the *curtain*. Here, usually in the form of a horse-shoe, only flatter.

Citadel   A fort with four, five or six *bastions* raised on the most advantageous ground in a town and placed to command it, commonly divided from the town by means of an *esplanade*.

Counterguard   A work placed in front of the *bastions* or *ravelins* to cover the opposite flanks from being seen from the *covert-way*.

Counterscarp   The exterior *talus* of the ditch, on the further side from the body of the place and facing it.

Covert-way   A space going round the works adjoining the *counterscarp* of the ditches.

Crown-work   A work not unlike a crown in shape with two fronts and two branches. The fronts are composed of two half-bastions and one whole one.

Curtain (wall)   That part of the body of the fortress that joins the flank of one *bastion* to another.

Escarp   The inner side of the ditch (nearest the fortress) separating besiegers and besieged.

---

[1] Much of this material has been based on Smith, *An Universal Military Dictionary*.

Esplanade   The sloping of the parapet of the *covert-way* towards the field. It is therefore the same as the *glacis* of the *counterscarp*. Often taken to mean the empty space between the *glacis* of a citadel and the first houses of the town.

Flèche   A work of two faces often constructed beyond the *glacis* of a fortified place, designed to keep the enemy as far away as possible.

Glacis   The part beyond the *covert-way*, serving as a *parapet* and terminating in an easy slope towards the outside of the fortress.

Gorge   The interval between the extremity of one flank of a *bastion* and the other.

Hornwork   A construction composed of a front and two branches, the front being made into two half-bastions and a *curtain*. Hornworks took possession of rising ground at a distance from the main fortifications.

Lunette   A work made on both sides of a *ravelin*. Or a work made beyond the second ditch, opposite to the place of arms. These differed from ravelins only in their situation.

Mine   An underground cavity in which a quantity of explosive could be lodged and detonated. The attacker could make mines under important parts of the defender's works, or visa versa.

Orillon   Part of a *bastion* near the shoulder that served to cover the retired flank from being seen obliquely. Sometimes faced with stone, on the shoulder of a casemated bastion to cover the cannon of the retired flank to hinder them from being dismounted by the enemy's cannon.

Outworks   Fortifications outside the first enclosure. Also the approaches made by the besieger.

Palisade   Stakes of strong split wood placed in the ground in the *covert-way* and parallel to the parapet to secure it from being surprised.

Parallel   That part of the besieger's trenches that surrounded the whole front attacked, deriving the name from the fact that a parallel would generally have that geometric relationship to the face of the defences. They served to hold and protect those soldiers defending the besieger's workmen and artillery.

Parapet   The part of the *rampart* of a work raised above it. It offered cover to the troops placed there to defend the work.

Rampart   An elevation of earth raised along the faces of any work to cover the inner part of that work against the fire of the enemy.

Ravelin   A work placed in front of the *curtain* to cover it. It prevented the flanks from being exposed from the side and consisted of two faces meeting an outside angle.

Redoubt   A work of various forms placed beyond the *glacis*.

Star-fort   A *redoubt* formed by a number of re-entering and salient angles that flank each other.

Talus   Slopes made both on the outside and inside of every work in such a way as to prevent dislodged earth from rolling down.

Vauban works   Fortifications constructed by, or in the style of, Marshal Vauban, the most famous French military engineer of the late 17th century.

Bibliography

Manuscript Sources

Manuscript	Accession Mark	Location
Constant Rebecque, Journal of	Coll 66	Algemeen Rijksarchief, The Hague
Gneisenau's Papers	Rep 92	Geheimes Staatsarchiv Preussischer Kulturbesitz, Berlin
Records of the Hanoverian Army and King's German Legion	various	Niedersächsisches Hauptstaats- archiv, Hanover
Murray Papers	7406-35	National Army Museum, London
Prussian War Archives	GStA, IV HA	Geheimes Staatsarchiv Preussischer Kulturbesitz, Berlin
Raglan Papers (FitzRoy Somerset)	A 24-31	Gwent County Record Office
Scovell Papers	WO 37/12	Public Record Office, London
Wellington Papers	WP, various	Hartley Library, University of Southampton

Printed Sources

Periodicals

anon, 'Ausgezeichnetes Benehmen einiger Preussischen Artilleristen in den Belagerungskrieg v. 1815', *Militair-Wochenblatt*, No. 18, 1816.

d'Avout, Vicomte, 'L'Infanterie de la Garde à Waterloo', *Carnet de la Sabretache*, January & February 1905, Paris, 1905.

Baring, George, 'Erzählung der Theilnahme des 2. Leichten Bataillons der Deutschen Legion an der Schlacht bei Belle Alliance', *Hannoversches militärisches Journal*, Hanover, 1831.

Forbes, Archibald, 'The Inner History of the Waterloo Campaign', *Nineteenth Century*, vol XXXIII, March 1893, London 1893.

Forst, Dr. H., 'Die Osnabrücker bei Waterloo', *Mittheilung des Vereins für Geschichte und Landeskunde von Osnabrück*, Vol XX 1895, Osnabrück, 1895.

Hafner, Dietrich, 'Hans Carl Ernst Graf von Zieten', *Militärisches*, Vol. I: January 1896, Leipzig

Nostitz, Graf von, 'Das Tagebuch des Generals der Kavallerie Grafen von Nostitz. II. Theil', *Kriegsgeschichtliche Einzelschriften*, Vol. 6, Berlin, 1885.

Pflugk-Harttung, Julius von, 'Das I. Korps Zieten bei Belle-Alliance und Wavre', *Jahrbücher für die deutsche Armee und Marine*, January-June 1903, Berlin.

Pflugk-Harttung, Julius von, 'Das I. preussische Korps bei Belle-Alliance', *Jahrbücher für die deutsche Armee und Marine*, July-December 1905, Berlin.

Pflugk-Harttung, Julius von, 'Die Gegensätze zwischen England und Preussen wegen der Bundestruppen 1815', *Forschungen zur Brandenburgischen und Preussischen Geschichte*, Vol. 24, Leipzig, 1911.

Pflugk-Harttung Julius von, 'Hinter der Schlachtlinie von Belle-Alliance', *Historisches Jahrbuch*, Vol. 36, Munich, 1915.

Pflugk-Harttung, Julius von, 'Von Wavre bis Belle-Alliance', *Jahrbücher für die deutsche Armee und Marine*, Berlin, 1908.

Pflugk-Harttung, Julius von, 'Wellington und Blücher am 17. Juni 1815', *Jahrbücher für die deutsche Armee und Marine*, January-June 1911, Berlin, 1911.

Pflugk-Harttung, Julius von, 'Zu Blüchers Brief an den König von Preussen vom 17. Juni 1815', *Jahrbücher für die deutsche Armee und Marine*, Berlin, 1904.

Pflugk-Harttung, Julius von, 'Zu den Ereignissen des 18. Juni 1815', *Forschungen zur Brandenburgischen und Preussischen Geschichte*, Vol.19, Leipzig, 1906.

Plumhoff, Fritz, 'La garde meurt et ne se rend pas', *Zeitschrift für Heereskunde*, Vol. XLV, No. 293, Berlin, 1981.

Poten, B. von, 'Des Königs Deutsche Legion 1803 bis 1816', Beiheft zum *Militär-Wochenblatt*, Vol. 11, Berlin, 1905.

Rehmann, Prof. Dr. (ed.), 'Das 2. Neumärkische Landwehr-Infanterie-Regiment. Seine Errichtung und seine Kriegstätigkeit 1813, 1814, 1815', *Schriften des Vereins für Geschichte der Neumark*. Vol. XXI. Landsberg a. W., 1908.

Scriba, von, 'Einige allgemeine Bemerkungen über den Feldzug im Jahre 1815 und besonders über die Schlachten von les Quatre Bras und Waterloo', *Internationale Revue über die gesamten Armee und Marine*, Berlin, 1892.

Books

Albedyll, Georg von, *Geschichte des Kürassier-Regiments Königin (Pommersches) Nr. 2.*, Vol 2, Berlin, 1904

anon, *The Crisis and Close of the Action at Waterloo*, Dublin, 1833.

anon, *Geschichte des 1. Westfälischen Husaren-Regiments Nr. 8*, Berlin, 1882.

anon, *Geschichte des 1. Oberschleisischen Infanterie-Regiments Nr. 22. 1813–1886*, Berlin, 1884.

Bagensky, Karl von, *Geschichte des 9ten Infanterie-Regiments genannt Colbergsches*, Berlin, 1842.

Beitzke, Dr. H., *Hinterlassene Schriften des Dr. Carl Friccius*, Berlin, 1866

Blesson, L., *Beitrag zur Geschichte des Festungskrieges in Frankreich im Jahre 1815*, Berlin, 1818.

Bornstedt, Major von, *Das Gefecht bei Wavre an der Dyle am 18. Und 19. Juni 1815*, Berlin, 1858.

Bothe, Heinrich, *Geschichte des Thüringischen Ulanen-Regiments Nr. 6*, Berlin, 1865.

Bredow, von, *Geschichte des 2. Rheinischen Husaren-Regiments Nr. 9*, Berlin, 1889.

Chandler, David, *Campaigns of Napoleon*, New York & London, 1966.

Charras, Jean Baptiste Adolphe, *Histoire de la campagne de 1815. Waterloo.*, Paris, 1869.

Chesney, Col. Charles C., R.E., *Waterloo Lectures: A Study of the Campaign of 1815*, London, 1907; reprinted London, 1997.

Ciriacy, F. von, *Der Belagerungs-Krieg des Königlich-Preussischen zweiten Armee-Korps an der Sambre und in den Ardennen*, Berlin, 1818.

Clausewitz, Carl von, *Der Feldzug von 1815 in Frankreich*, Berlin, 1835.

Conrady, Emil von, *Leben und Wirkung von Carl von Grolman*, Part 2, Berlin, 1895.

Costello, Edward (Brett-James, Anthony ed.) *The Peninsula and Waterloo Campaigns*, London, 1967.

d'Elchingen, Le Duc, *Documents inédits sur la campagne de 1815*, Paris, 1840.

Dalton, Charles, *Waterloo Roll Call*, London, 1890, revised 1904.

Damitz, Carl von, *Geschichte des Feldzuges von 1815 in den Niederlanden und Frankreich*, 2 vols, Berlin, Posen & Bromberg, 1837–38.

De Bas & T'Serclaes de Wommersom, *La campagne de 1815 aux pays-bas*, 3 vols, Brussels, 1908.

De Bas, F., *Prins Frederik der Nederlanden en zijn tijd*, Vol. 3, Part 2, Schiedam, 1904.

Delbrück, Hans, *Das Leben des Feldmarschalls Grafen Neithardt von Gneisenau*, Vol. 2, Berlin, 1920.

Dörk, E.M., *Das Königlich Preussische 15. Infanterie-Regiment Prinz Friedrich der Niederlande, (früher Graf Bülow von Dennewitz) in den Kriegsjahren 1813. 14. und 15.*, Eisleben, 1844.

Dudley Ward, C.H., *A Romance of the Nineteenth Century*, London, 1923.

Dziengel, Johann David von, *Geschichte des Königlich Preussischen Zweiten Ulanen-Regiments*, Potsdam, 1858.

Ebertz, Georg Wolfram von, *Hundertjährige Geschichte des Grenadier-Regiments König Friedrich III. (2. Schlesisches) Nr. 11 1808–1908*, Stuttgart, 1908.

Eck, von, *Geschichte des 2. Westfälischen Husaren-Regiments Nr. 11*, Mainz, 1893

Elting, John R., *Swords Around A Throne*, New York & London, 1989.

Epner & Braun, *Geschichte des Ulanen-Regiments Grossherzog Friedrich von Baden (Rheinisches) Nr. 7*, Berlin, 1909.

Esposito, Brigadier General Vincent J. & Elting, Colonel John R., *A Military History and Atlas of the Napoleonic Wars*, New York, 1964; reprinted London 1999.

Fleischman, Theo & Aerts, Winand, *Bruxelles pendant la bataille de Waterloo*, Brussels, 1956.

Förster, *Geschichte des Königlich Preussischen Ulanen-Regiments Graf zu Dohna (Ostpreussisches) Nr. 8*, Berlin, 1890.

Fraser, Sir Wm., *Words on Wellington*, London, 1889.

Gleig, Mary E. (ed), *Personal Reminiscences of the Duke of Wellington*, Edinburgh & London, 1904.

Gleig, Rev. G.R., *History of the Life of Arthur Duke of Wellington*, Vol II, London, 1858.

Goltz, Georg Friedrich Gottlob, *Geschichte des Königlich Preussischen dritten Ulanen-Regiments*, Fürstemwalde, 1841.

Gottschalck, Max, *Geschichte des 1. Thüringischen Infanterie-Regiments Nr. 31*, Berlin, 1894.

Gourgaud, Gaspard, *La campagne de dix-huit cent quinze*, Paris, 1818.

Granville, Castalia Countess, *Lord Granville Leveson Gower*, London, 1916.

Grosser Generalstab, *Das Preussische Heer in den Jahren 1814 und 1815*, Berlin, 1914.

Grouchy, Marquis de, *Mémoires de Maréchal Grouchy*, Paris, 1873.

Guretzky-Cornitz, *Geschichte des 1. Brandenburgischen Ulanenregiments (Kaiser von Russland) Nr. 3, vom Jahre 1809–1859*, Berlin, 1866.

Gurwood, John (ed), *Dispatches of Field Marshal The Duke of Wellington*, 12 vols., London, 1837–39.

Harkort, F., *Die Zeiten des 1. Westfälischen (16.) Landwehrregiments*, Hagen, 1964.

Hay, Capt. Wm., *Reminiscences 1808-1815 under Wellington*, London, 1901.

Henckel von Donnersmarck, Graf, *Erinnerungen aus meinem Leben*, Zerbst, 1846.

Hofmann, General von, *Zur Geschichte des Feldzuges von 1815*, Berlin, 1851.

Hope Pattison, Frederick, *Personal Recollections of the Waterloo Campaign*, Glasgow, 1873.

Houssaye, Henry, *1815*. 3 vols., Paris, 1914.

Hudleston, F.J., *Warriors in Undress*, London, 1925.

Hyde Kelley, W., *The Battle of Wavre and Grouchy's Retreat*, London, 1905.

Isenbart, Wilhelm, *Geschichte des Herzoglich Nassauischen 2. Regiments*, Berlin, 1891.

Jackson, Basil, *Notes and Reminiscences of a Staff Officer*, London, 1903.

James, W.H., *The Campaign of 1815, chiefly in the Flanders*, London, 1908.

Jennings, Louis J., *The Correspondence and Diaries of John Wilson Croker*, 3 vols, London, 1885.

Kolb, Richard, *Unter Nassaus Fahnen*, Wiesbaden, 1904.

Kortzfleisch, Gustav von, *Geschichte des Herzoglich Braunschweigischen Infanterie-Regiments*, Vol. 2, Brunswick, 1898.

Kraatz-Koschlau, M.T. von, *Geschichte des 1. Brandenburgischen Dragoner-Regiments Nr.2*, Berlin, 1878

Leszczynski, Rudolf von, *50 Jahre Geschichte des Königlich Preussischen 2. Posenschen Infanterie-Regiments Nr. 19*, Luxembourg, 1863.

Lettow-Vorbeck, Generalmajor von, *Napoleons Untergang 1815*, Berlin, 1904.

Lewinski & Brauchitsch, *Geschichte des Grenadier-Regiments König Wilhelm I. (2. Westpreussischen) Nr. 7*, Glogau, 1897.

Liddell, Col. R. S., *The Memoirs of the Tenth Royal Hussars*, London, 1891.

Lippe-Weissenfeld, Ernst Graf zur, *Geschichte des Königlich Preussischen 6. Husaren-Regiments (ehedem 2. Schlesischen)*, Berlin, 1860.

Mach, A. von, *Geschichte des Königlich Preussischen Zweiten Infanterie- genannt Königs-Regiments*, Berlin, Posen & Bromberg, 1843.

Malet, M. Albert, *Louis XVIII et les Cent-Jours à Gand*, Paris, 1902.

Malmesbury, Earl of, *A Series of Letters of the First Earl of Malmesbury, His Family and Friends from 1745 to 1820*, 2 vols., London, 1870.

Mercer, Cavalié, *Journal of the Waterloo Campaign*, London, 1870, 1927; reprinted London, 1989.

Mueller, Hugo von, *Geschichte des Grenadier-Regiments Prinz Carl von Preussen (2. Brandenburgisches) Nr. 12*, Berlin, 1875.

Müffling, Freiherr Friedrich Carl Ferdinand von, *Aus meinem Leben*, Berlin, 1851; (available in English as *Memoirs of Baron von Müffling*, London, 1997).

Müffling, Freiherr Friedrich Carl Ferdinand von, *Geschichte des feldzuges der englisch-hannövrisch-niederländisch-braunschweigischen Armee unter Herzog Wellington und der preussischen Armee unter dem Fürsten Blücher von Wahlstadt im Jahr 1815*, Stuttgart and Tübingen, 1816.

Neff, Wilhelm, *Geschichte des Infanterie-Regiments von Goeben (2. Rheinischen) Nr. 28*, Berlin, 1890.

Ollech, General von, *Geschichte des Feldzuges von 1815*, Berlin, 1876.

Otto, Felix von, *Geschichte des 2. Schlesischen Jäger-Bataillons Nr. 6*, Berlin, 1902.

Paget, Sir Julian & Saunders, Derek, *Hougoumont – The Key to Victory at Waterloo*, London, 1995.

Paulitzy & Woedtke, *Geschichte des 4. Rheinischen Infanterie-Regiments Nr. 30*, Berlin, 1884.

Pflugk-Harttung, Julius von, *Belle Alliance*, Berlin, 1915.

Pflugk-Harttung, Julius von, *Das Preussische Heer und die Norddeutschen Bundestruppen*, Gotha, 1911.

Pflugk-Harttung, Julius von, *Vorgeschichte der Schlacht bei Belle-Alliance – Wellington*, Berlin, 1903

Plotho, Carl von, *Der Krieg des verbündeten Europa gegen Frankreich im Jahre 1815*, Berlin, 1818.

Ravenstein, Heinrich, *Historische Darstellung der wichtigsten Ereignisse des Königlich-Preussischen Zweiten Kürassier-Regiments*, Berlin, Posen & Bromberg, 1827.

Reeve, Henry (ed), *The Greville Memoirs – A Journal of the Reigns of King George IV and William IV*, 3 vols, London, 1874

Renouard, C., *Das Norddeutsche Bundes-Korps im Feldzuge von 1815*, Hanover, 1865.

Roessler, Alfred von, *Geschichte des Königlich Preussischen 1. Nassauischen Infanterie-Regiments Nr. 87*, Berlin, 1882.

Rössler, Philip von, *Die Geschichte der Herzoglich Nassauischen Truppen*, Wiesbaden, 1863.

Schlieffen-Wioska, Graf von, *Hundert Jahre Braunschweigische Husaren*, Part 1, Brunswick, 1909.

Schöning, Kurd Wolfgang von, *Geschichte des Königlich Preussischen Fünften Husaren-Regiments*, Berlin, 1843.

Schreiber, Gustav, *Geschichte des Infanterie-Regiments von Borcke (4. Pommerschen) Nr. 21*, Berlin, 1889.

Schwartz, Karl, *Leben des Generals Carl von Clausewitz*, Berlin, 1878.

Schwertfeger, Bernhard, *Geschichte der Königlich Deutschen Legion 1803-1816*, 2 vols., Hanover & Leipzig, 1907.

Shaw-Kennedy, General Sir James, *Notes on the Battle of Waterloo*, London, 1865.

Siborne, H.T., *Waterloo Letters*, London, 1891; reprinted London, 1993.

Siborne, Wm., *History of the War in France and Belgium*, 1815, London, 1894; reprinted as *History of the Waterloo Campaign*, London, 1995.

Sichart, A. & R., *Geschichte der Königlich-Hannoverschen Armee*, Vol. 5, Hanover & Leipzig, 1898.

Six, Georges, *Dictionnaire Biographique des Généraux & Admriaux Français de la Révolution et de l'Empire (1792–1814)*, Paris, 1934.

Smith, E.A., *Wellington and the Arbuthnots*, London, 1994.

Smith, Captain George, *An Universal Military Dictionary*, London, 1779.

Strafford, Alice Countess of (ed), *Personal Reminiscences of the Duke of Wellington by Francis the first Earl of Ellesmere*, London, 1903.

Stanhope, Philip Henry, 5th Earl, *Notes of Conversations with the Duke of Wellington, 1831–1851*, London, 1888.

Starklof, R., *Das Leben des Herzogs Bernhard von Sachsen-Weimar*, 2 vols, Gotha, 1866.

Stawitzky, E.H. Ludwig, *Geschichte des Königlich Preussischen 25ten Infanterie-Regiments*, Koblenz, 1857.

Stuckrad, Bruno von, *Geschichte des 1. Madgeburgischen Infanterie-Regiments Nr. 26*, Berlin, 1888.

Swinton, J.R., *A Sketch of the Life of Georgiana, Lady de Ros*, London, 1893.

Thielen, Herbert von, *Geschichte des Madgeburgischen Husaren-Regiments Nr. 10 1813-1888*, Hanover, 1888.

Thurn und Taxis, *Prinz August von, Aus drei Feldzügen 1812 bis 1815*, Leipzig, 1912.

Unger, W. von, *Blücher*. Vol. 2, Berlin, 1908.

Unger, W. von, *Gneisenau*, Berlin, 1914.

Varnhagen von Ense, K. A., *Leben des Generals Grafen Bülow von Dennewitz*, Berlin, 1853.

Voss, Generalmajor von, *Napoleons Untergang 1815*, Vol. II, *Von Belle-Alliance bis zu Napoleons Tot*, Berlin, 1906.

Wachholtz, Freiherr Ludwig von, *Geschichte des Herzoglich Braunschweigschen Armee-Corps in dem Feldzuge der alliirten Mächte gegen Napoleon Buonaparte im Jahr 1815*, Brunswick, 1816.

Wagner, *Plane der Schlachte und Treffen*. Vol. 4, Berlin, 1825.

Ward, Major B.R. (ed), *A Week at Waterloo in 1815*, London, 1906.

Wedell, Rudolph von, *Geschichte des Königlich Preussischen 18. Infanterie-Regiments von 1813 bis 1847*, Posen, 1848.

Wellington, 2nd Duke of, *Despatches, Correspondence, and Memoranda of Field Marshal Arthur Duke of Wellington*, (New Series), 8 vols, London, 1867–80.

Wellington, 2nd Duke of, *Supplementary Despatches, Correspondence, and Memoranda of Field Marshal Arthur Duke of Wellington*, 16 vols., London, 1857–72.

Wellmann, Richard, *Geschichte des Infanterie-Regiments von Horn (3tes Rheinisches) Nr. 29*, Trier, 1894.

Weltzien, Karl von (ed), *Memoiren des königlich preussischen Generals der Infanterie Ludwig von Reiche*. Part 2, Leipzig, 1857.

Zychlinski, Franz von, *Geschichte des 24. Infanterie-Regiments*, Part 1, Berlin, 1854.

Index